CHINESE MODERN

POST-CONTEMPORARY INTERVENTIONS

Series Editors: Stanley Fish and Fredric Jameson

CHINESE MODERN

The Heroic and the Quotidian

XIAOBING TANG

DUKE UNIVERSITY PRESS   Durham and London   2000

© 2000 Duke University Press All rights reserved

Designed by C. H. Westmoreland
Typeset in Carter and Cohn Galliard with Eras display
by Tseng Information Systems, Inc.
Title page art: Woodcut, "Pursuit of Light" (ca. 1940),
by Li Hua, originally published in *China in Black and White:
An Album of Woodcuts by Contemporary Chinese Artists,* New York:
Asia Press, 1944.
Library of Congress Cataloging-in-Publication Data appear
on the last printed page of this book.

For Fred,

who first explained to me Brecht's insight:

"Woe is the land that needs a hero"

(*Galileo,* Scene 12).

CONTENTS

List of Illustrations ix
Acknowledgments xi
Introduction 1

PART I

1 Trauma and Passion in *The Sea of Regret:* The Ambiguous Beginnings of Modern Chinese Literature 11
2 Lu Xun's "Diary of a Madman" and a Chinese Modernism 49
Excursion I: Beyond Homesickness: An Intimate Reading of Lu Xun's "My Native Land" 74
3 *Shanghai, Spring 1930:* Engendering the Revolutionary Body 97
4 The Last Tubercular in Modern Chinese Literature: On Ba Jin's *Cold Nights* 131

PART II

5 The Lyrical Age and Its Discontents: On the Staging of Socialist New China in *The Young Generation* 163
6 Residual Modernism: Narratives of the Self in the 1980s 196
7 The Mirror of History and History as Spectacle: Reflections on Xiao Ye and Su Tong 225
8 In Search of the Real City: Cinematic Representations of Beijing and the Politics of Vision 245
9 New Urban Culture and the Anxiety of Everyday Life in Late-Twentieth-Century China 273
Excursion II: Decorating Culture: Notes on Interior Design, Interiority, and Interiorization 295
10 Melancholy Against the Grain: Approaching Postmodernity in Wang Anyi's Tales of Sorrow 316

Afterword 341
Glossary 349
Selected Bibliography 357
Index 369

LIST OF ILLUSTRATIONS

1. Folk painting, *Tianjin cheng maifu dilei Dong Junmen dasheng xibing tu* (A depiction of Commander Dong winning a great victory over Western troops by laying mines in the city of Tianjin) (1900)   36
2. Commercial advertisement, "International Dispensary Co. Ltd." (ca. 1930)   117
3. Commercial advertisement, "The Central Agency, Ltd." (ca. 1930)   120
4. Woodcut, *Bodou* (Confrontation) (1933)   124
5. Film poster, *Nianqing de yidai* (The young generation) (1964)   168
6. Stage design, *Nianqing de yidai* (The young generation) (1963)   178
7. Stage design, *Nianqing de yidai* (The young generation) (1963)   192
8. Film poster, *Benming nian* (Black snow) (1989)   259
9. Film still, *Beijing nizao* (Good morning, Beijing) (1990)   263
10. Film still, *Beijing nizao* (Good morning, Beijing) (1990)   269
11. Peasant painting, *New Look of a Village* (1974)   281
12. Peasant painting, *The Whole Family Studies the Communiqué* (1974)   282
13. Peasant painting, *The Motor's Roar* (1974)   291
14. Peasant painting, *Old Party Secretary* (1974)   291
15. Photograph, *Bringing You the Colors of the World, Giordano* (1993)   292
16. Oil, *Dream Girl* (1985)   293
17. Photograph, "Xiandai jushi" (Calendar: modern living) (1997)   310
18. Photograph, "Jia / Home" (Calendar) (1997)   310

Following page 290

Plate 1 (fig. 15). Photograph, *Bringing You the Colors of the World, Giordano* (1993)
Plate 2 (fig. 16). Oil, *Dream Girl* (1985)

ACKNOWLEDGMENTS

Since the writing of *Chinese Modern* spanned more than an entire decade of my life, to compose a succinct acknowledgment on the eve of its publication looms as a sobering exercise in remembrance. I have all my friends, teachers, colleagues, students, readers, and editors to thank for being there and for allowing me to pursue the ideas that I present in this book. Fully aware that my memory may falter, I still wish to express my appreciation to the following individuals for encouraging me, commenting on earlier drafts, and/or assisting me in my research. I list their names to reflect the order in which the chapters were written and revised: Jeff Twitcell, Fredric Jameson, Leo Ou-fan Lee, Dawn LaRochelle, Hu Ying, Mary Scoggin, Gan Yang, Howard Goldblatt, Laurels Sessler, Li Tuo, Meng Yue, Ivone Margulies, Dipesh Chakrabarty, Lydia Liu, Judith Zeitlin, Norma Field, Prasenjit Duara, Paize Keulemans, Ted Huters, Patrick Hanan, Ma Tai-loi, Arif Dirlik, Xudong Zhang, Tang Xiaoyan, Dongming Zhang, Arjun Appadurai, Yingjin Zhang, and Wu Linqing.

Special thanks are due my parents, Tang Haibo and Xie Lingling, who never stop looking after me from afar. A major motivation for my investigating the dialectics of the heroic and the quotidian was indeed my desire to understand the passion and confusion that I have witnessed in the lives of my parents' generation of Chinese.

Over the years, audiences at Hong Kong University, the University of Colorado at Boulder, the University of California at Berkeley, Indiana University, and the University of Chicago heard presentations of some of the essays that in different form are presented in this volume. Students in my seminars at the University of Colorado at Boulder and at the University of Chicago read and discussed, always politely, several chapters. I enjoyed all of the queries and comments generated by these memorable occasions, and I hope that the final version will give rise to just as much, if not more, response and interest.

My research assistant, Jason McGrath, capably helped me prepare the manuscript in the final stages and did a superb job of proofreading, indexing, and asking the right questions. The excitement that Jason felt while going through the chapters, I hope, outweighed the tedium of standardizing an academic manuscript.

Yet the one person whose emotional and intellectual investment in the volume is at least as significant as my own is Elizabeth Baker, always my beloved first reader, critic, editor, and cheerleader. I sometimes feel that all the words that I wrote for this book came to life and began to make sense only with the gentle but searching touch that Liza would bestow on each one of them with her exquisite red pen. When my mood became agitated by either "the lyrical age" or "heroic melancholy" that I intimately probed, Liza would often calm me down by making me feel and taste the lasting joy of everyday life.

In addition to all the invaluable personal support, I am grateful for different forms of institutional aid. During 1996–97, a residential fellowship at the Chicago Humanities Institute allowed me to concentrate and achieve a conceptual coherence for what was emerging as a book project. One of the earliest essays was finished in the summer of 1991, when I received a Rockefeller postdoctoral fellowship at the Center for Psychosocial Studies, directed by Benjamin Lee. At the University of Chicago, the Center for East Asian Studies provided me with timely research and course development funds with which I could collect visual material and put it to use in my undergraduate teaching. When the manuscript was finished, Ted Foss and Jim Ketelaar at the Center graciously made available a subvention, with which color illustrations could be reproduced for this publication. I hope Ted will find this book both good and elegant.

Several chapters have been published before, and I would like to thank *PMLA, Modern Chinese Literature, East-West Film Journal, Public Culture, boundary 2,* and Westview Press for permitting me to republish my work. I know how deeply indebted I am to the editors and copyeditors of these journals and presses. All the previously published essays, however, were carefully revised, in some cases extensively, before their appearance here.

I was very fortunate to have the opportunity to work again with Reynolds Smith at Duke University Press. His enthusiasm for the project was reassuring from the beginning and made the publication process amazingly painless for me. The three readers for Duke University Press, although vastly distinct in style, were equally generous with their comments and suggestions. I may or may not have taken all of their advice, but I have great respect for their professional rigor. I would also like to thank Bob Mirandon for copyediting the manuscript and Pam Morrison for capably managing the production of the book.

Finally, I understand that any remaining errors in the book are entirely my own and that I am responsible for all my arguments. My ultimate responsibility, however, lies in revealing the contemporary relevance of the Chinese experience in a most remarkable century. This task will demand just as active a part from readers of this book as it has from its author.

A number of chapters of this book have appeared in previous publications, all in an earlier and shorter form.

Chapter 2. 1992, "Lu Xun's 'Diary of Madman' and a Chinese Modernism," *PMLA* 107.5 (October): 1222–34. Reprinted by permission of the copyright owner, The Modern Language Association of America.

Chapter 6. 1993, "Residual Modernism: Narratives of the Self in Contemporary Chinese Fiction," *Modern Chinese Literature* 7.1 (Spring): 2–34. Reprinted by permission of *Modern Chinese Literature*.

Chapter 7. 1992, "The Mirror of History and History as Spectacle: Reflections on Hsiao Yeh and Su T'ung," *Modern Chinese Literature* 6.1 and 2 (Spring/Fall): 203–20. Reprinted by permission of *Modern Chinese Literature*.

Chapter 8. 1994, "Configuring the Modern Space: Cinematic Representation of Beijing and Its Politics," *East-West Film Journal* 8.2 (July): 47–69. Reprinted by permission of the Program for Cultural Studies, The East-West Center.

Chapter 9. 1996, "New Urban Culture and the Anxiety of Everyday Life in Contemporary China," from *In Pursuit of Contemporary East Asian Culture* ed. by Xiaobing Tang and Stephen Snyder, Copyright © 1996 by Westview Press: 107–22. Reprinted by permission of Westview Press, a member of Perseus Books, L.L.C.

Excursion II. 1998, "Decorating Culture: Notes on Interior Design, Interiority, and Interiorization," *Public Culture: Society for Transnational Cultural Studies* 10.3 (Spring): 531–48. Reprinted by permission of Duke University Press.

Chapter 10. 1997, "Melancholy Against the Grain: Approaching Postmodernity in Wang Anyi's Tales of Sorrow," *boundary 2: an international journal of literature and culture* 24.3 (Fall): 177–99. Reprinted by permission of Duke University Press.

This volume is published with a subvention from the Center for East Asian Studies, the University of Chicago.

XBT, Hyde Park

INTRODUCTION

This study of modern Chinese literature and culture observes a chronological order in which a series of significant twentieth-century literary and visual texts are studied and interpreted. Varied in both focus and length, the study's ten chapters and two excursions delve into representations of virtually every decade of the past hundred years. Some works discussed here are canonical, but also included are texts that, although not as well-studied, bring into relief a particular issue or moment. One main objective of the book is to demonstrate the pleasure of engaging specific, complex texts along with the need to continually assemble an explanatory historical narrative. Through its exercises in intimate reading, *Chinese Modern* offers interpretations of dense fragments gathered from a yet-to-be-written cultural history of modernity in China.

While the chronological arrangement acknowledges a need to situate individual creative works along a historical continuum, the wide range of topics and materials engaged in this study illustrates, I hope, how rich and multilayered the symbolic domain of modern Chinese literature and culture has been in the twentieth century. The book's underlying concern is to recognize not merely the traces and memories of a profoundly traumatic age, but also the recurring excitements and anxieties that competing visions of the modern continue to generate. These memories and visions are retrieved through a patient inquiry into some of the central themes of modern Chinese literature and culture: formations of subjectivity, the rural/urban symbology, historical consciousness, individual responsibility, and social transformation. The dialectics of the heroic and the quotidian, which I pursue here as an interpretive framework, describe an embedded structure of ambivalence, whereby the maelstrom of modernity is understood both to stir in us passions for a utopian future and to make us long for a fulfilling everyday life that is however constantly postponed. I examine how heroic actions as much as quotidian reassurances amount to a production of meaning that is nonetheless called into question in twentieth-century Chinese history and consciousness; my central argument is that the dialectical movement of the heroic and the quotidian constitutes an inescapable condition of secular modernity.

The book is divided into two parts that reflect a prevailing sense of discontinuity or new beginning that the founding of the People's Republic, after decades of war and social turmoil, engendered in midcentury. Up until that rupture, my reading deals exclusively with literary works, all of them seminal texts for twentieth-century Chinese literature and culture. In the first chapter, which explores the ambiguous beginnings of modern Chinese literature, I discuss the invocation of mythical pathos in Wu Jianren's 1906 novel *The Sea of Regret,* arguing that the narrative presents an intricate study of war trauma and human resilience. The discourse of passion that sustains the narrative articulates a cultural politics of virtue, which is nonetheless compounded by libidinal desire and shares the psychic structure of obsessional neurosis. Its indeterminacy between hagiography and pathography makes the novel an apt instance of changing literary conceptions and practices in the century's opening years. The divergence between meaning and experience painstakingly negotiated by the text also makes it a core narrative of modern Chinese literature.

The other four chapters in Part I draw on several analytical approaches —one of them psychoanalysis—to cast a fresh light on important works by the canonical writers Lu Xun, Ding Ling, and Ba Jin. A constant theme is the psychological depth and ambivalence that intensely self-conscious, albeit disparate, experiences of the modern have enabled these writers to reach and represent. The chapters on Ding Ling and Ba Jin can be taken, in turn, as microscopic studies of revolutionary romanticism of the early 1930s in metropolitan Shanghai and a somber poetics of failure in the Chinese interior during World War II. My selection of these texts may appear random, with little relationship of direct influence revealed among them, but each narrative is an overdetermined historical intervention that provides a crucial link in modern Chinese literary and cultural practices. It is not my intention in these pages to construct a systematic literary history, although a sharply focused interpretation of any given literary text—Lu Xun's "Diary of a Madman," for instance—invariably involves our conception of the entire tradition of modern Chinese literature. The overwhelming challenge of such an intimate engagement with literary texts, it seems to me, stems from the uneven, multifocal histories that continually surface and demand our imaginative reconfiguration.

Between the book's two main parts, there is a noticeable shift from psychoanalyzing Ba Jin's novel of virtual interior monologue to dismantling a carefully orchestrated theatrical spectacle. This change also foreshadows a broadening scope of investigation. In addition to literary texts,

I introduce cinematic and other visual materials in the book's second part. The ecstatic "lyrical age" in the wake of a time of unbearable despair, as I show in my reading of the 1963 play *The Young Generation,* is nonetheless fraught with anxiety and even terror. It thrives on an aesthetics of exteriority that extends the politics of sublimation, timidly embraced by Ding Ling in her fiction during the early 1930s. The exhilarating new life projected on the socialist stage, upon close examination, appears painfully incoherent and manipulative. In revisiting characters that galvanized the passion of an entire generation of Chinese youth and more, however, I view the play as valuable testimony to the grand project of a Chinese modernity, particularly to its utopian yearnings. Part of what I call "revolutionary mass culture" from the socialist period, *The Young Generation* directly confronts the question of everyday life and advocates self-abnegating heroism as its effective overcoming.

For all of its blatant propagandist style and intent, revolutionary mass culture calls for critical decoding rather than dismissal—as do the fleeting images, logos, and narratives that bombard a consumer society. Both socialist realism and capitalist realism, their best specimens being political propaganda and commercial advertisements, stimulate our dormant or unconscious longings for a transformed, more fulfilling environment. Ultimately, they are two interchangeable forms through which an ideological system may be mounted to help society better absorb the raw impact of secular modernity. Chinese culture and history after midcentury privilege us to witness an extraordinary metamorphosis of mass culture, with its socialist past ingeniously cannibalized by ever more voracious consumerism. To better understand late twentieth-century China, indeed, we must keep in sight the utopia of the lyrical age and all of its discontents. Therefore, my analysis of *The Young Generation* is crucially placed, not least because the play dramatizes a fundamental problem that I explore throughout the book in different contexts. In addition, the play declaratively speaks for a period when literary production was coordinated by the state to hasten the demise of solitary and sentimental readers of novels and when art as an autonomous activity was institutionally realigned to be continuous with life.

On an allegorical level, the second half of the book retraces a gradual journey from the spectacle of collective euphoria to a disconsolate moment of melancholy reflection and nostalgia as the century's end approaches. With the collapse of utopia grimly confirmed in the aftermath of the Cultural Revolution (1966–1976), we observe a resurgence of intimate and personal narratives of trauma, one of which I present in great detail through the chapter on "residual modernism." The revival of a modernist refusal to conform finds its fertile ground in an increasingly disorienting urban landscape. Hence, a subsequent chapter on cinematic representations of Beijing, where two separate visions of the city are brought together to reflect on each other. This tension is further elaborated against a larger historical background in the chapter on the anxiety of everyday life, in which I argue that recent Chinese cultural history vacillates between two logics and two value orientations: a rural but wholesome communal life versus an urban, disconnected, and detail-centered existence. Such a cultural dilemma is not by itself unique, but the imaginative efforts to resolve it often acknowledge a specific historical condition and heritage. In the final chapter, I conclude that a postrevolutionary disavowal of all heroic efforts is at the root of Wang Anyi's expression of a global melancholy in the mid-1990s; her contemporary tales of sorrow, against a transnational landscape of postmodernity, openly mourn the lost possibility of passionate devotion.

The book's final two chapters bring us to the contemporary scenario and compel us to rethink the implicit story that we are invited to abstract from the volume as one grand narrative. This move toward historical review is part of what I intend to provoke through this series of intimate readings. Between Wu Jianren's *Sea of Regret* and Wang Anyi's *Sadness for the Pacific,* for example, a similar evocation of passion calls forth a felicitous discourse that gauges the emotional and psychic content of modern Chinese literature. It also is uncannily befitting that theater—the most expressive medium of the lyrical age—is now fondly recalled by Wang Anyi's narrator as her revolutionary father's youthful fascination and commitment. No doubt it would be difficult to construct a uniform historical narrative from these chapters, but each of them arrests a moment that will have to be reconciled with any future narration of the twentieth century in China.

One explanatory description of the basic structural movement that brings together these texts and ties them to me is the dialectical engagement of the heroic with the quotidian, or a global utopianism with everyday life. While utopian politics often exact a terrible human toll, everyday life is never a complete or completely exhilarating experience; one choice always seems to reveal an unbearable lack in the other. If the revolutionary commitment of modern Chinese literature expresses itself in the drive for a grand heroic life, then the frustrated desire to reclaim an everyday life, now either actively disremembered or helplessly out of synch with the times, constitutes its political unconscious. As Zhang Ailing, one of the century's most important writers, remarked in the 1940s when the Sino-Japanese war was dragging on in the Chinese hinterland, there are two types of literature: one extols what is exciting and high-flying in life, the other affirms the stable and harmonious. "Emphasizing the active, exciting parts of human life gives something of a superhuman flavor. Superhumans are born only in certain eras, whereas the stable in human life has an eternal quality. Even though this calm stability is often incomplete and is bound for destruction every now and then, it is still eternal. It exists in all ages. It constitutes the sacredness of humanity, and we can even say it is womanliness itself." What attracted Zhang Ailing as a writer are not heroes with extreme determinations, but "the vast majority of people who bear the burden of our time." "They have no tragic heroism, just desolation. Tragic heroism amounts to a completion, whereas desolation offers a revelation."[1] This private, often internalized, experience of revelatory desolation possesses its own beauty and grandeur, forming an integral part of what Charles Baudelaire in the 1840s anticipated as the "*autrement héroïque*," "the heroism of modern life."[2]

Yet, according to the dialectics, the stable and constant aspect of life is lived only when its ruination appears inevitable or complete, whereas high-flying aspirations often grow out of impatience with norms or realities. The complete revelation that Zhang Ailing hints at, therefore, arises when we grasp the necessary incompleteness of both the heroic and the quotidian aspirations in life. Indeed, through an acute awareness that her own era was disintegrating, a time when "old things are falling apart while new ones are emerging," Zhang Ailing eloquently defended her work as unmistakably modern and yet nostalgic, and her aesthetic pursuit as one of uneven contrasts. She also succeeded in firmly grasping the rest-

---

1. Zhang Ailing (Eileen Chang), "Ziji de wenzhang," in her *Liuyan* (Gossip), *Zhang Ailing quanji* (The complete works of Zhang Ailing), vol. 3 (Taipei: Huangguan, 1992), 18–19. For an English translation by Wendy Larson, which I consulted, see Kirk A. Denton, ed., *Modern Chinese Literary Thought: Writings on Literature, 1893–1945* (Stanford, Calif.: Stanford University Press, 1996), 436–42.

2. See Baudelaire, "De l'héroïsme de la vie moderne," in his *Oeuvres complètes* (Paris: Gallimard, 1961), 949–52.

less soul of a literary tradition that she participated in shaping. Hence, the heroic and the quotidian—two complementary visions of reality that constitute the inner dynamics of Chinese literature in the twentieth century. These twin impulses may be a variation on what Jaroslav Průšek once characterized as "the lyrical and the epic" in his pioneering studies of modern Chinese literature,[3] although the heroic and the quotidian comprehend more than stylistic qualities or implications. They designate distinct artistic sensibilities and competing fantasies of becoming modern, and, more importantly, they always belie each other.

In addition to my effort to reconstruct the inner logic of these works, a more immediate motivation behind *Chinese Modern* has been to render these modern Chinese texts more accessible and therefore more relevant by means of theoretical discourse. My continual engagement with theoretical writings is certainly not aimed at stripping modern Chinese literature or history of its specificity. On the contrary, my objective is to highlight the extent to which the deeper grains and layers of a text may remain out of focus without the intervention of a theoretical lens. Every reason is present to make our study of modern Chinese literature part of the critical rethinking of modernity that often begins with a theoretical investigation. In employing various interpretive frameworks and vocabularies in my readings, I also hope to define my position as a student of modern Chinese literature who writes in English and for a broad readership. Nonetheless, during my research, as my notes testify, I relied heavily on scholarship published in Chinese over the past decade. It has become increasingly clear that modern Chinese literary studies in the United States will benefit greatly from interacting with its ever more vigorous counterpart in China. Also, wherever possible, I introduce existing English translations of the central texts discussed, hoping to facilitate readers' access to this body of literature.

A related effort of this volume is to make comparative references to other literary and cultural traditions (from the meaning of sickness in modern Japanese literature to neorealism in Italian cinema, for instance). Comparisons may not always be comprehensive or in-depth, but they begin to suggest, I believe, a historical as well as imaginative affinity among literatures and cultures produced in apparently different places.

---

3. See Jaroslav Průšek, *The Lyrical and the Epic: Studies of Modern Chinese Literature,* ed. Leo Ou-fan Lee (Bloomington: Indiana University Press, 1980).

They also indicate the multiple sources and influences that combine in the making of modern Chinese literature and culture and in our conceptualizations of the formative process itself. For all of these reasons, I expect this book to speak to an audience beyond those who are strictly students of modern China; they will find here an unprecedented study that engages texts from practically every decade of the past century. After all, this book is as much about what we understand by "the Chinese modern" as it is about how we make sense of the ineluctable condition of modernity.

1

Trauma and Passion in *The Sea of Regret:* The Ambiguous Beginnings of Modern Chinese Literature

The momentous emergence of the modern Chinese novel was greatly accelerated in 1902 when Liang Qichao (1871–1929), in political exile in Yokohama, started the literary journal *Xin xiaoshuo* (New fiction) and in its inaugural issue published a manifesto-like article to expound on the vital connection between "new fiction" and social progress and democracy. Hyperbolic rhetoric aside, Liang Qichao in this essay presents a compelling argument that the popular novel should function, and therefore be respected, as the most effective medium for mass education and spiritual cultivation.[1] With its unsurpassed capacity for expressing emotion and depicting reality, the novel is extolled as the highest form of literature. This rather pontifical revaluation, according to the literary historian Chen Pingyuan, ushered in a structural adjustment to the native aesthetic order and helped push novelistic narratives to the center of literary discourse and production during what is commonly referred to as the late Qing period.[2] The unprecedented social and cultural prominence

---

1. Liang Qichao, "Lun xiaoshuo yu qunzhi zhi guanxi" (On the relationship between fiction and the governance of the people), in his *Yinbingshi heji-wenji* (Collected writings from the ice-drinker's studio: collected essays) (Shanghai: China Books, 1936), 10:6–10. For an English translation, see Kirk A. Denton, ed., *Modern Chinese Literary Thought: Writings on Literature, 1893–1945* (Stanford, Calif.: Stanford University Press, 1996), 74–81. For a discussion of Liang Qichao's contribution to the modernization of Chinese fiction, see E. Perry Link Jr., *Mandarin Ducks and Butterflies: Popular Fiction in Early Twentieth-Century Chinese Cities* (Berkeley: University of California Press, 1981), 125–33.

2. Chen Pingyuan, *Ershi shiji Zhongguo xiaoshuo shi: di yi juan 1897–1916* (History of twentieth-century Chinese fiction: volume one, 1897–1916) (Beijing: Peking University Press, 1989), 1–22, esp. 15. Also see his *Zhongguo xiaoshuo xushi moshi de zhuanbian* (The transformation of the narrative pattern in Chinese fiction) (Shanghai: Shanghai renmin, 1988), 155–63.

granted to the popular novel, in retrospect, prepared a necessary condition for the beginning of modern Chinese literature at large, even though not all that was initiated would later be recognized as legitimate or relevant.[3]

In direct response to Liang's tireless trumpeting as both a theorist and an enthusiastic practitioner of the new fiction, the modernization of the Chinese novel forged ahead in the first decade of the twentieth century, often turning fiction into an open forum for either direct social commentary or political fantasy. This generic transformation was further aided by the contemporary influx of modern Western popular fiction (at first, mostly by means of Japanese translations) that demonstrated a new set of techniques, such as the rendering of narrative time, plot arrangements, and perspectival shifts.[4] Late Qing fiction or *xiaoshuo* (at the time the term also included drama) generated enormous creative energy because this once lowly literary form was now explicitly related to the reality of the modern world as well as its representation. The overwhelming volume of fiction writing from this period attests to a historical need for novelistic narration and, more importantly, for new narratable knowledge. Indeed, the numerous and ephemeral labels that accompany the new fiction point to a continual effort to name and order an estranged world and its hidden logic. The first five issues of Liang Qichao's *New Fiction,* for instance, introduced a dozen different types of *xiaoshuo* defined in terms of their subject matter, ranging unevenly from historical, scientific, and diplomatic to adventurous and detective.[5] If a general intersection of what David Der-wei Wang calls "confused horizons" took place in the late Qing conception of the novel, the seemingly unstoppable fictional output also signaled the active engineering of an epistemic restructuring, on the one hand, and a multifarious, often conflictual reality that the new fiction would have to encounter and represent, on the other. The

---

3. For a detailed study of this topic, see David Der-wei Wang, *Fin-de-siècle Splendor: Repressed Modernities of Late Qing Fiction, 1849–1911* (Stanford, Calif.: Stanford University Press, 1997).

4. See Chen, *The Transformation of the Narrative Pattern in Chinese Fiction,* 37–141.

5. For an informative discussion of the various types of fiction that were labeled during this period, see Chen Pingyuan, *Xiaoshuo shi: lilun yu shijian* (History of the novel: theory and practice) (Beijing: Peking University Press, 1993), 186–99. The Fiction Grove Society listed, for example, twelve different kinds of fiction that it had published by 1905.

ideal reader, consequently, was bluntly instructed to acquire encyclopedic knowledge and to respect the pedagogical seriousness of the new novel.[6]

However, the predominantly rationalist approach to fiction writing, which fueled Liang Qichao's "revolution in the realm of the novel,"[7] soon led to an awkward situation. The new fiction writers were so absorbed in popularizing new ideas and concepts that novels seemed more and more like political or philosophical treatises. Even more problematically, such compositions were often left unfinished either because no viable plot was present to continue or because a central argument had been made.[8] Also, from the start, the new fiction carried strong elitist and moralizing overtones insofar as its readership was largely imagined to be a nation of new citizens. While didacticism helped elevate the literary status of the novel, inattention to entertainment value rendered the once popular form of vernacular fiction increasingly abstruse and unpalatable to actual readers.[9] Already there appeared an ideological strife between a serious protoliterature of engagement and a literature for popular entertainment. This divide was to yield greater and longer lasting shock waves during the May Fourth period, when a thriving consumerist urban culture became one of the declared adversaries of the modernist New Literature movement. In historical hindsight, the intense enthusiasm for a new fiction at the turn of the century may illustrate how modernity was largely anticipated to be a mobilizing and morally uplifting mode of collective existence. The apo-

---

6. See "Du xinxiaoshuo fa" (The method of reading new fiction), *Xinshijie xiaoshuo-she bao* (Journal of the new world fiction society), nos. 6 and 7 (1907); collected in Jian Yizhi et al., eds., *Zhongguo jindai wenlun xuan* (Selections from early modern Chinese literary criticism) (Beijing: Renmin wenxue, 1962), 272–79.

7. This does not contradict the fact that in Liang Qichao's theorization of the effectiveness of fictional writing, emphasis also falls on the emotional impact of the novel, although it is an efficacy ultimately serving the purpose of social administration and democracy. For a helpful discussion of Liang Qichao's theory of the novel in terms of its intellectual sources, see C. T. Hsia, "Yen Fu and Liang Ch'i-ch'ao as Advocates of New Fiction," in *Chinese Approaches to Literature from Confucius to Liang Ch'i-ch'ao*, ed. Adele Austin Richett (Princeton, N.J.: Princeton University Press, 1978), 221–57.

8. This tendency was already indicated by Liang Qichao's own 1902 political novel *Xin Zhongguo weilai ji* (The future of new China). See my discussion of the novel in *Global Space and the Nationalist Discourse of Modernity: The Historical Thinking of Liang Qichao* (Stanford, Calif.: Stanford University Press, 1996), 117–37.

9. See Chen Pingyuan's documentation and analysis of the tension between elitist and popular fiction in his *History of Twentieth-Century Chinese Fiction*, 101–22.

ria in the new fiction discourse reveals that its passionate endorsement of a political modernity served to reduce, rather than reaffirm, the secular and fragmentary experience that called for novelistic representation in the first place.

For Wu Jianren (1866–1910), a prominent late Qing novelist, one mortal weakness of the rationalistic new fiction was precisely its departure from being novels. Specifically, Wu Jianren deplored the new fiction's inability to appeal to readers both intellectually and emotionally. In his preface to the first issue of *Yueyue xiaoshuo* (The all-story monthly), he critically assessed the achievements of the new fiction since Liang Qichao's revolutionary 1902 essay on the symbiotic relationship between the novel and social governance. Denouncing a facile conformity among fiction writers, Wu Jianren vented his frustration with reading an ineffective novel. "Of today's hundreds of thousands of new works and new translations that are called fiction, I dare not say that there are not any that reflect a concern with social governance; yet I have seen more than enough bizarre and fragmentary works, strenuous and unreadable translations. With publications like these, I do not know what others may think after reading them; as for myself, they all fail to move me emotionally."[10] Wu Jianren made these disparaging remarks in September 1906, when he and the translator Zhou Guisheng were invited to coedit the newly established literary journal *The All-Story Monthly*. By then, he had already published several novels in Liang Qichao's *New Fiction,* including parts of his widely acclaimed *Ershi nian mudu zhi guai xianzhuang* (Strange things witnessed in the past twenty years). His affiliation with Liang's journal, however, did not entirely define his profile as a popular novelist. On the contrary, although some of his own works may also seem "bizarre and fragmentary," Wu Jianren was never comfortable with a narrow understanding of new fiction as the forum for promoting modern cultural values and practices. He may be best remembered for his contribution to what Lu Xun once famously characterized as the "fiction of exposure" of the late Qing period, but the social criticism embedded in his exposé-style fiction did not always lend itself neatly to an agenda of program-

---

10. Wu Jianren, "*Yueyue xiaoshuo* xu" (Preface to *The All-Story Monthly*), *Yueyue xiaoshuo* (The all-story monthly), no. 1 (1906). Collected in Wei Shaochang, ed., *Wu Jianren yanjiu ziliao* (Research materials on Wu Jianren) (Shanghai: Shanghai guji, 1980), 320.

matic political reform.¹¹ Nonetheless, Wu Jianren never disavowed the grave social and moral responsibility on the part of a novelist. He firmly believed that all novels, be they historical or romantic, should serve a pedagogical purpose and lead their readers onto the proper "boundary of morality." For him, the value of a novel does not derive from its advocating the new over the old, but rather from its telling the good from the evil. "At such a moment of moral disintegration, we all hope to find a way to stop the general decline. We should then begin with nothing short of the novel."¹²

As if to demonstrate his conviction of the novel as a means of moral edification, Wu Jianren published in October 1906, independently of *The All-Story Monthly* that had come out a month before, a short novel titled *Henhai* (The sea of regret). A carefully constructed romantic tragedy that illustrates the novelist's understanding of the social content of human emotion and sentiment, the novel was an instant success. As A Ying documents in his pioneering study of late Qing fiction, its enormous popularity helped initiate and establish the subgenre of unfulfilled romance in modern Chinese fiction.¹³ The basic story line of *The Sea of Regret* itself was repeatedly adapted and rewritten for the greater part of the twentieth century, on stage and eventually in cinema.¹⁴ The sad tale of injured lives that unfolds in the novel conveys Wu Jianren's belief in the healing power of votive attachment, but it also voices a deep-seated anguish over the disintegration of the social and cultural fabric of life, now threatened from both within and without. It is a seminal narrative because it goes to great lengths to explore the internal journal of a displaced individual, and in the process it represents the psychological consequences of a traumatic encounter with the modern world.

---

11. See Lu Xun's discussion of Wu Jianren (Woyao), *Zhongguo xiaoshuo shilüe* (A brief history of Chinese fiction) (Beijing: Beixin shuju, 1937), 334–39. For an English translation, see Lu Hsün, *A Brief History of Chinese Fiction,* trans. Yang Hsien-yi and Gladys Yang (Peking: Foreign Languages Press, 1959), 377–81.

12. See Wu Jianren's "Preface to *The All-Story Monthly*," 321.

13. See A Ying, *Wan Qing xiaoshuo shi* (History of late Qing fiction) (Beijing: Dongfang, 1996), 202–06.

14. According to Wei, *Research Materials on Wu Jianren* (137–39), the plot of *The Sea of Regret* was remade for a theater production in 1914, then adapted into a silent movie in 1931, and again for the theater in 1947, the 1950s, and 1963.

The Writing of Passion

Contrary to the more confident, even militant, ethos of the reform-minded new fiction, Wu Jianren's first romance centers on the mental and emotional impacts of violent dislodging, depicting a subjectivity formed in fear. By means of exhorting devout passion as a stabilizing method in the face of a familiar world being shattered, *The Sea of Regret,* among other things, reclaims the writing of mythical pathos from the native literary tradition and turns it into a fundamental and yet equivocal theme for modern fictional discourse.

The immediate motivation for Wu Jianren to write *The Sea of Regret,* as Patrick Hanan suggests, was to counterbalance two contemporary texts of considerable impact.[15] The first was *Joan Haste,* a sentimental romance by the then-popular English novelist H. Rider Haggard. In 1901, an abbreviated rendition of the novel, in semiclassical Chinese, was serialized in a translation journal from Suzhou and attracted much attention, especially among educated male readers, who found in Joan an ideal combination of bold love and self-sacrifice. For a while, Joan, together with Marguerite of *La dame aux camélias* (by Alexandre Dumas fils, translated into Chinese in 1899), deeply enchanted a male romantic, if curiosity-driven, imagination and was idolized as the perfect embodiment of an affectionate, maternal, and universal femininity.[16] In the reformist elite culture at the time, the quiet infatuation with the sensual and emotional lives of these two fictional characters seemed to share the same intensity as the public and much-pronounced admiration for other heroic women figures, most notably Madame Roland of the French Revolution and Sofiya Perovskaya, the Russian anarchist.[17]

---

15. See Patrick Hanan, "Introduction," *The Sea of Regret: Two Turn-of-the-Century Chinese Romantic Novels,* trans. Patrick Hanan (Honolulu: University of Hawaii Press, 1995), 1–17.

16. For a discussion of Lin Shu's translation of *La dame aux camélias* and the masculine projection of a loving woman, see Rey Chow, *Woman and Chinese Modernity: The Politics of Reading Between West and East* (Minneapolis: University of Minnesota Press, 1991), 71–75, 121–28.

17. Liang Qichao wrote a moving biography of Madame Roland for his *Xinmin congbao* (New citizen journal) in October 1902, while the first influential biography of Perovskaya, by a Chinese student studying in Japan, appeared under the pen name Ren Ke in *Zhejiang chao* (The tide of the Zhe river) in September 1903.

In 1905, however, Lin Shu, the prolific translator of *La dame aux camélias* fame, outraged the reading public by putting out a full translation of *Joan Haste,* only the second half of which had been grudgingly divulged in the first rendition.[18] This new and complete translation caused a righteous uproar because it revealed that Joan, whom one commentator had adored as a "celestial fairy in the realm of passion," apparently had sexual intercourse with her lover, was impregnated sans marriage, and disgraced herself further by miscarrying. All these bodily details had been judiciously edited out by the two initial translators. Yet the outcry of disillusionment at the scandalous revelation had less to do with Joan's descending to the reality of human weaknesses and suffering than with the realization that she behaved improperly. The same commentator who worshipped the first immaculate Joan was compelled to bitterly denounce the new Joan as slutty, indecent, shameless, and selfish—in short, "a fraud in the realm of passion." The difference between these two incarnations, according to him, was that one Joan has pure passion (*qing*) but no lust (*yu*), and the other has mere lust in the guise of passion. After banishing the lustful Joan for good, the critic turned to inveigh against the meddlesome Lin Shu, accusing him of posing as a novelist and of churning out licentious translations that "bear the least benefit to society."[19]

Another critic, writing in the journal *New Fiction,* which by now had been relocated to an increasingly metropolitan Shanghai, seized the occasion to expound on the relationship between romantic fiction and the new society. Acknowledging the formative influence of fiction, Jin Songcen postulated that the various genres in new fiction, best represented by translations such as Harriet Beecher Stowe's *Uncle Tom's Cabin* (Heinu

---

18. A common misunderstanding is that the 1901 translation by Yang Zilin and Bao Tianxiao contains the first half of the original. The fact is that they started paraphrasing the text halfway through the novel, omitting unsavory details as they went along. See Wang Xuejun, "Ye tan *Jia'in xiaozhuan* liangzhong yiben: dui xinban *Lu Xun quanji* yitiao zhushi de buchong dingzheng" (Also on the two translations of *Joan Haste:* amendments to a note in the new edition of *The Complete Works of Lu Xun*), in *Lu Xun yanjiu dongtai* (Trends in Lu Xun studies), no. 4 (Beijing: 1988): 62–64. In addition, see Chen Xizhong, "Guanyu *Jia'in xiaozhuan* de liangzhong yiben" (On the two translations of *Joan Haste*), in *Wenxian* (Textual documents), no. 20 (Beijing, 1985): 255–58.

19. Yin Bansheng, "Du *Jia'in xiaozhuan* liang yiben shu hou" (After reading the two translations of *Joan Haste*), *Youxi shijie* (Playful world), no. 3 (1907); collected in Jian Yizhi et al., eds., *Selections From Early Modern Chinese Literary Criticism,* 526–28.

yutian lu) and Jules Verne's *Deux ans de vacances* (Shiwu xiao haojie) and *Le tour du monde en quatre-vingts jours* (Bashi ri huanyou ji), would have a positive impact on society because they erected new role models. "Therefore I am pleased to read today's new fiction, but I am terrified to read today's romantic fiction." The popular romances that caused his grave concern were none other than *La dame aux camélias* and *Joan Haste,* reckless foreign novels that, in his view, would only mislead the young and impressionable. The customs and mores suggested by these tales, he warned, would aid and abet rampant Europeanization and result in people abandoning their jobs and studies to frequent dance halls. In the end, the fearful society that became imaginable in light of romantic fiction meant not only the loss of a valuable national heritage, but, more disturbingly, a veritable disarray in social order and boundaries.[20]

Also in this essay, Jin Songcen found it necessary to generalize about romantic passion (*qing*) as part of human nature and a universal principle. The prevalence of *qing* explains why the expression of love and sentiment always occupies a key position in literature, be it Western or Eastern. "Given the difference and lack of communication between these two societies, it is the literary people's unavoidable duty to take advantage of the power of fiction to bring them together, employing passion as the common source." Since some novelists had failed to fulfill their obligation, and, worse, because romantic fiction now threatened the future of the country, the critic saw no option but to deny and demonize passion altogether. Evoking a central myth of Chinese culture, Jin Songcen argued that he would sooner see the heaven of passion remain broken, and any passionate awakenings be smothered with the help of Nüwa's stone, than witness what was bound to degenerate into unbridled carnality.

A fantastic figure in creation mythology, the goddess Nüwa is believed first to have given life to men and women in the world. Then, in the wake of a fierce agon between the gods of water and fire, which caused the vault of heaven to collapse, she, as a caring mother, mended the broken sky with colorful stones that she painstakingly melted and fused.[21] In the

20. Jin Songcen (Jin Tianyu), "Lun xieqing xiaoshuo yu xin shehui zhi guanxi" (On the relationship between romantic fiction and new society), in *New Fiction,* no. 17 (1905); collected in Jian Yizhi et al., eds., *Selections From Early Modern Chinese Literary Criticism,* 522–25.

21. For a modern narration of Nüwa's great deeds and identification of textual

folkloric tradition, Nüwa is usually associated with the themes of mothering, fertility, and healing,[22] but also with the spirit of dedication, even romantic devotion, in a despairing situation. Since the late imperial age, Nüwa has functioned persistently as a symbol of extraordinary dedication and endeavor, in no small part because of the wide-reaching impact of *Shitou ji* (The story of the stone; also known as *Honglou meng* [Dream of the red chamber]), particularly when Nüwa was paired with another mythical feminine spirit, the bird Jingwei.[23] Drowned in the eastern sea, the young daughter of the god of fire came back to life as a bird named Jingwei and was determined to fill up the sea with stones and twigs that she carried from the western mountain. In their Sisyphean efforts to mend heaven and fill up the sea, Nüwa the Ur-mother and Jingwei the faithful daughter are believed to have committed themselves to a passion that is at odds with reality. When Jin Songcen proposed to disrupt the heaven of passion so as to prevent men and women from engaging in dangerous free interaction, he was pointedly reversing the popular myth and viewing romantic passion as an ominous threat. It is significant that his endorsement of new fiction went hand in hand with his radical denunciation of new romances, for the unconscious anxiety preoccupying an elite-reformist social discourse at the time was precisely how to regulate the antihierarchical tendencies of sentiment and emotional exchange that would conceivably break loose when the dynastic order was done away with. Liang Qichao's initial exposition on the positive relationship between fiction and social governance, from this perspective, had hap-

---

sources, see Yuan Ke, *Zhongguo gudai shenhua* (Ancient Chinese myths) (Shanghai: Commercial Press, 1951), 54–60.

22. For a review of these dimensions of the Nüwa myth, see Jing Wang, *The Story of Stone: Intertextuality, Ancient Chinese Stone Lore, and the Stone Symbolism in "Dream of the Red Chamber," "Water Margin," and "The Journey to the West"* (Durham, N.C.: Duke University Press, 1992), 44–57.

23. Here is how the narrator in *The Story of the Stone* describes the heroic effort of Nüwa at mending a broken heaven: "Long ago, when the goddess Nüwa was repairing the sky, she melted down a great quantity of rock and, on the Incredible Crags of the Great Fable Mountains, moulded the amalgam into thirty-six thousand, five hundred and one large building blocks, each measuring seventy-two feet by a thousand and forty-one feet square." Translation by David Hawkes, *The Story of the Stone: A Chinese Novel by Cao Xueqin in Five Volumes* (London: Penguin, 1973), "The Golden Days," 1:47. Also see Hanan, "Stones in the Sea," in *The Sea of Regret*, 21–22 n.1.

pily envisioned literature as an unproblematic technology for advancing modernity. A blind spot in this agitating vision had been the messy and ambiguous status of romantic sentiment and longing, which Liang conveniently dismissed as a harmful legacy of traditional literature.

Not surprisingly, Jin Songcen's dismay with the romantic rendering of the Nüwa myth also found its explicit literary expression in at least two novels belonging to the contemporary political new fiction. Haitian duxiaozi's *Nüwa shi* (The Nüwa stone, 1904–05) and Qiu Jin's *Jingwei shi* (The stones of Jingwei, 1906, in the form of an incomplete *tanci* script) both advocate women's emancipation and revolutionary action, and in both narratives the mythological figures offer an edifying parallel to the dedication of the heroines to their respective political causes.[24] Yet while Nüwa and Jingwei are incorporated here as symbols of heroic perseverance in these texts, they more often are called upon to serve as accepted images of an individual's romantic devotion or, even, destiny. A number of novels written during this period evoke the myth of either Nüwa or Jingwei to highlight this mythical reinscription.[25]

Both the political and romantic appropriations of the mythical figure seek to elevate a human course of events and action. The mythical association consecrates an extraordinary dedication of the will, or of self-sacrifice, as, in and of itself, an admirable and therefore virtuous act. Once mythologized, even neurotic obsession has the potential of turning into a virtue, although the pathological origins of such a virtuous dedication are swiftly forgotten or repressed. The intent and structure of hagiographical narratives determine that a traumatic condition be overcome and turned into the source of sainthood rather than insanity or neurosis. For this reason, *The Sea of Regret* is all the more intriguing a literary

24. Catherine Gipoulon's French translation of Qiu Jin's text in *Pierre de l'oiseau Jingwei: Qiu Jin, femme et révolutionnaire en Chine au XIXe siècle* (Paris: des femmes, 1976) offers a contextualizing study, especially of the choice of *tanci* as the preferred medium (14–20).

25. For example, Zou Tao (Sixiang jiuwei)'s *Haishang chentian ying* (Shadow of the dusty sky in Shanghai, 1904) closely imitates *Dream of the Red Chamber* and evokes both Nüwa and Jingwei. Other titles include Fei Min's *Hen hai hua* (Flowers in the sea of regret, 1905), Xin Meizi's *Jingqin tianhai ji* (Story of Jingwei filling the sea, 1906), Wahun's *Butian shi* (Stones for mending the sky, 1906), and Wanshi's *Qingtian hen* (Regret of the passionate sky, 1906). Several popular pen names used by authors, such as "Wanshi" (Tough stone), "Wahun" (Spirit of Nüwa), and "Lian shi" (Welding stone), also refer to the stone myth.

text because it harbors as intensely a hagiographical intention as it does a pathographical narrative. Between the book's ideological statement or message and its narrative content, a persistent tension develops, revealing an incongruity that bespeaks the impossible task of making full sense of an overwhelming experience. This incongruity between hagiography and pathography is unconsciously explored in the novel and thereby endows the text with a deep ambivalence that is symptomatic of the Chinese experience of modernity. The same structural ambiguity can be found in two other, lesser texts that immediately preceded Wu Jianren's story.

Toward a Tragic Passion

The text that Patrick Hanan believes to have directly provoked Wu Jianren into writing *The Sea of Regret* was a slim volume, published in May 1906 by a certain Fu Lin under the suggestive title of *Qin hai shi* (Bird, sea, stone; translated as *Stones in the Sea* by Hanan).[26] The titular reference of this so far obscure novel is obviously to the Jingwei myth; its second chapter also refers to Nüwa in describing a happier moment: "The Heaven of Passion is repaired, as predestined lovers meet far from home" (317; 29).

Not much has been learned about the novel's author, Fu Lin, although the significance of his first-person narrative is widely recognized, even to the extent of being recommended as "the first true 'I-novel' in Chinese literature, a few years before the genre came into vogue in Japan."[27] Indeed, the nostalgic tone and confessional structure of the novel clearly emit all the generic signs of an intensely personal narration. Supposedly speaking from his deathbed, the mortally ill hero, Qin Ruhua, tells of his ultimately unfulfilled romance, recollecting, not without pride, his youthful

---

26. Hanan also determines that the first edition of *Stones in the Sea* came out in May 1906, a few months before Wu Jianren's *Sea of Regret*. See his "Introduction," *The Sea of Regret*, 1. The Chinese edition used here comes from *Qing bian* (Passion transformed) (Shanghai: China Eastern Normal University Press, 1993), a volume in the recent anthology of modern Chinese romantic fiction. In the following discussion, page references for *Stones in the Sea* and *The Sea of Regret* are included in the text, with the first page number referring to the Chinese edition of *Passion Transformed* and the second to Hanan's translation.

27. Hanan, "Introduction," *The Sea of Regret,* 10.

ingenuity at becoming intimate with his first and only love. Of the same age and in love since they were ten, the "predestined lovers" meet again in Beijing, where their two families happen to share the same residential compound. After much scheming and hand-wringing, including timely sickness, they get their fathers to agree to a marriage, although Ruhua's generally inattentive father stipulates that the wedding ceremony not be held until the groom turns sixteen.

What causes this almost frivolous love story to take a tragic turn is the violent intrusion of historical processes. Just when all that the precocious Ruhua needs is some patience waiting for his sixteenth birthday, despite the prevailing wisdom of the time that recommended twenty as the earliest marriageable age for men,[28] the turbulent Boxer movement spreads to Beijing, and, in the face of sweeping turmoil, the two close families go their separate ways. A specific reference to calendrical time is offered at this juncture, although the disturbing events in 1900 that lead to the ransacking and occupation of Beijing by a multinational army are described in an oblique, hearsay fashion. Yet the terror of a misguided rebellion is concrete enough for Ruhua's father, who deems it prudent to move the family south. After a tearful farewell with Aren his betrothed, whose father sees little threat in the virulently antiforeign and pro-Qing Boxers, Ruhua follows his own father and flees the capital; no sooner do they reach Shanghai than Ruhua spots a newspaper headline about the fall of Beijing. Tormented by an absence of news about Aren stranded in the north, Ruhua becomes depressed and withers away. When he finally sees her again, in a dingy Shanghai inn, Aren, accompanied only by her distraught mother, is dying. Her health is badly damaged when she swallows three drams of opium so as to avoid being sold into prostitution. Upon seeing Ruhua, she dutifully reports that she is still a virgin and, after voicing the belief that "so long as my dedicated spirit [*jingcheng*] re-

28. In a mock petition to the Qing court, an anonymous essayist at the time, citing Herbert Spencer and listing all of the social problems caused by hormonal urges, argued that it was inhuman to require a young man to reach twenty-four before he married. The proposed adjustments, however, were still age twenty for men and seventeen for women. See "Xini qingnian shang zhengfu qing chi jin zaohun shu" (A mock petition by a youth to the government to demand a relaxation of the ban on early marriage), collected in *Biji xiaoshuo daguan: wubian* (Grand exhibit of notation book fiction: collection five) (Taipei: Xinxing shuju, 1974), 3875–76.

mains intact, there's a chance we may meet in the next life," she chokes and expires (369; 96).

Sensing that he may soon follow Aren to the afterworld, Ruhua concludes that the lack of a free marriage system has done them in. The conclusion of the narrative, usually reserved for a moralizing message, turns into a bitter attack on the Confucian tradition, in particular its outmoded marriage customs.

> However, I blame neither Father nor the Boxer bandits for my ruin. Instead I hold Mencius responsible. But for his stale formula "by the parents' command and through the good offices of a go-between," I would long since have joined Aren in a free marriage. No matter how much turmoil the Boxers caused, she and I would still have been able to travel south together. . . . I hope above all else that one day this China of ours will change its marriage system and grant people their freedom, before the City of Wrongful Death claims countless more millions of aggrieved and anguished souls. That would be a beneficence of unimaginable, incalculable proportions. (371; 99)

Such an antitraditional protest is not entirely unexpected at this moment, for the narrator from the outset accuses the insensitive Mencius (311; 21–22), but his plea for a liberal marriage system undercuts itself when he refuses to link the cause of his demise to any specific historical agents. In his insistence that even war and social upheaval will not derail true love or personal happiness, there surfaces a juvenile willingness and need to believe in a given cause. Ruhua's resolution to advocate personal freedom and individual choice reveals its ideological nature since his experience obviously exceeds his rationalization or comprehension. Experience in excess of discursive capacity, conversely, indicates a general crisis and fragmentation. A degree of neurosis becomes discernible when the narrator steadfastly attaches himself to one piece of reality and invests in it all his psychic energy, resulting in what Freud describes as a neurotic ignoring of reality or a flight from it.[29] This neurotic obsession entails certain narrative content, even emotional appeal, but the subsequent claim to social

---

29. For Freud's discussion of neurosis and its difference from psychosis, see "The Loss of Reality in Neurosis and Psychosis," in *The Standard Edition of the Complete Psychological Works of Sigmund Freud,* trans. James Strachey (London: Hogarth Press, 1961), 19:183–87.

pertinence or even political protest appears markedly delusional. As one critic remarks, this eager transference of the causes for personal unhappiness onto some inimical but abstract external political force was common in late Qing fiction.[30]

The metaphysical force that justifies such an obsessional narrative, Fu Lin writes in a brief preface, is the mythical "passion" (*qing*) with which the universe is created and held together as a whole. He posits "passion" as a more comprehensive concept than "benevolence," which the late Qing philosopher Tan Sitong set forth as the ultimate meaning of nature as well as of the human world.[31] Fu Lin goes on to argue that although amorous attraction between the sexes is but a minor expression of such a cosmic principle, yet, since humans are the supreme beings in the universe, an obsession with passion, even to the extent of disregarding life and death, ultimately agrees with the true purpose of creation. The task of a good romance writer, therefore, is to closely depict all the emotional excitement caused by love in order to reveal the creator's secrets. Supported by this belief, Fu Lin recommends his own "romantic fiction" (*yanqing xiaoshuo*) to all those endowed with passion. In keeping with the proto-political sentiments of his times, he goes on to urge his readers to develop a love for their race and country, which will supposedly be a logical extension and fulfillment of their instinctual sexual yearnings (373; cf. 9).

Although the emphasis differs, in a concise preface to *The Sea of Regret*, Wu Jianren proposes the same *qing* as the fundamental principle that his novel is to illustrate. This much-discussed preface reflects Wu Jianren's deep interest in the human capacity for passion, and it lays the thematic foundation for his own tales of passion as well as subsequent popular romantic novels of the early Republican era.[32] As A Ying once

30. See Yuan Jin, *Yuanyang hudie pai* (The mandarin duck and butterfly school) (Shanghai: Shanghai shudian, 1994), 27.

31. For a bilingual text of Tan Sitong's philosophical treatise with an extensive background introduction, see Chan Sin-wai, *An Exposition of Benevolence: The Jen-hsüeh of T'an Ssu-t'ung* (Hong Kong: Chinese University Press, 1984).

32. In Wu Jianren's 1909 novel *Jie yu hui* (Ashes after the catastrophe), the narrator arranges for the virtuous widow, Zhu Wanzhen, to be rescued so as to hear an old nun expound on the difference between passion, lust, and desire. It is an offense to the all-embracing Buddha, according to the philosophical nun, to even claim that one has seen through passion, for that would only indicate a confusion of sexual desire with true passion. See *Ashes After the Catastrophe*, collected in *Passion Transformed*, 158.

commented, the philosophical foundation of Wu Jianren's fictional world was firmly laid in this novel.[33] Apparently fraught with ambiguity and couched entirely in traditional metaphysical concepts, Wu Jianren's discourse of passion is self-consciously concerned with maintaining social order and cultural continuity.[34] Passion, according to the authorial voice, "is something that we possess from birth, well before we know the meaning of the human world." This innate quality of passion or emotional attachment, moreover, "can be applied to any sphere of life, the only difference being in the manner of its application." In fact, the four cardinal virtues (loyalty, piety, parental love, and friendship) "all derive from passion" (5; 103). To convince the reader that much thinking went into the writing of the story, Wu Jianren reaffirms the hierarchical order of passions: the virtuous, the infatuated, and the lecherous. While the virtuous passion affirms the socially legitimate and foundational human relations, lechery is a self-indulgent abuse of one's emotion. As if anticipating accusations that the passion he promotes through the central character Dihua borders on "infatuation" or even "lechery," Wu Jianren singles out the case of chaste widows, arguing that "the occasions on which the widows remained unmoved were precisely those on which their passion was at its height" (5; 103–04). He stops short of naming which passion his romantic tale will exemplify, but he promises that it is definitely not about lechery or obsession.

Here the nun repeats the same understanding of passion as the foundation of social relations between father and son, husband and wife, emperor and subject. Wu Jianren's unfinished last novel, *Qing bian* (Passion transformed), also examines the force of passion in a changing and haphazard world. For a discussion of this text in terms of Wu Jianren's development as a novelist, see Mugio Tomie, "Go Kenjin no 'Kinjunen no kaigenjo' to 'Johen' ni tsuite" (On Wu Jianren's 'Strange things in the past ten years' and 'Passion transformed'), in *Shinmatsu shoseitsu kenkyu* (Late Qing fiction studies), no. 5 (1981): 60–70.

33. A Ying, *Xiaoshuo santan* (The third collection of essays on fiction) (Shanghai: Shanghai guji, 1979), 170.

34. For a commentary on, and also an example of, the confusion that Wu Jianren's discourse of passion may cause, see Mao Zonggang, "Lun Wu Jianren de wenxue xieqing yishi" (On Wu Jianren's literary awareness of describing passion), *Ming Qing xiaoshuo yanjiu* (Ming and Qing fiction studies), no. 4 (Nanchang: 1988): 234–43. See also Zhao Xiaoxuan, "Wu Jianren 'Xieqing xiaoshuo' de qinglun yu daodeguan" (On the discourse of passion and morality in Wu Jianren's "romantic fiction"), *Zhongwai wenxue* (Chung-wai literary monthly) 21.11 (Taipei: 1990): 148–79.

Both Wu Jianren's and Fu Lin's prefaces subscribe to the long philosophical tradition of "passionism" (*qing jiao*) that during the late Ming period rose to contest and complement a fully institutionalized Confucian code of social behavior and propriety. The late Ming fiction writer Feng Menglong went so far as to claim that all of the Confucian classics are based on a broad "passionism."[35] (Incidentally, in response to strong demand, a modern illustrated lithographic edition of Feng Menglong's *Qingshi leilüe* [A classified history of passion] was reissued by the Self-Strengthening Press in 1909.) True to the ethos of a period of "radical subjectivity," as Wai-yee Li characterizes the late Ming intellectual and literary life, Feng Menglong "celebrates the expansiveness and transformative power of *ch'ing* [*qing*] and at the same time insists that it must be reintegrated into schemes of order."[36] Historically, from the seventeenth century on, the development and growing popularity of vernacular fiction and drama are largely enabled by an aesthetic discourse on passion that affirms private sentiments (as either "authentic" or "natural"), on the one hand, and strives to legitimate new forms of social contact and intercourse on the other. The intensity of passion that vernacular fiction explores may index the extent to which libidinal energy is meticulously regulated by civilizational strictures or, simply, repressed. Yet even if it is made a fully ontological force, passion in this cultural context does not automatically translate into the modern Western notion of romantic love between individual subjects. Conflicts between the individual and society are not yet perceived as irresolvable, and passion in the final analysis functions as a moral imperative that secures its legitimacy through social acceptance and universal harmony. As a result, traditional romances always end on a comic note with true lovers happily united, either in this world

35. See both You Zilong (Feng Menglong), "Qingshi xu" (Preface to A history of passion) and Zhanzhan waishi (Feng Menglong), "Xu" (Preface), in Feng Menglong, *Qingshi leilüe* (A classified history of passion), ed. Zou Xuemin (Changsha: Yuelu shushe, 1984), 1–3. For a recent historical study of the concept of *qing* (passion), see Martin W. Huang, "Sentiments of Desire: Thoughts on the Cult of *Qing* in Ming-Qing Literature," *Chinese Literature: Essays, Articles, Reviews* 20 (December 1998): 153–84.

36. Wai-yee Li, *Enchantment and Disenchantment: Love and Illusion in Chinese Literature* (Princeton, N.J.: Princeton University Press, 1993), 93. See 89–93 for a discussion of Feng Menglong's thinking on *qing*. For an English translation of Feng Menglong, see Hua-yuan Li Mowry, *Chinese Love Stories from the "Ch'ing-shih"* (Hamden, Conn.: Archon Books, 1983).

or through fantasy, and such emplotment only testifies to the fundamental rationality of the larger universe.

This general avoidance of tragedy as irresolvable conflict, with the notable exception of *Dream of the Red Chamber,* apparently did not become a significant intellectual problem until the imminent collapse of the imperial tradition, which coincided with the arrival of the twentieth century. In 1904, Wang Guowei, inspired by a Schopenhauerian understanding of the human will as self-expression, published an essay that systematically discussed the tragic implications of perpetual desire and the impossibility of its full gratification. For Wang Guowei the imaginative critic, the function of literature, exemplified nowhere else but in *Dream of the Red Chamber,* is to reveal this tragic condition as an existential constant and to provide a way of deliverance from it.[37]

Soon after Wang Guowei's pioneering study, another critic also would recommend, drawing on a different intellectual source, tragedy as the preferred and more effective dramatic form for modern times. In an article published in Liang Qichao's influential *Xinmin congbao* (New citizen journal), Jiang Guanyun first relayed the contemporary Japanese criticism of the Chinese theater and then lamented the absence of tragedy in the native tradition. Only a tragedy given to portraying an indomitable "concentration of sincerity" (*jingcheng*) will be able to "inspire far-reaching ideals and cultivate a deep and reflective mind," whereas a crowd-pleasing comedy achieves nothing but the encouragement of licentious thoughts. The most respected plays by Shakespeare, observed the critic, are all tragedies. "If there are many tragedies in the theater, society will benefit from them and happiness will reign; if there are many comedies, society will have a negative influence and sadness will result therefrom."[38] Obviously, the critic wished to promote tragedy not because it might suggest the vulnerability or darkness of the human world, but because it would better serve the social purpose of encouraging the audience to emulate greatness. Tragedy became part of the reformist agenda, and as

---

37. Wang Guowei, *Honglou meng pinglun* (Commentary on *Dream of the Red Chamber*), collected in *Wang Guowei xiansheng sanzhong* (Three works by Wang Guowei) (Taipei: Guomin, 1960), 1–29. For a comprehensive evaluation of this groundbreaking essay and its limits, see Yeh Chia-ying, *Wang Guowei ji qi wenxue piping* (Wang Guowei and his literary criticism) (Hong Kong: China Books, 1980), 174–211.

38. Guanyun (Jiang Guanyun), "Zhongguo zhi yanju jie" (On the Chinese theater), *Xinmin congbao* (The new citizen journal), no. 17 (1905): 95–98.

serious drama it purportedly provided a more effective forum than popular entertainment for nation-building through didacticism. The promotion of tragedy, from a historian's viewpoint, constituted a crucial aspect of the modernizing of literary discourse during the late Qing, interjecting significant shifts in literary and aesthetic conceptions.[39]

What is intriguing and historically revelatory about Fu Lin's *Stones in the Sea,* therefore, is that it contains a tragic plot within an essentially comic notion of passion. The two young lovers obtain no happy ending in this world, but their tragic fate is nothing short of a testimonial of their deep passion for and dedication to each other. In this sense, Fu Lin's romantic novel accepts a new genre formula in which the comic justifications of passion are located outside or in spite of the characters' tragic fate and will have to be internalized as a spiritual compensation. This tragicomedy of passion, in which the experiential dimension is increasingly separated from the rational or the ideational, will reach an impasse in *The Sea of Regret;* it has its precedent perhaps in a 1903 short story by Pingdeng ge (Di Baoxian), a text that foreshadows both romantic novels by Fu Lin and Wu Jianren insofar as the threat of colonialism and a nationalist anxiety over the integrity of indigenous culture are brought together in a tragic love story.

The short story, simply titled "Tang sheng" ("Tang Sheng" or "A youth named Tang"), self-consciously alludes back to Pu Songling's classic *Liaozhai zhiyi* (Records of the strange from the Liaozhai studio) of the seventeenth century by labeling itself as a tale from the "new Liaozhai Studio." More significantly, it is the first story with which the journal *New Fiction,* in its seventh issue, introduced the subgenre of "romantic fiction" (*xieqing xiaoshuo*).[40] Romance evidently still fell largely into the category of the strange and extraordinary. Composed in classical Chinese, "Tang Sheng" also tells of the foiled romance of a young couple in the wake of the Boxer movement of 1900, except that the location is now set in the United States, and the love story has an international and anticolonial intricacy. The son of a wealthy Chinese merchant based in San Francisco, teenage Tang Sheng is in love with a beautiful American girl, Irene (Yiniang), daughter of a businessman from Chicago. Of the same age,

---

39. See Huang Lin, *Jindai wenxue piping shi* (History of modern literary criticism) (Shanghai: Shanghai guji, 1993), 14–15, 686–87.

40. "Tang sheng," *New Fiction,* no. 7 (1903): 117–22.

they grow up as siblings and in such intimacy that they often forget that one is from the Old Empire and the other from the New World. When the Boxer rebellion breaks out and American public opinion turns against a reportedly xenophobic China, the boy reacts strongly and shuts himself off from all of his friends, including Irene, who fails to cheer him up even by forecasting a Chinese renaissance after the current humiliation. Deeply disturbed, Irene protests that he should not transfer his resentment of America to her, since her heart already belongs to him and so will her body soon. In short, she considers herself Chinese. The proud boy, however, argues that, according to ancient teachings, the inequality in their situations makes them unlikely spouses; further, his cruelty in rejecting her only shows his great compassion because he is saving her from future insults and derision. Sensing the boy's stubbornness, the girl stumbles out and kills herself by filling her room with gas, leaving behind two suicide notes. In the note to her father, Irene blames Americans for her death and requests that all of her belongings be left to the boy. In the other note, for Tang Sheng who "knows and loves her," she deplores that heaven did not make her a Chinese or him an American. She also expresses the wish that her soul will not perish and that they will meet again in paradise. Upon seeing the note, Tang Sheng nearly dies of sadness and decides to contribute the money left by Irene to a Chinese grade school in San Francisco as a way of immortalizing her love for China.

In the lengthy authorial commentary, written in the same fashion as the acknowledged model of the Historian of the Strange, who in turn had followed in the footsteps of the Feng Menglong of *A Classified History of Passion*,[41] Di Baoxian first explains that the story was originally reported in a Chinese-language newspaper in San Francisco. The thrust of the commentary, however, comes from his summarizing a much longer essay that, put forward by another commentator, commends Tang Sheng for rejecting Irene in the interest of defending his nation and preserving his race. The original essayist suggested that marriage had been the method by which the white race had appropriated the property rights to Hawaii and New Zealand, where native women were often eager to marry white

---

41. For a study of the intertextual constitution of Pu Songling's Historian of the Strange, see Judith T. Zeitlin, *Historian of the Strange: Pu Songling and the Chinese Classical Tale* (Stanford, Calif.: Stanford University Press, 1993), chap. 2, 43–57; also see Wai-yee Li, *Enchantment and Disenchantment,* chap. 3, 89–151.

men. "Such calamity will strike wherever no firm racial boundary exists. How terrible! How terrible!"[42] Racial discourse and nationalistic sentiments incited by the story led the author to denounce the new tendency to fawn on foreigners in the wake of the Boxer fiasco. Reaffirmed as the hero of the story, Tang Sheng also becomes a model for emulation, and consequently there seems to be hardly anything tragic about either the young boy's emotional agony or, especially, Irene's death.

Both this short text and Fu Lin's first-person narrative rely on the same historical event as a major narrative turning point. The Boxer rebellion, as an incomprehensible eruption of external history, botches a budding romantic love only to reveal a larger meaning and the determinations of human emotions. *The Sea of Regret* by Wu Jianren, too, employs the same narrative device, but the traumatic experience of history is more closely integrated into the plot,[43] and the tragic sense of human passion becomes more problematic and less translatable into a comic rationality.

From Trauma to Neurosis

In her pioneering study of the plot structure in late Qing fiction, Milena Doleželová-Velingerová underscores the pivotal contribution that Wu Jianren makes to the development of the modern novel through *The Sea of Regret,* probably the most sophisticated "unitary plot novel" of its time. "Its typological peculiarity is already apparent in a purely external feature: the novel is much shorter than the novels with the string-plot or the novels with the cyclical plot, and the number of acting characters is reduced drastically." In addition, its "concentration on the intimate theme of love (the main erotic motif being coupled with that of parental love and filial piety) is a major feature pointing towards the development of the psychological novel." What further propels an inward turn in the narrative is the recognized frailty of the individual, now "placed against the elemental forces of history." In the end, Doleželová-Velingerová comments, "the individual suffers a complete defeat from the evil force of

---

42. "Tang sheng," *New Fiction,* no. 7 (1903): 121.
43. It is therefore for a good reason that A Ying included *The Sea of Regret* in his *Gengzi shibian wenxue ji* (Anthology of literature about the 1900 incident) (Beijing: Zhonghua shuju, 1959), 2:603–70.

social circumstances, a tragic theme which foreshadows many stories of modern Chinese literature."[44]

The modernity of *The Sea of Regret*, therefore, derives not merely from its more unitary plot, or from its attention to the hapless individual vis-à-vis historical violence, but also from the psychological responses and processes it probes. As Michael Egan demonstrates, a "psychological realism" in the novel makes it a modern text that parallels similar developments in the Western novel. Of the two central characters, the focus of such psychological portrayal rests on Dihua the heroine, "whose depiction is more modern in that it is oriented toward her state of mind, and the emotional turmoil she endures in the course of the novel." The specific techniques for representing her inner life include "frequent interior monologues, (and) the weaving into the text of rhetorical addresses and questions, and subjective semantics which point to Dihua."[45] Her fiancé, Bohe, by contrast, is presented in a more traditional light because it is often his action rather than emotion, and his exterior rather than interior, that define his part in the plot and document the adverse effects of history.

The plot of *The Sea of Regret* indeed bears striking resemblances to Fu Lin's *Stones in the Sea,* but it is distinct from its immediate predecessor in numerous significant, even radical, ways. First of all, Wu Jianren's story contains a carefully constructed symmetry that helps the narrator drive home the feeling of regret as an inescapable condition. As in the first story, *The Sea of Regret* also begins with a government official's family in Beijing, with its two sons. The older brother, who has no function in *Stones in the Sea,* is now the central character in the sense that the tragic fate befalling him and his fiancée becomes the primary plot; the younger brother, who is the first-person narrator in the earlier story, now plays a secondary but complementary role. In a brothel in Shanghai, Zhong'ai the younger brother, steadfast and morally incorruptible, will eventually encounter his childhood sweetheart and fiancée Juanjuan, who apparently succumbs to the unspeakable degradation from which Aren in

---

44. Milena Doleželová-Velingerová, "Typology of Plot Structures in Late Qing Novels," in *The Chinese Novel at the Turn of the Century,* ed. Milena Doleželová-Velingerová (Toronto: University of Toronto Press, 1980), 50–52.

45. Michael Egan, "Characterization in *Sea of Woe,*" in *The Chinese Novel at the Turn of the Century,* ed. Doleželová-Velingerová, 165–76. See 166 and 171 for the quotations.

Stones in the Sea escapes by poisoning herself. Zhong'ai's resolute decision to become a hermit in the end mirrors the pious devotion of Dihua, his brother Bohe's fiancée, who shaves her head and retires into a nunnery after Bohe dies an opium addict. Obviously, the first novel is more than altered or rewritten by Wu Jianren; it is structurally absorbed into the second narrative, and the grief and disconsolation that sickens the first-person male narrator in *Stones in the Sea* now inflicts itself evenly on Dihua the virtuous widow and Zhong'ai the illustrious husband-to-be.

A second major structural difference between these two novels lies in their separate narrative voices. While the profile of the first-person narrator in *Stones in the Sea* befits that of a clever and profusely sentimental, if ultimately narcissistic, teenager, the omniscient narrator of *The Sea of Regret* tells the story in a concise, controlled, and descriptive style, greatly elevating the prose of vernacular fiction. Wu Jianren's remarkable success in representing the inner life of the central character, Dihua, was readily recognized by his contemporaries. The critic Yin Bansheng, who had deplored the scandalous new translation of *Joan Haste*, hailed the author as having "a magic hand at description," whose "literary sensitivity" (*wenqing*) could be as fluid and penetrating as glittering mercury poured over the ground.[46] For essentially the same reasons, A Ying dismissed *Stones in the Sea*, another narrative set against the 1900 Boxer uprising, as drastically inferior to Wu Jianren's *The Sea of Regret*.[47]

In fact, more convincingly than Fu Lin's confessional "I-novel," *The Sea of Regret* establishes the psychic experience of anxiety and fear as a viable and legitimate subject for literary representation. While both narratives aim at expounding a redemptive attachment or passion (*qing*), Wu Jianren's symmetrical tale of foiled romances links emotional turmoil to an encounter with danger, shock, and terror. Furthermore, his psychological realism serves not so much a cognitive function (in the sense of exposing a certain condition as starkly "real") as a social purpose by exalting human will and determination at a moment of vast disarray and crisis. This moral concern determines the paradigmatic significance of *The Sea of Regret* in that the representability of the individual psyche is now intimately related to historical trauma.

46. Yin Bansheng, "Xiaoshuo xianping" (Random comments on fiction), originally in *Youxi shijie* (Playful world), 1906, collected in Wei Shaochang, *Research Materials on Wu Jianren*, 134–36.

47. See A Ying, ed., *Anthology of Literature About the 1900 Incident*, 1:23–24.

In this light, two more points of difference between this pair of romantic novels become revealing: the effect of a traumatic event and the symbolism of gender roles. In Fu Lin's *Stones in the Sea,* the Boxer movement erupts and cuts short the blissful intimacy of a teenage couple. This intrusion of a fearful and impersonal reality takes place only in the last third of the narrative, at a moment when the assiduous youth finally succeeds in securing family acceptance of his amorous longing. Yet, even to the end, he remains sheltered from any immediate danger. Rather, it is the historical movement as dislodging that inflicts a devastating loss from which the boy will never recover. His sentimentalized narrative only magnifies his utter inability to comprehend reality beyond his secluded world of adolescent romance. In *The Sea of Regret,* by contrast, the same eruption of historical reality occurs in the opening chapter; by the conclusion of it, Dihua, her mother, and her fiancé, Bohe, are already outside Beijing and settle for the night as refugees in an inadequate village inn. While the narrator in *Stones in the Sea* reads about the fall of Beijing from afar, all the central characters in *The Sea of Regret* directly encounter the senseless violence and horror. Dihua and her mother are traumatized by a frenzied crowd; Bohe is chased and shot by an Allied soldier; Zhong'ai witnesses his parents' decapitated bodies in their Beijing family compound. The initial escape from the besieged capital perforce brings together Dihua and Bohe, whose families have carefully kept them apart, for the sake of propriety, since their betrothal at the age of twelve. Such involuntary dislocation determines the structure of the narrative as both a fearful *journey* into the unknown and a wish to *return* to normalcy. The central narrative tension therefore rests on the growing disparity between the need to assert a return (at least its possibility) and the experience of a forced journey. It rests on the choice of seeking refuge in oneself when external reality is recognized as overwhelmingly hostile and discontinuous.

Indeed, "the sea of regret" into which Wu Jianren plunges his characters points to a new psychological, as well as neurological, reality of hyperstimulation that may well be a defining feature of modern life.[48] Underlying the central pathos of "regret" is an experience of trauma,

48. See Georg Simmel's essay "The Metropolis and Mental Life," in *Classic Essays on the Culture of Cities,* ed. Richard Sennett (New York: Meredith, 1969), 47–60; and, more recently, Ben Singer, "Modernity, Hyperstimulus, and the Rise of Popular Sensationalism," in *Cinema and the Invention of Modern Life,* ed. Leo Charney and Vanessa Schwartz (Berkeley: University of California Press, 1995), 72–99.

both in the clinical sense of physical injury or neurological hyperstimulation, and as a psychoanalytical concept that explains the formation of anxiety or neurosis. An actually experienced situation of helplessness, according to Freud's 1926 work on anxiety, may be called a "traumatic situation," in relation to which "external and internal dangers, real dangers and instinctual demands converge."[49] Faced with such global threat, the individual subject may collapse into a panic or traumatic state that entails a temporary functional breakdown. Or, more often, a flight into neurosis occurs. Besides birth and the loss of a love object, a typical traumatic situation that gives rise to an intense feeling of helplessness and anxiety is the experience of modern warfare.[50] And war is indeed the enveloping condition under which Bohe, Dihua, and her mother find themselves as refugees. This traumatic situation therefore determines the rest of the narrative as constituting an anxiety-driven response, which also lends itself to provoking a larger and more symbolic question of choice and survival.

Before turning to its culturally deliberate choice in the form of neurotic insistence, we need to examine more closely the traumatic situation re-created in the novel. For it is at this critical moment that historical experience achieves specificity, and modernity manifests itself ominously as containing an utter shock when two technologically unequal worlds collide in violent juxtaposition. The larger historical background being the confrontation between the nativist Boxers, mostly equipped with nothing but fists and spears, and technologically advanced Allied forces, it soon becomes apparent that the immediate source of widespread panic and helplessness among the natives lies in the supernatural power of Western weaponry that introduces an accelerated sense of time and space. After all, the Boxer movement and its defeat in 1900 most effectively dramatized the deadly, disenchanting force that the modern rifle held over magic, sorcery, spiritual force, and martial arts (figure 1). Since the mid-nineteenth century the rifle had in fact been used by some Qing government troops,[51] but its symbolic association with modernity as a traumatic

---

49. Sigmund Freud, *Inhibitions, Symptoms and Anxiety,* rev. and ed. by James Strachey (New York: Norton, 1989), 101–04.

50. See Freud's 1919 essay, "Introduction to *Psycho-analysis and the War Neurosis,*" *Standard Edition,* 17:207–10. Another important essay on this topic by Freud was written in 1915, "Thoughts for the Times on War and Death," collected in *Freud: On War, Sex and Neurosis* (New York: Arts and Science Press, 1947), 245–76.

51. During the 1868 suppression of the Nian rebellion in northern China, for in-

event was starkest when Allied forces began systematically puncturing the Boxers' supposed invulnerability to bullets. In this aspect, *The Sea of Regret* may also be read as one of the earlier literary works dealing with an important psychic suffering of the twentieth century: war trauma and neurosis.

Within the novel, the trauma of witnessing the destructiveness of an alien technology most severely afflicts Dihua's mother, Miss Bai, who for this purpose functions as an indispensable auxiliary character. Suffering from a clear case of traumatic neurosis, she serves to demonstrate the catastrophic effect of seeking refuge from war. After numerous breakdowns, she dies an anguished death halfway through their tortuous trip south. The traumatic moment that sets off her nervous attack occurs when a panicked mob of refugees appears from nowhere and completely disorients Dihua, her mother and Bohe. "A crowd of people suddenly came surging toward them. There was no knowing how many there were, but they were all running for their lives and screaming at the top of their lungs: 'Help! The hairies are coming!'" (18; 121–22). Apparently fleeing from a hysterical fear of a phantom, the rampaging crowd sweeps Bohe away in an unknown direction. Dihua and her mother, riding inside a small, rented carriage, are "terrified out of their wits" at the incomprehensible sight, and they find themselves dragged headlong into a state of helplessness (21; 126).

This sudden eruption of danger distresses Miss Bai so severely that she subsequently displays standard symptoms of autonomic dysfunction, and she continually experiences flashbacks of the terrifying circumstances. The same evening, she wakes from a nightmare screaming for help. In her violent dream, she sees the same crowd that surrounded them during the day still chasing her, with a man slashing at her with a sword (24; 130–31). On the surface, her traumatic neurosis results directly from being hyperstimulated by the hysterical crowd, but what launches the crowd into panic is the rumored horror of being hunted by the invading Allied troops. Just before the crowd scene, in Bohe's eager conversation with other refugees at a roadside inn in which he tries to gauge the danger of their situation, the power of a Western rifle is vividly relayed with ap-

---

stance, Li Hongzhang's armies used rifles and artillery newly purchased from Westerners. See Jonathan D. Spence, *The Search for Modern China* (New York: Norton, 1990), 188.

1. Folk painting, *Tianjin cheng maifu dilei Dong Junmen dasheng xibing tu* (A depiction of Commander Dong winning a great victory over Western troops by laying mines in the city of Tianjin) (1900). From *Zhongguo jindaishi cankao tupian ji* (Collection of pictorial references for modern Chinese history) (Shanghai: Shanghai jiaoyu, 1958).

prehension (18; 121). In his desperate search for Dihua after the riotous run, Bohe finds himself perilously within range of a foreign soldier's gun, and he has to run for his life (19–20; 124). (The family servant Li Fu is subjected to a similar danger-situation earlier, except that he is actually shot in the shoulder.) Later, during the siege of Tianjin, where Bohe is stranded by himself, he is chased, again by an Allied soldier, sustains a gunshot wound to his thigh, and has to stop the gushing blood with a handful of dirt (48–49; 163–64).

Miss Bai and Dihua are mercifully spared such a direct confrontation after the crowd scene. As panicked refugees, they remain at a distance from any actual violence, although that distance often proves to be precarious and allows them neither to detach themselves completely nor to make sense of their plight. Because they are in no position to even imagine the scale of the impending catastrophe, their sense of danger is all the more incapacitating. One evening during their journey down the refugee-jammed canal, "a crescendo of shouts arose outside, scaring both women." Dihua goes to the bow of their boat and looks up, only to be shocked by the view. "In the distance six or seven fires raged so fiercely that they lit up the whole sky with a ruddy glow, a glow that was reflected in the faces of the people watching from the boats. Amid the babble of voices, faint cries and screams were to be heard in the distance, and Dihua's heart began pounding violently" (42; 154). Although she is told that the fire may have been set by Boxers to burn down churches, Dihua withdraws into the cabin and reassures her mother, who is trembling with fear, that it is a mere accident on shore. A few days later, the same incomprehensible spectacle of violence erupts nearby. "Suddenly a random volley of gun shots rang out on shore, scaring Miss Bai out of her wits again. Dihua had never heard anything like it before, and she, too, was so frightened that her heart began to pound. At the sight of her mother's panic, however, she rallied and forced herself to offer comfort." This time she makes up her own explanation: "That was only the government army firing at the Boxer bandits...." (44; 157). Their whole flight south figuratively moves them ever more deeply into a danger-situation where their only possible relation to reality is anxiety or the constant expectation of danger. "A danger-situation," so describes Freud, "is a recognized, remembered, and expected situation of helplessness."[52] In this state of anxious expectation, a known, external danger is internalized and often triggers a neurotic danger, which is one still to be discovered and is usually symptomatic of a dissatisfied "instinctual demand." In other words, a danger-situation arises where anxiety signals not merely an external threat, but also an internal crisis, a challenge of the constitution of the self or ego from within. It exists where anxiety and neurosis, "a surplus of anxiety," reveal themselves as a symbiotic continuum. The narrator of *The Sea of Regret* keeps the female characters in this danger-situation most of the time and refuses to make their position as sheltered bystanders any less agonizing or traumatic.

In accordance with Dihua and her mother's position as passive witnesses to violence, the narrator offers little to make the events more sensible, although the story line of "escape" provides an effective framework,

---

52. Freud, *Inhibitions, Symptoms and Anxiety*, 102.

38 *Chinese Modern*

as A Ying comments, to "capture all the fright, rumors, terror, gunfire, and foreign troops."[53] Critics such as A Ying may complain that the novel does not cast the Boxers in a positive light, but the narrative shows a profound indifference to various political or ideological justifications of violence. The absence of a master narrative of collective action or historical rationality—nationalism or anti-imperialism—determines that the characters be unwilling witnesses to, rather than active participants in, the spectacle of group violence. The novel's psychological realism, to which we now turn, is therefore more than a stylistic achievement; it results from an overdetermined insulation of the focal characters from any collective alliance or identity. Such insulation leaves the individuals psychologically vulnerable to all violent disruptions of their world, which are inevitably experienced as trauma. Even the unfamiliar circumstances of the few village inns where they stay come as a shock to Dihua, who as a protected upper-class young woman has to overcome timidity and cope with poverty and what to her appears as an alien social reality—the peasants. The precarious distance from any site of action, in the end, allows for a new self-consciousness to emerge, for the traumatic hyperstimulation at once breaks down the insulation and forces the individual subjects to react to the crisis with utmost urgency. Such is the condition in which we find Dihua, a pious young woman whose subjectivity suggests a problematic convergence of virtue and sexuality.

Virtuous Passion, Virtual Erotics

As I suggested, the distribution of gender roles in the novel is anything but innocent. To convey the enormity of the loss, the journey is bound to turn into a painful process of decline and degeneration, which, in the case of Bohe, reaches a point of no return with his opium addiction and death. At the same time, the narrative also creates and institutes an interior life as the defensive mechanism against a chaotic condition over which no individual has any effective control. Obviously, this reactive interiority is designated to Dihua, who grows ever more determined to return life to its normal course and promised fulfillment. The implicit gender symbol-

---

53. A Ying, *History of Late Qing Fiction*, 57.

ism is even more striking if we recall the short story "Tang Sheng," in which a stubborn young man is chosen to embody the national pride of China, whereas Irene is the one to sacrifice her life in protest against an unjust reality. Through Dihua's transformation, most notably in her final withdrawal from secular life, her story documents an individual's defeat as much as it does a triumph of her will. Feminine chastity is now implicated in safeguarding the inner essence of the native tradition. Here, we enter a different aspect of the narrative than the danger-situation that incessantly generates anxiety. In contrast to Miss Bai's fit and fright, we see Dihua's virtuous passion; instead of a nervous breakdown, Dihua, apparently traumatized by violence and death, develops what may be described as a complex obsessional neurosis that functions as her surrogate self-identity.

Such a pathologizing view of Dihua compels us to return to Freud's observation that a neurotic anxiety inevitably indicates an unsatisfied instinctual demand. In the case of obsessional neurosis, according to a metapsychoanalytical Freud in *Civilization and Its Discontents* (1930), "the sense of guilt [*Schuldgefühl*] makes itself noisily heard in consciousness." "Every neurosis," Freud further asserts, "conceals a quota of [an] unconscious sense of guilt, which in its turn fortifies the symptoms by making use of them as a punishment." More specifically, neurotic symptoms, in psychoanalytical terms, are "substitutive satisfactions for unfulfilled sexual wishes."[54] From the outset, the plot development in *The Sea of Regret* formulates Dihua's subjectivity or self-conception predominantly through her feelings of guilt and self-blame; her virtuous devotion and passion, in the process, offer a refuge from her own desire, but devotion and passion also gradually acquire the intensity of virtual erotic excitement and pleasure. As unreleased sexual tension and energy constitute the etiology of Dihua's obsessional neurosis, the hagiographical account of her virtuous passion involves—in addition to a new selfhood/sainthood formed through denial and repression—a sympathetic description of her libidinal desire.[55]

54. Sigmund Freud, *Civilization and Its Discontents*, trans. by James Strachey (New York: Norton, 1961), 92–97.

55. Ever since 1905, when he published "My Views on the Part Played by Sexuality in the Aetiology of the Neurosis," Freud never completely gave up his analysis that the "modern nervousness" originates in the conflict between libido and civilization.

The sense of guilt that Dihua is enticed to feel initially derives from a "fear of the external authority" or a censorious super-ego,[56] which in the given cultural context is conveyed through concrete "maxims for young women" and "rules of propriety" that the much-protected girl grows up memorizing. (In the book's opening chapter we are told that after dutifully giving up her studies as she approaches puberty, Dihua forgets the specific wording of the classics but remains mindful of their general meaning [8; 108].) The first time that the narrator allows us into her vexed mind is the second night into the frightful journey, when Bohe comes down with a cold as a result of sleeping in the poorly insulated antechamber of the village inn. Because of this untimely sickness, the so far strictly external disarray turns into an exacerbatingly personal problem for Dihua. Her mother, Miss Bai, has asked a feverish Bohe to come inside and share the same and only platform bed (*kang*), but Dihua is too shy to sleep there, even though Miss Bai lies in the middle and sets up a low table as an additional boundary. Noticing that Dihua intends to sit up all night, Bohe gets up and offers to go out to the front room again, only to be stopped by Miss Bai, who admonishes her daughter for being too rigid with formalities when they are in such a desperate situation. After repeated urging, Dihua finally compromises and lies down with her clothes on.

> If I don't lie down, she thought, I'll be preventing Mother from getting any sleep. But this is such an unseemly situation, it makes me feel highly uncomfortable. If we'd married before we left, that would be one thing, but we're still bound by the rules of propriety, and I can't even personally ask him how he's feeling while he has cause to show concern for me. If I don't lie down, what a poor return that would be for all his kindness! But then again how could an unmarried couple sleep in the same platform bed? At the very thought she felt a sharp, prickling sensation down her spine. (13; 114)

56. Freud, *Civilization and Its Discontents,* 92–94. On p. 94, Freud writes, "As to a sense of guilt, we must admit that it is in existence before the super-ego, and therefore before conscience, too. At that time it is the immediate expression of fears of the external authority. It is the direct derivative of the conflict between the need for the authority's love and the urge towards instinctual satisfaction, whose inhibition produces the inclination to aggression." Two pages earlier, he also states that "the sense of guilt is at bottom nothing else but a topographical variety of anxiety; in its later phases it coincides completely with *fear of the super-ego*" (original italics).

Needless to say, tortured by such conflictual demands and uncertainties, Dihua gets no sleep that night. The "sharp, prickling sensation" she sustains down her back pointedly reminds her of the closeness of Bohe's body, but it also alerts her to the sense of being watched over by some piercing, though imagined, eye. This acute pain results from a heightened sense of conflict. In experiencing this psychosomatic pain, she also undergoes a self-formation, which can be articulated only as a fear of acknowledging herself and her own desire. This new self-consciousness or subjectivity, consequently, will derive its continual reassurance from ever greater pain or even self-immolation, because by subjecting herself to pain the subject actively transforms her own body into an object over which she can claim a victory of will.

Put differently, a masochistic will to self-affirmation necessarily constitutes the subjectivity formed in fear.[57] To secure recognition from others, the new subject will have to make her need for punishment a public event, through which she presents her pained body as an instance of willed self-abnegation. The paradox is that only through a demonstrable disavowal of herself will she be accepted as a self-willed subject. Hence, the ontological exigency embedded in Dihua's obsessional neurosis, which allows for a semblance of agency and is lauded as virtuous passion or acceptable self-sacrifice. "In conflict between her desires and her sense of duty," Freud comments on the frustrating consequences of monogamy, a married woman "again will seek refuge in neurosis. Nothing protects her virtue so securely as illness."[58] When, in the end, Bohe dies in a Shanghai hospital, for instance, Dihua blames herself for his demise and, with a pair of scissors, removes her ten fingernails and a lock of hair. "After wrapping up both items, she tucked them inside one of Bohe's sleeves.

---

57. "The sense of guilt, the harshness of the super-ego, is thus the same thing as the severity of the conscience. It is the perception which the ego has of being watched over in this way, the assessment of the tension between its own strivings and the demands of the super-ego. The fear of this critical agency (a fear which is at the bottom of the whole relationship), the need for punishment, is an instinctual manifestation on the part of the ego, which has become masochistic under the influence of a sadistic super-ego" (Freud, *Civilization and Its Discontents,* 94). For further discussion of masochism and the failure of the modern male subject in Ba Jin's *Cold Nights,* see chap. 4 below, "The Last Tubercular in Modern Chinese Literature."

58. Freud, "'Civilized' Sexual Morality and Modern Nervousness (1908)," collected in *Sexuality and the Psychology of Love,* ed. with intro. by Philip Rieff (New York: Collier Books, 1963), 23.

'Master Chen,' she said, 'if you are conscious in that other world, come back soon and take me away with you!'" In the wake of such symbolic self-immolation, she "began to wail, and all those present wept with her. Someone who knew her story remarked: 'And she was only his fiancée, too!' at which they were even more favorably impressed" (73; 199).

The evocation of virtue is a crucial ideological operation in *The Sea of Regret*, for the narrative is self-consciously hagiographical rather than pathographical. Through Dihua, virtues such as "sincerity" or "devotion" are mobilized from native cultural resources as a cardinal principle to cope with a comprehensive danger-situation. The symbolic richness of Dihua's hardship is evident if we speculate how the novel would work differently, should the daughter, rather than her mother, faint first during the mob scene and therefore become the mother's responsibility. Dihua in the narrative occupies a nodal point in the fabric of patriarchally delineated human relations, since she is a daughter as well as a fiancée. When stranded halfway between Beijing and Shanghai, she finds herself "worrying about her mother, missing her father, longing for her fiancé" (57; 176). If Dihua's taking care of her sick mother can be viewed as "natural" in regard to the biological as well as emotional bond between them, her devotion to Bohe then affirms a conscious and socially meaningful commitment. What the narrative constructs, significantly, is Dihua first as a good daughter and then as a good wife. To fulfill both roles, she has to be totally concentrated and selfless. As her mother's illness gets worse, Dihua decides to try an age-old method of curing one's parents with one's own flesh. After shearing a piece of flesh off her arm and offering it to the patient in a medicinal soup, Dihua still fails to save her mother. While grieving copiously, she begins to wonder:

> Perhaps her failure to cure her mother with that morsel of flesh showed that the ancients were lying, she thought. But how could their lies have been passed down over so many years without anyone seeing through them? No doubt the ancients weren't lying at all; it was her own heart that wasn't sincere [*cheng*] enough. At this thought she began to hate herself for her insincerity, banging her head against the bed and crying herself into a state of stupor. (59; 179)[59]

59. Dihua's reaction stands in sharp contrast to that of Lu Xun's Madman, whose central question is: "Is it right because it has always been like that?" See chap. 2 below.

The same belief in "sincerity" motivates Dihua in her caring for Bohe when he unexpectedly turns up as a depraved opium addict. In persuading her father to let her marry Bohe, Dihua reasons: "There's a saying of the ancients that springs to mind: 'Metal and stone will yield before a sincere [*cheng*] heart.' After we're married, I'll put my trust in a perfectly sincere heart, and perhaps, who knows, I may be able to inspire him to change" (69; 193). "Sincerity," or extraordinary devotion, becomes a source of strength; its evocation expresses the longing for an anchoring stability in a mutable and contingent world. More significantly, in quoting a cultural maxim about spiritual purity, the young woman effectively calls into place an inner realm of authenticity that, equated with the indigenous cultural tradition, both shields the vexed individual and requires her active defense. This interiorized zone has the same function as a set of core values that, ever more pronounced at a moment of crisis and confusion, serves to constitute a discourse of endangered authenticity, which, in turn, shares the structure of a neurotic reaction in the wake of a hyperstimulating trauma. The notion of "concentrated sincerity," for instance, also evoked in *Stones in the Sea,* derives from a fundamental concept in Chinese classics regarding "genuineness" and "truthfulness" in human interaction and emotion.[60] In other words, it belongs to an indigenous discourse on authenticity. The narrator's choice to let Dihua articulate her belief in the moving force of sincerity is therefore deliberate. It fully inscribes her into the established tradition of values and virtues. It also reveals that the virtuous passion she practices as a compensatory intensity in the face of a disintegrating world symbolically enacts the salvation of an entire cultural heritage. In this sense, the creation of Dihua in *The Sea of Regret* reflects a general anxiety over the continuity as much as

---

60. The earliest and most classic discussion of *jingcheng* occurs in a fable titled "The Old Fisherman" in the writings of Zhuangzi. Upon being asked by Confucius what he means by "genuineness," which he urges Confucius to cultivate and guard, the old fisherman answers: "The genuine is the most quintessential, the most sincere. What fails to be quintessential and sincere cannot move others." See A. C. Graham's translation in *Chuang-tzu: The Seven Inner Chapters and Other Writings from the Book of Chuang-tzu* (London: George Allen & Unwin, 1981), 251. Graham's translation of *jingcheng,* in my opinion, is an improvement on those by Herbert A. Giles ("the perfection of truth unalloyed") and Burton Watson ("purity and sincerity in their highest degree"), although all these translations shed light on the richness of the concept.

44 *Chinese Modern*

the purity of a threatened native culture, an anxiety that is best expressed through an overdetermined female character.[61]

Yet the origin of Dihua's virtuousness points to a sense of guilt that she feels toward Bohe's fall. Her passionate devotion to her fiancé is largely based on her own perceived indebtedness and is recharged continually insofar as she sees herself obligated to what she has personally incurred. After the first scene of unintelligible violence, when Bohe is swept away by the swarming crowd, Dihua first worries about his safety and then starts to blame herself. "Then again she thought: This is all my fault. So concerned about proper behavior that I even refused to speak to him. . . . If only I'd been willing to talk to him, he'd have been happy to join me, and none of this would have occurred. Oh, Cousin Bohe, I'm the one who did you in! If anything dreadful does happen to you, what am I going to do?" (23; 129). This self-blame she will carry even further when in a nightmare she sees Bohe pass by without speaking to her. Upon waking up, she wonders whether she has given their carriage driver a motive to murder Bohe for his money (34–35; 143–144). Constantly seeking indemnity in and through herself allows Dihua a masochistic sense of selfhood, for her extraordinary willpower gains acceptance and currency when she is supposedly repaying her debt—psychic or symbolic. Any subsequent agency or self-determination that she seems to achieve is always already circulating within an overarching relationship of indebtedness—"the sea of regret." If we stop here, we may be justified in criticizing a patriarchal system that subjects an individual to such an ineluctable net of indebtedness. We may even generalize about the victimization of women through a rhetoric of virtue and about the oppressive nature of traditional social order: "If feminine self-sacrifice was the major support of traditional Chinese culture, it is not surprising that, during a period of massive social transformations, the collapse of tradition would find its most *moving* representations in the figures of those who are traditionally the

---

61. Wu Jianren would express his cultural anxiety more openly in the preamble to his last novel, where he admonishes his readers to read his story "with Chinese eyes" and listen to the message "with Chinese ears." See *Qing bian* (Passion transformed), collected in *Passion Transformed*, 205–06. For a discussion of the moral and cultural choices embodied in female characters in late Qing fiction, see Chen Pingyuan, *History of Twentieth-Century Chinese Fiction: Volume One, 1897–1916*, 220–21.

most oppressed, figures that become 'stand-ins' for China's traumatized *self-consciousness* in every sense of the phrase."[62]

No doubt this is a persuasive instance of theorization, but it may flatten the unexpected and ambivalent content that goes into a traumatized self-consciousness, which is often recognized as contiguous with self-sacrifice or virtue, since it is the constitution and agency of the self that is thrown into crisis at a given moment of trauma and/or massive social transformations. In the process, Dihua's virtuous passion, for instance, is also intricately compounded by her sexual awakening. The intense sense of guilt makes it possible for Dihua to fantasize, as if to convince herself of what is lost, about a fully gratifying romantic relationship between herself and Bohe. Her experience of erotic desire is representable and legitimate, not only because it is a fantasy about their yet to be consummated marriage, but also because he is absent. The impossibility of its actual satisfaction, therefore, is a necessary condition for Dihua to assert her desire and anticipate a genuine happiness. This is the situation in which her thinking about Bohe develops into an obsession, and neurosis begins to substitute for sexual satisfaction.

> That night, under Bohe's bedding, Dihua's feelings uncontrollably grew into an infatuation [*qing ji cheng chi*]. She said to herself that although they were still not married, she was—at her mother's express command—sleeping in her fiancé's bedding; perhaps it was a sign of a "shared quilt" in their future. These fond thoughts clung to her mind and, before she knew it, had freed her, for the time being at least, from all her sorrows and cares. Instead she contemplated how much love and respect she would show him after they were married. . . . At this joyous prospect, she experienced a desire that could not be satisfied, a desire from which she drifted into a sound sleep. (38–39; 150)

Even after waking up, Dihua is still overwhelmed by what the narrator consistently calls *chixiang* or *chinian,* which can mean a wide range of thoughts and ideas (blind, silly, wishful, infatuated, obsessed, crazy), but in this context it describes a sexual arousal or obsession. The inten-

---

62. Chow, *Woman and Chinese Modernity,* chap. 4, "Loving Women: Masochism, Fantasy, and the Idealization of Mother," 170; italics in original.

sity of this longing is itself so pleasurable that Dihua, holding and fingering Bohe's bedding, experiences an erotic excitement. Such an amorous fantasy, however, does not disagree with her virtue because it centers on Bohe, who of necessity must not reciprocate. The object of her sexual desire is sanctioned by her betrothal and only synecdochically can be recalled into presence. This condition is further dramatized when Bohe is so sick and bedridden that Dihua has to bend over and feed him medicine mouth-to-mouth (71; 196). At this moment, eroticism is finally fused with a mothering instinct. Bohe's pale passivity, which may be viewed as a long-established formulaic position for the male character in traditional romances,[63] negatively reveals what the notion of virtuous passion seeks to disavow, namely, active satisfaction through sexual pleasure. Dihua's virtuous passion, on the other hand, has its precedent in numerous pious women (*jiefu*) canonized by the late imperial tradition. Through a virtual erotics it becomes clear that neurosis not only allows her a form of agency and self-sufficiency, but it also serves as a substitutive satisfaction for her nascent sexual desire. Thus a greatly complicated portrayal of a modern *jiefu*/saint. In acknowledging Dihua's sexuality and relating it to her piety, the narrator of *The Sea of Regret* interjects pleasurable experience at a moment of crisis and trauma and thus creates a lasting ambiguity in the narrative.

Partly because of the intriguing status of sexuality within the narrative, *The Sea of Regret* has given rise to continuous rereadings. In 1926, for instance, one enthusiastic commentator recommended the novel as appropriate reading material for high school students because of its thematic proximity to "modern life." This critic even claimed that Wu Jianren belongs in the same rank of classical novelists as Shi Nai'an (*Water Margin*) and Cao Xueqin (*Dream of the Red Chamber*).[64] In his 1939 *Zhongguo xiaoshuo shi* (History of Chinese fiction), Guo Zhenyi hailed *The Sea of Regret* as "an extremely refreshing problem novel" that attacks the traditional marriage system.[65] Yet a less sympathetic critic, years later, would denounce the novel as advocating a conservative "feudal understanding

---

63. See Li, *Enchantment and Disenchantment*, 108.

64. See Wei Bingxin, "Xu" (Preface) to the 1926 edition of *The Sea of Regret* (Shanghai: Shijie shuju), 1–2.

65. Guo Zhenyi, *Zhongguo xiaoshuo shi* (History of Chinese fiction) (Changsha: Commercial Press, 1939), 2:552.

of marriage,"[66] an assessment that by and large represented the then official view of late Qing and early Republican romantic fiction, which based itself on the May Fourth rejection of traditional forms and values.

These subsequent readings and rereadings of the text, like all interpretive exercises, reveal just as much about the process and condition of appropriating it as a relevant moment of history. The same observation applies to this book, for which the intricate relation between trauma and passion becomes a central issue. More directly, continued interpretations testify to the paradigmatic ambiguity that *The Sea of Regret* has at the beginning of twentieth-century Chinese literature. In reclaiming the writing of a mythical pathos and revitalizing the discourse of passion, Wu Jianren more than modernized the tradition of romantic fiction and inaugurated a literary genre that would flourish in the following decades, most notably in the popular romances of the Mandarin Duck and Butterfly school. It is his concern with the human consequences of a hyperstimulating world, rather than "a severe weakness for romantic love stories,"[67] that enriched and humanized the new fiction of the late Qing period. Against the grain of reformist fiction that strove for a new elevating master narrative, *The Sea of Regret* began to delve into a different realm, namely, heroic individual choices in everyday life. Its psychological realism that wavers, almost deliberately, between hagiography and pathography is a necessary rhetorical device to both capture the impact of a historical trauma and exhort the human efforts at healing and overcoming adversity. It leads to an anxiety-driven narrative that is deeply ambivalent, not the least because it focuses on the awakening of a self-consciousness that is feminine, which in the context is expressed through a complex discourse of passion that fuses virtue and sexuality. The "tragic theme" introduced by the novel and, according to Doleželová-Velingerová, foreshadowing many stories of modern Chinese literature, celebrates the triumph of human passion that nonetheless results in no gratifying, comic resolution. More than a story line or theme,

---

66. Ren Fangqiu, *Zhongguo jindai wenxue zuojia lun* (Essays on modern Chinese writers) (Zhengzhou: Henan renmin, 1984), 249–61.

67. See Link, *Mandarin Ducks and Butterflies,* 147–48. Here, Link lists Wu Jianren's influential romances as one cause for "the gradual degeneration of the new fiction" from 1905 through 1915. This process is described critically as a transition "from nation-building to time-killing to profit."

the narrative presents a tragic consciousness that will saturate modern romances and distinguish them from most late imperial love stories.⁶⁸ It is to become a highly symbolic narrative to the extent that it reveals hagiography and pathography as two deeply conflictual but mutually dependent operations in the representation of Chinese reality in the twentieth century. For while hagiography may allow a semblance of meaning, pathography registers a visceral experience that is only too immediate and overwhelming. This agonizing divergence between meaning and experience besets many a seminal text in the body of twentieth-century Chinese literature. Being one such central narrative, *The Sea of Regret* also belongs to the transitional moment of "beginning" insofar as it reworks a seemingly familiar plot and renders it utterly indeterminate, often against the author's pronounced determination.

68. For a discussion of the "tragic consciousness" in early Republican romances, see Chen Bohai and Yuan Jin, eds., *Shanghai jindai wenxue shi* (History of modern Shanghai literature) (Shanghai: Shanghai renmin, 1993), 376–77.

2

Lu Xun's "Diary of a Madman" and a Chinese Modernism

First published in the self-consciously avant-garde journal *Xin qingnian* (New youth) in 1918, "Kuangren riji" (Diary of a madman) almost immediately established its author, Lu Xun (1881–1936), as an emblematic writer of the then burgeoning New Culture movement, and it has since gained recognition as a prototypical text of social protest and criticism in modern Chinese literature. It also has been widely regarded as the first modern story in twentieth-century Chinese literature.[1] The short story, as the title promises, presents the fragmented and often imaginative writings of a deranged personality—a paranoiac who insists that all those around him are either disguised or unabashed cannibals, waiting to prey on him. The setting is a nameless village community that appears to be sealed off from the outside world, a milieu typical of most of Lu Xun's major stories yet to follow. From this suffocating "iron house," as Lu Xun would later characterize the oppressive reality of traditional China, the Madman lets out his cry of anguish and defiance. One of the earliest literary works to articulate antitraditionalism as a revolutionary ethos, "Diary of a Madman" provided the New Culture movement of the May Fourth period (1917–27) not only with a concerted theme but also with a new image and language.

The New Culture movement, as a far-reaching intellectual revolution, had unmistakable aspirations for Western modernity—its express ideological symbols being science and technology, general enlightenment, revolution, and democracy. "Diary of a Madman," as my reading in this chapter demonstrates, is a modernist text that critically underscores that longing. Such a reading necessarily challenges the conventional understanding of Lu Xun and incurs some theoretical difficulties. It seems to put an old-fashioned and essentially Western label on a key text in the

---

1. See, for example, Wong Yoon Wah, "The Influence of Western Literature on China's First Modern Story," in Wong, *Essays on Chinese Literature: A Comparative Approach* (Singapore: Singapore University Press, 1988), 52–66.

twentieth-century Chinese literary tradition, thus synecdochically rewriting that tradition into a dubious story about repetition—a practice that might even be suspected of subscribing to Western cultural hegemony. In addition, by throwing a modernist overcoat on Lu Xun, it may appear to be anachronistically attempting to distort or recast a historical reality. To suggest a modernist feature in Lu Xun, as a critic commented in 1996, would inevitably entail a reconceptualization of the course of modern Chinese literature in the twentieth century, since much historiography and interpretation of this tradition depend on reading Lu Xun as a realist founding father.[2] A clarification seems to be in order at the outset.

The Motility of Chinese Modernism

First of all, the term *modernism,* when applied to a Chinese text, cannot be taken simply as a periodizing concept. It should not be forced to suggest a facile repetition, in the historiographical sense, of Western modernism as either a literary movement or a cultural experience. On the contrary, the use of a culturally specific concept like modernism in the Chinese context works not so much to designate an identifiable historical moment as to highlight the absence of "high modernism," of any figure akin to, for instance, Proust or Joyce in the European canon. Although its denotation may vary considerably from context to context, modernism, in a general history of Western literature, describes the literary movements and production that flourished in the second half of the nineteenth century and the first quarter of the twentieth century. In a concentrated form, it articulates as well as interrogates the Western experience of modernity. To reconstruct a Chinese literary history based on the same pattern or to impose a modernist stage as an indispensable carte d'entrée into the modern world would result in what Gayatri Spivak theorizes as a "subaltern cognitive failure." Such a failure would stand as an effect of the "epistemic violence" that, according to Spivak, not only helps to objectify a different

2. Chen Fangjing, "Lu Xun de xiandai zhuyi tezhi: yige benshiji Zhongguo wenxue miaoshu ying yu shenhua de lunti" (The modernist feature of Lu Xun: a topic to be pursued in depicting Chinese literature in this century), *Lu Xun yanjiu yuekan* (Lu Xun studies monthly) (November 1996): 47–51. This brief article no doubt reflects a new and important development in the enormous Lu Xun scholarship that has been a virtual state-run enterprise.

other but also institutes the hegemony of a given form of knowledge.³ This epistemic violence necessarily accompanies an unequal power relation and founds its legitimizing ideology.

A case in point is the modern Chinese literary canon that, for most of the twentieth century, was shaped through a hegemonic imposition, although here a codified realism rather than modernism served as the master trope. A systematic valorization of realistic representation helped streamline the literary production and erect a critical paradigm. The history of Lu Xun studies up until the 1980s abundantly attests to the force of such ideological doctrine. Once widely acclaimed as the "Chinese Gorky," Lu Xun was revered in the 1930s and the early 1980s alike for his "most clearheaded realism."⁴ Critical realism is said to have bridged his early stage of revolutionary romanticism and his later, more mature period of socialism—a complete course of the Hegelian *Aufhebung* rerun in the Chinese field.⁵ A meaningful repetition of the "progressive" Western experience is thus prescribed in teleological narratives. Even classical Chinese poets, such as Li Bai (Li Po) and Du Fu (Tu Fu), would be neatly classified as either romantic or realistic and paired with their European counterparts.

The point, however, is not to lament the loss of an indigenous language. Although it is tempting to imagine that this unspoken language could have furnished Chinese writers with vindictive authenticity and ingenuity, nativism or obscurantism offers only an inadequate answer to the ineluctable interaction with Western modernity. What we as literary

3. Gayatri C. Spivak, "Subaltern Studies: Deconstructing Historiography," in her *In Other Worlds: Essays in Cultural Politics* (New York: Methuen, 1987), 202, 209.

4. See, for instance, Qu Qiubai, "Lu Xun zawen xuan xu" (Preface to selections of Lu Xun's random thoughts essays), collected in Li Zongying and Zhang Mengyang, eds., *Liushi nianlai Lu Xun yanjiu lunwen xuan* (Selected essays of Lu Xun studies in the past sixty years), 2 vols. (Beijing: Zhongguo shehui kexue, 1982), 1:120–27; Liu Dajie, "Lu Xun yu xianshi zhuyi" (Lu Xun and realism), in Li Zongying and Zhang Mengyang, *Selected Essays*, 1:192–98; Wang Yao, "Lu Xun sixiang de yige zhongyao tese: qingxing de xianshi zhuyi" (An important feature of Lu Xun's thinking: clearheaded realism), in *Beijing daxue Lu Xun danchen yibai zhounian jinian wenji* (Commemorative essays from Peking University on the centenary of Lu Xun's birth), ed. Wang Yao (Beijing: Peking University Press, 1982), 1–18.

5. See Li Zehou, "Jianlun Lu Xun sixiang de fazhan" (A brief essay on the development of Lu Xun's thought), in his *Zhongguo jindai sixiangshi lun* (Essays on modern Chinese intellectual history) (Taipei: Fengyun shidai, 1990), 521–59.

scholars should do instead is to historicize the language that frames our understanding and knowledge. The horizon of intelligibility, which is not static to begin with, should itself be open to interpretation and historical investigation. For all the literary or nonliterary terms we use and find convenient to use (*realism, romanticism, symbolism, modernism,* and even *postmodernism*) are as much a disobedient machine that twists and misstamps our experience as a functioning theoretical apparatus through which actual political, ideological confrontations on local and global scales are staged and played out.

Therefore, evoking modernism in our reading of Lu Xun's story serves at least a dual purpose: it calls into question a dogmatic realist appropriation of Lu Xun that in fact presupposes a Eurocentric historical paradigm (although in the guise of a revolutionary ideology); and, in causing the dominant critical paradigm to shift, it may reveal aspects of the text that will address our present concerns more directly. This paradigmatic shift must take place on two related levels: our understanding of Western modernism itself and our reconstruction of modern Chinese literary history.

Given that literary (or cultural) modernism is most likely to emerge at a moment of massive and rapid modernization, it best expresses what in Hegelian terms can be characterized as the "unhappy consciousness" of modernity. Modernity, observes Jürgen Habermas, bases itself on the idealist "principle of subjectivity" that, as a legitimizing ideology of the rising bourgeoisie, is historically institutionalized through the Reformation, the Enlightenment, and the French Revolution. All of these violent experiences of concentrated social change and discontinuity call forth a modernist "time-consciousness,"[6] whereby the "future" or historical progress turns into a central value and aspiration. With such intensified experience of evolutionary time, a fundamental philosophical problem for a post-Enlightenment secular society is then the securing of self-reassurance for the emancipated modern individual. Challenged by a bifurcation of experience such as public versus private, or work versus pleasure (which Habermas terms the "crisis of the diremption of life"),[7] modern subjectivity constantly has to assert its coherence, and in seek-

6. Jürgen Habermas, *The Philosophical Discourse of Modernity: Twelve Lectures,* trans. Frederick Lawrence (Cambridge: MIT Press, 1987), 13.
7. Ibid., 21.

ing self-affirmation it posits an other that is to be regarded and mastered as an object. An aggressive impulse is therefore built into modern self-consciousness. Hence, the colonial voyage to the "heart of darkness," as part of the Western experience of modernity, is inevitably also a journey of self-discovery.

Only a depoliticized representation of modernity will efface this constitutive presence of the other. Matei Calinescu, for instance, depicts one aspect of modernity as a self-referential experience of the self-centered subject. The foundation of modernist culture is therefore allegedly forged by an identity of time and self.[8] Not surprisingly, to propose a modernism in a culture that has not gone through the Western style of modernity and has in fact functioned as the other of this experience (modern Chinese history being a rich document of painful confrontations with a formidable West), we must come to terms with a subject that is neither the radically different other of the Western subject nor a simple replica of the Western consciousness. What produces and marks off this subaltern subject is, and can only be, its specific history—not simply the history of its pre-European experience preserved in a collective unconscious and inscribed on all levels of its present existence, but also a history of receiving the imperialist gaze, admiring the supernatural power of industrial civilization, and finally of looking back at and interacting with an imposing other. A modernism of the subaltern subject, therefore, is a historical necessity grown out of this interactive coexistence that is marked by a "nonsynchronous synchronicity"; the insurgence of such a subject has to be recognized by a remapping and reimagining of the imaginary world space.

In this context it is interesting to recall Fredric Jameson's 1986 essay "Third-World Literature in the Era of Multinational Capitalism." Although his reading of Third World literature as a national allegory "of the embattled situation of the public third-world culture and society" has provoked widespread critical interest and responses,[9] Jameson seems

---

8. Matei Calinescu, *Five Faces of Modernity: Modernism, Avant-garde, Decadence, Kitsch, Postmodernism* (Durham, N.C.: Duke University Press, 1987), 5. For a more general discussion of this modern condition, see Johannes Fabian, *Time and the Other: How Anthropology Makes Its Object* (New York: Columbia University Press, 1983).

9. See Fredric Jameson, "Third-World Literature in the Era of Multinational Capitalism," *Social Text* 15 (1986): 65–88. Aijaz Ahmad's critical response to Jameson's essay

to me justified in attempting to broach the West's drained discourse of subjectivity by inserting a literary production that incorporates the explosively, rather than implosively, political dimension of social life. The "essential operation" here, according to Jameson, is a historicizing "differentiation" that creates a tension between a complacent American public and a politically and culturally potent Third World text, not permitting the one to consume or subordinate the other.[10] His allegorical reading unsettles rather than gratifies a readership accustomed to a rapid recycling of fashions, not the least of which is politics. In this essay, as we will see shortly, Jameson also offers fresh insights into Lu Xun's "Diary of a Madman."

Similarly, constructing a Chinese modernism has a more local, though an equally far-reaching, function; it helps to bring about an epistemological break and to introduce challenge and crisis to a literary canon formed through a rigid official realism. Modernism appears to be a historically determined choice against an ossified and manipulative realist ideology. For a quick overview of the Chinese situation, where the bankruptcy of official realism was reflected in its stringency, we can turn to Robert Kiely, who visited many Chinese colleges and universities in the early 1980s to lecture on contemporary American writers. Reflecting on his rather revelatory experience, he wrote:

> Because of the censorship of Western literature since the 1950s and the virtual black-out during the Cultural Revolution (1966–76), the greatest curiosity I encountered was about literary trends and movements in the twentieth century. I soon learned that terminology, including literary jargon, has a distinctive flavor and political coloration in China. Terms like "streams of consciousness" or "romantic irony"—loosely bandied about in American classrooms—had an effect comparable to "abortion-on-demand" or "school prayer" in certain parts of the United States.[11]

---

can be read as a systematic expression of the dissatisfaction with Jameson's allegedly totalizing narrative. Aijaz Ahmad, "Jameson's Rhetoric of Otherness and the 'National Allegory,'" *Social Text* 17 (1987): 3–25. An abridged Chinese translation of Jameson's essay appeared in *Lu Xun Studies Monthly* in April 1993.

10. Jameson, "Third World Literature," 77.

11. Robert Kiely, "'Pernicious,' 'Pessimistic,' and 'Foreign': The Controversy Over Literary Modernism in the People's Republic of China," in *Notebooks in Cultural Analysis*, ed. Norman F. Cantor et al. (Durham, N.C.: Duke University Press, 1985), 210.

One of the many terms that consistently aroused interest was of course *modernism,* which, for Kiely's audience, meant "most twentieth-century literary and artistic innovations, including those now commonly referred to by Western critics as 'postmodern.'"[12]

The situation that Kiely describes prevailed in the early 1980s, but the general interest in understanding modernism persisted and was mirrored in academic and intellectual circles. In December 1987, for instance, an international conference on modernism and contemporary Chinese literature was held in Hong Kong to give recognition as well as publicity to modernism in China and to Chinese modernist poets and writers. Papers presented at the conference corroborate Kiely's observation. Ranging from symbolism, expressionism, and streams of consciousness to the theater of the absurd, black humor, *le nouveau roman,* and even Latin America's magic realism, all the Western (or, rather, nonnative) literary movements that do not claim to be traditional (socialist) realism fall into the category of modernism.[13] This seemingly indiscriminate classification forms a discursive strategy that was characteristic of the intellectual emancipation during the mid-1980s. Modernism in the wake of the Cultural Revolution signified that which had been eliminated and excluded as a dangerous and subversive heterogeneity, and its appropriation necessarily signaled a departure from, if not a rebellion against, the straitjacket of realism. In the Chinese context, in other words, modernism as a general label, no matter how vague and unspecified, was called upon to play the revolutionary role of producing new energies and imaginings.[14] Furthermore, modernism as an abstraction could serve contradic-

12. Ibid., 208.

13. For instance, in "Belated Modernism and Today's Chinese Literature," the innovative writer and playwright Gao Xingjian detailed a historical controversy over modernism that involved himself. Xie Mian, a prominent critic of contemporary Chinese poetry, used the term *modernism* to denote a period in which new content and new forms were introduced into Chinese poetry. In a statistically supported essay, "1978–1982: The Introduction of Western Modernism into China," Chen Sihe provided empirical data on the modernism debate. He, too, maintained no distinction between modernism and other literary schools, such as the avant-garde.

14. For a critical reassessment of the literary and cultural interest in modernism in the wake of the Cultural Revolution, see Xudong Zhang, *Chinese Modernism in the Era of Reforms: Cultural Fever, Avant-Garde Fiction, and the New Chinese Cinema* (Durham, N.C.: Duke University Press, 1997), 122–42. The "negative supplement" of modernism that Xudong Zhang describes is distinguished from a better-appreciated "avant-

tory political needs and interests; while it was promoted as the opposite of dogmatic traditionalism, the ideological state apparatus would also vigilantly resist it for its Western connotation.[15] The institutionalized denunciation of modernism—a simplified Lukácsian dismissal of modernist Western literature as a symptom of "morbid eccentricity" and of the bourgeois subject's inability to grasp the whole—functioned in the end to maintain an almost cynical instrumentalization of literary practice. From the late 1970s to the 1990s, every organized attack on modernism followed a paranoid rejection of so-called bourgeois liberalization, which, incidentally, could refer arbitrarily to anything from illegal pornography to Western Marxism. By laboriously deleting the notion of subjectivity from literary production, official realism helped to repress any desire either to cross a given epistemic boundary or to represent a heterogeneous reality. In short, it set up a self-consolidating other (the wretched West) as both evil and scapegoat. As Marshall Berman observes on the political significance of modernism in non-Western countries: what most Third World governments and propagandists "are projecting onto aliens, and prohibiting as 'Western decadence,' is in fact their own people's energies and desires and critical spirit."[16]

Against this background, it becomes clear that the motif of modernism, whether expressed through theoretical or literary practices, is one of many cultural strategies for radically reimagining, even transforming, social organization and control in an agrarian and authoritarian tradition (the two features may be logically linked). As part of the ongoing cultural revolution, reinvoked modernism must introduce a new language,

---

garde intervention," both of which, nonetheless, seem to belong to the same category of "Chinese modernism in the era of reforms."

15. During the 1980s both *xiandai zhuyi* and *xiandai pai* would stand for modernism, but *xiandai pai* often had a stronger connotation of a school or a self-conscious movement. The opposition between *xiandai pai* and *chuantong pai* was maintained mainly at the initial stage of general interest in modernism, when *chuantong pai* stigmatized those who were conservative and resistant to change. For an interesting attempt to compromise modernism with the established order, see Xu Chi's 1982 prediction that a Chinese modernism would be the natural offshoot of a modernized country and would incorporate both revolutionary romanticism and revolutionary realism. Xu Chi, "Xiandai hua yu xiandai zhuyi" (Modernization and modernism), *Wenyi bao* (Literary gazette) (November 1982): 6–9.

16. Marshall Berman, *All That Is Solid Melts into Air: The Experience of Modernity* (New York: Penguin, 1988), 125.

a new mode of textual production and reproduction. Its political impact is still to be derived from an "aesthetics of perceptual revolution."[17] With this understanding of modernism, not as a transhistorical trope but as a metaphor for historicizing a cultural transformation, we will approach Lu Xun's "Diary of a Madman" as a modernist text, a disruptive presence that challenges the given language of meaning. It is modernist not merely in its "literary effect," which is comparable to that of Western modernist literature, but also in the peculiar modernist time-consciousness that it introduces. The whole story can indeed be read as a manifesto of the birth of modern subjectivity as well as of a modernist politics in twentieth-century China.

The Madness of the Madman

The paranoid subject in "Diary of a Madman," the first-person narrator of the main text, suffers from a major mental derangement and stays virtually imprisoned in the house where his traditional extended family lives. His diagnosis, as well as the diary itself, is made known to the reader by another narrator, presumably a writer, who claims to have obtained the material from the Madman's brother. As a result, the diary entries are prefaced with explanatory remarks by this writer-narrator, who at the beginning informs the reader about the Madman's illness and eventual recovery.

In an early article about Lu Xun's indebtedness to modern foreign literature,[18] Lu Xun's brother Zhou Zuoren translates Nikolay Gogol's "Diary of a Madman" as "Fengren riji" instead of as "Kuangren riji," which later became the standard translation. Although both *fengren* and

---

17. This is how Fredric Jameson describes the modernist politics. See his "Reflections in Conclusion," in *Aesthetics and Politics: Debates Between Ernst Bloch, Georg Lukács, Bertolt Brecht, Walter Benjamin, Theodor Adorno,* ed. Ronald Taylor (London: NLB, 1977), 211.

18. Zhou Zuoren, "Lun 'A Q zhengzhuan'" (About "The true story of Ah Q"), in Li Zongying and Zhang Mengyang, *Selected Essays,* 1:9–13. For more comprehensive analyses, see Wen Rumin, "Waiguo wenxue dui Lu Xun 'Kuangren riji' de yingxiang" (The influence of foreign literature on Lu Xun's "Diary of a madman"), *Lu Xun yanjiu* (Lu Xun studies) (1983): 8:202–13, and Wong Yoon Wah, "The Influence of Western Literature on China's First Modern Story."

kuangren basically mean "madman," Zhou Zuoren was obviously making a point of underscoring the difference between *fengren* and the *kuangren* of Lu Xun's "Kuangren riji." Lu Xun himself was no less aware of the semantic difference between *kuang* and *feng*. In his youthful essay "Moluo shili shuo" (On the power of Mara poets) (1907), he postulated *kuang* as a Nietzschean self-affirmation that provides an essential regenerative energy for any thriving civilization. The word also characterizes talented individuals who contemptuously oppose themselves to a stagnant society and whose actions exceed the public's comprehension.[19]

Etymologically, *kuang* describes a hound gone wild that assaults, without distinguishing them, its master and its master's guests. On the basis of this signification, *kuang* has acquired over time a rich texture of meanings, including "madness," "the ecstatic," and "a wildly unrestrained person."[20] As an adjective—a usage that dates back to the *Shi jing* (The book of songs, eleventh to sixth centuries B.C.)—*kuang* is equivalent to "unrestrainedly outgoing, wildly defiant." In Confucius's *Analects,* it also occurs as a verb meaning to progress or aggress. *Feng,* an ideogramic word of much more recent origin, was initially a pathological term denoting the mad, the neurotic, the insensible, or the sheerly stupid; its two compounding parts tell of a severe migraine attacking a person rapidly and mysteriously like a gusting wind. *Kuang* is the archetypal metaphor for an explosive ecstasy (ex-stasis), a jumping off the right track, a transgressive crossing of the boundary—in short, a return to the primal or instinctual drive. It captures, to a certain extent, the inner experience of the alterity of reason, of what has to be repressed and marginalized as irrational; it acknowledges the deep discontents that a civilization necessarily breeds. In contrast, *feng* registers both an externalized, distancing knowledge of madness and a simultaneous containment of the eruptive forces through classification and categorization, if not, indeed, dismissal.

In the text of Lu Xun's "Diary of a Madman," this semantic difference is fully explored. The Madman is acutely aware that he is marked by the word *feng,* and in titling his diary "Kuangren riji" (so the writer-narrator

19. See Lu Xun, "Moluo shili shuo," in *Lu Xun quanji* (The complete works of Lu Xun) (Beijing: Renmin wenxue, 1981), 1:57; also see a discussion in William A. Lyell, *Lu Hsün's Vision of Reality* (Berkeley: University of California Press, 1976), 91–92.

20. See *Zhongzheng xingyi zonghe da zidian* (Zhongzheng comprehensive lexicographical dictionary), 5th ed. (Taipei: Zhongzheng, 1984), 0955, 1079, for detailed etymological and semantic interpretations for *kuang* and *feng*.

tells us in the preface), he may well be taking a final stand against the suffocatingly normative reality in which his brother and the villagers call him otherwise:[21] "'Get out of here, all of you!' he roared. 'What's the point of looking at a madman [*fengzi*]?' Then I realized part of their cunning . . . they had labelled me a madman [*fengzi*]. In the future when I was eaten, not only would there be no trouble but people would probably be grateful to them" (11).

The ecstatic *kuang* of the Madman belongs, if we refuse to regard it as clinical insanity, to what Michel Foucault describes as the fascinating yet "tragic experience of madness in a critical consciousness."[22] *Kuang*, unlike *feng*, is not an aphasic absence of signification but, on the contrary, a discursive energy that erupts and interrupts the normal and normalizing system of meaning. This eruption must necessarily dissolve "the first social censorship—the bar between signifier and signified"—to break down the socially instituted symbolic order and keep the signifying process a motile one.[23] By definition, then, *kuang* stands as a radical shift in the production of meaning from the chain of the signified to the mobile chain of the signifier. In other words, *kuang* switches the whole question from *what* reality is to *how* reality is constructed and represented through various sociosymbolic practices, not the least of which are our linguistic conventions. This epistemological break is precisely what takes place in the mind of Lu Xun's Madman. His *kuang* indicates a return of that which has been suppressed or erased from the horizon of allowed or conceivable experience. It represents a transgressive discourse not only because it goads the self-conscious subject to challenge the given boundaries but also because it drives the subject himself to all the limits, all the frontiers, of experience.

Predictably, in the mainstream literary discourse that absolutizes realis-

---

21. The English translation I use here is that by Gladys Yang, *Silent China: Selected Writings of Lu Xun* (London: Oxford University Press, 1973), 1–13. Nonetheless, I occasionally take the liberty of altering her translation to make it more literal and highlight aspects of the text that I am more interested in. I also have consulted William A. Lyell's translation in *Lu Xun: "Diary of a Madman" and Other Stories,* trans. William A. Lyell (Honolulu: University of Hawaii Press, 1990), 29–41.

22. Michel Foucault, *Madness and Civilization: A History of Insanity in the Age of Reason,* trans. Richard Howard (New York: Vintage, 1973), 28.

23. Julia Kristeva, "Revolution in Poetic Language," in *The Kristeva Reader,* ed. Toril Moi (New York: Columbia University Press, 1986), 113.

tic representation for its presumed social efficacy, pedagogical value, and mass appeal, much hand-wringing and headache are caused because of its inherent inability to take into full account the transgressive force of *kuang*. A brief examination of state-sponsored Lu Xun studies until the early 1980s (epitomized in Li Zongying and Zhang Mengyang, eds., *Selections of Lu Xun Studies Essays from the Past Sixty Years*) reveals a continuous attempt to trim the writer, posthumously, into a model realist.[24] Since the early 1940s, scholars have puzzled over ontotheological questions about the identity and class alliance of Lu Xun's Madman. Is he a clearheaded, intelligent, but understandably persecuted revolutionary against feudalism, or is he merely a madman who happens to be Lu Xun's mouthpiece? Opinions differ greatly—sometimes they even seem irreconcilable—but the consensus holds that the Madman is depicted realistically to expose feudalism as barbaric cannibalism in nature. After briefly reviewing the raging debate over the Madman's identity, one critic conclusively formulated the central issues: "Two questions are in effect raised: (1) Is the figure of Madman created in 'Diary of a Madman' a reflection of real life? (2) How does it reflect real life?"[25] Obviously, these two questions are ultimately the same one and presuppose only one positive answer. The whole interpretive enterprise fails to escape a deeply entrenched hermeneutic tradition underlying the rhetoric of realism, which—harboring in itself a rigid dichotomy between reality and reflection or, rather, between reason and madness—denies madness any access to truth or signification. Following this logic, the Madman is able to reveal the truth only when he takes a recess from his madness, and his experience makes sense only when it is transcended and elevated onto an allegorical level.

What is really at stake goes back to the basic ideological assumption

24. For a more recent review of this scholarly tradition, see Wang Furen, *Zhongguo Lu Xun yanjiu de lishi yu xianzhuang* (The history and present condition of Lu Xun studies in China), serialized in *Lu Xun Studies Monthly,* nos. 1–11 (1994).

25. Deng Yiqun, "'Kuangren riji' zhong kuangren xingxiang chuangzao de yishu tezheng" (Some artistic features in the creation of the figure of the madman in "Diary of a madman"), collected in *Lu Xun yanjiu ziliao* (Research materials in Lu Xun studies), 2 vols., ed. Lu Xun Studies Program at the Beijing Lu Xun Museum (Tianjin: Tianjin renmin, 1980), 1: 261. For a review of the discussion from the early 1950s to the 1980s of the class identity of the Madman, see Liu Fuyou, "'Kuangren riji' yanjiu gaishu" (General survey of the research on "Diary of a madman"), *Lu Xun Studies* (1984): 5:68–89.

that "Lu Xun pictures, in a highly realistic manner, the essence of a feudalist social system and reveals feudal moral rituals and teachings to be cannibalistic."[26] This definitive evaluation of Lu Xun as a revolutionary realist came in the late 1950s as the summit of a twenty-year campaign to make him serviceable to the new Communist regime. The general sociological paradigm for Lu Xun studies that was then set up eventually spread to dominate not only this particular subject but also the entire field of modern Chinese literature studies in China. Indeed, until the mid-1980s, literary criticism and history, at least in their public and publishable versions, were mostly constrained by the sociologically reductive and epistemologically crippling principle of unreflective and unmediated realism. The logic of transparency implied by this castrated realism demands that all social practices be subjugated to one center, or to the "cardinal contradiction" of class struggle, and all representations faithfully mirror a known reality. Indeed, we see here an almost classic case of abusing the realist principle of commitment to legitimize a "vulgar Marxist practice of reducing characters to mere allegories of social forces, of turning 'typical' characters into mere symbols of class."[27] It is at this point that we confront the conceptual inadequacy of an uncritical realism in dealing with a text like "Diary of a Madman." By shifting the critical focus from a supposedly extractable content to the multilayered texture of language and form, we confront once again the same question that haunts Lu Xun's Madman in a more intense way, namely, how a representation necessarily constructs a reality that it refers to and at the same time belies. With this perspective change, the historicity of the literary text itself may emerge as a legitimate object of investigation, and the relationship between literary articulation and its historical embeddedness demands much more intimate and careful reconstruction. In Jameson's words, the "a priori historical or ideological *subtext*," instead of a *mastertext*, "is not immediately present as such, not some common-sense external reality, nor even the conventional narrative of history manuals, but rather must itself always

---

26. Wang Shiqing, *Lu Xun zhuan* (Biography of Lu Xun) (Beijing: Zhongguo qingnian, 1959), 88. An English translation of this severely dated biography of Lu Xun came out, belatedly, in 1984 as *Lu Xun: A Biography,* trans. Zhang Peiji (Beijing: Foreign Languages Press).

27. Fredric R. Jameson, *Marxism and Form: Twentieth-Century Dialectical Theories of Literature* (Princeton, N.J.: Princeton University Press, 1971), 193.

be (re)constructed after the fact."[28] Of such a subtext the literary text stands as "the rewriting or restructuration," and it is often through such rewriting that a writer may arrive at an imaginary resolution of a real contradiction.

Reductive literary criticism as an institution, however, has been on the decline since the 1980s, thanks to a persistent, although constantly interrupted, movement toward more creative thinking. A new generation of critics and writers contended that a direct subjugation of literature to political instrumentalization leads inevitably to a failure to respect literature as a distinct social discursive praxis with its own logic and historical determinations. Together with this awareness surfaced widespread interest in the rhetoric of the autonomy of literature, in formalism, and in the textual analysis of New Criticism. This apparent depoliticization of literary studies paradoxically subverted the entrenched political tradition of reducing the individual to a faceless functionary in a revolutionary cause. It was an extension of what Václav Havel once called "antipolitical politics" in a totalitarian system. The critical urge to read a poem first as a poem, therefore, had the same implication and force as did the demand to treat a human being first as a human being. The political pertinence of such literary phenomena as the "misty poetry" of the early 1980s and the debate about "subjectivity in literature" a few years later can be partially measured by the furious response it provoked from the obese ideological state apparatus. The often vague, unnamable, and yet enduring desire to go beyond the imaginary projection of a different time and space is deeply disruptive to a highly hierarchized control over society. It is not surprising, therefore, to see Lu Xun's "Diary of a Madman" continually revisited by scholars, and the evolving approaches to the story themselves form a mini-history of paradigm shifts and negotiations.[29] Intense atten-

28. Fredric R. Jameson, *The Political Unconscious: Narrative as a Socially Symbolic Act* (Ithaca, N.Y.: Cornell University Press, 1981), 81.
29. The following is an incomplete list of published essays on various aspects of "Diary of a Madman" between 1978 and 1995. Even a cursory reading of these essays will show the different critical methods at work. Yan Jiayan, " 'Kuangren riji' de sixiang yu yishu" (The thought and art in "Diary of a madman") (1978), collected in Li Zongying and Zhang Mengyang, *Selected Essays*, 2:444–59; Gong Langu, "Lun 'Kuangren riji' " (On "Diary of a madman"), *Wenxue pinglun* (Literary review) (1980): 3:85–93; Zhang Huiren, "Yu lijie 'Kuangren' xingxiang youguan de liangge wenti" (Two issues related to understanding the figure of the madman), *Wenxue pinglun congkan* (Col-

tion to "Diary of a Madman" suggests that at the beginning of modern Chinese literature stands an enigmatic text that dramatizes the conflicts between conformity and individuality, between doctrine and interpretation. To return to this text and confront the Madman's *kuang* means to undertake the difficult task of reclaiming a radical tradition of transgressive politics.

---

lected publications of literary review) (1982), 11:309–22; Yan Huandong, "Kuangren yu 'Kuangren riji' xinlun" (The madman and a new essay on "Diary of a madman"), *Wenxue lunji* (Collected essays on literature) (1983), 6:170–91; Gao Songnian, "Guanyu kuangren de xingxiang ji qi chuangzao" (About the figure of the madman and its creation), collected in *Lu Xun yanjiu lunwen xuan* (Selected essays from Lu Xun studies), ed. Zhejiang Lu Xun Studies Society (Hangzhou: Zhejiang wenyi, 1983), 289–306; Li Danchu, "Lun 'Kuangren riji' de xinli miaoxie" (On the psychological description in "Diary of a madman"), *Lu Xun Studies* (1983): 6:119–30; Sun Hao, "Cong kuangren xingxiang shuoqi" (Beginning with the figure of the madman), *Wenxue luncong* (Journal of literary essays) (1984): 2:132–44; Wang Delin, "Kuangren xingxiang xintan" (New approach to the figure of the madman), *Lu Xun Studies* (1984): 3:80–86; Peng Dingan, "'Kuangren jiazu' chansheng de zhuguan suzhi yu wenxue, meixue yiyi" (The subjective elements of the creation of a "family of madmen" and its literary and aesthetic significance), *Lu Xun Studies* (1985): 9:112–29; Lu Ge, "'Kuangren riji' chuangzuo fangfa xinlun" (New essay on the creative method of "Diary of a madman"), *Lu Xun Studies* (1987): 11:80–100; Wang Chaohua and Xu Xiaocun, "Lun 'Kuangren riji' de yishu tese" (On the artistic innovation of "Diary of a madman"), *Lu Xun Studies* (1988): 13:275–91; Wang Furen, "'Kuangren riji' xidu" (A close reading of "Diary of a madman"), *Lu Xun yanjiu niankan* (Lu Xun studies annual) (1991–92): 265–85; Ling Yu, "'Kuangren riji' renwu xingxiang yu zhuti de shengcheng jizhi" (The generative mechanism of the character and theme of "Diary of a madman"), *Lu Xun Studies Monthly* (November 1992): 24–29; Shi Chengfang, "'Jingguan wanxiang, tihui yiqie': 'Kuangren riji' de shijian bianma" ("Observe the universe quietly and understand everything": The coding of time in "Diary of a madman"), *Lu Xun Studies Monthly* (March 1993): 12–16; Xue Yi and Qian Liqun, "'Kuangren riji' xidu" (A close reading of "Diary of a madman"), *Lu Xun Studies Monthly* (November 1994): 13–21; Qian Zhen'gang, "Lun 'Kuangren riji' zhong kuangren gousi de yishu gongneng" (On the artistic function of the creation of the madman in "Diary of a madman"), *Lu Xun Studies Monthly* (December 1995): 25–30.

Reading Between the Lines

The central as well as the canonical passage in "Diary of a Madman" is no less than a scene of reading; it is about a search for meaning, a reorganization of social space, and, indeed, a rewriting of history:[30]

> Everything requires careful consideration if one is to understand it. In ancient times, as I recollect, people often ate human beings, but I am rather hazy about it. I tried to look this up in history, but my history has no chronology and scrawled all over each page are the words: "Virtue and Morality." Since I could not sleep anyway, I read intently half the night until I began to see words between the lines. The whole book was filled with two words—"Eat humans." (6)

In characterizing the end of linear writing accompanied by the emergence of a pluridimensionality and a delinearized temporality, Jacques Derrida writes that "it is less a question of confiding new writings to the envelope of a book than of finally reading what wrote itself between the lines in the volumes."[31] A Derridean textual "grafting," or a Nietzschean genealogical tracing through etymology, opens a text to difference and unrelentingly undermines the plenitude that a sacred book supposedly enjoys. The Madman's reading is precisely such a transformation of a given text to bring forth another text within it, already inscribed, yet obliterated. The two words that surface here in a surrealistic fashion are the outcome of a violent movement of *différance*, only a repression or subordination of which could secure in the first place "the presence of a value or a *meaning* supposedly antecedent to *différance*, more original than it, exceeding and governing it in the last analysis."[32]

---

30. In the passage that follows, the Chinese character that I translate as "humans" in place of the "people" in Gladys Yang's translation is *ren*, which usually means the human species in general. By replacing "Eat people" with "Eat humans"—that is, by using a plural form that suggests persons rather than a mass—I want to emphasize not only that the Madman is contrasting humankind with other creatures, but that he is already aware of the modern subject as an autonomous individual. Lyell also translates the phrase in question as "Eat people." See Lyell, *Lu Xun*, 32.

31. Jacques Derrida, *Of Grammatology*, trans. Gayatri C. Spivak (Baltimore: Johns Hopkins University Press, 1974), 86.

32. Jacques Derrida, *Positions*, trans. Alan Bass (Chicago: University of Chicago Press, 1981), 29.

In the Madman's intense reading, a history without chronology—that is, the self-evident book of totality—is carefully perused, decoded, dismantled, and thereby forced to undergo an irreversible process of textualization. An entire textual tradition, as one critic puts it, is rejected.[33] From this almost violent reading, a new text emerges, one both historical and historicizing. The Madman sets out to consult history with the hope of obtaining an answer to his present concern. He wants to reach out and grasp some certainty about the meaning and purpose—in short, the rationality—of the present moment. But he ends up reading intently the pages that bear nothing but scrawled words or, rather, signifiers, for it is at the moment when he starts searching for historical reality that history ceases to be an external object. History for him becomes no more than the verbal traces of a previous attempt to represent and preserve a particular moment or structure. Now the question is no longer whether or not reality is truthfully represented but how a representation of the real is achieved and instituted. Those scrawled words, namely, no longer function as signs faithfully pointing to preexisting referents but turn into signifiers with their own force and energy. Set loose from that whole dimension of the signified that assumes various names, such as "truth," "meaning," or "reality," the signifier acquires its own materiality and returns to a disorienting and explosive play.

The play of the signifier following its disconnection from the signified stirs up the heterogeneous elements contained and repressed in the constitution of the sacred text. In the tradition of Western modernism, different attitudes toward this disconnection give rise to varied aesthetics and politics (from Rimbaud's to, say, T. S. Eliot's), but the final question invariably returns to history. With history now projected back from the present onto the past, its presumed reality promises to be dissolved into words. All of a sudden, the meaning of history, as the Madman discovers, is put into motion, and meaning itself becomes an open-ended process that goes on in the present and consists of a constant rereading and reinterpreting of pages of words from the past. Every such rereading, as Nietzsche argues in *On the Genealogy of Morals* (a work Lu Xun admired), must first disclose the violence and barbarism that went into

33. See Yi-tsi Mei Feuerwerker, "Text, Intertext, and the Representation of the Writing Self in Lu Xun, Yu Dafu, and Wang Meng," in Ellen Widmer and David Der-wei Wang, eds., *From May Fourth to June Fourth: Fiction and Film in Twentieth-Century China* (Cambridge, Mass.: Harvard University Press, 1993), 167–93, esp. 171–77.

establishing a previous representation of the real as either true or natural. The Madman's insertion of the two words "Eat humans," therefore, signals a revolutionary return of the repressed to the discursive field. It is not merely a contention over possession of the past but a struggle to own the present, which for the Madman is a matter of life and death.

The Madman, in and through his reading, carries out with one stroke the twofold task of transforming the text and liberating the signifiers. He thereby initiates a new technique of interpretation that has been associated with Marx, Nietzsche, and Freud in the modern Western intellectual tradition. The new interpretive strategy—as exemplified in Marx's analysis of the term *commodity*, Nietzsche's genealogical approach to all cultural values, and Freud's mapping of the unconscious—both modifies the space of signifier distribution and rearranges the signifiers to expose the "other thing" that a text is saying at the same time. The interpreter gains access to this hidden inscription when a new economy of signs dismantles the existing process of ideological reproduction, which, for the Madman, is the dominant value system that legitimizes repression and barbarism in the name of "virtue and morality." A similar radical reassessment of all values led Nietzsche to conclude that it was in "the sphere of legal obligations, that the moral conceptual world of 'guilt,' 'conscience,' 'duty,' and 'sacredness of duty' had its origin: its beginnings were, like the beginnings of everything great on earth, soaked in blood thoroughly and for a long time."[34] The critical radicalism of Lu Xun's story, or its "totalistic iconoclasm,"[35] at the turn of the century, therefore, rests not so much on the revelatory force of the statement that the traditional gemeinschaft is soaked in violence and injustice as it does on the introduction of desire into language, engendering a new form of discourse. It unleashes an imaginative energy that always unsettles the dominant discursive order.

At this point, it becomes necessary to situate Lu Xun's "Diary of a Madman" in the general discussion of the possibility of a popular ver-

---

34. Friedrich Nietzsche, *On the Genealogy of Morals*, trans. Walter Kaufman and R. J. Hollingdale (New York: Vintage, 1968), 65. See also Min Kangsheng, "'Kuangren riji' zhong Nicai de shengyin" (The voice of Nietzsche in "Diary of a madman"), *Lu Xun Studies* (1988): 12:299–315.

35. This term comes from Lin Yü-sheng, *The Crisis of Chinese Consciousness: Radical Antitraditionalism in the May Fourth Era* (Madison: University of Wisconsin Press, 1979), 116–21.

nacular literature in the late 1910s. Initiating the notion of "literary reform" in 1917, Hu Shi, another leading figure among New Culture intellectuals of the May Fourth period, called with a resounding determination for a new modern literature: "We ought to use the living language of the twentieth century instead of the dead words from three thousand years ago."[36] The "living language" is the spoken vernacular (*baihua*), and Lu Xun's "Diary of a Madman" was one of the first literary works written in modern vernacular Chinese. To a large extent, Hu Shi's modernistic skepticism toward the past and his critical awareness of the formative force of language directly begot Lu Xun's Madman.

At the forefront of the New Culture movement, therefore, "Diary of a Madman" embodies this emerging critical attitude toward language, and it offers itself as an archetypal text of deconstructive reading. In this sense, it is a key text that unambiguously articulates a potent discursive strategy in modern Chinese culture. Throughout the diary, various practices that constitute and participate in everyday life are subjected to a powerful estrangement, so that their naturalness or legitimacy is called into question. At one point, the Madman's brother ushers in a physician to examine the patient. By reading the doctor's movements and prescriptions as a meaningful text, the Madman demonstrates his bracketing of what is part of the accepted and practiced sociosymbolic order. When Doctor He feels his pulse, the Madman decides that the physician is a butcher in disguise, trying to find out how fat the prey is. By repeating Doctor He's promise, "You'll be fine in a few days," he brings forward and explores the double, even conflicting, meaning of "being fine/profitable" (*hao*). "By fattening me of course they'll have more to eat. But what good will it do me? How can it be 'fine'?" (7). When the Madman takes "fine" to mean "profitable," the basic question becomes who will profit from his being fine. Thus questioned, "to be fine" means either to fit in better with the instituted cannibalistic machinery or to be able to take part in cannibalism. Also, in Chinese the word for "fine" can mean "good," the opposite of "evil." In bracketing "good," the Madman comes to realize that by challenging the concept of what makes a "good man" (*haoren* is translated as "a good

---

36. Hu Shi, "Wenxue gailiang chuyi" (Some modest proposals for the reform of literature), in *Hu Shi wencun* (Selected works of Hu Shi) (Taipei: Yuandong, 1971), 1:17. For an English translation, see Kirk A. Denton, ed., *Modern Chinese Literary Thought: Writings on Literature, 1893-1945* (Stanford, Calif.: Stanford University Press, 1996), 123–39.

son" [13]), he is to be labeled an "evil man" (*e'ren* is loosely rendered as "a bad character") and imprisoned, punished, and eventually murdered by communal "justice." "When our tenant spoke of the villagers eating an evil man, it was exactly the same device. This is their old trick" (12). It is a "trick" as old as history itself, the trick of justifying violence against the rebel, who is first marginalized and then condemned as either abnormal or eccentric.

In a gesture of projection that necessarily implicates his anxiety and desire, the Madman produces his own new text. The desire to name traverses language and makes it at once the space for engagement and the site of possible fulfillment. The Madman's playful manipulation of language both to distort and to displace existing texts (e.g., his mixing up *Catalog of Flora and Fauna* and *Supplements to the Catalog,* his anachronistic juxtaposing of Yiya and Jie Zhou, two historical and legendary figures belonging to different times), apparently a symptom of his madness, fulfills his urge to express himself—to break down the existing chain of signs and make his own voice heard. In speaking a language different from that of the encasing context—namely, the preface provided by the writer-narrator—the Madman shows the disruptive force of language itself.[37]

The Madman writes in his own language, employing a syntax that is itself both colloquial and logical. The passage preceding his diary frames the text and, through the medium of language, forms an ironic play with notions of the present and the past. Fredric Jameson notices that the story in effect offers "two distinct and incompatible endings. . . . One ending, that of the deluded subject himself, is very much a call to the future, in the impossible situation of a well-nigh universal cannibalism. . . . But the tale has a second ending as well, which is disclosed on the opening pages."[38] The prefacelike passage that introduces the story reassures the reader that the Madman "has recovered some time ago and has gone elsewhere to take up an official post." In other words, he has returned to the system against which he once desperately revolted with all his strength. Between these two incompatible endings, Jameson sees a tension surfacing and concludes that "by way of a complex play of simultaneous and antithetical messages . . . the narrative text is able to open up a concrete perspective

---

37. Wang Furen suggests in his insightful "A Close Reading of 'Diary of a Madman'" (see n. 28 above) that what the Madman achieves is a Brechtian *Verfremdungseffekt.*

38. Jameson, "Third-World Literature," 77.

on the real future."³⁹ This tension in fact exists on the level not merely of temporality but also of linguistic experience. The introductory passage, composed in a semi-esoteric, classical style, functionally establishes a present moment or reality with which a contemporary reader is invited to identify. The reader is assured of a safe distance from the stormy events to follow, which have by now been historified and put into proper perspective. Though the preface narrator assumes an aesthetic tranquillity and an equally detached scientism, he nevertheless judgmentally excludes the Madman's diary from the order of reality. He expresses the common view of paranoia as a mental disorder that, one hopes, can be cured. "The writing was most confused and incoherent, and he had made many wild statements" (3). Yet this present moment of the preface is saliently marked as past because the language that constructs it was widely pronounced "dead" and "archaic" at the time when the story was composed. During the first quarter of the century the classical Chinese language was associated with a decaying and impotent tradition that had to be discarded and replaced by a new language born of a culture of new youth. The new living language is what the Madman speaks and writes.

In other words, the preface, composed in a narrative past (similar to the French preterit),⁴⁰ constitutes a hierarchized and sensible "reality," whereas the diary entries, without dates or a coherent linear narrative, seem to be written in and about a perpetual and motile present. The presentness of the preface is a hollow and ornate construction, and the new writing, which in the story is fictively anterior to the preface's present but historically posterior to it, not only subverts the solidity of the tradition of old writing but also suggests the irrevocability of the new writing—that of the Madman. Furthermore, this tension between the two modes of writing points to a more fundamental complexity in modern Chinese literature. What Lu Xun demonstrates in "Diary of a Madman" is a critical recognition of an impossible promise of realist fiction. As Marston Anderson observes, Lu Xun realizes, through his self-conscious play with his own storytelling, that realism "risks making authors accomplices to the social cruelty they intend to decry. The realist narrative, by imitating at a formal level the relation of oppressor to oppressed, is captive

39. Ibid.
40. See Roland Barthes's discussion of the use of the preterit in the novel as an ideological construction securing a given social order in his *Writing Degree Zero,* trans. Annette Lavers and Colin Smith (New York: Noonday-Farrar, 1968), 29–40.

to the logic of that oppression and ends by merely reproducing it."[41] "The very first story that sets the new literature movement in motion," concurs Yi-tsi Mei Feuerwerker, "is also filled with self-doubts about the nature and effectiveness of its own literary enterprise."[42] At the origin of modern Chinese literature, the limits of realism are already grasped and underlined. To those limits a modernist reconceptualization of language is offered as a preferable alternative. The realist writer-narrator of the preface, although sympathetic, belongs in the final analysis to the existing social order and shares no common language with the Madman.

The Madman's deconstructive reading and the emergence of a new language, however, take place not in an original nowhere but, rather, "between the lines." In September 1919, against the grain of a general enthusiastic rhetoric of "awakening"—"enlightening," or "reviving" the nation from a blind complacency—Lu Xun wrote, not without bitter sarcasm, that "the first awakened has always been, by either a malicious person or a mindless crowd, oppressed, persecuted, conspired against, exiled, and eventually murdered."[43] In fact, the awakening metaphor, which contains the light/darkness opposition and easily gives way to another hierarchical power structure, is also part of what the Madman stubbornly questions. The initial moment of his transgressive *kuang* can be located in the night when he perceives a bright moon that he has not seen "for over thirty years." Thus, the first entry in the diary reads: "Tonight the moon is very bright. I have not seen it for over thirty years, so today when I saw it I felt in unusually high spirits. I begin to realize that during the past thirty-odd years I have been in the dark" (4). But the fact is that he is still in the dark when he sees the bright moon. Leo Ou-fan Lee rightly points out that the "recurring image of the moon gives rise symbolically to a double meaning of both lunacy (in its Western connotation) and enlight-

---

41. Marston Anderson, *The Limits of Realism: Chinese Fiction in the Revolutionary Period* (Berkeley: University of California Press, 1990), 91.

42. Yi-tsi Mei Feuerwerker, "Text, Intertext, and the Representation of the Writing Self," 177. See also David Der-wei Wang's discussion of "Diary of a Madman" in his *Fictional Realism in Twentieth-Century China: Mao Dun, Lao She, Shen Congwen* (New York: Columbia University Press, 1992), 4–10, where he argues that the text through its narrative strategy "leads us to the ideological and epistemological conditions of a realist discourse" (7).

43. This Lu Xun text was discovered in the 1970s. See *Research Materials on Lu Xun Studies*, 2:2.

enment (in its Chinese etymological implication)."[44] But there is also a twist in the enlightenment rhetoric. For if the moon is a metaphor for the Madman's inner illumination, it is at the same time metonymic of the vast surrounding darkness that stands for what both threatens and calls for enlightenment. The visibility of the moon, unlike that of the sun, has a parasitically interdependent and no less antagonistic relation with that which tends to obscure or obliterate it. What is in or of the moon depends on what is around or even against it. The awakening, in other words, is not itself an unqualified blessing. It is much less like awakening from a nightmare than becoming critically conscious of the darkness of the night. Metaphorically, the moon is a differentiated presence, a solitary site that both accepts and resists what defines its boundaries. Following the same line of skeptical thinking, Lu Xun would pose the well-known rhetorical question in the preface to *Nahan* (Call to arms) (1923), his first collection of short stories: "Imagine an iron house without windows, absolutely indestructible, with many people fast asleep inside who will shortly die of suffocation. But you know that since they will die in their sleep, they will not feel the pain of death. Now if you cry aloud to wake a few of the lighter sleepers, making those unfortunate few suffer the agony of irrevocable death, do you think you are doing them a good turn?"[45]

In opposition to the moon, the sun, whose radiant light is expected to prevail, never becomes bright for the Madman. "The sun is never out and the door is forever closed. Just two meals every day" (12). The three actual confrontations between the Madman and others—most notably, between him and his brother—all take place in the early morning, a transient moment that links the night and the day and yet ineluctably gives in to daylight. Daylight, whose presence presupposes the absence of the moon, is always depressing to the Madman. "Today there is no moon, I know that this is a bad omen. This morning when I went out cautiously, Mr. Zhao had a strange look" (4). Enlightenment for the Madman, then, is not so much a spreading of light to banish obscurity or murkiness as it is an individual perception of the encroaching dark, of which the enlight-

---

44. Leo Ou-fan Lee, *Voices from the Iron House: A Study of Lu Xun* (Bloomington: Indiana University Press, 1987), 54.

45. Lu Xun, "Preface" to *Call to Arms,* in *Selected Stories of Lu Xun,* trans. Yang Hsien-yi and Gladys Yang (Beijing: Foreign Languages Press, 1972), 5.

ened remains a part, often in an oppositional margin. "Diary of a Madman" can never be a rationalized "program of political struggle" for the revolutionary masses, nor does it "reflect," as dogmatic realism hastens to argue, "the awakening process people undergo to realize the unbearability of feudal oppression, their strong will to struggle and their determination to fight feudalism to the end."[46] On the contrary, the Madman, almost painfully following his own epistemology of suspicion, will in the end come to see himself as part of the darkness. His last horror is the realization that he has all the time been engulfed in the tradition of cannibalism and may well have eaten pieces of his beloved sister. Even his self-identity, which he has clung to as the last site of resistance, is thrown into uncertainty because the past irrepressibly returns. The only way out that he can see, therefore, lies not in the present but in a remote future that has yet to begin with the now, with "saving the children." The Madman, a modern "bearer of a full critical consciousness," as Anderson names him,[47] heroically tears down the illusive opposition between light and dark and refuses to be overshadowed by either. He is the solitary warrior that Lu Xun later celebrates in *Yecao* (Wild grass), the rebel who will always raise his javelin of skepticism and toss it forward, not to confirm or probe but to challenge and displace.[48]

The concluding line of "Diary of a Madman" strikes me as explosively elliptic. "Save the children . . ." (13). Who will save them from what? From becoming cannibals? So that they, as the "real human beings," will be spared, start a new era, and consequently own a present time to be neither ashamed of nor proud of, with no history to escape from or identify with? Or save them from being devoured by ourselves? So that when they grow up and become acquainted with a 4,000-year history of cannibalism, they will only be shocked to find that they have all the time been eating their own kind? Or, in yet another possibility, must the children be saved from being eaten and from becoming eaters of others? Who, in that case, is to accomplish this redemptive task, and from what vantage point can such a salvation defy both history and the present?

Just as intriguing is the ultimate absence of the Madman in the story. We are told, indirectly by his older brother, that he has recovered from his mental lapses and is away from the village waiting for an official post.

46. Wang, *Biography of Lu Xun*, 88.
47. Anderson, *The Limits of Realism*, 88.
48. See *Yecao* (Wild grass), collected in *The Complete Works of Lu Xun*, 1:525–27.

His diary is the only trace we have of his madness as well as of his existence. He may have returned to being normal, but he may also have been devoured, both figuratively and literally, by the villagers. It is through his absence that the Madman keeps us from studying him as a realistic object, from regarding him as an identifiable other. With his physical presence removed, we are compelled to directly encounter the Madman's inner world and subjectivity. We find ourselves reading between the lines and trying to imagine the condition under which he wrote down his intimate fears and visions. Our reading of the Madman's diary, therefore, is largely driven and determined by a desire, incited by the narrative framework, to overcome his absence, to make present a past moment as it was actually lived. Such also is the Madman's obsession when faced with a history book without chronology.

The ambiguity of the Madman's last words, therefore, derives from the structure of the story as a whole, in which the reading of the text is prescribed as a continuous and open-ended process. From a comparative study of Lu Xun's thought, some may argue that this last sentence expresses his principle of hope and belief in evolution.[49] Others may conclude from a reductive understanding of social practices that Lu Xun is calling for action to overthrow the entire cannibalistic system. It seems to me, however, that this sentence poses not so much the hope or possibility of a better future as it does the modernist problem of history. History is that which can never be undone. The children must be saved from being severed from the past, however nightmarish it may be, and also from being preyed upon by the historically determined present. One keeps history alive and dead, present and removed, at the same time by continuously rereading and rewriting it. By reading and rereading the past—as a text, as a space filled up with tension and forces—one can distance it so that it both intervenes in and yet submits itself to the present. At this juncture the modernist obsession with language and with the condition of meaning comes in and asserts itself as deeply political. A modernist politics, in the end, invariably begins with examining how a given representation of reality is always already outmoded.

---

49. For a discussion of Lu Xun's belief in evolution, see Susanne Weigelin-Schwiedrzik, "Lu Xun und das 'Prinzip Hoffnung': Eine Untersuchung seiner Rezeption der Theorin von Huxley und Nietzsche," *Bochumer Jahrbuch zur Ostasienforschung* (Bochum: Brochmeyer, 1980), 414–31, esp. 426.

Excursion I

Beyond Homesickness: An Intimate Reading of Lu Xun's "My Native Land"

The initial and hermeneutically challenging difficulty of reading Lu Xun's 1921 short story "Guxiang" (My native land) lies in its very title. A stock phrase in Chinese language and cultural semantics, the two-character compound commands a rich cluster of variations such as *guli, guyuan, gutu,* and *guguo.* One of the earliest and most memorable usages of the phrase *guxiang* occurs in Sima Qian's (ca. 145–86 B.C.) *Shi ji* (Records of the historian), in which the triumphant return of Liu Bang (ca. 247–195 B.C.), founding Emperor Gaozu of the Western Han dynasty, to his hometown at the end of his life is described in great detail. During a feast to which he summons all his old friends, neighbors, and relatives, the aging Gaozu is stricken with deep sorrow, lets tears stream down his face, and explains to those present: "The traveler always pines for his native land [youzi bei guxiang]."[1] This candid revelation by a legendary hero of his private feelings contains such mythopoetic power as to have shaped an emotive pattern and permeated a collective pathos. Ever since the high Tang period of the eighth century, when poetic giants excelled in elevating homesickness to an archetypal human longing, *guxiang* as subject matter has been fully developed into a fertile field for cultivating com-

---

1. See Burton Watson, trans., *Records of the Historian: Chapters from the Shih chi of Ssu-ma Ch'ien* (New York: Columbia University Press, 1969), 141, where the sentence is translated as "The traveler sighs for his old home." Before this moment, Gaozu sings a song that he composes at the banquet: "A great wind came forth; / The clouds rose on high. / Now that my might rules all within the seas, / I have returned to my old village. Where shall I find brave men / To guard the four corners of my land?" For the original text, see *Shi ji jin zhu* (Records of the historian with contemporary annotations), annotated by Ma Chiying (Taipei: Commercial Press, 1979), 1:343. Incidentally, the French translation of Gaozu's saying by Édouard Chavannes sheds a different light on the notion of *guxiang* than Watson's rendition of it as "old village": "Le voyageur s'afflige en pensant à sa terre natale." Chavannes, trans. and annot., *Les mémoires historiques de Se-ma Ts'ien* (Paris: Librairie d'Amérique et d'Orient, 1967), 2:397. This difference will become relevant in the discussion below.

munal sentiment as well as artistic and literary sensibilities. The image and concept of *guxiang* best indicates a primary structure of feeling and frequently provokes a melancholic nostalgia that reaches metaphysical heights while also suggesting allegorical dimensions. Literally meaning "old country," the phrase pits an existential temporality against an external and emphatically rural, often even pastoral, landscape. Like all such key words in a signifying language, *guxiang* describes as well as prescribes a mode of human relationship and experience. In articulating a vital attachment and sense of belonging that is predicated on a spatio-temporal displacement and the subsequent possibility of nostalgia, the phrase, with its layered associations, encodes and transmits a complex conception of home, communal life, and the private self.

The richness and invocatory power of such an overcharged expression may be illustrated by the range of choices available for rendering it into another language. The accepted and widely used English translation of Lu Xun's "Guxiang," by Yang Hsien-yi and Gladys Yang, is titled "My Old Home," whereas a French version, put out by Peking Foreign Languages Press in 1974, reads "Mon village natal."[2] If these two titles may already activate starkly distinct images and memories, an earlier German translation, "Die Heimat" (1948),[3] evokes yet another and much more intense feeling of homesickness and devotion. The implication of the German word is evidently different from the English "hometown," which is the title that William Lyell gave to his recent translation of the same story.[4] The inevitable mismatch in capturing the associative content of the title "Guxiang" was duly noted by Chi-chen Wang, who, as one of the earliest English translators of Lu Xun's work, published *Ah Q and Others: Selected Stories of Lusin* in 1941. In a footnote, Wang explained that *guxiang* can be town or country and it "indicates an indefinite region or district

---

2. The Yang and Yang English translation was initially also sponsored by Peking Foreign Languages Press (1st ed. 1956), but it has since been republished by Norton (New York, 1977). The Yang and Yang version was collected in the anthology *Modern Chinese Short Stories and Novellas, 1919–1949,* ed. Joseph Lau, C. T. Hsia and Leo Ou-fan Lee (New York: Columbia University Press, 1981), 11–16.

3. O. Benl, trans. "Die Heimat," in *Story/Erzahler des Auslands* 3 (August 1948), referred to by Irene Eber, "Selective Bibliography," in *Lu Xun and His Legacy,* ed. Leo Ou-fan Lee (Berkeley: University of California Press, 1980), 279.

4. William A. Lyell, trans., *Lu Xun: "Diary of a Madman" and Other Stories* (Honolulu: University of Hawaii Press, 1990), 89–100.

rather than any specific place." For him, "there is no better equivalent for the Chinese term" than "My Native Heath," although "heath" admittedly sounds more Scottish than English.[5]

This studied use of "heath" in translating Lu Xun's story, however, turned out to be too idiosyncratic to gain sustained currency. Nonetheless, Chi-chen Wang's deliberation brings to the fore a crucial component of what stands as a paradigmatic narrative in modern Chinese literature, namely, the recognition of landscape. This recognition has to overcome an initial estrangement or misrecognition, and it is then achieved through a withdrawal or a journey that increasingly turns inward. At the end of the journey an imaginary land appears where the narrating, autobiographical subject is able to reconcile the ineluctable lapse of time with an altered human geography. The sense of recognition arrives as a therapeutic relief and leads to a miraculous discovery of an inner home, an imaginary landscape that derives from and yet transcends the old country. This transformed landscape symbolically gives a new life to the narrator because it now turns into a source of spiritual resilience. The native land, in short, engenders another birth, a self-conscious regeneration. On this account and for reasons that will become apparent later, I propose to translate the title of Lu Xun's story as "My Native Land," intending for each word to designate an indispensable aspect of the encounter between the subject and its inescapable other, between historical time and altered space.

Aside from the need for recognition, the motif of journey, and the epiphany in coming upon an imaginary homeland, Lu Xun's story as a paradigmatic narrative also voices the anguish and despair of the first generation of modern, educated Chinese. The encounter with an unrecognizable landscape quickly translates into an examination of the historical conflict between different realities and knowledge systems. The narrating subject's impulse to distinguish a familiar landscape from the unfamiliar one compels him to adopt a mode of realist representation, through which the distance between reality and anticipation acquires a social and moral valence. This moralized perception of difference enables a strikingly detailed human portraiture in the story to appear as metonymic of a disappointing reality. On a metafictional level, therefore, the narrative

5. Chi-chen Wang, trans., "My Native Heath," *Ah Q and Others: Selected Stories of Lusin* (New York: Columbia University Press, 1941), 3 n.1.

of "My Native Land" can even be read as a fable of the condition of possibility for realist fiction in modern Chinese literature.

The goal of this reading exercise is to closely follow the imagery, logic, and reasoning that underlie the story, and to unpack the dense and complex narrative. Our intimate reading will be digressional and sympathetic, because we will try to experience the narrative as if from within. An intimate relationship with the text demands that we be transformed by the experience of reading, decoding, and reassembling the text. It also implies that the text is produced anew and brought to bear on matters and conditions that are of our own concern. Entering the text is no doubt the first step toward placing both the text and ourselves in the ongoing interpretive process. In our reading, we will be concerned with what may be called a "homesickness complex" and its sublimation within the story. We will also encounter questions of subjectivity, language, sexuality, memory, and fantasy. What we will be exploring intimately is indeed the condensed psychobiography of a modern Chinese male consciousness.

Approaching the Homeland

The following are two renditions of the well-known first sentence of "My Native Land."

> Braving the bitter cold, I travelled more than seven hundred miles back to the old home I had left over twenty years before. (Yang and Yang, 54)

> Braving the bone-cold weather, I was headed back to my hometown, a hometown from which I was separated by over six hundred miles and more than twenty years. (Lyell, 89)[6]

---

6. Both translations have their strengths, although William Lyell's rendition uses more idiomatic American English and offers a better read. In the following discussion, I indicate which translation I quote with the translators' names and a page number. I put "cf." in front of the reference to indicate where I modify the translation to make it closer to the original. The page numbers given for the Yangs' translation are to the Norton edition, 1977, 54–64; for Lyell's translation, page numbers refer to the 1990 University of Hawaii edition. I also replace the Wade-Giles system for transliteration in the Yang and Yang translation with the now standard *pinyin*. For the Chinese version, see *Lu Xun quanji* (The complete works of Lu Xun) (Beijing: Renmin wenxue, 1981), 1:344–58.

Readers with some knowledge of Lu Xun would know that this story has a definitely autobiographical framework. It is largely based on Lu Xun's trip to Shaoxing in December 1919 to bring his mother, wife, and second younger brother to Beijing, where he had been working as a minor government clerk. The "over twenty years" of separation refers to his first leaving home at age seventeen. According to his 1922 narration, in 1898 the teenage Lu Xun (then Zhou Shuren) had left his hometown for Nanjing in the hope of "taking on a new path, fleeing to a fresh place, and searching for different people."[7] That initial leave-taking was a determined flight toward something new and different; it was also the origin of the narrating subject's fated relationship to an old home, a distant native land. For the formation of a native land necessarily presupposes a departure from, even an active rejection of, the land and the symbolic universe of which the returning visitor was until that moment of separation an involuntary part.

In recounting his current return, the narrator begins with the first-person pronoun, much in the same way that Lu Xun called attention to the autobiographical subject through its opening sentence in the self-preface to his first collection of short stories *Nahan* (Call to arms, 1923). Appropriately, the original first sentence in "My Native Land" is so structured that, between the subject *wo* and its destination *guxiang,* it places the description of a spatio-temporal separation and the effort to overcome it. Between "myself" and "my native land" now lies a large narrative space that bespeaks the impossibility of the narrating subject achieving a complete return. Once separated, the narrator and his native land cannot but maintain the relationship between a subject and an object, although the subject, as we will witness, is not always the active or agential one as might be expected. To some extent, his native land necessarily participates in the formation of the narrator's selfhood or subjectivity. An absent presence, the native land has become the other that is always within the narrating subject and in terms of which he needs to tell his story and narrate his origin. It thus stakes a permanent claim on his existence and self-consciousness. No matter how far he may drift away from this landscape, he cannot escape it, just as he is not equipped to step outside his own body.

7. This is a literal translation of part of Lu Xun's own preface to his *Nahan* (Call to arms). See *The Complete Works of Lu Xun,* 1:269–76; for an English translation of the text, see Yang and Yang, *Lu Xun: Selected Stories* (New York: Norton, 1977), 1–6.

Even more strikingly, the original first sentence ends with a directional co-verb *qu* (to go) that puts the narrator in an intriguing position. For this verb suggests that the present narration about this trip home in the past is conducted away from the hometown. (The implied perspective would be radically altered should the co-verb be *lai* [to come], which is syntactically possible and would place the narrator in contiguity with, not away from, his hometown.) The word choice conveys a detachment with which the narrator, in anticipating the end of his travel, views his homecoming as a transitory return or even a business trip. The centrifugal mobility that the verb institutes betrays a condition of rootlessness with which the narrating subject will have to come to terms during and through his journey. The happy conventional plot of the prodigal son is therefore instantly canceled; neither is much sense of relief or pride conveyed at returning to one's roots.

Still further removed is the likelihood of the kind of royal treatment that the Emperor Gaozu must have received. On the contrary, the detachment embedded in the first sentence already points to the structure of a hard and unsentimental adult world that the narrator now inhabits. For he will soon divulge the less-than-inspiring purpose of his trip as to "move away from this familiar countryside to the strange and faraway place where I now earned my keep" (Lyell, 90). He comes home to take a final leave, because the old family compound—the concrete site and symbol of reassuring propinquity and closeness—has been sold, and the transaction is to be completed before the end of the year. This commercial change of hands is to render the native land even more abstract and to make the narrator an indifferent outsider to it as much as he is to the "strange and faraway place" where he makes a living. His coming home is indeed to witness yet another loss, but this time it bears the weight of a more comprehensive and thorough disenchantment.

The disenchantment, stemming from the exposed fragility of sentiment in the face of commercial exchange, is compounded by the growing gap between reality and memory as the narrator approaches his destination.

> As we drew near my former home the day became overcast and a cold wind blew into the cabin of our boat, while all one could see through the chinks in our bamboo awning were a few desolate villages, devoid of any sign of life, scattered far and near under the sombre yellow sky. I could not help feeling depressed.

Ah! Surely this was not the old home I had remembered for the past twenty years? (cf. Yang and Yang, 54)

"Approaching my hometown" is always an intense moment that incites the remembering subject to anticipate; it is also an emotional occasion for overdetermined interpretation and self-explanation. "Drawing near" in space helps to activate distant and buried memories about the landscape and one's past existence. The moment of approaching is therefore a liminal one in that it sets into motion all static categories and compels the subject to become aware of his own transformation and difference. It accelerates the precarious procedure of investigating depths—inside as well as outside. Whatever the homeland scenery appears to be in its present condition, its concrete reality, when subjected to a comparison with the remembered and internalized native land, cannot but embody externality and strangeness. The inner homeland, as the narrator goes on to acknowledge, is always abstract and unrepresentable. "The land that I remembered was not in the least like this. My native land was far more lovely. But if you asked me to recall its peculiar charm or describe its beauties, I had no concrete images, no words to describe it" (cf. Yang and Yang, 54).

A sense of facing an impassive reality arises when the abstract native land reveals itself to be other than and in excess of the scenery before one's eyes. Reality sets in to signal an inadequacy, a failure to live up to or reproduce an imaginary intensity and plenitude. Critical realism, in turn, ultimately amounts to a representational effort to underscore reality as apathetic failure and to throw into relief the disparity between the observed and the anticipated. The realistic portrayal is an implicit decoding in terms of a utopian and different other—or a preexisting empty frame, as Roland Barthes once called it. "To describe is thus to place the empty frame which the realistic author always carries with him (more important than his easel) before a collection or continuum of objects which cannot be put into words without this obsessive operation."[8] This process of framing and matching, initiated at the moment of approaching the scene of unimaginative reality, will reach a dramatic point when the narrator reads the physiognomy of his childhood friend Runtu. Thus, more than an emotional excitement, "approaching my hometown" awakens a cognitive impulse that drives realist discourse.

8. Roland Barthes, "Painting as a Model," *S/Z*, trans. Richard Miller (New York: Hill and Wang, 1974), 54.

This cognitive operation of realism will help the narrating subject establish a critical relationship to the impoverished scene of reality that he enters. It gives rise to a hermeneutic exercise through which the first-person narrator constantly seeks signs and offers explanations. "At dawn the next day I reached the gateway of my family compound" (cf. Yang and Yang, 54). From the broken stems of withered grass up on the tile roof to the disquieting silence and deserted rooms—all yield a sign of disrepair and decline. When the mother comes out, the narrator sees what is not shown or obvious but what may be expected. It is this sensation of seeing the unseen and hearing the unsaid that accords the narrator a sobering sense of confronting the truth of reality. "Though mother was delighted, she was also trying to hide a certain feeling of sadness" (Yang and Yang, 55).[9] Even the manner in which she asks him to rest and have some tea makes him suspect a pointed avoidance of the topic of relocating. With his mother is his eight-year-old nephew, Hong'er, who meets the narrator for the first time and observes the guest with curiosity from a timid distance.

A multiple network of inquiring gazes thus quietly connects family members of three separate generations. The most notable absence at the moment appears to be the father—the narrator's as well as Hong'er's father. The narrator will later recall his own father as a benevolent but distant figure, while Hong'er seems to be searching for a surrogate father in examining his uncle, who is apparently a stranger. In some fundamental modern Chinese narratives, such as Lu Xun's "Diary of a Madman" and Ba Jin's *Family*, the absent or enfeebled father often embodies an inexplicable failure that has both collective and personal pathogens. It is a symptomatic absence that reflects the bankruptcy of patriarchal authority, or the impossible condition of locating a father figure in one's biological father.[10] Lu Xun's own writing about the illness and death of his father effectively turned the pained paternal body into a symbol of national suffering. In the present situation between the narrator and Hong'er, a new bond will be formed that differs from and appears more modern and more hopeful than the traditional father-son lineage that Runtu continues to practice.

9. The less literal translation of this sentence by Lyell reads: "Though she was obviously happy to see me, I also read hints of melancholy in her face" (90).

10. See chaps. 4 and 5 for further discussion of the symbolism surrounding the father figure.

82 *Chinese Modern*

    At last, the conversation between mother and son comes to the details of moving. "I said that rooms had already been rented up north, and I had bought a little furniture; in addition it would be necessary to sell all the furniture in the house here in order to buy more things" (cf. Yang and Yang, 55). Almost imperceptibly, the emotionally charged return visit winds down to become as plain as buying and selling used furniture. There is an increasing weariness about describing business transactions in an adult world. On this practical level of livelihood, the narrator has no more attachment to the old house or his native land than to the salable household goods. Again, the logic of commercial exchange serves to wipe out the depth and emotional investment that goes into the notion of "native land." Mundane worries and calculations momentarily keep the final farewell from reaching its global proportion and make the prospect more manageable.

Remembering the Homeland

Yet the dull concreteness of the adult world is interrupted as soon as the mother speaks of Runtu, almost as an afterthought, when she enumerates relatives and friends they should visit before departing. The mere mention of Runtu's name triggers, "as if through a flash of lightning," spectacular childhood memories and releases the anamnestic image of a "young hero." "At this point a strange picture suddenly flashed into my mind: a golden moon suspended in a deep blue sky and beneath it the seashore, planted as far as the eye could see with jade-green watermelons, while in their midst a boy of eleven or twelve, wearing a silver necklet and grasping a steel pitchfork in his hand, was thrusting with all his might at a *zha* which dodged the blow and escaped between his legs" (Yang and Yang, 55). In contrast to the gray and desolate landscape of reality, this magic vision conjures up a fantasy land where the primary colors are intense and vibrant, the space is infinite, and the action of a young boy is playful and yet heroic. This is also an imaginary scene recalled because, as it becomes clear later, the narrator as a young boy never had the chance to visit Runtu by the ocean. Nor did he ever witness the escape of a crafty creature called the *zha*. Yet this childhood fantasy is now remembered as anamnestic of a different and removed existence that is ever more vivid and meaningful than the present gloominess. It participates in a truly utopian vision, if only because such a gorgeously fulfilling life was never to be achieved but merely anticipated. Still, the remembered fantasy releases a romantic longing for infinity that abnegates the mundaneness and fragmentation of the adult world. More importantly, essential to this vista — at least from the perspective of the nostalgic subject — is a child's purposeful but disinterested play.

Once awakened, childhood memories usher in a stream of objects, scenes, occasions, wishes, and narratives, through which the mind's eye is refocused and "I seemed to see my beautiful native land" again (cf. Yang and Yang, 58).[11] A forgotten language, or indeed a different sign system, has to be excavated and set up as the frame before the narrator can bring his native land into focus. Or, to extend Jacques Lacan's metaphor, the "archival documents" of childhood memories, in which the unconscious as hidden truth "has already been written down," are now released and made readable.[12] In recounting his acquaintance with Runtu more than thirty years ago, the narrator assumes the position of a cultural anthropologist and describes a bygone world with its rigorous customs and rituals. He explains the prayer and analogical thinking that go into Runtu's name, which amounts to an ingenuous overcoming of a feared deficiency. Even before his first appearance, Runtu already excites anticipation because all the young narrator cares about is that Runtu knows how to "set up traps and catch small birds" (Yang and Yang, 56). To the narrator, the name "Runtu" from the beginning signifies a mode of free and creative play that is lacking from his own day-to-day schooling.

When he finally arrives from the countryside, the boy Runtu brings not only a new friendship, a rare opportunity to play, but also a fresh and figurative speech. He introduces an adventurous outside world to the teenage narrator, who with his everyday schoolmates would normally have "nothing to look out on but the square patch of sky that was visible above the high walls of a family courtyard" (Lyell, 93). The names and nouns that Runtu utters, because they possess no specific referents but only exotic associations for the listener, turn into a colorful chain of signifiers: husks, pheasants, hornchicks, paddychicks, bluebacks, ghost-

11. Again, compare with the more elaborate Lyell translation: "For a fraction of a second, I even seemed to recapture that beautiful homeland I thought I had lost" (93–94).

12. Jacques Lacan, "The Function and Field of Speech and Language in Psychoanalysis," in his *Écrits: A Selection,* trans. Alan Sheridan (New York: Norton, 1977), 50.

scarers, *Guanyin* hands, badgers, porcupines, jumperfish, and the *zha*. To recapture the impact of this new experience, the narrator coins a linguistic sign *zha* and uses it to refer metonymically to an imaginative reality and playfulness unknown to him. "I had no idea then what this thing called *zha* was—and I am not much clearer now for that matter—but somehow I felt it was something like a small dog, and very fierce" (Yang and Yang, 57). The concocted word and image of *zha*, intimately associated with young Runtu and his magic world, becomes the sign par excellence of a different realm of reality from what the narrator finds familiar and uninteresting.

Together with his string of new nouns, Runtu also supplies a series of ministories, without which the exotic birds and fish would hardly come to life. What the young narrator misses, as a boy from the small town, are such narratable experiences and adventures. "I had never known that all these strange things existed: at the seashore there were shells all colors of the rainbow; watermelons were exposed to such danger, yet all I had known of them before was that they were sold in the greengrocer's" (Yang and Yang, 57). The fruit at the greengrocer's is already an abstraction, because it is removed from the environment in which it grows, and also because it is a commodity to be purchased through monetary exchange. It shrinks into the flattened, uniform residue of an organic life cycle that involves human time and labor. The heaps of fruit in a store may convey the idea of abundance, but they also display a splendid poverty of experience. This deceptive appearance of a marketplace seems to stimulate young Runtu during his trip to town, but there is no story to tell, nor much depth to look into. "I don't know what we talked of then, but I remember that Runtu was in high spirits, saying that since he had come to town he had seen many new things" (Yang and Yang, 56). Not surprisingly, the exciting "new things" that first strike Runtu never become concrete enough or even get named by the narrator as a young child. Intrigued by the rich experience of the visitor from another realm of reality, he only has time to feel embarrassed by his eventless and restrained life. In light of Runtu's enticing tales, his world appears unbearably narrow and abstract. After his visit is over, Runtu still asks his father to bring "a packet of shells and a few beautiful bird feathers," but all the young narrator can do in return, again, is to send him "some things a few times" (cf. Lyell, 93)—abstract objects that remain unnamed or simply unspecifiable.

Runtu's visit to town, incidentally, also reminds us that the generic notion of *guxiang* may refer to an area larger than the countryside. For the narrator, his native land obviously includes the small town where he grows up. His nostalgia for "guxiang," or what may be called a prototypical "homesickness complex," therefore describes a primordial attachment to a certain life form or stage that is not necessarily bound to a rural setting. Since the formation of a native land is one of the first signs of coming of age that signals irreversible entrance into adulthood, the nostalgia for one's native land is often more concretely expressed as a longing for one's lost childhood. Their similar psychotropic impact brings together one's native land and childhood, because both may be made into depositories of a mythical contentment free of anxiety, or into metonyms of an imaginary plenitude prior to the strictures of the symbolic order.

More generally, a visit to one's native land may turn into a sentimental journey and yield a lyrical literary topic only when the prospect of achieving reconciliation with oneself becomes problematic and is put on trial. The ensuing pathos of lament or regret underscores a fundamental misrecognition and brings to the fore the incoherence or discontinuity in one's life experience, now magnified and given a physical contour in the external landscape.[13] The journey deep into past territories as inscriptions of the unconscious also prompts intense self-review and a global reflection on one's condition of existence. Often, as the narrating subject fondly recalls, in vivid detail, an innocent and playful childhood, we detect a disillusionment with and questioning of the cold, harsh reality of the adult world.

As a narrative genre, which Lu Xun was first to name and characterize in 1935, modern Chinese native-land literature (*xiangtu wenxue*, or literary nativism) often sublimates anxiety about entering the adult world into a critical thrust against modern urban culture; it has the basic structure of transforming a private reminiscence into an expression of utopian longing. In straightforward terms, Lu Xun describes the necessary condition of displacement for native-land literature to be written. "Before a writer sets out to write native-land literature, he finds himself already exiled from his home, driven by life to a strange place. What can he do but recall his father's garden, a garden which does not exist any-

---

13. For a discussion of the ethos of nostalgia in modern Chinese literature, see David Der-wei Wang, "Towards a Poetics of Imaginary Nostalgia," in his *Fictional Realism in Twentieth-Century China: Mao Dun, Lao She, Shen Congwen* (New York: Columbia University Press, 1992), 249–53.

more?"¹⁴ The motivation and rhetorical operation of such narratives is therefore the seeking, in childhood memories, of an imaginary compensation for present dissatisfaction. As a literary form devoted to reliving absent scenes and private moments, native-land literature cannot fail to be a hypersubjective form of writing. It is a kind of writing that draws on the "archival documents" of the unconscious and helps the narrating subject recognize, as Lacan would suggest, his unconscious not merely as his history, but also as "the discourse of the other."¹⁵ Herein lies the symbolic function of native-land literature. As a literary form that explores the incidental and remembered fragments of experience, native-land literature compels as well as accomplishes an inquiry into the realm of the unconscious. In engaging in the discourse of alterity, nostalgic writings antithetically outline large and external forces that drive memories and desires inward and into the unconscious. Native-land literature, in other words, may be both the symptom of civilizational discontent and its cure. It is a therapeutic writing because it allows for a contemplative subjectivity and opens up access to other visions of social life and the future. Sustained literary interest in the subject matter of homeland or homesickness only testifies to the great need for such a therapeutic relief in twentieth-century China.¹⁶

According to one representative analysis, Lu Xun's own native-land narratives (including other stories such as "New Year's Sacrifice" and "In the Wineshop") depict a second loss: one returns home to lose it again and perhaps even for good. In these stories the alienation of the male visitor from his homeland is often taken as an allegory of "the antagonism between a modern intellectual, cultivated in Western civilization and ideas, and the stagnant communal society that is still locked in traditional Chinese culture and thought patterns."¹⁷ Indeed, native-land lit-

---

14. Lu Xun, Preface to *Xiandai Zhongguo wenxue daxi* (Compendium of modern Chinese literature), 10 vols., ed. Zhao Jiabi (Shanghai: Liangyou tushu gongsi, 1935–36), 2:9.

15. Lacan, "The Function and Field of Speech and Language in Psychoanalysis," 52–55.

16. For a comprehensive anthology, see *Tiandong cao: yi guxiang* (Chinese asparagus: remembrances of the native land), ed. Deng Jiuping and Yu Haiying (Beijing: Zhongguo duiwai fanyi, 1995). To some extent, even the *xiangtu* literary movement in Taiwan during the early 1970s expressed the same psychological need.

17. Yang Jianlong, "Lun Lu Xun de xiangtu qingjie yu xiangtu xiaoshuo" ("On Lu

erature is also bound to be a self-consciously allegorical mode of writing, upon which depends the salient and substituting translatability between private sentiments and social commentary. Finally, native-land literature must rely on realist techniques to satisfy its descriptive impulse, while its ethos is recognizably lyrical, and its ultimate vision deeply utopian.

(Mis)Recognizing the Homeland

If the journey through one's native land leads to the innermost childhood memories being discovered as the unconscious, either incidentally or through concentrated efforts, the contemporary reality of one's hometown does not emerge fully until one as a visitor is looked at and recognized (or rather misrecognized) as a stranger. A failure to recognize, which Lacan points out as essential to self-recognition and knowledge,[18] occurs to redefine the subject's position and his relationship to others. When the narrating subject arrives at his family compound, he is greeted by his mother and nephew as a family member. Hong'er examines his uncle with curiosity, but since no other identification is possible, nor is there the need for mutual recognition, no description follows. During the conversation between Hong'er and the narrator, the young boy learns that he will soon be taking a train ride and a boat trip and will leave this place. The narrator makes a point of asking whether Hong'er likes traveling, but is the young boy fully aware of and prepared for the consequences of this expected departure?

> "Oh! Like this? With such a long moustache!" A strange shrill voice suddenly rang out.
>
> I looked up with a start, and saw a woman of about fifty with prominent cheekbones and thin lips. With her hands on her hips, not wearing a skirt but with her trousered legs apart, she stood in front of me just like a compass in a box of geometrical instruments. (cf. Yang and Yang, 58)

Xun's native-land complex and native-land fiction"), *Lu Xun yanjiu yuekang* (Lu Xun studies monthly), no. 134 (June 1993): 29–36, esp. 32.

18. For one version of Lacan's theorization, see "Subversion of the Subject and Dialectic of Desire," in *Écrits: A Selection,* 306–07 where the original French description is given as *"un méconnaître essentiel au me connaître."*

The first jolting description of the narrating subject as a stranger thus results from an instance of mutual misrecognition. The pronouncement of the loud woman abruptly makes the narrator realize, as if looking in an unflattering mirror, how other people in town may and will (mis)recognize him—with shock and disbelief. Moreover, with her comment about his "long moustache," the woman forces him to see himself first as a body fragment and then as an adult male, images grotesquely irreconcilable with the longing and private child whom he has just recalled as his own self. In reaction to such fragmentary identifications, the narrator grows defensive and engages in a similar misrecognition; the less than pleasing features that he notices first are therefore her "prominent cheekbones and thin lips."[19] This misrecognition, which consists in reducing the object of observation to a fragmented body, follows a synecdochic procedure and institutes a realistic recognition—the revelatory astonishment at seeing reality as less than the imagined fullness or plenitude. Even though the narrator already experiences such a painful encounter with reality on approaching an unrecognizable landscape, the moment of mutual misrecognition still shakes him profoundly, because he now perforce sees himself being seen and undergoes the primal "deflection of the specular *I* into the social *I*."[20] The human body grows to be a more bitter record of ruinous reality than does landscape.

Seeing how flabbergasted the narrator is, the unexpected stranger goes further and stakes her claim to familiarity and even physical intimacy: "Don't you recognize me? Why, I held you in my arms before!" (cf. Yang and Yang, 58). At this turn of intimate misrecognition, childhood or infancy turns into a liability, and the narrator's identity or selfhood is psychologically arrested in and held hostage to a helpless infant body. Only with his mother's helpful hints does the narrator recall that the woman before him is Second Sister Yang, who, as the Beancurd Beauty, used to attract many customers to her bean curd shop. However, "probably because of my tender age, I must have been immune to the alchemy of her charms, for I had forgotten her completely" (cf. Lyell, 94–95). Once again, the present situation delivers a blunt reminder of the remoteness of his childhood. As if in a psychoanalytical minidrama, Sec-

---

19. For Lacan's classic discussion of the impact of a "fragmented body" vis-à-vis the Gestalt of a subject's total body, see his "The Mirror Stage as Formative of the Function of the I as Revealed in Psychoanalytic Experience," in *Écrits: A Selection*, 1–7.

20. Ibid., 5.

ond Sister Yang plays the part of a "bad mother," who is cold, seductive, and domineering. The most insidious aspect of her character is her close symbolic association, as well as semiotic association, with the narrator's natural mother. She held him as a baby; she is introduced by the mother; and, while exiting the scene, she steals the mother's gloves. The shrewd, compasslike woman makes it clear that the narrator no longer can claim innocence from adult sexuality, even when he is at home with his mother; yet she also derives pleasure from subjecting him to an infantile position. Assaulted by her flirtatious teases and mockery (calling him, inappropriately, "Elder Brother Xun," and alleging that he now possesses three concubines), the narrator falls speechless, apparently as the result of an incapacitating confusion over which language to speak and which identity to assume. "Knowing there was nothing I could say, I remained silent and simply stood there" (cf. Yang and Yang, 59; Lyell, 95). Her outrageous behavior is so disconcerting that the narrator's wit and knowledge (including his learned references to Napoleon and Washington) appear helplessly pale and pointless.

The unscrupulous Second Sister Yang threatens the integrity of the narrator's self-conception by imposing on him two incompatible roles: an amiable baby boy vis-à-vis a lascivious adult man. Her entrance into the scene, preceded by her "shrill voice," puts the narrator in a defenseless position from the start. In that initial moment, she easily dominates the situation by first voicing her surprise at how drastically the narrator's appearance has changed. The narrator, surprised by her piercing gaze, never manages to set himself entirely free.

Yet a similar scene of (mis)recognition soon repeats itself, with different intersubjective dynamics at work. "One very cold afternoon just after lunch I was sitting and drinking tea when I heard someone come in from the outside. When I turned around to look I couldn't help but start with surprise. I scrambled to my feet and rushed over to welcome him" (Lyell, 95). This time the narrator takes the initiative, although the sense of being approached and the element of surprise are still present. In actively directing his look and recognizing the other person, the narrator assumes control over the unfolding scene. However, the same crisis of language and communication erupts, because the problematic relationship between a gazing subject and his object of observation persists. Besides, in this instance it also becomes abundantly clear to the narrator that recognition involves no less than perceiving reality as a painful failure.

It was Runtu. Although I recognized him right off, he was not at all the Runtu who lived in my memory. He seemed twice as tall now. The round and ruddy face of yesteryear had already turned pale and grey, and it was etched with deep wrinkles. The rims of his eyes were swollen and red just like his father's. I knew that most farmers who worked close to the sea got that way because of the wind. He was wearing a battered old felt hat, and his cotton clothes were so thin that he was shivering. His hands held a paper package along with his pipe. They were not the smooth and nimble hands that I remembered. Now they were rough, clumsy, and as cracked as pine bark. (Lyell, 96)

This description presents arguably one of the earliest and most memorable realist portraitures in modern Chinese literature. Its success has to do with the shock in recognition, for with striking strokes it makes visible a familiar stranger. The description of Runtu and of other details about him is motivated by a systematic comparison with the idealized image that the narrator cherishes in his memory. Through this filtering lens, Runtu's visage emerges as a vivid picture of the toll of a stark reality, the truth of which is its radical difference from our subjective wish or anticipation. The critical thrust of the portraiture originates in a sense of loss, a lament over the contrast between the adult Runtu in reality and the young boy in memory. At the same time, it relies on a sympathetic identification with the object of observation, because the stranger is vaguely recognizable. The humanist concern in realist representation has first to come from regarding the other as sharing the same human condition and vulnerabilities as the observing subject. It is this active and participatory sympathy that distinguishes the narrator's relationship with Runtu as separate from his reaction to Second Sister Yang, who forecloses a humane identification by disallowing the other to emerge as a full and self-sufficient person.

The shock of recognition, however, causes the narrator to feel excited as much as confused. "Delighted as I was, I did not know how to express myself, and could only say: 'Oh! Brother Runtu—so, it's you' . . ." (cf. Yang and Yang, 60). In his excitement, the narrator comes to realize the irrelevance, or unreality, of the mythical world that he associates with the young Runtu. The mental blockage he experiences results from the external reality that he cannot reconcile with his memory or imagination. His perception of reality as ruinous to human life leads him to see the inadequacy of language. "There was so much I wanted to say. There were so many words waiting to gush out one after the other like pearls on a string: hornchicks, jumperfish, *Guanyin* hands, *zha*—but at the same time I was aware of something damming them up inside me, so that they simply swirled around in my brain without a single one coming out" (Lyell, 96). No doubt the inside/outside tension, or the forced insulation of the inner world from outer reality, indicates a classical despair with the impossibility of action. In this case, however, the narrator is so fully conscious of what he wishes to say that his inability or unwillingness to utter the "pearls" of words may point to a deliberate refusal. His mythical world may be inadequate or unreal, and the *zha* may be sheer fantasy, but when they are endangered as such, only the narrator is in a position to defend them against the elemental forces of reality. The fear of witnessing his memory and language of fantasy invalidated by historical reality is sufficient to prevent the narrator from speaking. His silence protects an interiority that is sentimentally real and true.

Not until after the narrator reaches an emotional high point do we see Runtu react to the moment of reunion, which he humbly expects all along.

> He stood there, mixed joy and sadness showing on his face. His lips moved, but not a sound did he utter. Finally, assuming a respectful attitude, he said clearly:
> "Master! . . ."
> I felt a shiver run through me; for I knew then what a lamentably thick wall had grown up between us. Yet I could not say anything. (Yang and Yang, 60)

What we still do not know, from this account, is Runtu's observation of the narrator, whom he now deferentially addresses as "Master." In this scene of recognition, Runtu is the object of the narrator's close examination and is consequently read as the symptomatic sign of a general bankruptcy. Here is a situation that could lead to what Marston Anderson terms "the violence of observation" that Lu Xun desires to avoid in his fiction. According to Anderson, Lu Xun was acutely aware that "representational art risks making the victim into a mere object of the reader's curiosity or pity; in the process of reading, these emotions, which significantly are those of the observer, are satisfied, thereby camouflaging the true nature of the reader's involvement with the victim."[21] To prevent such facile recognition and, worse, moral complacency, Lu Xun employs various literary techniques in his fiction and institutes an "interpretive procedure" through which a narrated content is also evaluated self-consciously or even deconstructively.[22]

In the narrator's observation of Runtu, the limits of realist description are at once present and quickly overcome through the internal crisis that confronts the narrator. A shiver runs through him because of the shock of being (mis)recognized, a deliberate act by the other at that. The narrator/observer is again jolted by the object of his observation when he realizes that he is seen as different from what he takes himself to be. His shock and sadness is that of not being recognized and being kept outside. The honorific title that Runtu gives him confirms that the narrator inhabits a separate realm of reality, and that his very existence and status may be part of the "lamentably thick wall" separating two boyhood friends. Both the wooden Runtu and the brazen Second Sister Yang misrecognize the narrator, although he seems more self-assured and occupies a more active subject-position in one encounter than the other. Together, these two situations drive home his realization that he is a stranger in his native land. As a stranger, he cannot but be irrelevant to Runtu's hard life. Also as an irrelevant stranger, he will find nothing to talk about with Runtu, even if he tries to understand. "We chatted a bit more that night, but none of it amounted to anything. Early next morning he took Shuisheng and headed back home" (Lyell, 98). What contributes to Runtu's plight ("too many children, famine, harsh taxes, soldiers, bandits, officials, and gentryfolk" [Lyell, 97]) acknowledges too real and too overwhelming a referent to generate the same fantasy as did the interjection of mobile signifiers such as jumperfish or the *zha*.

As if to combat the sense of repetition that suggests itself through these two sobering scenes of (mis)recognition, the narrator believes that between Shuisheng, Runtu's fifth child, and Hong'er, a transformative bond and friendship develops as once occurred among the generation before them. Shuisheng appears to be a replica of the young Runtu of more than twenty years ago, whereas Hong'er is now the responsibility

21. Marston Anderson, *The Limits of Realism: Chinese Fiction in the Revolutionary Period* (Berkeley: University of California Press, 1990), 86.
22. Ibid., 76.

as well as the hope of his uncle—the narrator. When the two boys are together, Shuisheng is not at all the shy and timid child he seems to be in front of the adults. Just as a generation ago, Shuisheng's visit is brief and he does not come back, but he also promises Hong'er a playful trip to the countryside, which Hong'er begins to anticipate eagerly. Obviously, there is the concern that Shuisheng will grow up to be another adult Runtu, just as Runtu turns out to be no different from his own father. Yet there also is a chance that this younger generation will live its life differently. This is then the only tangible hope with which the otherwise disenchanted narrator will leave his native land a few days later.

Reconfiguring the Homeland

> As we set off, in the dusk, the green mountains on either side of the river became deep blue, receding towards the stern of the boat. (Yang and Yang, 62)

> As we proceeded upriver, the twilight-green mountains on either bank took on deeper hues and joined together in a single blue-green mass as they fled away into the distance behind the stern. (Lyell, 98)

Leaving at this juncture comes, once again, as a timely relief. More than disengaging the narrator from the emotional and intellectual agonies and self-doubt occasioned by his native land, the new departure frees him from the hectic final days of ridding the old family house of "old and used things of every imaginable size and description" (Lyell, 98). Besides, he is relieved to escape the pettiness and harassment of Second Sister Yang, who, in her effort to acquire a piece of furniture for free, does not hesitate to spoil the narrator's regard for Runtu. Now the steady movement away from the forlorn site of chaos introduces a fresh perspective, and a new scenery seems to set in. The depressing wintry landscape that he witnessed upon coming home, no more than two weeks ago, is miraculously transformed into a pleasing vista of spring. There is no sadness or regret; sentimentality gives way to a resolute serenity. Hong'er, however, seems to be more attached to the land than the narrator, because Hong'er still remembers Shuisheng's invitation to the countryside. Engrossed in thoughts about his new friend, Hong'er is allowed to put together a beautiful myth about his native land that he is leaving behind. "Hong'er and I leaned against the window and watched the dimming landscape" (Lyell, 98). In the passing scenery, two separate visions of the native land must be rising for these two quiet passengers.

"I was leaving the old house farther and farther behind, while the hills and rivers of my native land were also receding gradually ever farther in the distance. But I felt no attachment" (cf. Yang and Yang, 63). The old house and what it stands for are too real to leave any room for imagination. More accurately, the old house disillusions the narrator and deprives him of his fond memories. The "gentle slapping of water against the hull" (Lyell, 99), on the other hand, reassures the narrator that he and his mother and nephew are moving away. The flowing river nurtures an anticipatory excitement about departure, motion, change, and regeneration. It offers itself as an apt symbol for life, for unstoppable energy and hope. In soothingly moving the narrator into an open space, the river allows him to contemplate and put in perspective the landscape of his native land. It embodies a viable resolution that brings therapeutic peace, freshness, and completion.

The hope for a new life lies with the next generation, as Lu Xun's Madman famously voices, if mainly for the reason that the present generation and life are so inextricably injured and complicitous. Youth itself is reason for hope and change for the better. "They should have a new life, a life we have never experienced" (Yang and Yang, 63). Hong'er and Shuisheng should not be stymied by the same barrier that separates their forefathers. They should extend their friendship and nurture their closeness, but this commitment should not mean their living a miserable life together, either. Their life should be different to the extent that it is unimaginable, because the narrator cannot yet picture an ideal life. None of the three ways of living that he witnesses seems satisfactory. His own life is rootless, Runtu's benumbed, and Second Sister Yang's scurrilous: they are all burdened by the same hard and unfulfilled reality.[23] The new life should be a negation of adult life as it is known. It must consist of a

---

23. Chi-Chen Wang's translation of these dense and difficult sentences, in my opinion, is the most successful: "However, I did not want them to live, as a price for their continued companionship, the bitter and rootless life that I lived; I did not want them to live the bitter and wretched life that Yun-t'u lived; I did not want them to live the bitter and shameless life that others lived. They must have a new kind of life, a life that we of the other generation had not known." See Chi-chen Wang, "My Native Heath," 14.

communal, communicable existence, and yet it does not lack generative diversity. In essence, this visionary new life calls forth a utopian society where, with its guiding principle romantically modeled after a playful and carefree childhood, each and every individual will be different but equal.

Yet such a utopian reverie suddenly fills the pensive narrator with anxiety. His hope for a better future makes him question his own conviction, for his vision appears at once vivid and blurred, as may be true of all global fantasies. The prospect of a new life, because of its radical difference from the lived present, strikes him as "far off in the murky distance" and may demand the same devotion as an article of faith. More immediately, concentration on such a grandiose hope risks ossifying the "new life" into an immovable creed that blocks concrete, transformative action or discoveries in one's own life. For bad faith, as the narrator is keenly aware, may be a negative consequence of the gravity of faith. Nonetheless, the compelling utopian imagination causes him to ponder the next logical question: where lies the path that will lead us there? "In the dim moonlight, an emerald green plot of land by the sea appeared before my eyes. In the deep blue sky above it hung a moon, full and golden. 'Hope isn't the kind of thing that you can say either exists or doesn't exist,' I thought to myself. 'It's like a path across the land—it's not there to begin with, but when lots of people go the same way, it comes into being.'" (cf. Lyell, 100). The final landscape of fantasy is conjured up in the concluding paragraph to relieve a series of anxieties, immediate or global. Against the growing darkness, the brilliant vista of infinite space and depth serves as a possible site for the desired good life. As in a mirage, the sharply defined vision displays a timeless terrain in which no human subjects seem to be present, not even the "young hero" who so far is closely associated with the scenery. If the emptiness of the scene seems to suggest that no human life can yet do justice to the sublime truth of nature, the primary vigor and simplicity of the environment are also called upon, as it were, to provide irrefutable physical evidence of a bright future for humanity. For, after all, this fantastic landscape is the redemptive projection of an embattled human subject. And it offers a definite site to bury all ontological doubts.

For this reason, the scenery is necessarily specific and recognizable. A familiar landscape is sublimated into an imaginary homeland that coincides with the final horizon for hope and utopian anticipation. The departing narrator may always be haunted adversely by his native land, but, in the final analysis, he refuses to be totally disenchanted and insists on reconfiguring its symbolic elements into a reliable source for spiritual resilience and inner certainty. This symbolic reconfiguration culminates the narrative of "My Native Land" and determines its lyrical and uplifting conclusion. With this final upward turn, the sentimental journey undertaken by the narrator in "My Native Land" acquires a paradigmatic significance, because it illustrates the arduous but ultimately gratifying process of reclaiming an imaginary homeland. The necessity and origin of such an imaginary homeland is what Lu Xun persuasively conveys in this short story, which as a dense psychobiographical narrative offers an effective antidote for the homesickness prevalent among displaced modern Chinese intellectuals. The intense nostalgia that propels popular native-land literature is both acknowledged and redirected in this fundamentally sublimational narrative, in which therapeutic discourse directs a shocking recognition of the real homeland to its symbolic reconfiguration. This reconfiguration enables an open-endedness in the narrative insofar as it not only extends the native landscape to an ontological dimension, but it also shifts the promise of an imaginary homeland to the reader, however burdened with his or her own history. The relivable native land lies not in the past, but in the future, and it is to be reached collectively; it signifies nostalgia overcome. Such is the narrator's belief when he reminds us how a new path may be created on the surface of the earth.

3

Shanghai, Spring 1930:

Engendering the Revolutionary Body

In her novella *Yijiu sanling nian chun Shanghai* (Shanghai, spring 1930), Ding Ling (1904–86) tells two separate and yet related stories, the central idea of which, according to Tsi-an Hsia, is simple and straightforward: "how intellectuals discover the meaning of their lives in a mass movement."[1] Indeed, both stories, written and published in the second half of 1930, offer a less than refined sample of the then-popular "revolution and love" fiction churned out by the nascent literary Left. Many such narratives center on an often melodramatic conflict between collective cause and individual preferences, between a rising proletarian movement and private sentiment. In view of Ding Ling's entire writing career, critic Yi-tsi Mei Feuerwerker suggests that the *Shanghai, Spring 1930* stories, together with another 1930 novella on the same topic, show Ding Ling the author "negotiating a passage *from* love *to* revolution, from the focus on internal experience to the outer world of political reality."[2] More than a personal expansion of intellectual horizons, this seemingly inevitable passage reflects the historical experience of a generation of educated young men and women in the 1930s. It was also part of an international political culture that gathered much momentum during the decade of capitalism in crisis. In accord with the contemporary Old Left's effort to internationalize a worldwide revolutionary literature, Ding Ling, as well as Lu Xun, was translated as a representative Chinese progressive writer in journals such as *The Liberator* and *New Masses* in the United States.[3]

---

1. Tsi-an Hsia, "Enigma of the Five Martyrs," in his *Gate of Darkness: Studies on the Leftist Literary Movement in China* (Seattle: University of Washington Press, 1968), 175. Although Hsia is generally dismissive, sometimes even sardonic, toward this literary tradition, his study is meticulous and groundbreaking.

2. Yi-tsi Mei Feuerwerker, *Ding Ling's Fiction: Ideology and Narrative in Modern Chinese Literature* (Cambridge, Mass.: Harvard University Press, 1982), 53 (original emphasis).

3. Among the inspired readers of these radical publications was Tillie Olsen, a

It would be interesting to determine which Ding Ling was being so promptly promoted as a revolutionary writer in the United States in the early 1930s. For until 1930, which was actually fewer than three years after the publication of her first and fame-establishing short story "Mengke," Ding Ling in her writings had created a gallery of alienated, depressed, often tubercular and suicidal young women living on the fringes of the modern city. Her most memorable creation from this period is Miss Sophia (1928), whose anguished diary reveals a hypersensitive soul relentlessly tormented by self-doubt and questions, abstract and fundamental, about the meaning of life, love, sexuality, and death. Consumed by both ennui and passion, Miss Sophia embodies the existential angst acutely experienced by an entire generation of Chinese youth caught between the disintegration of traditional social structures and the emerging modern metropolis. For this reason, a contemporary critic perceptively attributed the importance and modernity of Ding Ling's writings to her sensitive portrayal of a representative "modern girl" in urban and Westernized China (the English-language term "modern girl" is used in the original text).[4] Another reason for Ding Ling's instant success as a young woman writer and spokesperson of her generation is the confessional mode of narration that she employed in most of her stories. Some prominent male writers of the late 1920s, such as Mao Dun, had also explored the "woman question" and had even demonstrated a "feminist consciousness,"[5] but Ding Ling's bold and penetrating exploration of female psychology—in particular, sexuality—was groundbreaking. Her refusal to allegorize her

---

young woman and budding writer from Omaha, Nebraska. See Deborah Rosenfelt, "From the Thirties: Tillie Olsen and the Radical Tradition," in *Feminist Criticism and Social Change: Sex, Class and Race in Literature and Culture,* ed. Judith Newton and Deborah Rosenfelt (New York: Methuen, 1985), 229.

4. Fang Ying, "Ding Ling lun" (On Ding Ling), in *Ding Ling yanjiu ziliao* (Research materials on Ding Ling), ed. Yuan Liangjun (Tianjin: Tianjin renmin, 1982), 237–45. Originally published in *Wenyi xinwen* (Literary news), nos. 22, 24, 26 (10, 24, 31 August 1931). The thesis of Fang Ying's article, i.e., the conflict between traditional society and modern capitalism being the cause of anomie for most of Ding Ling's characters, is influential and still present as an analytical paradigm in Meng Yue and Dai Jinhua, *Fuchu lishi dibiao: xiandai funü wenxue yanjiu* (Emerging from history: studies in modern women's literature) (Zhengzhou: Henan renmin, 1989).

5. See, for instance, David Der-wei Wang, "Feminist Consciousness in Modern Chinese Male Fiction," in *Modern Chinese Women Writers: Critical Appraisals,* ed. Michael S. Duke (New York: M. E. Sharpe, 1989), 236–56.

characters' experience only added to the poignancy of her expositional writing. Through a discourse of discontent, Ding Ling at once introduced a new literary sensibility and established the problematic female experience as a personalized form of social protest.[6]

From the beginning, the inescapable backdrop to Ding Ling's explorations into the inner depths of the dislocated "modern girl" was the city of Shanghai. Yet within three short years, the glamorous but "purely carnal society" that Mengke, the humiliated—albeit successful—movie actress, detected and detested in Shanghai would turn into a site of political action for the young revolutionaries described in *Shanghai, Spring 1930*. This change of the literary landscape also brought forth in Ding Ling's writings a different group of characters who began to demonstrate a new politics of the body and a new relationship to the modern city.

A Desire Named Shanghai

If in its popular image in the early 1930s, no doubt promoted by the multinational colonialist establishment, Shanghai was the decadent "Paris of the Orient" and a "paradise for the adventurers," at the same time it was revered by China's radicalized and city-bound youth as the bestirring "Moscow of the Orient." For the contemporary Chinese culture and consciousness, Shanghai was both a gigantic embodiment of Western-style modernity, probably in its most aggressive and grotesque form, and the site that brought forth its inseparable nemesis—a concentration of industrial power and political agency. Its modern dynamism derived from the raw capitalist transformation of a port city, cosmopolitan Shanghai also bred various ideological persuasions (such as anarchism, liberalism, nationalism, traditionalism, anti-imperialism, guild socialism, communism) that fiercely competed to impart intelligibility and symbolism to the sprawling cityscape and beyond.

One classic literary expression of the desire to comprehend the symbolism of Shanghai is Mao Dun's 1933 novel *Ziye* (Midnight). In the opening

6. For this reason, Tani Barlow observes that "Ding Ling wrote Chinese feminist fiction as a young writer, but over the course of her life she abandoned most of feminism's component elements." See Barlow, "Introduction" to *I Myself Am a Woman: Selected Writings of Ding Ling*, ed. Tani E. Barlow and Gary J. Bjorge (Boston: Beacon Press, 1989), 1.

paragraph, the realist-narrator, apparently strolling along the exotic Bund in a "heavenly May evening" of 1930, surveys the dynamic city from a distance.

> Under a sunset-mottled sky, the towering framework of Garden Bridge was mantled in a gathering mist. Whenever a tram passed over the bridge, the overhead cable suspended below the top of the steel frame threw off bright, greenish sparks. Looking east, one could see the warehouses on the waterfront of Pootung [Pudong] like huge monsters crouching in the gloom, their lights twinkling like countless tiny eyes. To the west, one saw with a shock of wonder on the roof of a building a gigantic neon sign in flaming red and phosphorescent green: LIGHT, HEAT, POWER.[7]

If an initial detached view of Shanghai would expose, even for an omniscient narrator, a monstrous field of ominous interrogation and intrigue, the same unsettling experience of visual incongruity was marketed as a fascinating instance of modernity, conceivable only through the most contemporary cinematic technique of montage. The 1934–35 edition of an annual English guidebook, catering to an emerging international class of tourists, thus peddled "Shanghai the bizarre, cinematographic presentation of humanity":

> Cosmopolitan Shanghai, city of amazing paradoxes and fantastic contrasts; Shanghai the beautiful, bawdy, and gaudy; contradiction of manners and morals; a vast brilliantly-hued cycloramic, panoramic mural of the best and the worst of Orient and Occident. . . .
>
> Behold! "The longest bar in the world!" The shortest street in the world with a blatant cacophony of carnality from a score of dance-halls; scarlet women laughing without mirth; virgins in search of life; suicides; marriages; births; carols of vested choirs; cathedral chimes; Communists plotting; Nationalism in the saddle; war in Manchuria!; it's a great old town, and how we hate it and love it.[8]

This intriguing "cinematographic presentation of humanity" is the theme as well as the technique of one of Ding Ling's best short stories. Written in 1929, "Daylight" (Ri) achieves a sweeping panoramic view of

---

7. Mao Dun, *Ziye* (Beijing: Renmin wenxue, 1988), 3. English translation by Hsu Meng-hsiung and A. C. Barnes, *Midnight* (Peking: Foreign Languages Press, 1957), 9.

8. *All About Shanghai and Environs: A Standard Guide Book (Edition 1934–35)* (Shanghai: University Press, 1935), 43–44.

this "boisterous metropolis, a colony that is semi-foreign, a place governed by numerous countries and inhabited by numerous races."9 Following the omnipresent narrator, we look over the city at daybreak and move swiftly, all within one long paragraph, from the industrial sweatshops to the financial district, from modern high-rises to putrid slums, from a decadent life of leisure to degrading hardship and despair. Daylight exposes the uneven urban landscape and gradually brings into focus a sickly young woman, named Yisai, who lives all by herself in one of the overcrowded apartment buildings in the International Settlement. She desperately needs some sleep, but the cacophony of the city makes sleep an impossibility. The rest of the story describes an uneventful and pointless day in Yisai's life. At the sound and stench of the night-soil truck, she grows sympathetic to the misery of the multitudes, but, moments later, she is assaulted once again by boredom. She becomes aware of her weak body and grows restless. The sulking face of the intrusive maid completely ruins her day, which also makes her realize that only fantasy can give her some solace. "As a result, she would often start daydreaming while she was cursing and start cursing while daydreaming" (583). Her foul mood continues and helps drive away two ghostly visitors who barely can manage to engage the dejected hostess in a coherent conversation.

Without much of a plot, "Daylight" is instead the prelude to a possible story about the city. It depicts the wearied life of a Weltschmerz-stricken young woman against the uncontrollable expanse of the city, in which even political passion quickly becomes the object of mockery. Youth, as much as the imposed interiority, becomes pathologized and demands therapeutic release. A cinematic juxtaposition highlights the disjuncture between two perspectives: a painfully self-conscious but apathetic individual against the vibrant, repetitive, and unreflective city life around her. Thanks to the visual structure of the narrative, these two extreme forms of life in the city are brought together, if only to problematize each other. Yet there is no explicit message or judgment in the story. On the contrary, this sketchlike description of different dimensions of city life seems to be in search of a story, of a logical or even causal connection between the urban landscape and the interior of Yisai's dreary world. The story

9. Ding Ling, *Ding Ling wenji* (Collected works of Ding Ling) (Shanghai: Yiwen shudian, 1936), 576. Page references in the text are to this edition.

conveys a vague longing for action, a desire to break free of the imprisoning subjectivity and participate in urban narrativity. The narrative ends as the heroine languidly drifts into sleep at dusk. With a final comment—"Tomorrow everything would come and go one more time just as before" (586), the absence of either action or purpose in her life becomes an obvious theme and suggests the need to interrupt this incapacitating pattern of repetition.

The search for a purposeful life and narratability becomes the motive in Ding Ling's subsequent writings. In *Shanghai, Spring 1930* (I), we see a paradigmatic choice being set up and made. Through the action of Meilin, who is an educated woman of the post-May Fourth era now confined to her comfortable bourgeois home, a transfer of political alliance is carried out. Her final decision to leave her house without first telling her husband (who is a self-obsessed writer with considerable fame) and to join another man in a street demonstration is reached as both the climax of the story and the resolution to her boredom. Meilin participates in collective action so as to free herself of submission to a "so gentle and yet so tyrannical" love. When at home, she increasingly feels like a prisoner of her impervious husband, Zibin. Out of desperation,

> Meilin would wear a new outfit every day, green ones, red ones. She went out regularly with Zibin, but got neither pleasure nor gratification from it. She imagined that each person she saw on the crowded streets had a more meaningful life than she. Meilin did not want to die. Quite the contrary, she wanted to really live and she wanted to be happy. It was just that she could not find the right direction and she needed guidance from someone. (218–19; 129)[10]

In this description, the statement that "Meilin did not want to die" may sound abrupt, but it constitutes an intertextual response to the series of suicidal female characters that peopled Ding Ling's earlier fiction. There, the young women always felt excluded from a presumably happy life that everyone else was living, and their only connection to the bustling crowd was their death as a voiceless protest.[11] "No one would give me a dollar

---

10. The page reference following the semicolon refers to "Shanghai, Spring 1930," translated by Shu-ying Ts'ao and Donald Holoch, in *I Myself Am a Woman*. In most instances, I have modified the Ts'ao/Holoch translation.

11. Following Durkheim's classical study of suicides in modern society, the suicide

for free," so laments Yisa, a young woman stranded in Shanghai, in her diary ("The Diary of a Suicide"), "just as no one would show me any attachment for free. I am not jealous of anyone, because everyone else is a better person than me" (148). For Meilin the new heroine, however, this moment of observing others in the street leads to a different resolution: she wants to partake of this happiness and needs to find someone to take her there.

This mentor figure that Meilin awaits is a young man named Ruoquan, who used to be a writer as well. At the beginning of the narrative, however, his conception of society has undergone some radical changes, and consequently he renounces literature as useless and even harmful to those young people "who have just reached adolescence and are most subject to melancholy." Sentimentalist and individualist writings, according to Ruoquan, would only serve to "drag the young people into their own gloom" and make it impossible for them to see "the connection between society and their sufferings" (190–91; 116). His new mission consists in debating political issues in study groups, holding meetings to bring together workers and college students, and orchestrating rallies in the street. In contrast to the pale and solitary Zibin, Ruoquan is a committed young man, full of energy and hope.[12]

On one level, *Shanghai, Spring 1930* (I) has the structure of metafiction, for it is decidedly a narrative about the writing of fiction, and, with the help of a moral discourse, it reflects on its own condition of possibility. Irony or ambiguity is no longer an intended effect for this mode of writing. On the contrary, the clarity that Ding Ling now strives for in her fiction allows her repositioning as a political writer and brings about a new sense of authority. The act of writing, to which some of her earlier diarists resorted as the sole means of self-affirmation, is now contextual-

---

they contemplated can be seen as either an "anomic" or "egoistic" type, because both types indicate a lack of social bonds and integration. Critics have traced this dejection at the sight of unattainable happiness to the influence of Gustave Flaubert's *Madame Bovary,* a novel that Ding Ling had read repeatedly at a young age. See, for example, Feuerwerker, *Ding Ling's Fiction,* 25–27.

12. According to Jaroslav Průšek, Ruoquan's comments in Ding Ling's story sum up the basic character of a new literature that puts much emphasis on subjectivism and individualism. See his influential essay "Subjectivism and Individualism in Modern Chinese Literature," in Průšek, *The Lyrical and the Epic: Studies of Modern Chinese Literature,* ed. Leo Ou-fan Lee (Bloomington: Indiana University Press, 1980), 1–28.

ized. Reconfigured, too, is the scene of literary creation. As Tani Barlow comments, "speaking as a revolutionary writer, rather than as a woman, Ding Ling felt empowered to criticize the masculine world of 'bourgeois' literature."[13] This masculine world of bourgeois values and aesthetics, inhabited by Zibin, who, incidentally, suffers from a major writer's block, is challenged and revealed to be faulty by a revolutionary discourse, which is what informs Ruoquan. Meilin's experience of boredom and fulfillment, therefore, becomes interpretable largely in terms of her association with the two men in her life. She is, as Laura Mulvey would argue, the "bearer," "not maker, of meaning" in either of the symbolic orders defined by male fantasies and obsessions. She embodies and demonstrates a positive value, but she is never allowed to generate or determine it.[14]

By the end of the story, Meilin succeeds, with the guidance from Ruoquan, in achieving a sense of being socially useful. She does not yet show much understanding of the objective of her assignment, but she has sufficient reason to commit herself and follow instructions. By identifying with a political community, she now has a different relationship to the city from which, until recently, she felt distant, even excluded. We are not given a direct description of her new excitement and gratification in the city. Instead, we read, with her astonished husband, a note from Meilin. "Zibin, I simply can't hide the truth from you anymore. When you read this letter, I will probably already be on __ avenue, as assigned by the collective to carry out a __ movement" (238; 138). The political parade as a demonstration of solidarity gives Meilin access to public space and provides her with a new cognitive structure by means of which she is able to map, experience, and eventually narrate her surroundings. As a result, she speaks a new and more assertive language. In her note to Zibin, Meilin asks to have "a rational discussion" with her husband when she returns from the demonstration. "We should both criticize each other very sincerely and thoroughly. I have a lot of things to tell you, some about myself and some about you" (238; 138).

Shanghai, Spring 1930 (I) thus ends with a moment of impending confrontation, with Meilin marching down the street and Zibin heaving furious sighs at home. The political demonstration is not described, but the

---

13. Barlow, "Introduction" to *I Myself Am a Woman*, 30.
14. See Laura Mulvey, "Visual Pleasure and Narrative Cinema," in her *Visual and Other Pleasures* (Bloomington: Indiana University Press, 1989), 14–26.

private home is irrevocably reorganized. Resolved in this format, the conflict between "revolution and love" in much of the left-wing literature at the time reflected the competition between two ways of appropriating the city. Both terms of the antinomy—"revolution" as experience of collective power, and "love" as successful socialization through personal freedom—are central ideological constructs in the legitimizing discourse of modernity. More specifically, these are two symbiotic aspirations generated by the modern industrial-commercial metropolis, which, in its daily self-reproduction, necessarily relies on the large congregated population. The modern city, before its postindustrial suburbanization, is therefore a centripetal field of narrativity that germinates variations on the two prototypical plots: collective destiny and romantic encounters.

Apart from its universal features as a modern metropolis, Shanghai, the "crucible of modern China," was in the second half of the 1920s and early 1930s in a transitional stage, during which a growing proletariat rapidly developed a political consciousness and became mobilized. "It was during this era in Shanghai, amidst all the glamour and suffering, that Chinese nationalism and modernization took on a new meaning."[15] Nationalism, as the hegemonic unifying political discourse in post-May Fourth China, was evoked to mobilize students, factory workers, merchants, and ordinary city-dwellers in anti-imperialist demonstrations such as the May Thirtieth movement in 1925 and at subsequent annual rallies commemorating that historical event. At the same time, nationalist ideology fueled the drive to regiment and modernize the city. With the establishment of a Nationalist government in Nanjing in 1927, administering and policing Shanghai became part of the renewed effort to institute a new civic order and experiment with the nationalization project. "Much the same impulse to 'police' social behavior on the one hand, and to 'train' people's habits on the other," characterized both the mission of the Public Security Bureau (established on 22 July 1927) and the New Life Movement (launched in February 1934).[16]

15. Betty Peh-T'i Wei, *Shanghai: Crucible of Modern China* (Hong Kong: Oxford University Press, 1987), 206.

16. See Frederic Wakeman Jr., *Policing Shanghai, 1927–1937* (Berkeley: University of California Press, 1995), 232. The Public Security Bureau was established in Shanghai as a police force administered by the Special Municipal Government. "As a force representing the Chinese people and the new national government, it would also strive to recover long-lost sovereign rights by establishing the authority of the Chinese state

Yet the perilously discontinuous political landscape of Shanghai, reflected in its three different municipal jurisdictional bodies (the International Settlement, the French Concession, and the City Government of Greater Shanghai), continually derailed an urban everyday life that the new civic order intended to establish. Anti-imperialist nationalism, too, turned out to be a historical blind alley in the metropolis because a normalized urban life, in promoting and regulating consumer behavior, would spell a dead end to the insurgent nationalist movement. For nationalism to continue to be a viable political ideology, in other words, the modern city would have to be resisted as such, and everyday life would have to be nationalized and reclaimed by a national public and form. If the nationalist program of policing Shanghai was a doomed effort at creating an exemplary modern disciplinary society, with the New Life Movement as its most systematic ideological expression, then the revolutionary insurrection was no less a modernizing project whose ultimate task was to give order to the same postdynastic and urbanizing society. The choice of revolution over love, therefore, pointed to both a collective and a personal redemption. It suggested a deeply utopian vision of overcoming the experiential fragmentation fostered by the city on the one hand, and of participating in a national life and identity on the other. It also expressed a newly reinforced cultural anxiety to mobilize and keep tractable the human body that was now subjected to the monstrously disjunctive modern city. In short, commitment to revolution mandated a corporeal reorientation.

The Question of the Romantic Body

The force and anxiety of such a historically determined politics become much more evident in *Shanghai, Spring 1930* (II), where the tension between collective identity and individual freedom is no longer a simplified intellectual choice or discussion, as is faced by Meilin, but manifests itself more as a bodily adjustment. Although Meilin also has to undergo some training in order to better participate in the collective work, by the sec-

---

over those parts of the city it ruled. Its efforts to bring law and order to Republican Shanghai were thereby viewed as a crucial test of the overall effectiveness of the new régime" (14–15).

ond installment of the novella, the individuated human body becomes further problematized in the negotiation between love and revolution, and a new body has to be engendered for the individual to overcome the apparent impasse. Central to the new technology of the body is its disciplining, which the narrative represents without ambiguity as a masculine attribute and practice. The female body, by contrast, is now shown to be incapable of such retraining and becomes identifiable only through its association with sensuous details. An emerging political struggle over the body, paradoxically, is not able to articulate itself unless it subscribes to a hierarchical language and imagery of gender roles and divisions.

The story about Mary and Wangwei in *Shanghai, Spring 1930* (II), therefore, is both subtler and more complex than the first part of the novella. Instead of tantalizing the reader with a conceivable triangular affair, the narrative decidedly revolves around the life of two lovers and their eventual parting. Nor is there prolonged didactic commentary on the function of literature or the social responsibility of a writer. By closely narrating Mary's arrival in Shanghai to live with Wangwei, her growing frustration with a hardly attentive lover, his doomed efforts at molding her into a revolutionary companion, Mary's final decision to move out, and Wangwei's arrest during an anti-imperialist rally at the end, Ding Ling presents a much more nuanced psychological portrait of the young couple. In the process, the narrator follows Mary and Wangwei through a series of urban settings—streets, restaurants, theaters, makeshift offices, department stores—foregrounding the cityscape as a key participant in the story's unfolding. Just as the liberating city space has initially fostered their uninhibited love, so the same vast and multidimensional environment lends validity to their divergent senses of reality and relations to their own bodies. The body in the city becomes a major and concrete theme of the narrative.

It is tempting to try to gauge the degree to which the writing of the story was affected by the author's own situation at the time. For the greater part of 1930, Ding Ling was pregnant with serious health problems, whereas her husband, Hu Yepin, a young and enthusiastic poet and would-be Communist, was frenetically involved in a mass of politically subversive, hence dangerous, literary and extraliterary activities.[17] Just as

---

17. In Tsi-an Hsia's rather disapproving account, Hu Yepin, upon returning to Shanghai in the early summer of 1930, "plunged into his new life with zest and aban-

with Mary in the novella, Ding Ling during this period was largely kept out of her husband's exciting and secretive world. She also had her confusion and misgivings about a writer's total devotion to the public realm, and she managed not to join, as did Hu Yepin, the League of Left-wing Writers, a Communist organization promoting revolutionary literature and radical young writers, in May of the same year. As a result of her forced domestic confinement, historian Jonathan Spence suggests, Ding Ling was perforce to encounter two separate realities.[18] It was her experience as a woman, or more directly, the experience of her reproductive female body, that for a while remained undisciplinable and turned Ding Ling into a detached observer. Her pregnancy became a constant reminder of a reality in excess of political enthusiasm or sublimation.[19] Such corporeality apparently was too messy a matter for Hu Yepin, the young husband and expectant father. Shortly before he was executed, together with twenty-two others, by the Nationalist government police in February 1931, Hu Yepin finished a short story in which a young revolutionary recommended abortion as a necessary personal sacrifice so that a young couple could continue devoting their lives to the collective cause. The woman, in Hu Yepin's romantic imagination, is readily persuaded and ends up consoling her husband: "Once there is a baby, our work will be hindered. We cannot have the baby."[20]

In his meticulous study of this group of writers-cum-martyrs, Tsi-an Hsia concludes that Hu Yepin's high-flying absorption in political action stood in contrast to Ding Ling's momentary hesitation, which allowed her to "see at least the charms, problems, and meanings of a nonrevolutionary life."[21] This nonrevolutionary life to which Ding Ling was con-

---

don. . . . He taught at a summer school, presumably for workers, and was elected a member of the Executive Committee of the League [of Left-wing Writers], chairman of its Board of Correspondence with Workers, Peasants, and Soldiers, and a member of the delegation to the Soviet Congress to be convened in Kiangsi [Jiangxi]" (*The Gate of Darkness,* 177).

18. Jonathan D. Spence, *The Gate of Heavenly Peace: The Chinese and Their Revolution, 1895–1980* (New York: Penguin, 1981), 268.

19. For an interesting discussion of related issues, see Wolfgang Kubin, "The Staging of the Interior: Ding Ling's Short Story 'A Man and a Woman,'" in *Woman and Literature in China,* ed. Anna Gerstlacher et al. (Bochum: Brockmeyer, 1985), 275–91.

20. "Xisheng" (Sacrifice, 1930), quoted and translated in Hsia, *The Gate of Darkness,* 178.

21. Hsia, *The Gate of Darkness,* 182. Hsia continues, "The occasional psychological

fined is now represented in her narrative, not without its concrete pleasures, as the opposite of a socially meaningful life. It defines the life that Mary in *Shanghai, Spring 1930* (II) lives. It is a life that, instead of making the human body transcend its immediate surroundings, firmly consigns it as such to the urban spectacle. In short, it is an idle life, most susceptible to the consumerist exploitation of the body, a life that lacks grand spiritual sublimation. By ascribing this nonrevolutionary life to a female body, Ding Ling both acknowledged the corporeality of her own gender and, more importantly, created a trope through which to imagine and prescribe her self-transformation. For this reason, her portrayal of Mary in the story is wrought with ambiguity. The narrator is at once sympathetic and denunciatory, intimate and penetratingly critical.

At the same time, this nonrevolutionary life that seems to consume the female body brings up the question of the body and its incorporation into the revolutionary cause. Since a revolutionary life cannot be disembodied, what significance should be accorded to the revolutionary's body? Onto the figure of Wangwei, to which we now turn, Ding Ling would inscribe as an answer the political regimentation of a liberated body, a body that must first learn how to resist the seductive cityscape through self-discipline and ascetic practices.

It is therefore not surprising that the revolutionary romance should open with a description of the pleasurable physical sensation that Wangwei, "a likable, bronze-complexioned young man," dreamily experiences one early spring morning in Shanghai of 1930. We see the hero of the story, apparently exhausted from working late the night before, lie in bed and languidly fall asleep again. His apartment's interior is hardly noticeable, except as the extension of an embracing spring scenery. "At dawn on an early spring day, a moist breeze swept in softly through the broken window, brushed everything gently, and left quietly. The pale light of the sky reached into every corner and coated the room with a dreamy hue. The bustling noises of the city had not yet arisen. It was a good time for some peaceful sleep . . ." (240; 139).

This, then, is a moment *before* the noisy cycle of urban life, a fleeting

---

subtleties, the little tremors of a sensitive mind that enliven her writings are absent in his. His eagerness for revolution made it impossible for him to dwell on such trivialities or on anything or any person that was doomed to be swept away by the surging tides of history" (182–83).

but emphatic moment of nature's revival and harmony that precedes the symbolic space of the dynamic city. This is also a private moment *before* Wangwei assumes his political identity and activity. His contented body, obviously susceptible to pleasure, both affirms his sensitivity and serves as a metaphor for his self-consciousness. For he can allow himself this momentary aesthetic relaxation because he knows that he is all by himself, and that he does not yet have to reenter the city. A similar instance of positive pleasure occurs in the first part of the novella when Ruoquan, the mentor figure who guides Meilin into collective action, ventures to a public park on the outskirts of Shanghai to meet secretly with the apparently distraught woman. Once inside the park, the same spring breeze caresses Ruoquan with a tenderness completely absent in the swarming city. Attracted by the surrounding lush green, he "walked aimlessly across the undulating grass for quite a way, almost forgetting why he had come" (230; 134).[22] For both dedicated young men, however, such pleasurable indulgence of their bodies cannot be a purpose in itself. Leisure must function as a productive respite in that it better prepares them for their subsequent total devotion to work.

The initial intimate account of Wangwei's apartment and his relaxed body, while establishing as the central figure a romantic young man in the city, also forebodes the end to what Leo Ou-fan Lee has described as "a romantic decade," to which the image of a sensitized, libidinal body was central and during which "the vogue of self-exposé—laying bare the author's innermost secrets, emotional and sexual—all but carried the day."[23]

The romantic outburst of private emotions and desires in the turbu-

---

22. A more pointed description of Ruoquan in the park is worth quoting at length here: "Ruoquan stood up straight, unbuttoned his suit jacket, inhaled deeply, and felt refreshed right away. The tension and exhaustion he usually felt left him without a trace. Anyone arriving at this verdant carpet of grass, leaving behind the noise of the world, bathing in the spring breeze, embraced by the morning sun, would invariably relax, forget everything and unshoulder all cares. They would casually lay their bodies in nature, extend their limbs, and allow the serene environment to give them such pleasure until they could not remember who they were" (229; 134). In Ding Ling's 1929–30 novel *Wei Hu* (Wei Hu), description of physical pleasure constitutes a basic motif of romantic love. The heroine Lijia is mostly defined by her beauty and uninhibited sexuality.

23. Leo Ou-fan Lee, *The Romantic Generation of Modern Chinese Writers* (Cambridge, Mass.: Harvard University Press, 1973), 263.

lent 1920s was very much predicated on an intensified awareness of the individual body and its determined separation from society and society's ritualized practices. It was the cultural expression of the body in revolt against traditional discipline mechanisms. The newly ontologized body not only became a rich source for self-definition, but it also provided a personalized site for generating and manifesting political and national, even cosmic, significations. Yu Dafu's relentless allegorization of hypochondriac melancholy, for instance, highlighted the impossibility of an individual even beginning to relate his frustration, physical as well as psychic, in a shared language. Such was the fate of the series of young women that Ding Ling painted with great sympathy in her early fiction. A convalescent Miss Sophia's resolve to leave again and go "somewhere where no one knows me, where I can squander the remaining days of my life" amounts to a desperate protest against the displacement of a young generation (62).[24] As Mao Dun observed in 1933, Miss Sophia, at once an "emblem of the conflicting attitude toward sexual love experienced by young women emancipated since May Fourth," was also a deeply wounded lone rebel denouncing her own times.[25]

In many of the literary expressions from this romantic period, the liberated body, after a brief outburst of passion, would often grow into a focal symptom of a disarrayed society's failure to productively integrate its youth, together with youth's newly released energy and enthusiasm. The inescapable urban setting, where new practices of the self as a sign of being modern were experimented with and encouraged, offered a spatial parallel to the disjuncture that besieged the individual. Just as the city was positively modern only to the extent that it embodied a radical difference from the vast rural hinterland, so bold proclamations of the desiring subject often served to reveal its limitedness or even its irrelevance to society at large. Indeed, the romantic celebration of the self in the immediate post-May Fourth era, or what Yu Dafu lauded as "the discovery of individual personality,"[26] was largely an urban event, deriving much of

---

24. "Shafei nüshi de riji." See its English translation, "Miss Sophia's Diary," in *I Myself Am a Woman*, 81.

25. Mao Dun, "Nüzuojia Ding Ling" (Woman writer Ding Ling), *Wenyi yuebao* (Literature and arts monthly), no. 2 (15 July 1933); collected in *Research Materials on Ding Ling*, 253.

26. Quoted in Lee, *The Romantic Generation*, 262.

its modernity from an implicit valorization of the cosmopolitan city as a civilizational vanguard against the countryside as intransigent tradition. As a result, the romantic imagination was ultimately defined less by the possession of poetic inspiration or talent than by the frequent onslaught of a Weltschmerz that a sensitive soul and body suffered. From its very start, in other words, the romantic journey of sentiment was to seek an imaginary compensation for the individuated body that now became susceptible to defeat and despair. Even Guo Moruo, the most ebullient poet of May Fourth romanticism who would imagine himself to be a wild celestial hound and declare "I am I! My ego is about to burst," had to first endure a dark period in his life when the only solution to his existential crisis appeared to be death.[27]

By the time that Ding Ling began a story by describing the hero waking up in a Shanghai apartment in the spring of 1930, however, the tempest of the romantic age had been overtaken by a much more violent storm of political upheaval. The romanticized body had proved to be too fragile when faced with bloody revolutions and counterrevolutions. It had died a pathological death in Mao Dun's 1928 short story "Zisha" (Suicide), where a Miss Huan, pregnant from her brief but passionate love affair with a young revolutionary, decides to hang herself when she realizes that she is all alone and unable to cope with that grim reality. Tormented by anguish, she utters a bitter verdict on romantic rhetoric for having ill-prepared her for society. "Lies, lies—liberation, freedom, brightness—everything is a lie! . . . I shall announce to the world the crimes of those fraudulent ideas of liberation, freedom, and brightness. I shall announce it with my own death!"[28] She does die, but not without suggesting, at the last moment, that personal redemption may come from joining the "tide of history."

Indeed, the swirling tide of history had brought about revolution, its miserable failure notwithstanding, as an even grander, more global passion. To dialectically negate its romantic pathos and sentimentality, the

---

27. See David T. Roy, *Kuo Mo-jo: The Early Years* (Cambridge, Mass.: Harvard University Press, 1971), 87.

28. Mao Dun, "Suicide," in his *Yexiangwei* (The wild roses) (Shanghai: Dajiang shupu, 1929), 76–77. For a contextual reading of this story, see Yu-shih Chen, *Realism and Allegory in The Early Fiction of Mao Tun* (Bloomington: Indiana University Press, 1986), 144–49.

"literary revolution" of the early 1920s would necessarily transform itself into a "revolutionary literature."²⁹ Along with this much-trumpeted *Aufhebung* (a theoretical catchphrase at the time, with its Chinese transliteration) of literary practice, a Hegelian sublimation of details became an integral part of the new aesthetic of representing collective action.³⁰ The role and function of the writer had also undergone significant changes; the idea of an expressive, if also lonely, romantic poet was now replaced by that of a proud advocate of the recently discovered faith in the collective. The revolutionary mass as an emergent subject of history quickly supplied a cause for, and reignited the imagination of, young urban intellectuals who had witnessed their own impotence or superfluousness only too well in war-torn China. For this post-1911 Revolution generation of Chinese, the political enterprise of a proletariat-led national revolution offered direct social integration on the one hand, while it made available a powerfully explanatory language, because of its global implications, for their own anxiety and discontent on the other.

Against this background, Ding Ling's maturation into a revolutionary writer by 1930, as Meng Yue and Dai Jinhua pointedly comment, was almost a historical necessity. It answered her epistemological as well as existential need to release herself and her female characters from the dark vacuum left behind by a spate of bankrupt ideologies, not the least of them being romantic individualism.³¹ Trapped in this vacuum, early Ding Ling had had to turn inward and repeatedly explore, as Tani Barlow put it, the depths of the "generally 'dark' quality of female consciousness."³²

---

29. Cheng Fangwu, "Cong wenxue geming dao geming wenxue" (From a literary revolution to a revolutionary literature), dated 23 November 1927, collected in Zhang Ruoying, *Zhongguo xin wenxueshi ziliao* (Documents from the history of Chinese new literature) (Shanghai: Guangmin shuju, 1934), 380–87. For an English translation, see Kirk A. Denton, ed., *Modern Chinese Literary Thought: Writings on Literature, 1893–1945* (Stanford, Calif.: Stanford University Press, 1996), 269–75.

30. For a highly relevant discussion of the implication of the Hegelian philosophizing of the detail, see Naomi Schor, *Reading in Detail: Aesthetics and the Feminine* (New York: Methuen, 1987).

31. See Meng and Dai, *Emerging from History*, 126. For a contextual study of the discourse of individualism during the May Fourth period, see Lydia H. Liu, *Translingual Practice: Literature, National Culture, and Translated Modernity, China, 1900–1937* (Stanford, Calif.: Stanford University Press, 1995), 77–99.

32. Barlow, "Introduction" to *I Myself Am a Woman*, 25. Ding Ling's exploration

Thus, the potent symbolism of the title of her first collection published in 1928: *In Darkness*.

The Training of the Male Body

When Wangwei appears at the beginning of *Shanghai, Spring 1930* (II), he and his body have undergone a radicalization similar to what Ruoquan experienced in the first part. In Wangwei's words, he has consciously "plebeianized" (pingmin) himself (252; 144). Motivated by a "change in his outlook on life," he finds less and less time to worry about his clothing or physical appearance. To him, plebeianization means frequenting dingy and unsanitary restaurants of the working class, exhausting himself in working for an underground society that promotes proletarian literature, and diligently studying the newspapers "in order to sort through the information on world economy, to seek reports on the development of revolution in China and collect evidence of the daily weakening of the ruling class" (267; 151). Sometimes he gets a headache from having to compose work reports or outlines of a plan, for "only three months before he had still been a student prone to melancholy, who could easily and very quickly produce moving, clever, and sentimental lines in a poem of equal length" (268; 152). His extensive involvement in "practical struggles," incidentally, also enables him to better deal with a private frustration caused by his lover Mary's absence. No longer an artistic young man, Wangwei is now a dedicated intellectual.[33]

---

of "female subjectivity," according to Barlow, led her to the "extraordinarily sensitive issues of sexual repression and expression, homoeroticism, female Don Juanism, sexual politics, and the generally 'dark' quality of female consciousness."

33. In his 1908 essay on "'Civilized' Sexual Morality and Modern Nervousness" (*Sexuality and the Psychology of Love* [New York: Collier Books, 1963]), Freud makes the following observations: "An abstinent artist is scarcely conceivable; an abstinent young intellectual is by no means a rarity. The young intellectual can by abstinence enhance his powers of concentration, whereas the production of the artist is probably powerfully stimulated by his sexual experience. On the whole I have not gained the impression that sexual abstinence helps to shape energetic, self-reliant men of action, nor original thinkers, bold pioneers and reformers; for more often it produces 'good' weaklings who later become lost in the crowd that tends to follow painfully the initiative of strong characters" (24). What happens to Wangwei at the end of his story seems to make this paragraph even more relevant.

The love story between Wangwei and Mary, now briefly narrated as prehistory from his perspective, is a typical episode from the bygone romantic age.[34] It was unconstrained modern love between a young boy in his aimless *Wanderjahre* and a capricious young girl equally unclear about what she was looking for in life. After an initial encounter, the exchange of a few letters was sufficient to arouse a "much stronger desire" in him, which expressed itself as an unbearable "physical pain" and drove him from Shanghai to Beijing.[35] There, following the example of many contemporary young men and women boldly tasting personal freedom in the city, they swiftly moved in together and consummated their passionate, if doomed, romance. Shortly after, Mary went home to visit her parents and never came back, and Wangwei, duly panicked, turned to a "new hope" that much excited him. Gradually, he would even forget her, for now he had no time to be idle or fantasize. The libidinal drive that had once overpowered him was now both regulated and transferred onto other, more global pursuits. If the romantic years allowed much *aestheticization* of his body, the new political age demanded its *asceticization* for it to be productive and accessible to a public life.

At this juncture, Mary announces her return to Wangwei's life through a peremptory telegraphed message, which instantly "revived many hopes and dreams in him and brought back memories of the sweet past" (243; 140). Upon her return, Wangwei is compelled to confront his largely repressed romantic past, his sexuality, and his new self-image. Much of the rest of the narrative, therefore, depicts the gradual process in which Wangwei and Mary realize that they are no longer compatible and are in fact miserable together. Mary, as much as Wangwei, sees no remedy to their strained relationship unless she takes the pains to "deny herself

34. In his case study of the "romantic generation," Leo Ou-fan Lee concludes, "the literature of the 1920s was filled with stories of how an independent Nora met and flirted with a pale and pensive young man at a cafe or how a group of nature-loving girl students bumped into a handsome art student doing a landscape painting at the West Lake near Hangchow" (34). This basic plot of "the freedom to love" appears in all of Ding Ling's three "revolution and love" stories: *Wei Hu* and *Shanghai, Spring 1930* (I and II).

35. *Collected Works of Ding Ling*, 242. The English translation collected in *I Myself Am a Woman* has some curious omissions. Missing is the telling phrase "physical pain" (shenti shang de tongku), which, incidentally, is also truncated in a mainland edition of *Ding Ling daibiaozuo* (Representative works by Ding Ling), ed. Jiao Shangzhi and Liu Chunsheng (Zhengzhou: Henan renmin, 1988), 83.

and become a person with a mind like his" (298; 166). Although the central consciousness of the narrative is Wangwei's, much sympathetic room is given to explaining Mary's frustration and her reasoning. A constant criss-crossing and clashing of two perspectives, as Meng Yue and Dai Jinhua suggest,[36] engender the dynamics of the narrative and bring into relief a wide range of hierarchical values embodied by Wangwei and Mary: reason/emotion, work/pleasure, public/private, political/personal, collective/individual, mind/body, heroism/hedonism, masculine/feminine. What the narrative tension reveals, perhaps against Ding Ling's authorial intention, is an understanding that revolutionary movement, just like modern industry or routinized office work, first has to develop a work ethic reinforced by a mode of regimenting the sexualized human body. It has to invent its own version of what Freud calls "the economics of the libido" so as to maximize the productivity of the body.[37]

This ideologically justified need to control the body becomes more pronounced soon after Mary's arrival. On the same evening, as they enjoy a leisurely dinner in a Cantonese restaurant and confess how much they missed each other, Wangwei cannot help but appreciate the physical attributes of the sensuous woman with him. His probing gaze over her body is enough to arouse his erotic imagination. "She had taken off the hundred-and-twenty-yuan coat and was wearing only a thin, light green, tight-fitting, soft silk *qipao* that delicately revealed the intriguing parts of her body" (figure 2). As Mary continues her small talk, Wangwei finds himself distracted by a growing "discomfort." "A bodily instinct pressed upon him, making him wish that at this very moment he could jump upon her, press her down, and enjoy once again the ecstatic intoxication on her beautiful flesh. For he did not have the need to express his love in words. Several times he said, 'Let's eat up quickly!'" Yet Mary, elegantly sipping wine and tea, is enjoying the pleasant intimacy of the restaurant with her lover too much to notice Wangwei's turgid impatience. "Wangwei, on the other hand, gradually fell silent. He was suffering from a desire that, aroused by love, could not yet be fulfilled. He tried to hold himself together, he felt his entire body burning hot, and red capillaries filled up his eyes that seemed ready to burst in flames. He remained quiet,

---

36. Meng and Dai, *Emerging from History*, 128–31.
37. See Sigmund Freud, *Civilization and Its Discontents*, trans. James Strachey (New York: Norton, 1961), 28–29.

2. Commercial advertisement, "International Dispensary Co. Ltd." (ca. 1930). From *Lao yuefenpai guanggaohua* (Advertising images in old calendars), special issue of *Hansheng* (Echo magazine), no. 63 (Taipei: Hansheng, 1994).

trying not to listen to her, to be vulnerable to her seduction, because he was really feeling more pain than pleasure" (253; 144).

The self-control that Wangwei exercises here, however, is not nearly as momentous as what he is about to achieve. If at this moment he manages to contain his reactivated sexuality by diverting his thoughts to other irrelevant and trivial things, when he suddenly remembers that he has an important meeting to chair later that evening, his decision to leave behind an amorous Mary in his bare apartment comes as a remarkable triumph. It is a triumph of his will over his body; it marks the priority now given to a new source of excitement, the achievement of which consists in postponing, and ultimately sublimating, the immediate gratification for which his body yearns. The meeting that he hurries to attend, of which there will be a series of timely repeats in the story, functions as a ritual, as an act of good faith that convinces Wangwei of his own ability to displace the libido and to productively devote his body to a greater cause. The meeting is also a form of public life, to which Wangwei now entirely submits himself. The fact that Wangwei is constantly exhausted and unavailable, emotionally as well as physically, to a desiring Mary becomes one effective way for him to safeguard his commitment through disciplining his body.[38]

It would be a fallacy, as Michel Foucault reminds us, to think of the revolutionary commitment that absorbs Wangwei as merely repressive.[39] To the contrary, it is a discourse of sublimation that legitimizes a new technology of the body and delegates to it new functions as well as symbolic contents. The evocation of political identity is an ingenious part of what Foucault describes as the "subtle, calculated technology of subjection (*assujetissement*)" that answered the urgent need for controlling "multiplicity" in the modern liberal state. It is a technology that provided a "guarantee of the submission of forces and bodies" that became a sociological reality with the demise of the sovereign body of the king.[40] The same time that an individuated and juridical subject was called forth as such, it also was subjected to a disciplinary power in the form of systematic classification, normalization, and externalization. For "the real, corporal disciplines constituted the foundation of the formal, juridical liberties." Discipline as a new modality of power, with its "set of physico-

---

38. "It was never enough for Mary, but when she saw that Wangwei was exhausted, she would curtail her excitement. Wangwei would be so tired that his eyes would be red, his head pounding, his joints stiff. Once home he would always fall asleep as soon as he reached the bed, which was something that Mary also felt sorry about" (275; 155).

39. See Michel Foucault, "Part Two, The Repressive Hypothesis," in his *History of Sexuality, Vol. I: An Introduction* (New York: Vintage, 1980), 15–49.

40. Michel Foucault, *Discipline and Punish: The Birth of the Prison,* trans. Alan Sheridan (New York: Vintage, 1979), 221–22.

political techniques," mobilizes the body so as to regulate it, inscribes on it political signification so as to restrict it. The asceticism practiced by Wangwei, therefore, helps to incorporate the body into the political, and the private into the public. As the narrative continues and the rift between the two lovers widens, Wangwei's body is represented as more and more immune to the instinctual force that inflicted intense "physical pain" at the beginning. The pleasure he now enjoys is more of an intellectual nature, partly derived from a conscious resistance against immediate bodily gratification. The same intellectualized pleasure enables him to invest his body with global significance and eventually to mobilize it as a political statement in a street demonstration. When confounded by the possibility that Mary may leave him someday, Wangwei decides that he should overcome the loss by making himself even busier. His faith now unassailable, he refuses "to change his thinking due to the coming and going of a woman in his life" (290; 163).

While Wangwei's body undergoes conscientious training, Mary throughout the story remains the same sensuous woman and is always portrayed in the deliberate and decorative detail of the private sphere.[41] Her "dignified and exciting" body, which she narcissistically appreciates in a mirror, is her self-consciousness and individuality (figure 3). Her decision to leave Wangwei amounts to a refusal, by a city woman in the post-May Fourth era, to relinquish what the romantic age has made available to her. The two reasons she gives for her departure in her farewell note (his unfaithfulness to love and his obsession with work) point to the centrality of romantic love in her existence (302; 167). By allowing Mary a last chance to voice her anguish and, more significantly, by introducing the reader into her private world of feminine pleasure and sensuousness, the narrator explores, rather than dismisses, the young woman's sensibility and dilemma. In doing so, Ding Ling's narrative presents more than an ideological difference between Mary and Wangwei. A sociology-based reading of both parts of Ding Ling's novella may lead to the conclusion that the growing number of educated women, such as Mary and Meilin, in the 1930s still had little access to the workplace and were forced to con-

---

41. For a relevant discussion of the suppression of the detail as femininity in Chinese political modernity, see Rey Chow, "Modernity and Narration—In Feminine Detail," *Woman and Chinese Modernity: The Politics of Reading Between West and East* (Minneapolis: University of Minnesota Press, 1991), 86–120.

3. Commercial advertisement, "The Central Agency, Ltd." (ca. 1930). From *Lao yuefenpai guanggaohua* (Advertising images in old calendars), special issue of *Hansheng* (Echo magazine), no. 63 (Taipei: Hansheng, 1994).

front, primarily as consumers, the new commodity of leisure in metropolitan Shanghai.[42] Their bodies, in other words, may not have been subjected to the same degree of corporal retraining first undertaken by the male population in an emerging disciplinary society. As a result, the Chinese Noras that Lu Xun described in 1923 were still besieged by boredom and a lack of socialization.[43]

If the irreducibility of Mary's sentient body indicates both an interiority not yet externalized and engenders a desire to fulfill herself in romantic love, an aesthetics of details centered on the body is corroborated by much of what the metropolis has to offer. During the same time that Wangwei grows resistant to the lure of the city through his intellectual belief, Mary is continually enlivened by the urban spectacle. For her, the city cannot be abstracted into a metaphysical structure or concept; rather, it embodies a way of life that sustains itself on concrete details, designs, and objects. Her relation to the city therefore lies not in distancing herself, but in intimate immersion. "In the enjoyment of love, Mary was forever insatiable. She'd drag him out onto the street to look for little restaurants that they had never been to before, or sometimes they would go to larger ones. After dinner they would take a leisurely walk along the brilliantly illuminated, bustling streets because it was still too early for the late movie" (272; 154).

When finally seated in a deluxe movie theater, Mary would sooner enjoy and fantasize about its interior decorations than follow the story unfolding on the screen. "Of the one yuan she spent to attend the movie, eighty cents was for the soft, cushioned chair, the shiny brass banisters, the velvet curtains, and the pleasing music. Only a country bumpkin

42. In the text, we find a description of how Mary spent her day consuming popular culture while Wangwei went to his "work." "Her interest focused entirely on herself. She would read tabloid papers, read about girl students or campus queens, sports celebrities, movie stars, and pimps and prostitutes. Wangwei disapproved and sometimes, unable to put up with it, would say to her, 'Mary! I don't think this is good entertainment . . . ?'" (277–78; 156).

43. For a discussion of the May Fourth understanding of Nora from Ibsen's *A Doll's House,* see Elizabeth Eide, "Ibsen's Nora and Chinese Interpretations of Female Emancipation," in *Modern Chinese Literature and Its Social Context,* Nobel Symposium (32), ed. Goran Malmqvist (Stockholm, 1977), 140–51. Also see Eide's 1985 essay "Optimistic and Disillusioned Noras in the Chinese Literary Scene, 1919–1940," in *Woman and Literature in China,* 193–222.

would come solely for the movie." To Wangwei, however, cinema as a bourgeois entertainment was condemnable because it "so easily numbed people's minds and influenced society for the worse." He put up with such senseless diversion only because he loved Mary and wished to compensate for his absence during the day (274–75; 155).

In tracing the historical metamorphosis of the privileged artist-flâneur into a department store-bound flâneuse in nineteenth-century Paris, Priscilla Ferguson comments that the emergence of commercial arcades fatefully transformed the practices of the city street. "No woman can disconnect herself from the city and its seductive spectacle. For she must either desire the objects spread before her or herself be the object of desire, associated with and agent of the infinite seductive capacity of the city."[44] The infinite seductive capacity of the city that now fascinates Mary the flâneuse in Shanghai of the 1930s (across its sizable French Concession?) also originates in the presence of other people, to whom she in turn constitutes an intriguing and performative other. For Wangwei, however, in order to successfully resist the seductive city, he cannot acknowledge an onlooking or indifferent crowd. He has to construct a collective *us* versus a reactionary *them*. The urban spectacle becomes a conspiratorial illusion because it depends on a constant and manipulative proliferation of empty forms to conceal an impoverished content. The trivial and sensuous objects that define an aesthetic experience for Mary, furthermore, are but an exploitation of the body as sensory fragments on which the modern city flourishes. Wangwei's critique of the city, in agreement with modern political radicalism, has to begin with a rhetoric of collective identity and destiny. His poetic vision of its transformation, too, calls upon a climactic "surge of roaring waves" or an "erupting volcano" that would destroy the phantasmagoric city in raging flames.[45]

Such an apocalyptic vision, composed of vivid images of natural forces,

---

44. Priscilla Parkhurst Ferguson, *Paris as Revolution: Writing the Nineteenth-Century City* (Berkeley: University of California Press, 1994), 84. See also 112–13.

45. Toward the end of the narrative, Wangwei was assigned to give a public speech downtown. Before the secretly planned demonstration, he paced up and down the street to examine the situation. "He felt an excitement that he couldn't suppress, as if he were seeing a surge of roaring waves toppling the mountains and churning up the seas. He also imagined an erupting volcano engulfing the city in its raging flames. It was possible that this might happen immediately, since so many people were ready for it! And he, he would accelerate the great storm and ignite the flame!" (305–06; 169).

often underlies a revolutionary psychology and seems to articulate a prevalent frustration with another aspect of the urban experience: the routinization of daily life. As much a spirited consumer in the city as she can be, Mary in the story is also a modern housewife in training.[46] Through this domestic domain, or rather in Wangwei's fierce resistance against it, we see a patriarchal gender division being endorsed, as if in an absentminded oversight, by the politicized public life that elates Wangwei. His impatience with everyday life and refusal of leisure, however, are symptomatic more of a fear than a self-confident rejection. They betray a fear of what is not yet part of the socially and semiotically regulated public space. The private home, as much as the seductive city spectacle, is threatening because it stands for what has not been fully infiltrated by the new discipline mechanism. In the narrative structure of *Shanghai, Spring 1930* (I and II), banal everyday life and its attendant domesticity are readily represented as effeminate and accessory. Mary's lack of a political consciousness, as in the case of the besieged writer Zibin, is illustrated by her sole wish to build a happy home. As a result, Wangwei has to reinforce his efforts at self-discipline by removing himself from his apartment, by being constantly *absent* from the scene. The spectacular explosion that he envisions consequently indicates, rather than vengeance, a desire to force open and share the private and intimate spheres of life. Only a unitary application of the body would give coherence to everyday life and, at the same time, prevent the body itself from receding from public life. The causal relation between a "masculinization of the body politic" and a male domination of the public space and discourse, which Gillian Rose retraces in her study of women in everyday spaces,[47] once again proves to be an instrumental component of the modern experience, even when the body is now devoted to a revolutionary cause (figure 4). In fact, from its very birth during the great French Revolution, the modern revolutionary body has been dominantly represented as male, public, and in continuous need of

46. "Mary did not go out and run around anymore. She waited for Wangwei, and while he was out even cleaned the room for him. She wanted to move to a better place and see about getting one or two pieces of finer furniture" (296; 164).

47. See Gillian Rose, "Women and Everyday Spaces," in her *Feminism and Geography: The Limits of Geographical Knowledge* (Minneapolis: University of Minnesota Press, 1993), 17–40. Rose also observes that "a history of the white masculine heterosexual bourgeois body in Euro-America can therefore be told in terms of a series of denials of corporeality" (32).

124 *Chinese Modern*

4. Woodcut, *Bodou* (Confrontation), by Yefu (1933). From *Zhongguo xinxing banhua wushi nian xuanji* (Anthology of new Chinese woodcuts in the past fifty years) (Shanghai: Renmin meishu, 1981).

disciplining.[48] The historical specificity of Wangwei's body, in the final analysis, derives not so much from its embeddedness in Chinese cultural tradition, as from its eager acceptance of a modern universalism that rests, as I suggest elsewhere, on a global imaginary of identity.[49]

    48. See Dorinda Outram, *The Body and the French Revolution: Sex, Class and Political Culture* (New Haven, Conn.: Yale University Press, 1989), esp. 164.
    49. See my discussion of Chinese nationalism and its necessary subscription to a global imaginary of identity in *Global Space and the Nationalist Discourse of Modernity:*

To better illustrate the unitary application of the body that revolutionary discourse allows, Ding Ling inserts another romantic couple into her narrative as a contrast to the failure of Mary and Wangwei. This second pair strikes a happy union between a plebeianized intellectual and an "unaffected, healthy" tram conductress who possesses a "simple, correct understanding of politics" (246; 142). Peripheral though they are in the story, their successful romance nonetheless signifies the central ideal of a political and disciplined existence, which also justifies Wangwei's analysis of his difference from Mary in terms of social class and history. Between Mary's sensuous and, as is indicated by her exotic name, Westernized body and the naturally healthy and native body of the working-class woman, a social physiology is constructed that interprets the human body as a direct demonstration of historical and social forces. Fundamental to it is the contrast between a liberal, pleasure-oriented body and a disciplined, socially productive body.

> If Mary were a peasant girl, a factory worker, or a high school student, then they would get along very well because there would be only one idea, one outlook on life. He could lead her and she would follow. Yet Mary was from a relatively well-to-do family and had never experienced hardship. Her intelligence made her all the prouder and her education confirmed her attitude toward life, which was a hedonist pursuit for pleasure. She believed in herself and would yield to no one. (276; 156)

A deep ambiguity, however, surfaces when such a comprehensive and historicizing analysis still cannot explain away Wangwei's longing for Mary's "flawless beauty." It is his body, for all the disciplining it receives, that refuses to deny the reality of what Mary has come to embody. After she leaves him, Wangwei tries to keep himself occupied, "but as soon as he lay down on his bed alone, he could not help but miss her sorely" (305; 168–69).

The Body as Enunciation

In the end, the question of the body dramatically reasserts itself in the closing scene when, in the commotion of a quickly dispersed political

---

The Historical Thinking of Liang Qichao (Stanford, Calif.: Stanford University Press, 1996).

rally, Wangwei is arrested, hurled into a police patrol wagon, and finds himself landing on top of other demonstrators who have met the same fate. "As he looked out through the wired mesh, he spotted an elegant lady by the entrance to a big department store. Ah, it was Mary!" Indeed, Mary, "gorgeous and graceful as ever," had apparently just finished shopping in the company of a handsome young man. Through such extraordinary coincidence, her primary function in the narrative is both disambiguated, so to speak, and ideologically condemned as embodying no more than the bourgeois idea of a conspicuous consumer. At this sight, a stunned Wangwei for some curious reason feels relieved and bids a mental farewell: "Good, she is happy again. After all, she is that kind of person, and I don't have to worry about her anymore. So long, Mary" (309; 170–71).

With this final moment of recognition, the narrative reexamines Wangwei's revolutionary body with a turn of irony. Two dramatized forms of body experience are brought together. Side by side with Wangwei's heroic body, dragged through the street and forcibly thrown onto a political collective, is Mary's carefully protected and consumerist body, evidently insulated against the disturbance nearby. Each directly participates in a signifying spectacle in a public space and dramatizes one potential use of the human body. Yet both bodies are objectified—one through political insurgence, the other by the cityscape and, more specifically, by the male gaze. The politicized body is now explicitly male, whereas the female body remains resolutely indifferent. At this point, we see an almost complete inversion of the gender distribution in the first part of the novella, where it is Meilin who actively seeks a political life, much to the chagrin of her self-obsessed husband, although her new social identity, as we have seen, relies much on the strong presence of her mentor Ruoquan.

The deep irony of this final scene of aborted action, therefore, lies in the close juxtaposition of two now disparate bodies, which until recently were intimately connected; they problematize as much as rely on each other for their own signification, and yet there is an unequal exchange. Mary never looks back, and we see Wangwei, from behind the barred window, look at and recognize Mary. The male political hero, obviously, is privileged with a subject position from which he can observe and make a judgment, but such a vantage point quickly collapses when his body is subjected to brutalization on the one hand and disallowed differentiation on the other. Collective action and political violence combine to moralize his body and prevent it from activating its own memory or acquiring its own private history. It is abstracted into disembodied conceptuality. As soon as he feels relieved, therefore, Wangwei is also compelled to denounce his former lover as despicable and of a different social class. The female body, given no chance to return the male gaze, is apparently condemned to a morally indifferent corporeality. At the same time, however, it projects a concrete image of personal happiness and freedom. Wangwei's last glimpse of Mary, "like a queen from a distant land," captures what he has consciously denied himself, and it epiphanically illuminates, before he joins in a collective chanting of "Down with . . . ," what his body was once capable of and perhaps what it still desires, independently of his will and passion. The handsome young man by her side now is indeed his alter ego. Thus, the irony of recognition. At the last moment, Mary unexpectedly emerges as the narrative's central character because she becomes at once the object of a judgmental gaze and the object of desire. Wangwei's pursuit of a political life fulfills itself at the moment when his body is used in a public performance, whereas Mary's individual negotiation with various demands on her sensuous body still firmly anchors her in the narrativity of the city space. His is a story that closes with a certainty he always strives for, but her story remains open-ended, if only because it is nothing out of the ordinary and resides in the private sphere.

The eventual merging of Wangwei's disciplined young body into the political collective as itself a body of symbolic plenitude concludes the narrative of *Shanghai, Spring 1930* and comes as the culmination of his conscious self-transformation. His individual and indulgent body that we initially observe in a private apartment eventually succeeds in acquiring as well as enacting social meaning in a public space. As a metaphor, Wangwei's changed relation to his body illustrates the invention of a "politicized body" in revolutionary China, which was to provide a material semiotic component for ordering everyday reality and signifying the power of the body politic for years to come.[50] A politicized body is the body as public enunciation, as the unmediated site for the exercise and demonstration of power. Upon this semiotically charged body, many a spectacle will have to be staged so that it extends and eventually be-

50. See Ann Anagnost, "The Politicized Body," in *Body, Subject and Power in China*, ed. Angela Zito and Tani E. Barlow (Chicago: University of Chicago Press, 1994), 131–56, esp. 150.

comes identical with the public realm. Constant mobilization, through corporal semiotics and physico-political techniques, becomes a necessary means to keep such a body from imploding or succumbing to inertia.[51]

The turn to such an empowering externalization marks a new stage in Ding Ling's career as a writer, which in many ways parallels, if also magnifies, the course of the Left literary movement as a radical outgrowth of the liberal-humanist May Fourth tradition. For Ding Ling, writing in the early 1930s, the nodal point of literary practice was how to reclaim the romanticized body from an earlier discourse of interiority and eventually to dissolve in public life the same body, now retrained to be purposeful rather than idly imaginative, productive rather than acutely sensitive. More specifically, the newly plebeianized intellectual, inspired by an ideologized collective, should not only be able to resist sensuous details and libidinal urges, which we see in Wangwei's coping with Mary and his own "physical pain," but also to cultivate a different sensory appreciation of disagreeable poverty as an authenticating social reality, as is the realization of another Wangwei-type young man during an oddly agitating day of his life.[52] What the romanticized body needed to overcome, in other words, is an aesthetic that centers on the individuated body and a sensibility that valorizes inner depth and self-exploration. In the given historical context, this body was readily identified as Western, urban, and bourgeois, the opposite of a nationalist and proletarian evocation of a collective subject of history, in which belongs the adequately disciplined working-class woman sketched in *Shanghai, Spring 1930* (II), who also happens to be nameless.

The ideological campaign of the Left in the early 1930s to proletarian-

---

51. Jeffrey N. Wasserstrom offers an interesting discussion of the theatrical aspect of the student protest "repertoire" developed in Shanghai in the decades after the May Fourth movement in his *Student Protests in Twentieth-Century China: The View from Shanghai* (Stanford, Calif.: Stanford University Press, 1991). For a concise version, see his "The Evolution of the Shanghai Student Protest Repertoire; Or, Where Do Correct Tactics Come From?" collected in *Shanghai Sojourners,* ed. Frederic Wakeman Jr. and Wen-hsin Yeh (Berkeley: Institute of East Asian Studies, University of California, 1992), 108–44.

52. In the short story, "Yitian" ([One day], 1931, in *Collected Works of Ding Ling,* 673–88), Ding Ling tells of how a young writer Lu Xiang tries to overcome his distance from political reality by constantly examining and negating his immediate responses to the dismal condition, spiritual as well as physical, of the working class. For a close analysis of the story, see Yi-tsi Mei Feuerwerker, *Ding Ling's Fiction,* 81–88.

ize the writer and make literature accessible to the working masses drew heavily on a poetics of spectacular collective action mandated by an optimistic historical vision. It also projected a new public life that would appropriate urban modernity through a disciplining of the individual body. The desire to endow literary practice with political significance entailed a deeply utopian project, which was profoundly contradictory and as liberating as it was limiting.[53] In the summer of 1931, Ding Ling once again showed herself to be in the vanguard of the Left literary movement by finishing the novella *Shui* (Flood) to offer a commanding view of a hungry crowd of peasants, "roaring with a passion for life" and rising against social injustice compounded by natural disaster.[54] The most significant achievement of the new novella, according to an approving critic at the time, was its prompt attention to "major contemporary events," which would demand any writer to look beyond "the trivialities of daily life." For this reason, *Flood* was hailed as indicating the birth of a new type of fiction as well as a new type of writer.[55]

53. In her study of the long but also loose relationship between the radical tradition in the United States and Tillie Olsen, Deborah Rosenfelt focuses on three contradictions of the literary policies of the Old Left. See Rosenfelt, "From the Thirties: Tillie Olsen and the Radical Tradition," 216–48. Her summary of the heritage of the Old Left is worth quoting in full here: "First, the left required great commitments of time and energy for political work, on the whole valuing action over thought, deed over word; yet it also validated the study and production of literature and art, providing a first exposure to literature for many working-class people, fostering an appreciation of a wide range of socially conscious literature, and offering important outlets for publication and literary exchange. Second, although much left-wing criticism, especially by Communist Party writers, was narrowly prescriptive about the kind of literature contemporary writers should be producing, it also inspired—along with the times themselves—a social consciousness in writers that deepened their art. Third, for a woman in the 1930s, the left was a profoundly masculinist world in many of its human relationships, in the orientation of its literature, and even in the language used to articulate its cultural criticism; simultaneously, the left gave serious attention to women's issues, valued women's contributions to public as well as to private life, and generated an important body of theory on the woman question" (224–25).

54. *Shui* (Flood), *Collected Works of Ding Ling*, 395.

55. He Danren, "Guanyu xinde xiaoshuo de dansheng: ping Ding Ling de *Shui*" (On the birth of a new fiction: review of Ding Ling's *Flood*"), *Beidou* (The Big Dipper) 1:2 (January 1932), reprinted in *Research Materials on Ding Ling*, 246–51. Here is how He Danren defines a new writer: "At the present, a new writer is one who understands class struggle correctly, identifies with the interests of the mass of workers and peasants, and, equipped with dialectical materialism, clearly sees the force and future

This proved to be a powerful prophecy. With her new interest in depicting revolutionary peasant life, Ding Ling's literary journey, and soon the tortuous journey of her life, ventured beyond the imaginational geography of Shanghai and began an earnest search for a redemptive political modernity.⁵⁶ Yet Shanghai, "city of amazing paradoxes and fantastic contrasts," would continue to exist and offer the same phantasmagoric spectacle, to be either celebrated by the New Sensationists of the 1930s or narrated with nostalgia by modern romance writers such as Zhang Ailing of the 1940s. When the great city of urban modernity did reappear, ever so fleetingly, in Ding Ling's fateful story "In the Hospital" (1941), Shanghai was a faint memory, a remote past that hardly bore any relationship, much less resemblance, to the heroine's new communal life in the Communist border region. There the aspiring young nurse, professionally trained in Shanghai, found herself hospitalized and would have to survive on humiliation and self-disciplining. Her body, too, still had to learn how to be useful and adapt to a new normativity.⁵⁷

---

of the working mass: only the fiction written by such a writer can be deemed as new fiction" (247).

56. It is by no accident that Ding Ling's life should provide a central organizing element for Spence's historical narrative *The Gate of Heavenly Peace*. One critic has called Ding Ling a paradigmatic searcher for "complete emancipation" (the emancipation of the self and the collective) in modern Chinese literature. See Chen Huifen, "Chedi jiefang de zhuiqiu zhe he tansuo zhe" (A searcher for and explorer of complete emancipation), *Wenxue pinglun congkang* (Journal of literary criticism), no. 29 (1987): 87–127.

57. Ding Ling, "Zai yiyuan zhong," *Representative Works by Ding Ling*, 214–34. Translated by Gary Bjorge as "In the Hospital," in *Modern Chinese Stories and Novellas, 1919–1949*, ed. Joseph S. M. Lau, C. T. Hsia, and Leo Ou-fan Lee (New York: Columbia University Press, 1981), 279–91.

4

The Last Tubercular in Modern Chinese Literature: On Ba Jin's *Cold Nights*

Secretly I don't believe this illness to be tuberculosis, at least not primarily tuberculosis, but rather a sign of my general bankruptcy.
—Franz Kafka to Felice Bauer, 1917

The opening paragraph of Ba Jin's (1904–) last novel *Hanye* (Cold nights, 1947) presents a starkly modern spatiotemporal regime and its problematic relationship to an individual subject. It describes a momentary suspension of reality during an air raid, from which the murky landscape, gradually coming into focus, appears to be nothing but imminently catastrophic. By instilling a sense of routinized emergency, however, the urgent siren that had sounded and trailed off, *before the beginning,* also suggests a paradoxical situation of permanent contingency. Against such an inimical background, the protagonist of the novel finds himself unable to concentrate, paralyzed by some internal agony.

The historical time was the winter of 1944–45, the darkest hour of World War II when Japanese airplanes were systematically bombing Chongqing, wartime capital of the Nationalist Republic of China. The constant threat of air raids over the city effectively wiped out, in addition to a civilian sense of time and space, all credibility of any uplifting rhetoric or hope for a final victory. By then, the war had apparently instituted disarray as itself a kind of order in the hinterland city, and crisis exigencies had turned into routine exercises of repetition. Resistance and national salvation over the years had ossified into an abstract cause and as such seemed increasingly vacuous and incapable of mobilizing or even unifying the nation. This moment of pervasive despair and vulnerability, which Ba Jin as a war refugee lived through in Chongqing, prompted the veteran novelist to ponder the fate of individuals violently dislodged by the war. Increasingly, Ba Jin, writing in the mid-1940s, turned his attention to a realm of unheroic reality that seemed to remain beneath, or unsublimated by, various overlapping constructs of subjectivity, such as discourses of enlightenment, nationalist mobilization, and the sovereignty of the modern nation-state. A more mundane, bitter, and somatic reality surfaced to highlight the bankruptcy, or at least irrelevance, of all overarching systems of symbolic meaning.

The first paragraph of *Cold Nights* thus firmly sets up the narrative mode of the novel and introduces the reader to an instance where the embattled subject is no longer meaningfully attached to the environment as its responsive agent. On the contrary, he is apparently a withdrawn and pensive subject.

> The emergency air raid siren had sounded nearly half an hour ago; the faint drone of airplanes could be heard in the sky; the streets were quiet without a trace of light. Rising from the stone steps in front of a bank's iron gate, he walked down to the sidewalk and raised his head to look at the sky. It was ashen, like a piece of faded black cloth. Save the dark shadows of some imposingly tall buildings across from him, he could not see a thing. Woodenly he kept his head raised for quite a while, not really trying to hear anything or see anything, but only, as it were, to pass some time. Yet time seemed to be bent on thwarting him by passing very slowly—so slowly that he felt as though it had stopped moving altogether. The chilly night air, gradually penetrating his thinly-lined gown, suddenly made his body shiver in spite of himself. Only at this did he lower his head and heave a painful sigh. He said to himself in a low voice: "I cannot go on doing this anymore."[1]

---

1. Ba Jin, *Hanye* (Cold nights), first published in 1947, revised and collected in *Ba Jin wenji* (Collected works of Ba Jin) (Beijing: Renmin wenxue, 1962), 14:3. An English translation by Nathan K. Mao and Liu Ts'un-yan, *Cold Nights, a Novel by Pa Chin* (Hong Kong: Chinese University Press, 1978), was based on the original 1947 edition. Mao and Liu claimed that the revision by Ba Jin of his own works "reflects his attempt to adapt to the trends of Chinese politics in the 1950s and 1960s" ("Preface," xi). This was evidently the case. See Olga Lang's "Epilogue" to her pioneering *Pa Chin and His Writings: Chinese Youth Between the Two Revolutions* (Cambridge, Mass.: Harvard University Press, 1967), 263–82, for a critical analysis of the systematic revisions carried out by Ba Jin himself in order to make his writings acceptable to the new Communist regime. It also is true that the changes are "only minor stylistic and political" ones (Mao and Liu, xi). A comparative reading of the two editions of *Cold Nights* suggests that the revision has actually made the novel a better read. This observation does not deny, however, that the textual revisions are deeply symptomatic of the heteronomous status of literary discourse in modern China. Given the fact that Ba Jin's works are

After one initial sentence registering the gloomy surroundings, the narrative quickly dissociates the protagonist from a declared situation of emergency and enters his private field of vision and perspective. Obviously inured to the predicted air raid, he finds his immediate enemy to be the seemingly frozen time, which, in frustrating his wish, also constitutes his passive relationship to the external environment. Time ceases to be a valuable resource; neither does it seem to possess a directional flow. The individual's internalized experience of time, at this moment, separates him from the historical present and becomes metonymic of his self-consciousness. From the very beginning, he is effectively removed from any position to claim membership in a collective identity. Instead, he is assaulted by a growing sense of personal failure that seems to drive him further into interiority.

Yet this insulating interiority is hardly a reliable safe haven, for his train of thoughts, however empty they may be, are suddenly interrupted when he involuntarily shivers because of the invasive cold air. His body, markedly clad in a "thinly-lined gown," serves to reattach the individual, not to the given spatiotemporal regime as a condition of collective destiny, but rather to a more immediate and irreducible physicality. At such a rude awakening, he lowers his head and perforce sheds, so to speak, his disembodied musings. His is already a demoralized body that inscribes a reality no longer of the same order as the communal and nationalizable experience of danger incurred by enemy invasion. It is this frail, pained body that both determines the forced reflexivity of the individual subject and incites its aspiration as well as its despair. Upon his articulation of a desired self-transformation ("I cannot go on doing this any more"), an intrusive voice responds pointedly: "Then what are you going to do? Do you have the guts, a softy like you?" Startled, the man looks around, only

---

now widely available only in their revised version and that the same revisions are kept intact, with the author's approval, in an exhaustive 25-volume edition of *Ba Jin quanji* (The complete works of Ba Jin) (Beijing: Renmin wenxue, 1986–93), the 1962 version of the text of *Hanye* should be regarded as the definitive edition and is therefore used here. Mao and Liu's English rendition, which, incidentally, is inadequate in some respects, is also consulted. (For a detailed analysis of the inadequacies of this English translation, see Jane Parish Yang's critical review in *Chinese Literature: Essays, Articles, Reviews* 2.2 (1980): 288–93.) Further citations of Ba Jin's text will be given as internal page references, with the first number indicating the Chinese original and the second the English translation.

to realize that no one is about and that it is his own voice contradicting him (3; 1).

An imagined dialogue follows, and from here the novel proceeds to narrate the existential angst and irreversible decay of the tuberculous professional proofreader, whose full name, not revealed for the first time until the fourth chapter, is Wang Wenxuan. As we soon find out, the other voice that challenges Wenxuan at the beginning echoes his wife's opinion of him, now apparently internalized as reproof of his failure. By contrast, Zeng Shusheng, his lover from college and common-law wife of fourteen years, stands as a splendid success in her career as a bank clerk. More resourceful financially as well as socially, she capably shoulders the responsibility of sending their son to a private prep school and eventually of supporting the whole family, which also includes Wenxuan's doting mother. The mother, determinedly disapproving her daughter-in-law's modern lifestyle and openly jealous of the younger woman, seizes every opportunity to demean Shusheng and instigate estrangement between the couple. The feud and incessant bickering between Shusheng and Wenxuan's mother, as a result, continually torments Wenxuan, whose indecisiveness and malleability only frustrates the two women in his life and drives them further apart. As the war crisis deepens, Shusheng decides to leave Chongqing, without her family, to pursue an elusive happiness and self-fulfillment. In the end, when the war is suddenly won and over, this miserable family completely falls apart. Wenxuan dies an excruciating death on the day that a victory celebration is held in the city, and a few months later, in a cold winter night, Shusheng comes back to the old apartment to learn about his demise and the subsequent vanishing of her son and mother-in-law.

A complex and richly symbolic novel, *Cold Nights* is generally considered to be the author's masterpiece. With this tragic story, as C. T. Hsia observes in *A History of Modern Chinese Fiction,* Ba Jin finally established himself as a "psychological realist of great distinction" by fully presenting "the naked human condition of suffering and love."[2] Suffering and love, or rather suffering because of love, predominate the life of Wang Wenxuan, probably the last and best-known tuberculous patient portrayed in modern Chinese literature. Yet the nakedness of the human condition is

---

2. C. T. Hsia, *A History of Modern Chinese Fiction, 1917–1957* (New Haven, Conn.: Yale University Press, 1961), 381–86.

heavily mediated through overlapping discourses of meaning and social determinations of identity. What collapses in the course of the novel, as our reading will show, is the complex construct of subjectivity legitimized by a series of modern practices and ideologies, such as individuality, romantic love, the nuclear family, and finally the nation-state. Each of these fundamental modern institutions is brought to crisis as Wang Wenxuan's body is corroded by tubercle bacilli and his world plagued by uncertainty and hopelessness. The painful disease, which continually prevents the invalid from assuming the position of a valid subject, loses all of its romantic connotations and closely mirrors a general bankruptcy that leads to the death of the individual. Tuberculosis in this case not merely yields a symptom or metaphor, but also suggests its own diagnosis, demanding an etiological analysis of sickness as *both* meaning *and,* ultimately, the undoing of meaning.

In the character of Wang Wenxuan, therefore, Ba Jin creates a virtually schizophrenic antihero whose failure to attach himself meaningfully to any forms of identity, social as well as private, is aggravated by and reflected in his tuberculosis. The disease functions as no less than a surrogate identity. It drives his fears and desires inward, breeds *ressentiment,* and offers masochism as a desperate escape. It also offers him a somatic language, by means of which the invalid Wang Wenxuan is forced to interpret and ultimately to invalidate his world with a vengeance. The significance of the last tubercular in modern Chinese literature thus lies in a demythologizing dialectic of failure and success.

Tuberculosis as Symptom

"Nothing is more punitive," so warns Susan Sontag, "than to give a disease a meaning—that meaning being invariably a moralistic one. Any important disease whose causality is murky, and for which treatment is ineffectual, tends to be awash in significance."[3] Tuberculosis and cancer are the two master diseases of modernity, the metaphoric meanings of which Sontag succinctly reconstructs in her influential book *Illness as Metaphor.* Whereas TB as a disease of the recent past signified an intriguing mix-

---

3. Sontag, *Illness as Metaphor and AIDS and Its Metaphors,* first published in 1978 and 1989, respectively (New York: Doubleday, 1990), 76.

ture of delicacy, spirituality, willful romanticization, and simultaneously a failure of will, cancer as a still unconquered threat most often evokes paranoia and bewilderment. Sontag's central contention is that "illness is *not* a metaphor, and that the most truthful way of regarding illness—and the healthiest way of being ill—is one most purified of, most resistant to, metaphoric thinking."[4] Nonetheless, she underscores a modern predilection for giving disease at least a psychological explanation. In a secular world after the Enlightenment, "psychologizing seems to provide control over the experiences and events (like grave illnesses) over which people have in fact little or no control. Psychological understanding undermines the 'reality' of a disease."[5] However, one may also argue that psychological discourse, just as previous notions of cosmic predestination or retribution, enriches the reality of illnesses by endowing them with a symbolic depth and interpretability. A disease psychologized may yield a more intense experience.

To liberate oneself from all lurid disease metaphors, which Sontag takes to be the first step toward a healthy acceptance of death as natural, one would have to develop a different relationship to one's own body. The body would have to be delivered not only from fear, agony, and the urge to moralize, but also from social symbolism in general. It would become a truly autonomous body, signifying nothing but itself, and inscribing no other meaning than its own physiological reality. Such a blanched body, in rendering superfluous all human imaginative efforts at coping with and transcending pain, death, and eventually life itself, would spell the end to sickness as a form of subjectivity, which is no less than what sustains metaphoric thinking about diseases. The same self-sufficient body would also suggest that modern subjectivity, its creative but rancorous expression identified by Nietzsche as *ressentiment,* may itself be a sickness incurred by the perceived impossibility of reconciling consciousness with action, or words with deeds. In this sense, Sontag's plea to end all metaphoric uses of illness is a call for action rather than contemplation. It voices a deeply utopian project of positive demystification, of freeing the individual body from "the fantasy of inescapable fatality."[6]

With such utopian emancipation, however, the possibility always exists of a historical reversal, or, simply, a repetition that belies it. The fantasy

---

4. Ibid., 3.
5. Ibid., 55.
6. Ibid., 87.

of inescapable fatality seems to be able to either give rise to or cast doubt over a rhetoric of liberation. For if an overt exploitation of illness as part of a moralizing semiotics compelled Sontag to envision a self-sufficient body and a fear-free landscape, then Ba Jin's critical attention to individuals afflicted with tuberculosis and to the symbolism of diseases in general, by contrast, followed an earlier period of celebrating new life, youth, and a desiring body. Sickness as meaning, as the troublesome details of life, became the focus of Ba Jin's writings when he turned to look into "little people and little things," as summarized by the title of a collection of his short stories published in 1945.[7] Mournful "groaning," so some critics observe, now defined a deliberate mode of writing that came in to replace the romantic writer's earlier exuberant style in the tradition of an uncompromisingly antagonistic "*J'accuse*."[8]

For most of his writing career, Ba Jin was constantly inspired, as he stated in a later preface to his 1931 novel *Family,* by Georges Danton's motto: "Have courage, have courage, always have courage!"[9] An effective combination of anarchist rejection of patriarchal institutions, romantic affirmation of the individual, and utopianism in the tradition of the French Revolution made Ba Jin enormously popular among the young educated readers of the 1930s and his pen name a synonym for a radically modern imaginary and passion. With voluminous trilogies such as *Revolution* (unfinished), *Turbulent Stream, Love,* and *Fire,* as Olga Lang points out in her study, Ba Jin "helped to create among the intellectuals an emotional climate that induced them to accept the Chinese revolution."[10] Indeed, his combative writings, up until the early 1940s, can be read as a figurative genealogy of the revolutionary spirit in twentieth-century China. The heroes in Ba Jin's early fiction are mostly young

---

7. *Xiaoren xiaoshi* (Shanghai: Wenhua shenghuo, 1945). This was Ba Jin's last collection of short stories before the founding of the People's Republic of China in 1949. It took the author well over three years, from March 1942 to November 1945, to finish the five stories in the slender volume. During this period, Ba Jin was forced by the ongoing war to travel across southwest China. See Ba Jin, "Houji" (Postscript) to *Xiaoren xiaoshi,* 52.

8. See Chen Sihe and Li Hui, "Ba Jin chuangzuo fengge de yanbian" (On the evolution of Ba Jin's writing style), in *Ba Jin zuopin pinglun ji* (Essays on Ba Jin's works), ed. Jia Zhifang et al. (Beijing: Zhongguo wenlian, 1985), 83–114, esp. 107.

9. See "Preface" to the 5th ed. (May 1936), *Family,* trans. Sidney Shapiro, with intro. by Olga Lang (New York: Doubleday, 1972), 7.

10. Lang, *Pa Chin and His Writings,* 265.

rebels and idealists, who, always compassionate, altruistic, and ready to act, abundantly display the characteristics longed for by the visionary May Fourth generation. Their ebullient and expressive vitality, according to one critic's comprehensive analysis of the different "life forms" constructed in Ba Jin's oeuvre, stands in contrast to the decay of the old as much as to "the abject life" lived by the weak and resigned.[11]

Although the two central and opposite "life forms" in Ba Jin's fictional world, the exuberant and the decadent, explicitly convey the author's judgment and values, it is in presenting a third form of "abject life" that Ba Jin is most successful and sophisticated. The reason, Zhang Minquan explains, is that the author always retained a rich and multidimensional childhood memory of the hapless and resigned, and that the mode of these people's lives better enabled realist representation.[12] With a seemingly sudden shift of his attention to wasted and unfulfilled lives in narratives such as *Qiyuan* (Leisure garden, 1944) and *Cold Nights,* Ba Jin indeed noticeably modified his conception of literary realism. Realistic description would no longer function as a sign of imminent and desirable changes, or merely set up a stage for idealistic and heroic intervention. On the contrary, the previous ideology of rationality implied in realist discourse now gave way to a recognition that reality as an encompassing and complicitous mass of attachments defies rationalization. Writing, as the writer-narrator of *Leisure Garden* realizes with increasing urgency, is rather a compensatory act and answers a desperate need to console oneself with a happier and simpler imagined life. It registers the writer's utopian desire and serves as an imaginary solution to real and insurmountable contradictions.

Yet literary realism is at its most powerful when it confronts reality as failure, especially when it deals with *death* as the horizon of life that cannot be transcended. Such disillusionment with reality was the basic structure of feeling at the origin of modern Chinese literature, and it underlies virtually all of the narratives of the self that we find in, for instance, Lu Xun, Yu Dafu, and early Ding Ling. Ba Jin's 1944 novel *Leisure Garden* continues this tradition of exploring the difference between the first-person narrator and the world that he acutely witnesses in its disin-

---

11. Zhang Minquan, *Ba Jin xiaoshuo de shengming tixi* (The life forms in Ba Jin's fiction) (Shanghai: Shanghai wenyi, 1989), 1–15. The Chinese for these three "life forms" are "congshi shengming," "fuxiu shengming," and "weidun shengming."

12. Ibid., 50–51, 140–41.

tegration. Toward the end of the narrative, several deaths occur around Mr. Li, the writer-narrator, despite his inspired attempt to offer a heartwarming ending to the novel on which he has been working. Almost by accident, the purplish face of a drowned young man confronts the writer-narrator and drives home a dimension of reality that could hardly be sublimated: "Such is death! So quick, so simple, and so real!"[13] If sudden death at this point is for the first-person narrator largely a traumatic event—in Lacanian terms, the horrifying eruption of the unsymbolizable Real in *Cold Nights*—the death of the protagonist becomes a prolonged and conscious process of expectation. By painstakingly narrating Wang Wenxuan's demise, Ba Jin not only gives voice to the muted agony of an abject existence, but he also pushes to its limit the realist representation of depth and subjectivity.

To a large extent, the maturity and psychological subtlety that Ba Jin achieves in *Cold Nights* depend on the basic plot of the narrative, namely, that of an individual's life as failure. Such a summary abstraction may help us isolate what Fredric Jameson has named an amphibious "ideologeme." As the raw material or Saussurian *langue* underlying complex cultural expressions and systems, an ideologeme describes a dual formation rather than a statement: "as a construct it must be susceptible to both a conceptual description and a narrative manifestation all at once."[14] An ideologeme, in other words, makes representable and also gives significance to certain apparently unconnected experiences; it has the capacity of generating both the abstract and the concrete. The abstractable message of the novel in question, therefore, cannot substitute for the complexity of its narrative manifestation, for the same reason that a sociological classification of Wang Wenxuan cannot replace or diminish his experience. An emphasis on the fundamentally narrative character of apparently disembodied ideologemes, as Jameson reminds us, "will offer the advantage of restoring the complexity of transactions between opinion and protonarrative or libidinal fantasy."[15] It is on the narrative level, on the level of imaginative operation where the author engages and negotiates an ideologeme, that the failure of an individual life, as a theme, yields successful

13. *Qiyuan* (Leisure garden), first published in 1944, collected in *Collected Works of Ba Jin*, 13:186.
14. Fredric Jameson, *The Political Unconscious: Narrative as a Socially Symbolic Act* (Ithaca, N.Y.: Cornell University Press, 1981), 87.
15. Ibid., 88.

symbolic construction and commentary. Libidinal fantasy, too, becomes manifest only when the narrative is read as a complex explanation of the individual's complete and self-willed failure.

As we have seen, *Cold Nights* opens with a description of the uncertain present in which Wang Wenxuan finds himself transfixed during an air raid. This initial moment of immobility, however, signals a deeper malaise, a deadly syndrome that results from the failure of both the environment and the individual. For this pathogenic condition of despair, tuberculosis provides a perfect metaphor, because it was still a largely incurable disease in wartime China and remained "awash in significance." One way to read the multiple meanings of tuberculosis in *Cold Nights* is to see it as psychosomatic, as a willed illness through which Wenxuan inflicts physical pain on himself so as to displace the larger anxieties in his life. Such masochistic willing—paradoxically, the exercise of a weak will—seems to be the revenge of Wenxuan, who has internalized, as we see from the very beginning, his wife's calling him a "softy." Combining a willed disease with a disease of the will, tuberculosis seems eventually to offer him the only possible way to relate to others and identify himself.

The first indication of the onset of tuberculosis does not occur until the ninth chapter, where we find a description of how on one ordinary rainy day Wenxuan trips on his way to work and has to leave for home early because of a rising fever. From then on, he successively demonstrates all of the standard physical symptoms of pulmonary and then laryngeal tuberculosis that end in his anguished and voiceless death. Up until this ill-fated rainy day, however, Wenxuan has actually been enjoying a brief period of peaceful domestic life—at least since the last crisis between him and his wife, Shusheng, was, to his mind, miraculously resolved. The miracle that would bring Wenxuan this short-lived domestic bliss actually involves using his pained body as an object of pity and sympathy. It establishes a behavioral pattern and determines his subsequent return to a stage of infancy in exchange for compromise and security. Moreover, the incident reveals the psychic structure of Wenxuan's private life as that underlying a masochist's universe.

The miraculous resolution of a major crisis in the marriage of Wenxuan and Shusheng, which occurs even before the novel begins, takes place two nights after the couple had a fight and she moved out on him and his mother in a fury. Earlier during the day, Wenxuan meets his wife in a fancy coffee shop and tries, to no avail, to talk her into going home with him. He does manage, nonetheless, to bring their hearts closer by reminiscing about their college days and their shared memories and visions. They both had hoped to devote their lives to education, to build new schools in the countryside and run them like a family (31; 18). Yet such happy recollections of past idealism only demoralize them further about their current situation.

Dejected, Wenxuan returns home by himself, but his mother allows him no quiet by badmouthing her independent and unconventional daughter-in-law. Not daring to refute his mother, who treats him like a helpless child wronged by the outside world,[16] and yet wanting to defend his wife, Wenxuan has only himself to blame: "His heart seemed to be drifting in some empty space searching for a haven. He felt that he had not suffered enough pain or endured enough misery. He wanted to scream, to cry bitterly, to experience intense pain, or to be beaten mercilessly. Anything, except to remain quietly by his mother's side" (40; 22).

With such masochistic urges, Wenxuan leaves home, bumps into an old friend in a tavern, commiserates with him, and drinks until he feels ill. Before he can find his way home late that night, he loses control, opens his mouth, and "the supper he had eaten earlier shot out like a cataract." This pathetic scene of Wenxuan throwing up in the street dramatizes the connection between physical pain and the formation of his ego. Suffering turns him into an object of curious gazes in a public place, but it also emboldens him and allows him a rare sense of self-centeredness. Overcome by pain, "he had nothing to do with his surroundings anymore. At this moment, he would not have turned around or even noticed, had someone dropped dead right next to him" (47; 28). Involuntary disgorging, indeed, will eventually develop into a central trope of self-expression for Wenxuan.

While he is absorbed in vomiting, his wife Shusheng happens to pass by and recognizes him.

"Are you sick?" she asked.

He shook his head. His breathing had gotten smoother, but tears were

---

16. The description here is pertinent to what I discuss below: "His tears won her sympathy, and her rage subsided. She looked at him lovingly, as if he were still her young child who had been wronged by others and had come home to cry in front of her" (37–38; 22).

coming out again. They were tears of gratitude and sorrow, different from those that had been caused by his vomiting. . . .

"Are you really going to walk me home?" he asked in a quavering voice. He looked at her as if intimidated.

"If I don't, I'm afraid you will go drinking again," she replied, smiling. He felt warmer, and much more relaxed.

"I will never drink again," he sounded like a child and then let her support him all the way home. (48–49; 28–29)

Thus, even to his own surprise, Wenxuan succeeds in persuading Shusheng to go home with him, not through adult, discursive reasoning, as he had tried earlier, but by demonstrating his body in pain and by underscoring his passivity. Since the demonstrative or persuasive feature of masochism, according to Theodor Reik's classical study, consists in the masochist's exhibition of pain, embarrassment, and humiliation,[17] to convince Shusheng to stay for good, Wenxuan has to undergo yet more suffering in order to bring together the two feuding women in his life. When they reach their candlelit home, his mother, not realizing that Wenxuan is sick and that Shusheng is with him, tries to cheer him up by saying that he should marry another woman once the war is over and he makes a fortune. As soon as she sees Shusheng, however, the mother turns sarcastic and, on learning that Wenxuan has been drinking and has thrown up, is greatly upset. She is alarmed because she believes that her husband, Wenxuan's father, had died from alcoholism. "I've never allowed you to touch alcohol since you were a kid. How come you still went out and drank?" She first demands an answer. Then, "speaking gently as if to a spoiled child," she asks what happened, but she seems to be hurt more because he has brought back his wife.

"When did you come across her?" she pressed him for an answer, another emotion having made her oblivious to her son's physical pain.

"Why don't you let him go to sleep?" Shusheng could not help interrupting her again.

Ignoring the young woman, the mother continued to demand a full explanation from her son.

17. Theodor Reik, *Masochism in Modern Man*, trans. Margaret H. Beigel and Gertrud M. Kurth (New York: Farrar, Straus, 1941), 72–83. The other two features of masochism, according to Reik, are the special significance of fantasy and the element of suspense.

"I . . . I . . . ," he struggled with words. Something churned violently inside him and shot up from his stomach. He tried to force it down, but lost control instead and started disgorging noisily, sputtering vomit on both himself and his mother. (53; 31–32)

At this sorry sight, the mother relents and gives her daughter-in-law permission to take Wenxuan to bed. As Shusheng is tucking him in, he realizes that he had not enjoyed such attentive care in years and becomes "as submissive as an infant." Before he falls asleep, however, he reaches out, grabs her hand, and makes his suffering into a negotiating device: "Please don't leave me . . . whatever I did was for you . . ." (54; 32).

What Wenxuan enacts here is no less than a contract with Shusheng and, by extension, with his own mother. A masochist contract, in Gilles Deleuze's psychoanalysis of masochism, forms a crucial strategy to protect the masochist's world of fantasy and symbols from reality or even from its hallucinatory return. Central to this masochistic imagination is the banishment of the father who has proved to be ridiculously weak and inadequate. By giving up every right over himself to the torturing woman, "the masochist tries to exorcise the danger of the father and to ensure that the temporal order or reality and experience will be in conformity with the symbolic order, in which the father has been abolished for all time."[18] With his father conspicuously dead and absent, Wenxuan is now contractually attached to the two competing women to the extent that he must continue his self-infantilization and let them define the order of his reality and experience, at least as far as his domestic or libidinal life is concerned.

At this point, as Deleuze points out, the masochist's relationship to his women is desexualized, and it is the father image in him that stands to be expelled. What this process actualizes is "the transference of the law onto the mother and the identification of the law with the image of the mother."[19] Following such a psychoanalytical interpretation, it is not accidental that Wenxuan's father is recalled, by the mother, only as a negative example to prohibit any resemblance between father and son. It also becomes significant that Wenxuan and Shusheng's thirteen-year-old

---

18. Gilles Deleuze, *Coldness and Cruelty*, in *"Masochism: Coldness and Cruelty" by Gilles Deleuze and "Venus in Furs" by Leopold von Sacher-Masoch*, trans. Jean McNeil (New York: Zone Books, 1989), 66.

19. Ibid., 91.

son (Xiaoxuan, or Young Xuan) appears to be an exact duplication of his pale and reticent father. Never close to his mother, Xiaoxuan enjoys being with his doting grandmother much more. Indeed, as we will discuss, the two women function as different types of mother, the bad and the good, and bring into relief the masochist's deepest fear and desire.

A systematic psychoanalytical reading may yield a metanarrative of the absent father in terms of abrupt historical changes and their impact on the traditional symbolic system as well as the individual psyche. The expulsion of the father from the symbolic order is already staged, if we go back to Ba Jin's earlier works, through distinct plots in *Leisure Garden* (where two fathers, one indulging and the other self-indulging, both fail in their paternal responsibility to their sons) and *Family* (where the eldest son of the grandchild generation has to assume, with great ambivalence, the function of his deceased father). Such prevalence of absent or inadequate father figures reflects the negation of patriarchal authority on the one hand and the weakening of the law on the other. Wenxuan, born in the year when the monarchy was overthrown (he was thirty-four years old in 1945) and educated with the new ideas of the May Fourth period, is therefore bound to inhabit a world where the image and likeness of the father is "miniaturized, beaten, ridiculed, and humiliated." Moreover, "what the subject atones for is his resemblance to the father and the father's likeness in him: the formula of masochism is the humiliated father."[20] In this light, Lu Xun's paradigmatic influence at the origin of modern Chinese literature is all the more astounding when we realize that the core narrative he provided in "Diary of a Madman" describes a Confucian family from which the father is nonetheless deleted and abolished. For the same reason, we can better appreciate the psychoanalytical implication of their statement when Meng Yue and Dai Jinhua compare the significance of the New Culture movement of the May Fourth era to that of the 1911 Chinese Revolution. Both effect a "massive, prominent symbolic patricide": one in the political field of patriarchal rule and order, the other in the realm of culture and values.[21]

As a result of this irrevocable patricide, "the masochist experiences the symbolic order as an intermaternal order in which the mother represents

20. Ibid., 60.
21. See Meng Yue and Dai Jinhua, *Fuchu lishi dibiao: xiandai funü wenxue yanjiu* (Emerging from history: studies in modern women's literature) (Zhengzhou: Henan renmin, 1989), part I, 3–6.

the law under certain prescribed conditions: she generates the symbolism through which the masochist expresses himself."[22] Part of the symbolism for self-expression, for Wenxuan, is no less than to present his own body as being subjected to increasing pain. His tuberculosis, therefore, is as much a physical disease as it is a desire. It functions as what Lacan calls the *objet petit a,* which indicates an irreducible otherness internal to the psychic apparatus that at once impedes and enables, as an obturator, the subject's constitution. Such a presence allows a perverse pleasure, even a semblance of agency, with the subject's repeated efforts to contain and confront an inherent displeasure or lack.[23] The interest of Ba Jin's novel, it should be evident by now, lies not in a clinical case study of tuberculosis. The disease is itself turned into a symptom of larger cultural anxiety, or of the internal pain exacted by the new symbolic order into which the invalid now retreats. Tuberculosis, as in the case of the Jewish patient Franz Kafka, becomes what Sander Gilman calls a "test case" that shores up the individual's "fundamental inability to control the cultural language of his time."[24]

Wenxuan's fever, cough, and eventually his spitting of blood therefore function as more than mere clinical symptoms. They serve as the only effective language that helps him communicate his inner self as he grows ever more reticent. Such somatic signs also reinforce the contractual relationship that he has entered with his mother and his wife. In exhibiting his sick interior, Wenxuan's ailing body compensates for his inarticulateness and masochistically relates him to others. The blood he coughs up, more specifically, continues and even ritualizes the symbolism of vomiting that was established earlier. It is also the most powerful means of verbalization available to him. Much agitated by the incessant

22. Deleuze, *Coldness and Cruelty,* 63.
23. See Jacques Lacan, *The Four Fundamental Concepts of Psycho-Analysis,* ed. Jacques-Alan Miller, trans. Alan Sheridan (New York: Norton, 1977), 103–04, 144–45. For an explication of Lacan's notion of the *objet petit a,* see Slavoj Žižek, *Enjoy Your Symptom! Jacques Lacan in Hollywood and Out* (New York: Routledge, 1992), 48–49. On p. 22, Žižek elaborates that "the very gesture of renouncing enjoyment produces inevitably a surplus enjoyment that Lacan writes down as the 'object small a.'" According to Žižek, this surplus enjoyment (*jouissance*) derived from renunciation "gives a clue to so-called 'primal masochism.'"
24. Sander Gilman, *Franz Kafka: The Jewish Patient* (New York: Routledge, 1995), 238. See the chapter, "Tuberculosis as a Test Case" (169–228) for a discussion of the meaning of the disease and Kafka's discourse on it.

quarreling between his mother and his wife on another night, Wenxuan quietly leaves the apartment again, not bold enough to speak his mind: "I am going to die and you two are still bickering." When he returns home much later, all pale and shaken, he finds that the two women have reached a truce. Upon Shusheng's solicitation, he anxiously tries to describe what he has just witnessed, but "phlegm spurted out before his words." "'Blood! Blood! You spat out blood!' Terrified, the two women cried in unison, and together they carried him to bed and laid him down" (101; 59).

Between Masochism and *Ressentiment*

The dramatic moment of Wenxuan spitting blood in front of his mother and his wife qualitatively changes his life as a tubercular and its symbolic mechanism as well. For this is the moment when he at last makes public his fatal illness and, more important, his despair. Now officially an invalid, he, as much as the people around him, is confronted with the question of how to treat and make sense of his disease. In the process, Wenxuan's masochism, rather than his tuberculosis, makes possible a general psychopathological study of the modern Chinese male subject.

Tellingly, Wenxuan's mother and his wife, who throughout the novel consistently represent separate generations, suggest two different approaches to his ailment. The mother, with her strong belief in traditional values and practices, decides that Chinese medicine will best serve her son. Shusheng, a determined practitioner of the May Fourth humanist and liberal ideals, urges Wenxuan to see a doctor trained in modern Western medical science. As for the patient himself, however, the rich symbolism of what treatment to seek boils down to two mundane and practical considerations: he does not want to disobey his mother, and, moreover, Western medicine is more costly than a Chinese herbal cure. Even though he finds the Chinese doctor's diagnosis—exhaustion plus too strong an element of fire in his liver—less than convincing, Wenxuan comforts himself by putting his faith in the long native tradition of medical practice (102; 59–60). When later his condition worsens and he starts to lose his voice, he finally goes to a crowded modern hospital, only to be turned away by the steep price of a standard fluorescent examination prescribed by the doctor (230; 132).

The two doctors in the novel, peripheral as they are, nevertheless highlight the paradigmatic difficulty of making a choice on Wenxuan's part. Dr. Zhang, who significantly is related to Wenxuan's mother, is older, amiable, reassuring, and he visits his patient at home, whereas the nameless doctor in the hospital, equipped with a cold stethoscope, appears at best indifferent and impersonal. The contrast between them serves to suggest a focal cultural opposition between tradition and modernity, or that between organic community and organized society, which is also reflected in the antagonism between the mother and her daughter-in-law. Both doctors fail to save Wenxuan's life, and an outbreak of cholera will abundantly expose the inadequacy of either medical institution: the epidemic immobilizes Dr. Zhang himself as a helpless patient and paralyzes the city's hospital system. The outbreak, a small-scale replica of the ongoing war, creates a crisis situation that renders choices by an individual both more urgent and less tenable. When both terms of a conceivable binary opposition are brought into question through violence, choices can hardly be made through privileging one term over the other. This impossible situation lies at the heart of Wenxuan's despair.

What further compounds the individual's dilemma in a moment of crisis, moreover, is not so much the difficulty of making a choice as the inevitable failure of any decision, including the decision not to choose. In the case of Wenxuan, the larger decision in his life has to do with his mother and his wife. This is forcefully suggested early on in the novel when an anxiety dream of Wenxuan's, which he refuses to believe to be a dream, makes up the entire second chapter. In this highly prophetic dream, Wenxuan is heroically determined, against the urgings of his wife, to go back to the city to look for his mother when war breaks out, interrupting their ordinary conjugal life and sending interminable streams of refugees from the city. Shusheng wants him to stay with her and their son, telling him that they are his responsibility, but Wenxuan is not to be dissuaded, shouting, "I can't abandon her and run away all by myself" (17; 9). In the end, Shusheng resolutely leaves him, his mother remains forever out of reach, and Wenxuan wakes up desperately fighting a phantom crowd of strangers. The basic structure and tension of the novel, encoded in this dream text through intricate condensation and displacement, thus revolves around Wenxuan's doomed effort to reconcile the two women and two moral duties.

What this dream produces, in fact, is a "masochist text" that underscores the incompatibility of different conceptions of the individual subject at a moment when the presumed validity or legitimacy of the individual is brought into question. Masochism in psychoanalytical terms can be read as "a story that relates how the superego was destroyed and by whom, and what was the sequel to this destruction."[25] Kafka's literary discourse, for instance, over his experience of tuberculosis as a male Jew in turn-of-the-century Prague offers such a masochist text. For Kafka, according to Sander Gilman's study, masochism "comes to be an acting out of the conflict felt between the claims lodged against the individual and the inability of that individual to counter these claims completely because of the underlying incompleteness, the transitoriness of all constructions of the self."[26] The original and most comprehensive masochist text, conceived by Leopold von Sacher-Masoch (1836–95) under the title *The Heritage of Cain*, was to examine the entirety of human history through six dominant themes: love, property, money, the state, war, and death.[27] (These six forces that propel the cycling of a masochistic history are also clearly present in what generates the anxiety dream to which Wenxuan wakes up in a cold sweat.) Presiding over a masochist's world determined by the six uncontrollable forces are heroines who, in Deleuze's reading of Sacher-Masoch, have in common "a well-developed and muscular figure, a proud nature, an imperious will and a cruel disposition even in their moments of tenderness and naiveté."[28] These women fall into three archetypes that closely correspond to a mythic view of the evolution of human history in three stages, a prevalent historiographical convention to which Sacher-Masoch as a nineteenth-century writer apparently subscribed.[29] Such a tripartite model of human evolution, obviously, is not what structures the meaning system in *Cold Nights*. Nor is it entirely how Wenxuan relates to the women in his world. Instead, as has been suggested, his masochistic universe is governed by two mother figures, two strong-willed women who, in enacting the symbolic order as intermaternal for the masochist, themselves symbolize different conceptions of the individual and claims against him.

From Shusheng's perspective, since Wenxuan the "softy" always wants

25. Deleuze, *Coldness and Cruelty*, 130.
26. Gilman, *Franz Kafka*, 22.
27. See Deleuze, *Coldness and Cruelty*, 11, 38.
28. Ibid., 47.
29. See ibid., 47–55.

to be nice (the literal meaning of "laohaoren"), he ends up constantly compromising himself, even masochistically so, just to avoid conflict with others and to divert the tension between being a son and a lover/husband. "He could not bring together his mother and his wife, or choose one between the two. He always tried to muddle through or put off reality" (172; 98). For her, Wenxuan's fatal mistake is that he never thinks about himself and, worse, always turns his weakness into passive aggression.[30] If Shusheng's criticism of Wenxuan is in agreement with her liberal-humanist conception of the self, Wenxuan's failure seems to be complete when his mother also blames him for "not thinking about himself," for being a "softy." Both women complain that he is unnecessarily sacrificing himself for the sake of the other person.[31]

What vivacious Shusheng consciously embodies in the novel, on one level, is the May Fourth tradition of liberal-humanist ideas about personal freedom, happiness, and self-fulfillment. Her distinct cultural identity was acquired, emphatically, through her modern university education. It is now faithfully reflected in the critical choices that she makes in her life. Never close to her own son, Xiaoxuan, she admits that she is not a good mother; she does not ever acknowledge the existence of her parents or other relatives. She is a modern individualist par excellence in that her selfhood is affirmed through freeing herself first from all family ties and eventually from all moral scruples. She is, in Deleuze's analysis of the three women examined by Sacher-Masoch, the uterine, hetaeric woman. Dedicated to love and beauty, "she is modern, and denounces marriage, morality, the Church and the State as the inventions of man, which must be destroyed."[32] Her final decision to leave the endangered wartime capital Chongqing, in her own words, is based on her belief that she is still young and hopeful; it constitutes a triumphant sacrifice of the sacrifice that is expected of her as a mother and wife. "I am active, and love excitement. I need to lead a passionate life." "I am not a bad woman," she states in a long letter to Wenxuan in which she demands to be relieved of her obligation as his common-law wife, to annul, in other words, the contract between them. "My only fault is that I pursue freedom and happiness" (239–43; 138–39). In reality, Shusheng's success owes much to the fact that she works as a clerk in a commercial bank and is vigorously pursued

30. See her letter to Wenxuan, 235–36; 135–36.
31. See, for instance, 165, 196; 100, 120.
32. Deleuze, *Coldness and Cruelty*, 48.

by her superior, Director Chen, a savvy, strong, and handsome banker, the exact opposite of Wenxuan. Her job in effect stipulates—more than a complete abandonment of her previous dreams as an educator—the suspension of idealism itself. Thus, her financial resourcefulness and unrelenting pursuit of personal happiness ultimately constitute her failure, for they involve a suppression of her utopian desires, or her socially significant ideals. "Don't talk to me about the ideals we used to have," so pleads Shusheng in her last letter to Wenxuan. She is away and thriving in the frontier town of Lanzhou, while he lies dying in besieged Chongqing. "Living in an age and a life like ours . . . we are in no position to talk about education or ideals any more" (242; 139).[33]

Needless to say, Shusheng's ideological valorization of the self and individual choice also leads to a concept of personal responsibility. Thus, she expects Wenxuan to be her equal and companion, two roles that would also serve as the foundation of her love for him. Yet, his inability to maintain an equal footing, most concretely demonstrated in his sickness and financial dependence, finally makes her realize that no such foundation exists. "Together we are not going to be happy, for there is not anything connecting us. . . . I can only pity you, but can no longer love you. You were not such a weakling before" (236–37; 135–36). In this context, it becomes extremely revealing that *only* after Shusheng had left him and unilaterally dissolved their marriage contract was Wenxuan able to experience, for the first and sole time in the novel, sexual desire. Initially, it was her attractive face, now vividly recalled, that excited his imagination. Then it was the ambivalent meaning of her action (her regular letters inquiring about his health and her sending him money) that intrigued Wenxuan and led him to fantasize about her life. At this moment, she again became a woman with her free choice, and he, "an invalid nearing his death, experienced a healthy man's desires." Yet "his urges tortured him all the more because even he himself knew that they could not be satisfied, not in the least" (256; 146).

If Shusheng acts as the hetaeric, bad mother in the masochistic world, Wenxuan's biological mother encompasses all the maternal functions of

33. For a defense of the character Zeng Shusheng from a feminist perspective, see Liu Huiying, "Chongchong fanli zhong de nüxing kunjing: yi nüquan piping jiedu Ba Jin de *Hanye*" (The difficult situation of a woman facing various barriers: a feminist interpretation of *Cold nights* by Ba Jin), in *Zhongguo xiandai wenxue yanjiu congkan* (Journal of modern Chinese literature studies), no. 52 (1992), 3:107–15.

nurturing and protecting. To Wenxuan's mother, the law of the father is also transferred. The good mother, whom Deleuze describes as "cold, maternal, severe" and, above all, "oral,"[34] is to triumph in the end, and it is her alliance with the son that forms the foundation of the masochist's realm of reality. The love that his mother expects from Wenxuan rests precisely on his being weak and dependent, on his behaving like a submissive child who completely surrenders his responsibility. Unlike Shusheng, the mother does not produce a written statement of her beliefs, but she is vocal and articulate, if often vociferous. Aided by her traditional education, her values are systematic and contradict what Shusheng stands for on almost every point. The mother resents, for instance, the fact that Shusheng holds a job in a bank because she thinks it is improper and humiliating. As much as an expression of the premodern gender hierarchy (in terms of a masculine claim to the public workplace and an equation of domesticity with feminine virtue), her frustration also amounts to a denunciation of the modern capitalist commodification of labor as generalized prostitution. Herein lies the ambiguity of the exchange between the mother and Shusheng: while the young woman heatedly protests being sneered at as an enticing "flower vase" in the bank office (92; 54), she also painfully realizes, in a different context, that she is being degraded and taken advantage of (32; 19).

The mother's most bitter complaint against the young woman, however, is that she is not a good mother to Xiaoxuan ("Then I suppose you will be free to fool around with your boyfriends. I've never seen a mother like you" [96; 56]), and that she and Wenxuan never had a proper wedding. For her, Shusheng is both a disqualified mother and an illegitimate wife—two negative attributes that only serve to reinforce the mother's own authority and legitimacy. When Wenxuan musters the courage to explain that he and Shusheng understand each other, the mother turns a deaf ear to such a feeble plea of romantic love. She firmly believes that,

---

34. See Deleuze, *Coldness and Cruelty*, 51–55, 66–67. In *Cold Nights*, noticeable instances occur in which the mother is described as expressing her feelings through an oral urge. Besides the fact that she constantly worries about her son's diet and feeds him food and medicine, she often gnashes her teeth (yaoya qiechi) when she talks about her daughter-in-law (cf. 96; 56 and 160; 92). At one point, the description becomes most explicit: "'I'd rather die and we all die, than see her again!' She gnashed her teeth, as if she were gnawing at that young woman's flesh. After this outburst, she returned to her room, paying no more attention to him" (152; 88).

now in the position of mother-in-law, she has the right to discipline the young woman (159; 92).

Finally, the mother perceives her relationship to her son as one of vertical control and subordination, and her love for Wenxuan is therefore as protective as it is possessive. Shusheng's conception of love, however, presupposes a horizontal relationship of equivalence and mutual responsibility among liberated and liberal subjects. From these two types of love ensue two very different conceptions of the individual and the individual's duty, and two very different economies of desire and its satisfaction. Furthermore, these two forms of love are metaphoric of two opposing ideologies and social institutions: Confucian familism versus liberal individualism. The narrative actually contains a moment of metacommentary when Shusheng is made aware of the fatal consequences of these two conflicting loves; she has seen a production of Cao Yu's play *Yuanye* (The wilderness, 1937) and is now reminded of the tragedy befalling the filial son/husband (184; 105). Her decision is eventually to escape from this emotional dilemma in a flight to freedom, to sacrifice the sacrifice. It is at this point in *Cold Nights* that the psychological structure of masochism necessarily extends and lends itself to a discourse of cultural and political entrapment.

Caught in the middle of such conflicting demands and attachments is Wenxuan the invalid, for whom the flight to freedom is never a viable choice. While tuberculosis is deployed as a symptom of his masochistic anxiety, he is also enabled by his tuberculous body to arrive at a protopolitical gesture of disavowal. His ailing body and the prospect of his own death as an individual continually compel Wenxuan to distance himself from both his mother and his wife; his illness also leads him to deconstruct various institutions of authority. The incessant bickering between the bad and the good mothers incites Wenxuan to ever more intense masochistic pleasure in inflicting pain on himself. At the same time, the profusion of the official discourse of the sovereign nation-state, which the suffering patient finds impervious to and irreconcilable with his own life, leaves him seething in *ressentiment*. Such a transition, from weakness as displacement to the Nietzschean *ressentiment,* seems to be an integral part of the formation of the masochist's ego. While the sadist, in Deleuze's analysis, externalizes his ego and posits it as the superego, the masochist nurtures his ego through multiple disavowals in the aftermath of the superego's removal.[35] The masochistic ego emerges as such when it converts its weakness into a source of strength and disavows the mother, with the father already abolished. What Deleuze uncovers in Sacher-Masoch's description of sexual perversion, in other words, is no less than a rewriting of the Hegelian fable of the master and the slave, the triumph of an internalized self-affirmation, or the revenge of "the weak as weak" that Nietzsche would denounce.

For Wenxuan, therefore, masochism and *ressentiment* are of homological value in shaping his personal and social existence. His monotonous job as a proofreader consists mostly of double-checking texts that never make much sense to him. With much poignancy, he realizes that he is demeaned by money and the need to survive. Early in the novel, Wenxuan found himself tackling an impossible translation that bore hardly any resemblance to the language he knew, but he had no right to make changes. While he kept his eyes mechanically moving over words that looked like a "bundle of entangled hempen cord," his thoughts would wander away: "I'm finished. All my happiness is robbed by the war, by life itself, by those lofty and pretentious slogans, and by the proclamations that are posted all over the streets" (75; 44). Such demurral, however, would always remain internal and audible only to himself. "Yet there was no point. He had protested like this thousands of times, but no one had heard him, and no one ever knew that he would even entertain such a resentment. To his face as well as behind his back, people would call him a 'softy.' He himself would also prefer the position of a softy. It had been like this for several years now" (75; 43–45).

As his tuberculosis worsens and a general collapse looms, Wenxuan's relationship to the official discourse of patriotism, or what may be called the dominant political economy of the sign, also changes. In the final stage of his illness, when he almost loses his voice because of laryngeal tuberculosis but is still working in the publishing house, Wenxuan one day accidentally spills some of his blood on a proof sheet from a propagandist book trumpeting the impressive progress that China as a modern nation-state has been making. Tubercular blood-spitting at this point becomes a

35. See Deleuze, *Coldness and Cruelty,* chap. 11, "Sadistic Superego and Masochistic Ego," 123–34. On p. 124, Deleuze writes: "The masochistic ego is only apparently crushed by the superego. What insolence and humor, what irrepressible defiance and ultimate triumph lie hidden behind an ego that claims to be so weak."

revelatory supplementation, signifying the eruption of a much more immediate and brutal reality than what its ideological representation allows or maintains. As the ultimate form of asserting himself through pain, blood-spitting for Wenxuan metaphorically constitutes a deconstructive writing that inserts radical difference and exposes any systematic imposition of meaning as inherently incomplete and incoherent.

> He tried to wipe it off with a piece of waste paper, but he had to do it very lightly, for he was afraid that he might break the fragile paper. Removing the waste paper, he found that among the sentences celebrating the improvements in people's living conditions was still a faint trace of his blood. "Because of your lies, I am going to bleed to death!" He thought angrily, and almost wanted to tear that page to shreds. Yet he did not dare. He looked at the stain for a while, sighed, and turned over the page when he at last finished proofreading it. (264; 152)

The indelible blood stain on the printed page thus registers a double failure. On the one hand, it debunks the legitimizing narrative of the nation-state by inserting what has been written over or erased. Wenxuan's attempt to wipe off the trace of his blood turns into a critical gesture of bracketing, or putting under erasure, the assertive text proper. In the process, the ideological self-representation of the nation-state is revealed as at best artificial and necessarily incompatible with the raw and objectal experiences of the individual. On the other hand, Wenxuan's fear, his inability to develop his awareness into political action, may also be read as a failure on the part of the individual. His most bitter protests and complaints, either political or domestic, are often uttered through an interior monologue. His capacity for passive inner musings offers an index of Wenxuan the "softy's" failure in his social as well as his personal life.

Such complete failure may also constitute what Fredric Jameson detects as an "authentic *ressentiment*" in the narratives of George Gissing. There is an "exclusive preoccupation in Gissing with the anxieties of money, the misery of hand-to-mouth survival, the absence of independent means or a fixed income." This preoccupation with the mundane aspects of life serves the purpose of blocking Gissing's characters from ever entering the position of desiring subjects, because, in Jameson's reading, the novelist understands that any achieved desire or wish is bound to be inauthentic in an age of universal commodification, while at the same time "an authenticity at best pathetic clings to images of failure."³⁶ As a result, "the whole system of success and failure has been undermined from the outset by a narrative strategy which may thus be read as something like the final form of *ressentiment* itself."³⁷ Instead of a bourgeois "commodity desire," the modern nation-state is now challenged by Ba Jin's novel as the dominant system of success and failure.

Wenxuan's failure and *ressentiment,* in the final analysis, are inevitable not so much because of the sovereignty of the nation-state now brought into crisis by imperialist aggression, as because of his constitution as a modern subject in the tradition of liberal individualism. Throughout the novel, the narrator repeatedly observes that, although they once shared the same youthful ideals and visions, Wenxuan and Shusheng seem to belong to two different historical ages and are no longer contemporaries (59, 35; 186, 106). Shusheng's success is also her personal failure, not only in that her idealism has to be compromised, but also because when she comes back to Chongqing at the end of the war and finds no one but former neighbors living in what used to be her home, she has to face the emptiness of her survival and success. She is the lonely survivor, which truthfully reflects her individualistic refusal to be burdened by any attachments, be they familial or sentimental. Her story, just like that of Mary in Ding Ling's *Shanghai, Spring 1930,* is the one to be continued and further negotiated.

Wenxuan's failure, conversely, succeeds in revealing the incongruity between ideological claims upon the individual subject and its actual condition of existence. The different periods that Wenxuan and Shusheng seem to occupy, therefore, are actually two related aspects of the same modern discourse of liberal individualism. Hence, the importance of their shared liberal education and spiritual genealogy. From its inception, as Wendy Brown has argued most succinctly, modern liberalism contains a "general incitement" to a Nietzschean *ressentiment* among all liberated and liberal subjects.

> It is not only the tension between freedom and equality but the prior presumption of the self-reliant and self-made capacities of liberal subjects, con-

---

36. Jameson, "Authentic Ressentiment: Generic Discontinuities and Ideologemes in the 'Experimental' Novels of George Gissing," in his *Political Unconscious,* 204.

37. Ibid., 205.

joined with their unavowed dependence on and construction by a variety of social relations and forces, which makes *all* liberal subjects, and not only markedly disenfranchised ones, vulnerable to *ressentiment:* it is their situatedness within power, their production by power, and liberal discourse's denial of this situatedness and production, which casts the liberal subject into failure, the failure to make itself in the context of a discourse in which its self-making is assumed, indeed, is its assumed nature.[38]

Wenxuan's tuberculosis, his masochism, and ultimately his death all make it impossible for him not to be aware of his own situatedness, of the distance between his consumptive body and the production of him as a modern subject. His attachments to the modern discourse of liberal individualism, just like his attachments to the two women in his life, are indeed mortally wounded. Haunted by death and with his energy depleted, Wenxuan knows that he would rather not go on living, "but no one would allow him to give up" (230; 132). He has to die a most excruciating death at the moment when the war ends and the entire city is out celebrating a hollow national victory. This moment of jubilation is wrought with ambiguity insofar as it also registers the masochist's final vengeance in his accusatory death. The essence and the aim of masochism as a cultural metaphor, as Theodor Reik once commented, is "victory through defeat."[39]

The Death of the Last Tubercular

Nevertheless, death proves to be much too great a terror for Wenxuan, no matter how hard he tries to attach himself to others as an infant, to his inner self and fantasies, or even to the nation as a cause. The vision of his decomposing body drives home the realization that he will face death all by himself and that no redemptive system of meaning could spare him the visceral fear and existential despair that he experiences alone.[40] In his

38. Wendy Brown, "Wounded Attachments: Late Modern Oppositional Political Formations," in *The Identity in Question,* ed. John Rajchman (New York: Routledge, 1995), 214.
39. Reik, "Victory Through Defeat," *Masochism in Modern Man,* 427–33.
40. The following describes a brief period when Wenxuan's disease was apparently stabilized and his life with his mother made routine, but he also knew that he was

death, therefore, it is the complete failure to sublimate the individual's pain that becomes the central issue, and the validity of the moral economy is brought into question. "When he finally expired, his eyes were half closed, showing their whites, and his mouth wide open, as if he were still demanding 'justice' from someone. It was about eight o'clock in the evening. Out on the streets was the blaring sound of gongs and drums. People were celebrating victory, aiming firecrackers at a giant dancing dragon" (285; 166).

The insulation of the deathly inside from the festive outside, of the individual from the collective, is unmistakable. Wenxuan's death transforms the psychic depths of an individual, which the novel explores with great patience, into a larger and more universal question of social meaning and justice. The symptomatology of the novel, in other words, gives way to an etiological analysis, which explicitly acknowledges the desire for cure and salvation. The moral discourse that underlies the novel finally makes itself audible and unavoidable.

In fact, two other deaths directly described in the novel seem to point to the same direction of social criticism. When Wenxuan's schoolmate Tang Baiqing, after some heavy drinking one night, throws himself in front of a roaring truck, he has bitterly blamed society for failing him and his youthful aspirations (96–100; 56–59). Tang Baiqing's disillusionment with life and subsequent suicide, initially triggered by his young wife's death at childbirth, epitomize the utter despair and vulnerability of a generation of educated Chinese, who found their May Fourth optimistic ideals continually betrayed and crushed by war, by poverty, and by death as the ultimate unreason. The second death, that of Old Zhong, an older, fatherlike colleague of Wenxuan's, occurs when the outbreak of cholera claims as its casualties numerous individual lives in the city. His abrupt death more focally exposes the failure of society to function and protect its members. In the perfunctory burial of Old Zhong, Wenxuan

---

slowly approaching death: "'What else can I do other than eat, sleep, and be sick?' He asked himself constantly. Forever unable to come up with an answer, he gave up thinking about it with a wry smile of despair. Once he seemed to find an answer. The dreadful word 'death' sent cold shivers down his spine and made him shudder. He began to see his own body rotting, with worms crawling all over it. For many days thereafter he did not dare to let his imagination wander again. His mother could not comfort him: this was his secret. Nor could his wife give him any more solace, although she kept sending him brief notes (at least once a week)" (227–28; 130–31).

sees both his future and the social implications of his own fate (271–73; 157–58).

These two deaths, together with the prolonged and acutely experienced death of the protagonist, introduce to moral discourse another related issue: the question of retribution. All of the main characters in the novel ask, one way or another, the impossible question "Why do we deserve to suffer?" When the mother expressed frustration at the misery of life during the war, Wenxuan reasoned: "We have never robbed or stolen from anyone. Never hurt anyone either. Why shouldn't we continue living?" (81; 47). Later, when Wenxuan was the one who indicated that he might as well die to save all the trouble, his mother countered with the same reasoning: "Stop thinking like that. We have never stolen, robbed, murdered, or done anything unjust to others. Why shouldn't we live?" (155; 89). With the same belief in a sensible moral economy, Shusheng would ask Wenxuan to understand her decision to pursue her own happiness: "Living in an age and a life like ours, I, as a woman, have never hurt anyone or done anything wicked, and yet what could I do?" (242; 139). In each of these cases, retribution or justice is never of a cosmic order; rather, it is a principle deeply embedded in a vision of justice for the human world. It is as protest against the bankruptcy of such principles and moral economy that Wenxuan's death acquires social pertinence and revelatory force.

With his final gesture of voiceless accusation, Wenxuan also dies as the last tubercular in modern Chinese literature. His agonizing death simultaneously culminates and puts an end to a long tradition of using tuberculosis as a metaphor for an enfeebled nation, a benighted populace, an individual's existential angst, or a continually thwarted sensitive mind. From Lu Xun's bony Little Shuan ("Medicine") to Yu Dafu's ailing and nostalgic writer ("Blue Smoke") to Ding Ling's willful Sophia ("Miss Sophia's Diary"), the tuberculous individual in Chinese literature has always been a symptom of a deeper malaise. Literary representations of sickness or physical deformity invariably express an understandable desire for social etiology and transformation. The development from an expressive symptomatology to a more comprehensive and methodical discourse of etiology seems to be inevitable. At the origin of modern Chinese literature, Lu Xun's conception of literature as a medicinal discourse proved to be paradigmatic and far-reaching. Similar politicization (in fact medicalization) of literary practice also occurred in Meiji Japan when, as Karatani Kojin suggests, the successful institutionalization of modern Western medicine and the nation-state made it necessary to represent subjective interiority on the one hand, and to depict society "as ailing and in need of a fundamental cure," on the other.[41]

Evidently, the modernity of all such literary representations of disease is grounded in the belief, implicit or explicit, that a cure can and should be achieved through social engineering. We cannot afford to gloss over the utopianism in the longing for a healthy and carefree human existence, even though we also have to recognize what Karatani Kojin describes as the "pernicious" nature of such a systematic eradication of disease. The modern "mirage of health" constitutes a secular form of theology, according to Karatani Kojin, "which sees the cause of illness as evil and seeks to eliminate that evil. Though it has eliminated various sorts of 'meaning' which revolve around illness, scientific medicine is itself controlled by a 'meaning' whose nature is even more pernicious."[42]

The disappearance of a sick antihero in modern Chinese literature after Ba Jin's *Cold Nights* is therefore no historical accident but an overdetermined event that radiates multiple significations. The removal of a sick body from literary discourse indicates a paradigmatic shift, through which the focus of literary representation schematically changes from the individual to the collective, from the interior to the exterior, from the contemplative to the active. Instead of an individual passively contemplating his pain and suffering history as a betrayal of what he is promised, a collective subject is now believed to be actively transforming the course of history. Such is the fundamental logic of socialist realism, for which sickness can be only a political allegory rather than a form of concentrated experience of individuality. The absence of individualized experience of pain thus metaphorically bespeaks the death of the individual. For the collective body is never ill and is always optimistic. This vision of social health and happiness infused Ba Jin, rejoicing in the still young People's Republic, with optimism about the new socialist regime and compelled him to stress the historical specificity, or outmodedness, of his writing.

41. Karatani Kojin, "Sickness as Meaning," in his *Origins of Modern Japanese Literature,* translation ed. by Brett de Bary (Durham, N.C.: Duke University Press, 1993), 111. See also "The Discovery of Interiority," 45–77.

42. Karatani, "Sickness as Meaning," 108.

> I once cursed the old society with such pathos, and cried out against injustice on behalf of those individuals. Now in great happiness and jubilation I sing praise of our new society rising like the morning sun. . . . Constant progress in science and our superior social system have conquered tuberculosis. It no longer causes much fear among us. I read *Cold Nights* in the last two days again and felt like having had a nightmare, but such nightmares are gone and are gone forever.[43]

Ba Jin's rereading of his novel in 1961, even his rereading of this rereading in 1981, was largely inspired by the hope that the individual body would be always sheltered from uncertainty and trauma. For this reason, the author has insisted that the novel is a book full of hope rather than despair, and that its main point is to criticize and denounce a dying society.[44]

The death of the last tubercular, Wang Wenxuan, thus historically accompanies the end of the liberal ideology of the state and of its tortured relationship to individual subjects. The *ressentiment* to which all liberal subjects are inevitably incited also comes to an end when the self-making of the individual is no longer the issue in the socialist regime. The new hero, free of disease and interiority, will attest to the success of sublimation through participation in a national identity and the socialist project of construction. Such sublimation, as we have suggested in our reading of Ding Ling, is based on a constant politicization of the body. While there is no sick body anymore, the human body is subjected to direct inscription of social meaning. It is a signifying body to the extent that it has to remain positively charged and externalized as part of an imaginary social body of plenitude. Such is the condition for sublimation, through which the individual's fear of death is alleviated because the individual body is, in fact, dissolved. In the end such a sublimational mechanism may prove too much to impose, because even if the human body is no longer capable of pain, it is still susceptible, in the end, to death.

43. Ba Jin, "Tan *Hanye*" (On *Cold nights*), in *Collected Works of Ba Jin*, 14:448.
44. See Ba Jin, "Guanyu *Hanye*" (About *Cold nights*), in *Chuangzuo huiyi lu* (Reminiscences about my writing) (Hong Kong: Joint Publishing, 1981), excerpted in *Ba Jin yanjiu ziliao* (Research materials on Ba Jin), ed. Li Cunguang (Fuzhou: Haixia wenyi, 1985), 1:537–45. During the late 1950s and early 1960s, Ba Jin was criticized for having created such a pitiful character and giving readers no hope in *Cold Nights*. A representative expression of such criticism, even though it is enormously sympathetic, can be found in Yu Simu, *Zuojia Ba Jin* (On the writer Ba Jin) (Hong Kong: Nanguo, 1964), esp. 275–76.

5

The Lyrical Age and Its Discontents:
On the Staging of Socialist New China in
The Young Generation

Only by radically remoulding the teaching, organisation and training of the youth shall we be able to ensure that the efforts of the younger generation will result in the creation of a communist society.
—V. I. Lenin, "The Tasks of the Youth Leagues" (1920)

In hindsight, it was not out of a personal whim that, in December 1963, Chairman Mao decided to publish ten more of his classical-style poems, all of which were then prominently publicized in *The People's Daily* on 4 January 1964 as part of the ritualized national salutation to the new year. The majority of these newly released works had been composed after 1959, except for one that was written in April 1949 to commemorate the triumphant capture of Nanjing, capital of the Republic of China, by the People's Liberation Army. In the centrally controlled symbolic machinery of the socialist People's Republic, which was soon to celebrate its fifteenth anniversary, such an official issuing of Mao Zedong's poetry was carefully designed to speed up the production of political incentives and energy. In its wake, profuse exegeses and celebrations would follow, elevating the poet's voice and vision into the source of universal inspiration. The elliptical poetic texts would often be expounded on as applicable policies, concrete exhortations, and eventually as philosophical verities. The last couplet of Mao's 1961 "Reply to a Friend," for instance, consists of fourteen characters in the original: "And I am lost in dreams, untrammeled dreams / Of the land of hibiscus glowing in the morning sun."[1] When Guo Moruo, the poet laureate of the state at the time, prof-

---

1. *Ten More Poems of Mao Tse-tung* (Hong Kong: Eastern Horizon Press, 1967), 10–11. The translation here was adopted from the official journal *Chinese Literature*, published by Peking Foreign Languages Press, May 1966.

fered his interpretation, the radiant "land of hibiscus" became more than a time-honored praise of the southern landscape. It now reflected the glorious future of socialist China and, by extension, of the entire globe to be brightened by an impending world revolution.[2]

Such optimistic confidence seemed precisely what the new poems were intended to regenerate in the nation. In fact, the publication of this group of poetic works by Mao marked the height of what literary critics have come to describe as the "expressive" or "lyrical age" (*shuqing shidai*) in modern China.[3] The onset of this deeply romantic period was conveniently dated, in January 1957, by the inauguration of a government-sponsored journal, *Shikan* (Poetry), which grandly introduced itself by publishing eighteen of Mao's earlier poems. This event further welded the systematic production of poetry in New China with Mao Zedong's revolutionary poetics of magnificence.[4] In the same winter, an upsurge in the socialist revolution had reportedly brought about advanced collectivization in the Chinese countryside, and the socialist transformation of society at large had also been accomplished at a furiously faster pace than expected or planned. With the launching of the ambitious second Five Year Plan (1957–62), the young People's Republic declared itself at a new stage of peaceful construction. The strategic objective was to rapidly modernize the country and to demonstrate the superiority of socialism by catching up with England and surpassing the United States in the shortest time possible. For a brief period, the imminence of a socialist paradise enthralled the popular imagination and excited many a utopian

---

2. See Guo Moruo, "'Furongguo li jin zhaohui': du Mao zhuxi xin fabiao de shici 'Da youren'" ("The land of hibiscus glowing in the morning sun": reading Chairman Mao's newly published poem "Reply to a friend"), *People's Daily*, 16 May 1964.

3. See Li Yang, *Kangzheng suming zhi lu: shehui zhuyi xianshi zhuyi (1942–1976) yanjiu* (The path of resisting destiny: a study of socialist realism [1942–1976]) (Changchun: Shidai wenyi, 1993), esp. 145–92. Also see Zhang Geng's assessment of dramatic works from this period in his introduction to the officially sanctioned *Zhongguo xin wenyi daxi, 1949–1966: xiju ji* (Compendium of new Chinese arts and literature, 1949–1966: the drama collection), 2 vols., ed. Zhang Geng (Beijing: Zhongguo wenlian, 1991), esp. 1:6–7. The play *Nianqing de yidai* (The young generation) that is discussed later is collected here, 1:805–46.

4. See Zhang Jiong, "Mao Zedong yu xin Zhongguo shige" (Mao Zedong and poetry in new China), *Dangdai zuojia pinglun* (Review of contemporary writers), no. 6 (1993): 4–12. Mao's exuberant idealism and romanticism, according to the author, had a deep impact on poetic discourse during the early years of the People's Republic.

fantasy. It was apparently an age of great passion and expectations, an age in which the boldest dreams about human happiness were collectively dreamed, and the most ordinary moments in life gloriously poeticized. In April 1958 a mass campaign to collect new folklore was under way, enthusiastically endorsed by Mao Zedong himself, who pointed out that new Chinese poetry would flourish when workers in the field of poetry first drew on a native tradition and, more importantly, combined realism with romanticism.[5] Soon after, the formula of "dialectically bringing together revolutionary realism and revolutionary romanticism" was theoretically presented as the sole viable method of literary production for the great, rhapsodic socialist epoch.[6] For this new literary style, Chairman Mao's poetry, which consistently "articulates a sublime heroics,"[7] already provided a brilliant example.

The euphoric lyrical age, according to the critic Li Yang, became historically possible when the unprecedented socialist transformation of society allowed a genuinely national subject to emerge and take center stage. Only after the People's Republic had consolidated itself as a modern nation-state, "only after we had found our subjectivity as Chinese, could we begin historical creation and turn into a lyrical subject."[8] The defining feature of this lyricism, from the mid-1950s to the eve of the Cultural Revolution in 1966, was its fervent celebration of the populist identity of the nation. What enabled the lyrical subject to emote and rhapsodize was the joy of direct participation in a collective life and national destiny.[9] This belief in immediate access to eternal rejuvenation would in turn help enliven everyday life with metaphysical expectations and reveal global significance in all mundane details. Negated in one stroke, therefore, were the prose of the world and individual finiteness and uncertainty. Appropriate for a culture of lyrical exuberance and transcen-

---

5. See editorial, "Da guimo de shouji quanguo min'ge" (Collect folklore in the country on a large scale), *People's Daily,* 14 April 1958.

6. See Zhou Yang, "Xin minge kaituo le shige de xin daolu" (New folklore has broadened a new path for poetry), *Hongqi* (Red flag), no. 1 (June 1958): 33–38.

7. Ban Wang, *The Sublime Figure of History: Aesthetics and Politics in Twentieth-Century China* (Stanford, Calif.: Stanford University Press, 1997), 188. See pp. 188–93 of Ban Wang's book for an insightful reading of the symbolic significance of Mao Zedong's poetic discourse.

8. Li Yang, *The Path of Resisting Destiny,* 158.

9. See ibid., 169.

dence, poetic vision would invariably prevail over narrative temporality, and poetic diction and imagery offered the master medium of expression and communication. More than aestheticizing politics alone, it was a triumphant moment of aestheticizing everyday life in the socialist mode. "Just as Chairman Mao is a statesman-poet," as Ban Wang points out, "the party-state is an aesthetic state."[10]

The nationally incited urge to enact a poetic life was probably most observable in modern spoken drama (*huaju*), where from 1962 through 1965 a series of plays about either contemporary life or the revolutionary heritage were carefully developed and produced to achieve national impact. The staging of the nation in the form of theatrical spectacle was a purposeful enterprise and a phenomenal success. The achievements were so momentous that in March 1964 the Ministry of Culture held an award ceremony, for the first time ever, to commend some twenty plays and productions of modern drama in the previous year. As if to bear witness to astonishing progress on the ideological front, Chairman Mao, usually accompanied by other leaders of the nation, watched the production of twelve new plays from August 1963 through November 1964.[11] Given the prominence it enjoyed, this extraordinary moment may well be described as the golden age in modern Chinese drama, although it also was the historical occasion that Jiang Qing, Mao's wife and a one-time film actress, would seize to prepare for her own entry onto the national political stage. One of the prizewinning plays that Mao did not manage to see during this period was *Nianqing de yidai* (The young generation), a four-act modern drama originally produced by three Shanghai-based theater groups in the summer of 1963. In October of the same year, Yao Wenyuan, an energetic literary critic who would later be bitterly denounced, together with Jiang Qing, as a member of the infamous "Gang of Four," penned an effusive essay to cheer the latest harvest in the burgeoning field of modern drama, exalting the play as "the song of youth in the age of socialist revolution."[12]

---

10. Ban Wang, *The Sublime Figure of History*, 192.

11. See headline reports in the government-sponsored journal *Xiju bao* (Journal of drama) from August 1963 to December 1964.

12. See Yao Wenyuan, "Shehui zhuyi geming shidai de qingchun zhi ge: ping *Nianqing de yidai*" (The song of youth in the age of socialist revolution: on *The young generation*), *Wenyi bao* (Literary gazette), no. 311 (October 1963): 8–15. One of the earliest positive reviews of the play, published in June 1963, already recognized its thematic

The lauded socialist song of youth is definitely lyrical, and *The Young Generation* reads like a good specimen of the imagination and logic of that bygone time. What I attempt to do in this chapter is conduct an archaeology of the lyrical culture by also uncovering the deep anxiety and discontents that it desperately wished to suppress. This excavation project therefore involves the careful task of reconstructing not only what was staged and visible, but also what determined the theatrical spectacle and representation. The anxiety, as much as the lyricism embedded in the play, may still be abundantly pertinent, insofar as we continue to find ourselves confronted with the same dilemmas of modernity.

The Politics of Lyricism

By one contemporary account, *The Young Generation* may well have been the most popular of all the modern-style plays recognized by the Ministry of Culture in 1964.[13] Within less than two years of its first production, a definitive version of the play was published by the Chinese Drama Press (with an initial printing of 24,000 copies). In addition to the nearly sixty theaters across the nation that put on the play, it also was adapted into various regional opera productions and *tanci* performances, and finally it was made into a much-awaited movie (figure 5). Obviously its quick ascendance to the limelight on a national scale foreshadowed the path that would be taken by the "model theater" groomed by Jiang Qing during the Cultural Revolution. The original author of the play, however, remained unusually reticent during this exciting transmutation, although he dutifully went through all the stages of revision and adaptation. In sharp contrast to other newly laureated playwrights, Chen Yun, as far as

---

timeliness. See Su Kun, "Yichu yinren zhumu de xinxi: jianlun 'Nianqing de yidai' zhuti de xianshi yiyi" (An important new play: on the contemporary meaning of the theme of *The young generation*), *Shanghai xiju* (Shanghai drama), no. 45 (June 1963): 14–16.

13. According to the *Journal of Drama* (no. 184 [April 1964]: 30–31), by March 1964, fifty-eight theater groups had put on *The Young Generation* in twenty-seven cities, compared to fifty-three for *Nihong dengxia de shaobing* (On guard under the neon lights), forty-some for *Qianwan buyao wangji* (Never forget), and twenty-eight for *Lei Feng*. During December 1963 alone, forty-seven theaters were playing *The Young Generation*. In the same month the play was also adopted into seven different local operas (Peking, Shanghai, Canton, etc.) that together put on 122 productions.

5. Film poster, *Nianqing de yidai* (The young generation) (1964). From *Dazhong dianying* (Popular cinema) (Beijing, June 1965).

one can tell, never offered any platitudinous statements about his motivation or inspiration.¹⁴ Amazingly little was made known about the writer

14. For instance, two other award-winning writers, Hu Wanchun and Cong Shen, did not hesitate to reveal to the public either how they were inspired by Chairman Mao's teachings or what they learned from writing the play. See Hu Wanchun, "Chuxie huaju de ganxiang" (Thoughts at writing modern drama for the first time), *Journal of Drama*, no. 184 (April 1964): 25–26; Cong Shen, "*Qianwan buyao wangji* zhuti de xingcheng" (The formation of the theme of *Never forget*), *Journal of Drama*, no. 184 (April 1964): 27–28.

who helped shape the idealist profile of an entire generation of Chinese youth.

Its overwhelming popularity aside, the play was certainly the most influential and most paradigmatic of the new drama on contemporary life. The heated discussion and philosophizing it generated almost immediately after its debut testify to the ideological need it fulfilled. One of the earliest commentaries on *The Young Generation* welcomed it for its "thought-provoking theme," which was to treat the education of young people as an integral part of the continuing class struggle, domestic as well as international.[15] Together with several other prizewinning plays, *The Young Generation* raised and answered "questions with which millions of people are concerned," one authoritative critic stated. All of the new plays, better than any other literary genres, helped define and dramatize the "major themes" of the historical situation, but this work in particular "has not only excited countless young people, but also touched numerous parents." What it put forth to the audience was therefore an urgent question that had to be addressed seriously by the entire society: "how to cultivate and educate Communist successors and how to lead the young people onto the revolutionary road."[16] Another commentator more pointedly directed a rhetorical question to the target group of the play: "What is the meaning of the 'young generation'? And what kind of 'young generation' should we make?"[17]

Evidently "the young generation" was more than an apt title for a play about educating the young. It acknowledged a grave social reality, namely, the coming of age of the generation that grew up with the

---

15. See Wen Ping, "Faren shensi de zhuti: du huaju *Nianqing de yidai*" (A thought-provoking theme: a reading of the play *The young generation*), *Journal of Drama,* no. 176 (August 1963): 22–24. Ouyang Wenbin in another essay attributed the forcefulness of the play to its editorializing style and philosophical profundity. See his "*Nianqing de yidai* qianlun" (A brief essay on *The young generation*), *Shanghai xiju* (Shanghai drama), no. 51 (December 1963): 5–7.

16. See Hou Jinjing, "Guanxin he tichu qianbaiwan qunzhong suo guanxin de wenti: duju mantan" (Notice and address issues that millions of people are concerned with: remarks on recent plays), *Journal of Drama,* no. 184 (April 1964): 19–24.

17. See Yang Haibo, "Ba geming de huoju ju de genggao ranshao de gengwang" (Raise higher the revolutionary torch and make it burn harder), *Journal of Drama,* no. 178 (October 1963): 1–3. The same article was reprinted in the bimonthly *Zhongguo qingnian* (Chinese youth), nos. 21–22 (October 1963): 15–17. A forum on *The Young Generation* is featured in this combined issue, including a lengthy plot synopsis.

People's Republic. By singling out this generation for theatrical treatment, in turn, the play articulated a deep uneasiness about the identity and political orientation of contemporary youth. In this sense, the "thought-provoking theme" that *The Young Generation* introduced was actually an intensified awareness of youth as a problem, of the need for greater social guidance and political authority. It also initiated a new discourse about the family structure and everyday life during a self-consciously socialist era. Soon after *The Young Generation* appeared in Shanghai, a play called *Zhu ni jiankang* (To your health) was produced in Harbin, in northeastern China; it quickly became the next national sensation and won the same prize as the previous play, although not without a revised, more alarmist title, *Qianwan buyao wangji* (Never forget).[18] In addition to these two prominent dramatic works, a movie was promptly made to present and resolve a similar family problem in which a college-educated youngest son is humbled and taught how to respect his father, older brother, and working-class family origins.[19]

Of all the stage and filmic representations of the youth question, however, it is *The Young Generation* that remains the most lyrical and, as we will discuss, the most dramatic. It was widely praised for its profound dialogues and poetic language. One director, for instance, projected the artistic style of the play in these schematic terms: "youthful revolutionary enthusiasm; lucid philosophical theorizing; a vigorous and refreshing basic tone; lyricism in the style of a poetic essay."[20] Only such an impassioned style of lyrical poetry, noted the director, would do justice to the ethos of contemporary youth and simultaneously reflect an uplifting Zeitgeist. Yet the director was also perfectly aware of the gravity of the dramatic conflict at hand. The intended effect was to compel the audience to think "what attitude a revolutionary youth should have toward the

18. For the first version of the play, see Cong Shen, *Zhu ni jiankang* (To your health), *Juben* (Scripts), (October-November 1963): 2–63; see also Cong Shen, *Qianwan buyao wangji* (Never forget) (Beijing: Zhongguo xiju, 1964). For a critical analysis of the play, see Xiaobing Tang, "*Qianwan buyao wangji* de lishi yiyi: guanyu richang shenghuo de jiaolü jiqi xiandaixing" (The historical significance of *Never forget:* on the anxiety of everyday life and its modernity), in *Zai jiedu,* ed. Tang Xiaobing (Hong Kong: Oxford University Press, 1993), 184–95.

19. For the script, see Hu Wanchun and Fu Chaowu, *Jiating wenti* (Family problem) (Shanghai: Shanghai wenhua, 1964).

20. See Xu Xiaozhong, "*Nianqing de yidai* daoyan zhaji" (Directorial notes on *The young generation*), *Journal of Drama,* no. 182 (February 1964): 35–39.

revolutionary cause, and how to inherit the revolutionary tradition and carry on the cause."²¹ The director's observations, therefore, shed light on the political designs behind the lyrical style, and they reveal direct connections between a high-spirited lyricism and a possible legitimacy crisis in the revolution. In this instance, lyricism becomes a technical solution, a strategy of mobilization that serves to engage and coordinate the young population. It belongs to the modern technology that relentlessly aestheticizes politics and that programs popular sentiment and its gratification in a mass society. The lyrical subject, too, is the creation of what Louis Althusser calls the ideological state apparatus that operates to systematically interpolate the individual in an imaginary relationship to the real condition in which he or she exists.²²

Although, as we learn from Althusser, what constitutes the real condition of existence cannot always be readily grasped, the ideological function of lyricism appears more and more deliberate when we realize that *The Young Generation* intersected with a number of historical developments underpinning the lyrical age. By 1963, when the play was first put on, the socialist New China had weathered a series of severe political crises, not the least among them the disastrous consequences of the Great Leap Forward of 1958 and the Sino-Soviet split. A more direct challenge had come about even earlier in the restless 1956–57 political season, when urban dwellers and intellectuals, in part bestirred by the 1956 Hungarian uprising, made their dissent and discontent heard. The opposition was quickly suppressed as a "bourgeois rightist counterattack" on the proletarian dictatorship, but the necessity of continuously deepening the revolution in order to safeguard its achievements was brought home. The following massive failure of the Great Leap Forward led to widespread famine, and Mao Zedong the visionary and his "storming approach" were forced to the second front.²³ Yet while his utopian economics was discredited, Mao soon reasserted his leadership on the ideological front by warning against a happy obliviousness to the protracted and fierce class

---

21. Ibid., 35.

22. See Louis Althusser, "Ideology and Ideological State Apparatuses," in his *Lenin and Philosophy and Other Essays,* trans. Ben Brewster (New York: Monthly Review Press, 1971), 162–65.

23. See Lowell Dittmer, *China's Continuous Revolution: The Post-Liberation Epoch, 1949–1981* (Berkeley: University of California Press, 1987), for a discussion of the difference between an "engineering" and a "storming" approach, esp. 6–11.

struggle during the socialist period. His concern was that the more pragmatic "engineering approach" had created "in a peacetime context a new type of cadre, whose narrow professional/bureaucratic interests caused one to lose sight of the revolutionary mission."[24] Remembering the original mission subsequently became a key component in political reasoning and discourse.

Mao Zedong's deep fear for the future of the revolution was also greatly compounded by the de-Stalinization of the Soviet Union since the mid-1950s and by the pro-American liberalization policies adopted by Josip Tito's Yugoslavia. Revisionism now posed a real danger from within, threatening to derail the revolution just as ominously as imperialist aggression, embodied by American forces stationed in Taiwan, Japan, and South Korea, would from without. In short, the grim geopolitical situation seemed to demand that the nation be once again mobilized to defend the revolution's gains, if not its very existence. China had to stand independently of the two superpowers and unite with the oppressed but increasingly independent Third World nations across Asia, Africa, and Latin America. The vision of a world revolution was therefore an integral part of the Chinese lyrical age because it grew out of a geopolitical realignment. Moreover, it supplied an ultimate mission of commitment and made lyricism possible by introducing a discourse of infinite deferral. This global aspiration found its vivid expression in one of Mao's better-known poems, dated 9 January 1963:

> The Four Seas are rising, clouds and waters raging,
> The Five Continents are rocking, wind and thunder roaring.
> Away with all pests!
> Our force is irresistible.[25]

To ensure that such a cosmic task was accomplished and the revolutionary cause continued, campaigns of varying scales were waged one after another, now often envisioned as a massive offensive rather than as guerrilla warfare. The lyrical age was first of all an age of politicized passion. At the outset of 1963, a "socialist education campaign" was started in the countryside and would become a test run of the systematic mobilization

24. Ibid., 44.
25. "Reply to Comrade Kuo Mo-jo: To the Melody of *Man Chiang Hung*," in *Ten More Poems of Mao Tse-tung*, 1967, 22–23.

during the upcoming Cultural Revolution.[26] In February, top leaders of the nation, the Party, and the People's Liberation Army (PLA) offered aphoristic sayings and calligraphy to urge every Chinese to learn from Lei Feng, an exemplary soldier and Good Samaritan. Less than a year later, the example set by Lei Feng was supplemented by that of the PLA itself, and when the nation was called upon to emulate the army,[27] military uniforms and paraphernalia turned into proud fashion statements. With the publication of *Quotations from Chairman Mao* in May 1964, the campaign to collectively "study Chairman Mao's works" gained momentum and would further institutionalize a standard political parlance for the nation. During the same riveting period, two equally far-reaching movements unfolded, both adding credibility to the doctrine of self-reliance and the vision of utopian modernity. Dazhai and Daqing, a production brigade and an oil field, respectively, were promoted as model units for the agricultural and industrial battlefronts. While these mobilizations reinforced the socialist triumvirate of the workers, peasants, and soldiers, a continual but much quieter campaign had been under way. It first sought to return a large number of rural young people, who had migrated to industrial cities during the Great Leap Forward, to the countryside. By early 1964, the "return to the village" initiative (*huixiang*) had grown into a full-fledged social movement to relocate urban youth throughout the underdeveloped interior (*shangshan xiaxiang*).[28] Then hailed as an act that would revolutionize traditional values and practices, millions of educated urban youth settling in the remote areas would indeed change the social and cultural landscape of the nation. Some fifteen years later, the same displaced generation would fight their tortuous way back, only to radically reconfigure the human and political geography of the country

---

26. For an early but still informative study of this campaign, see Richard Baum and F. C. Teiwes, *Ssu-ch'ing: The Socialist Education Movement of 1962–1966* (Berkeley: Center for Chinese Studies, 1968).

27. Editorial, "Quanguo douyao xuexi jiefangjun" (The whole nation must learn from the People's Liberation Army), *People's Daily*, 1 February 1964.

28. Editorial, "Zhishi qingnian shangshan xiaxiang shi yifeng yisu de geming xingdong" (Educated youth going to the countryside is a revolutionary act to change traditional practices), *The People's Daily*, 20 March 1964. For a good study of this topic, see John Gardner, "Educated Youth and Urban-Rural Inequalities, 1958–66," in *The City in Communist China*, ed. John Wilson Lewis (Stanford, Calif.: Stanford University Press, 1971), 235–86.

yet again. Finally, partially in response to the concern dramatized by *The Young Generation,* in the summer of 1964 a brief campaign "to train successors to the revolutionary cause" intervened, heralded by a stern critique of "Khrushchev's phony Communism" and its historical lessons for the world revolution.[29]

Yet these were not all of the bestirring activities that demanded constant political enthusiasm and recharging. Those two heady years, 1963 and 1964, also witnessed increasingly thunderous marches and parades across Tiananmen Square as well as other public spaces all over China in spirited support of the civil rights movement in the United States. Every instance of resistance against American imperialism, be it in Vietnam, Cuba, Panama, or Zaire (the Congo), would have the resolute backing of the Chinese and was lauded in massive demonstrations. For three consecutive days in January 1964, for example, "workers in drama in the capital assumed their fighting position and marched to the streets and Tiananmen Square" to voice their moral support for the valiant Panamanian people.[30] Imaginary international solidarity, obviously, supplied a new source of energy for the lyrical age and made the lyrical subject a new revolutionary cosmopolitan.

The flow of emotional energy, therefore, had to be constantly redirected in order to maintain its vital force, and the capacity for lyrical response and agitation had to be continually enhanced. For it is not so much the content of lyricism as the ability to practice revolutionary lyricism, not the *énoncé* but the act of enunciation, that completes the ideological interpolation of the lyrical subject. This political economy of passion sustaining the lyrical age, however, ran a very real risk of exhaustion, even though physical fatigue and pain were always welcomed as signs of passionate devotion. As if acutely aware of this possibility, a February 1963 essay in *Zhongguo qingnian* (Chinese youth), an organ of the Communist Youth League, specifically advised its young readers on "how to

---

29. See Stuart R. Schram, "Introduction: The Cultural Revolution in Historical Perspective," *Authority, Participation and Cultural Change in China,* ed. Stuart R. Schram (Cambridge: Cambridge University Press, 1973), 77–85. Schram's introduction provides a concise historical survey of the period discussed in this chapter.

30. See "Woguo xijujie jianjue zhichi Banama remin de fan Mei aiguo zhengyi douzheng" (The drama circle in our country firmly supports the Panamanian people's patriotic struggle against America), *Journal of Drama,* no. 181 (January 1964): 3.

cultivate and maintain robust revolutionary enthusiasm."[31] In its effort to stimulate revolutionary passion among the young, the same journal serialized a discussion, for the greater part of 1963, of what constituted a correct understanding of "happiness." Toward the end, it became apparent that a rigid opposition was set up between self and collective, bourgeois hedonism and proletarian asceticism, material satisfaction and revolutionary determination. The main thrust of most writings, however, was to convince the reader that "you are actually happy." "Young comrades, we now live in a happy country. We must not live in happiness without knowing what it is," so concludes a severe essay denouncing bourgeois decadence and hedonism. The culminating metaphors that the author employs are graphic and indicative of the volatile "polemical symbolism" that would saturate public discourse and practice during the forthcoming Cultural Revolution.[32]

> If we ignore our current happy life and abandon the broad road of revolutionary happiness, if we instead seek happiness in the enjoyment of a materialistic life, or worse, in the cesspool of bourgeois decadence and degeneration, then we will sink to the bottom and become a pitiful bug in life. To soar in the open sky like a brave eagle, and to glide over waves like a seagull in the hurricane of revolutionary struggle: this is our chance to be heroes and offer our talent to the revolution. . . .[33]

The destiny of the young, as advocated in this 1963 essay, lies in seeking happiness in perpetual commitment and confrontation. Yet, at the same time, this youthful restlessness must be made productive and harnessed to a foundational purpose or institution. It must be socialized and stopped from growing into a blind antiestablishmentarian and self-destructive impulse or energy. The meaning of youth, so explained a recitational poem from the same period, was "to strive forward, work selflessly, and always remain modest." Collectively written by the May

---

31. "Zenyang peiyang he baochi wangsheng de geming reqing" (How to cultivate and maintain robust revolutionary enthusiasm), *Chinese Youth*, nos. 3–4 (February 1963): 2–5.

32. See Dittmer, *China's Continuous Revolution*, 81–90.

33. Gan Feng, "He zichan jieji xiangle zhuyi huaqing jiexian: tan zenyang zhengque kandai wuzhi shenghuo" (Stay clear of bourgeois hedonism: on how to correctly view material life), *Chinese Youth*, no. 16 (August 1963): 13.

Fourth Literary Society at Peking University, the poem, "Let youth shine forth," ends with a crescendo of directives:

Female chorus: Offer it to our motherland,
  Our fiery life!
Male chorus: Offer it to the world,
  Our brilliant youth!
Together: Offer it to the future,
  The principle of our existence:
  Forever revolution![34]

The Re-enchantment of Necessity

The central conflict of the play *The Young Generation* seems to revolve around contrasting perceptions of happiness. All of the action takes place in the living room of the Lin family home in an industrial suburb of Shanghai (figure 6). The time is the beginning of summer, when the main character, Xiao Jiye, a 27-year-old geologist, returns from his prospecting team stationed in the frontier region of Qinghai to verify the team's recent discovery of a rare mineral resource. His old classmate Lin Yusheng, now also a teammate, is already back in Shanghai on sick leave, supposedly suffering from disabling rheumatoid arthritis in his knees. While Xiao Jiye, three years older, is passionate about his work and can hardly wait to go back to the field, Lin Yusheng much prefers life in the city and even forges a medical report in order to stay in Shanghai. The dénouement is not reached until Yusheng's misdeed is exposed, and a long-held family secret is subsequently revealed. In the process, all members of the Lin family (his parents, younger sister, and girlfriend), as well as Xiao Jiye's grandmother, play an indispensable role in accordance with each character's symbolic composition and function. The play ends with a rousing scene where everyone is gathered onstage to send Lin Yusheng back to the prospecting team, his younger sister Lin Lan to the countryside, and other graduating students of the Geological Institute to remote areas, including Qinghai and Tibet. Among the older generation left be-

---

34. The May Fourth Literary Society of Peking University (recorded by Li Guanding, Yang Kuangman, Wang Yi), "Rang qingchun shanguang (jiti langsong shi)" (Let youth shine forth [recitational poem]), *Shikan* (Poetry), no. 71 (February 1964): 46.

hind, incidentally, is Xiao Jiye the tireless young man, recovering from the removal of a tumorous growth in one leg.

As Kai-yu Hsü comments in an anthology, the play, by "treating the problem of getting young people to work in faraway places, touches a sore issue known as the 'rustification of the young generation,' or the endless task of fighting the corrupting influence of city life." For this reason, Hsü observes, "it has continuing significance in the People's Republic," even in the reform era of the 1980s.[35] The corrupting influence of city life inflicts its damages mainly on Lin Yusheng, although its seemingly resourceful agent is a shadowy Young Wu, who never appears onstage. By making Young Wu an absent presence, critics have long agreed, the playwright showed great ingenuity in highlighting the constant and invisible danger of bourgeois ideology and lifestyle.[36] Symptoms of Yusheng's infirmity extend beyond the forged document he submits as an excuse. They include signs of his being a deft urban consumer and his conception of a happy life. Yusheng makes his first entrance by pushing onto the stage a bicycle draped with shopping bags. He is getting ready to celebrate his girlfriend Xia Qianru's birthday with canned food, dessert, and a fancy dress.[37] The future he anticipates for himself and Qianru is one of stability and high cultural entertainment: "During the day we go to work together. After we come back in the evening, we can listen to music, read a novel or some poetry, go to a movie. On weekends we can go to the park, or get together with some friends. . . . Of course we'll

---

35. Kai-yu Hsü, introduction to *The Young Generation*, in *Literature of the People's Republic of China*, ed. Kai-yu Hsü and Ting Wang (Bloomington: Indiana University Press, 1980), 628.

36. See Yao Wenyuan, "The Song of Youth in the Age of Socialist Revolution," *Literary Gazette* (October 1963): 14. Nonetheless, Yao Wenyuan also thinks that the audience should be clearly informed of what becomes of Young Wu, the despicable "representative of bourgeois forces."

37. In the 1963 version, Lin Yusheng is the first person onstage in act 1. This was changed in the 1964 edition, where Xiao Jiye appears first in order to set a different tone for the play. See Chen Yun, *Nianqing de yidai* (The young generation), *Scripts*, no. 104 (August 1963): 2; Chen Yun, Zhang Lihui, and Xu Jingxian, *Nianqing de yidai* (The young generation) (Beijing: Zhongguo xiju, 1964), 2. Except for minor rearranging and rewording, these two versions show no significant differences. Nonetheless, they will be compared continually in this chapter, with the first version referred to as the original edition, and the second as the revised edition. The page reference immediately following a citation refers to the revised edition.

6. Stage design, *Nianqing de yidai* (The young generation) (1963). From *Xiji bao* (Journal of drama) (Beijing, November 1963).

have to do a good job at our work. We definitely will have to score some successes in our careers" (21).

This picture of routinized urban existence, however, appears to Xiao Jiye—the positive role model that the play creates—to be unbearably banal, trivial, and selfish. During the first exchange between these two friends, Yusheng asks Jiye whether he still writes poetry. This allows Jiye a chance to describe, with full lyrical rhythm, his life as a geologist: "Life in the field is itself poetry! High mountains, dark forests, deserts and rivers, everywhere is poetry, everywhere is a struggle" (7). What the one-time poet does not tell Yusheng about is the leg injury that he suffered in an accident, which is another reason for his coming back to Shanghai at this point. In act 3, at a high point of the clash between their divergent approaches to life, Jiye and Yusheng engage in a heated debate about their worldviews. With mounting eloquence, Jiye charges Yusheng with insulating himself complacently in his own little universe, reminds him of the mission to bring happiness to millions of other people, and warns him against putting his own interest before that of the country. The danger of Yusheng's behavior, Jiye orates, comes from his not wanting to continue the revolution. "The danger also lies in the corruption of your mind by individualism before you even know it. It will take away your ideals, wear down your fighting will, and drag you deeper and deeper into the bourgeois quagmire" (75).

The "bourgeois quagmire" into which the young generation must be prevented from sliding was a stock political phrase during this period of revolutionary lyricism. As used by Xiao Jiye here, it more often describes the inertia and banality of everyday life in secular modernity than it does a clearly identified hostile force. The image of a sucking "quagmire" (*nikeng*) directly denounces the narrow private world (*xiao tiandi*) that threatens to substitute for the global will and vision of a revolutionary foot soldier. It articulates an almost idealist fear of impurity, contamination, and unwholesomeness. This implicit elitism is most strident when pursuits of material satisfaction are frequently condemned as vulgar and in bad taste. When Jiye criticizes Yusheng for obsessing about his personal happiness, he makes it clear that the point is not whether self-interest is legitimate or not, but that a morally better existence is one that is fully integrated into a collective cause. He goes on to invalidate the concept of legitimacy by arguing that an individual right, even if it is legitimate, needs to be subordinated to the putative interests of the nation-state (74).

Part of the reasoning here reflects an entrenched Confucian tradition of moralizing human behavior and relations. This philosophical tradition and discursive habit, reinforced by a Leninist opposition between society at large and the socialist state, finds in legitimate self-interest nothing but a moral betrayal of, or even a latent threat to, the collective good.[38] The fear of impurity, at the same time, also expresses a deep-seated cultural anxiety over a possible loss of national identity and distinction. For "bourgeois individualism," while rejected as incompatible with proletarian ideals, is primarily constructed as a Western infection and malaise. The

---

38. See, for instance, Yao Wenyuan's analysis of Lin Yusheng's notion of "legitimate individualism" in his "The Song of Youth in the Age of Socialist Revolution," *Literary Gazette* (October 1963): esp. 10. The two key texts that determined the vanguardist critique of everyday life during this period were Lenin's "'Left-Wing' Communism—An Infantile Disorder" and "The Tasks of the Youth Leagues," both written in 1920 and collected in Robert C. Tucker, ed., *The Lenin Anthology* (New York: Norton, 1975), 550–618, 661–74. Lenin's concern with the continuation of the communist revolution in everyday life had a major impact on the policies adopted by the Tenth Plenum of the Eighth Congress of the CCP in the fall of 1962.

"quagmire" is doubly reprehensible, therefore, because it is foreign and heterogeneous, as much as synonymous with degeneration and capitulation.

Moreover, the same marshy area of danger also includes personal feelings and attachments, which will only mire any resolute action. When Lin Yusheng's girlfriend, Xia Qianru, engages in self-examination, for example, she characterizes her recent emotional dependence as having fallen into a "thick and deep quagmire" (89). Earlier in the play, her involvement with Yusheng makes her rather compliant to his plan of remaining in the city, although she also feels constant pangs of conscience. At one point, Qianru reveals her hesitations to Lin Lan, Yusheng's younger sister, who bluntly questions why she should be so submissive. "You will understand it when you fall in love with someone," Qianru feebly explains. Upon this revelation, the eighteen-year-old high school graduate solemnly announces: "If this is what love is all about, I will never fall in love in my life. Never!" (44).

As the female and younger counterpart of Xiao Jiye, Lin Lan is also presented as a positive role model with abundant poetic passion, if only more zealous and excitable. Part of her function in the play is to glamorize the current policy of relocating educated youth from the city to the countryside. So she not only refuses to be tempted to study at a film school, but she also manages to miss the entrance exams for an agricultural institute by saving the life of a heart-attack patient. What she sets her mind and imagination on is "engaging in another revolution" on a collective farm in the mountainous Jinggangshan area. In the end, her enthusiasm is so contagious that Li Rongsheng, a "social youth" two years her junior, happily quits idling around and joins her in a new long march to the hinterland. Oftentimes serving as the comic relief of the play, Li Rongsheng is a minor character whose presence nonetheless reveals an incoherent core of social reality. His initial disdain for menial labor, criticized as an instance of bourgeois influence, darkly acknowledges the growing problem of providing jobs for urban youth. In addition, his lack of proper occupation, in spite of his working-class family background, brings to the surface a rigid social structure and stratification that is unable to recognize an individual with no institutional affiliation. This nonrecognition, just as in the case of denying legitimacy to individual interests, often translates into a political ambiguity or even suspicion of whomever remains independent in society. Hence, the use of awkward categories such as "social youth" or "people in society" when such terms actually designate those who are marginalized in the new socialist order and are supported by no particular work units.[39]

In many ways Lin Lan demonstrates onstage the upbringing and training of the Red Guard generation of the forthcoming Cultural Revolution. Her ardent idealism and self-abnegation identify her as a proud youth of the Mao Zedong era.[40] Her epigonic pain at having missed all the great historical moments adds to her impatience with an ordinary existence. She decides to go to the countryside because "Chairman Mao and the Party call upon us to aid the agricultural front" (13). Telling herself that "since our fathers are a generation of iron men, we must not be a bunch of cowards" (69), she longs to live "where Chairman Mao once lived, and where revolutionary martyrs shed their blood" (93). In this exuberant high school graduate, we find an ideal person envisioned by the lyrical age: while her passion constitutes her thinking, her motivation acknowledges no internal origin. Allowing herself no interiority or self-reflection, she derives confidence and pleasurable reassurance from continually striving to merge into a grand collective subject. Her happiness lies in becoming a faithful seed—wherever she is sown, she will grow, blossom, and yield fruit (104). More concretely, she expresses her anticipation of the revolutionary future through an unwavering respect for her father, a respect that entails nothing short of filial piety. (To this structure of familial subordination and its implications, we will return in the next section.)

The creation of Xiao Jiye and Lin Lan as inspiring characters onstage

---

39. It is clear that a Leninist resistance to society is revealed by such loaded demographic categories. In its official as well as popular usage, "society" often indicates an impure, complicated, and damaging influence on the morale of an emerging new order. See, for example, Hou Jinjing, "Notice and Address Issues that Millions of People Are Concerned with," *Journal of Drama,* no. 184 (April 1964): 19–24. When explicating the significance of the play *Never Forget,* the critic emphasizes that "every worker, and every member of the cadre will have to remain in a web of contacts with various social relations (relatives, friends, and people from the same hometown). As a result, all these social groups will form an extremely complicated relationship in our everyday life" (21).

40. See Mi Hedu, *Hongweibing zhe yidai* (The red guard generation) (Hong Kong: Joint Publishing, 1993), esp. 58–67. For a psychological portrayal of the Red Guard generation, see also Anita Chan, *Children of Mao: Personality Development and Political Activism in the Red Guard Generation* (Seattle: University of Washington Press, 1985).

historically answered the question of how the young generation ought to socialize and integrate itself into the revolutionary enterprise. Social integration for youth could be achieved only through political mobilization, since the existing social structure was not viewed as stable but rather as in the permanent process of exciting transformation. Youthfulness and social movement, therefore, formed the basis of a rhapsodic confidence of the lyrical age, to which *The Young Generation* was self-consciously erected as a magnifying mirror. Far from random, for example, was the playwright's decision to focus on graduates from a geology institute, because in the early 1960s Liu Shaoqi, then president of the People's Republic, had in a memorable phrase romanticized their future occupation as contiguous with revolutionary warfare: "Geological workers are the guerrillas for the period of peaceful construction."[41] This peculiar metaphor calls forth a central myth of the lyrical age, namely, that peace is to be waged with the same intensity and devotion as war. The source for the new lyricism, following this mythical thinking, lies not in routinized work or orderliness, but rather in constant motion and the excitement of overcoming inertia.

Within the play, the action is therefore meaningfully set at the beginning of summer, "the season when high school graduates decide either to go on to college or to work, and when college graduates are about to enter the real world; it is a time when young people are filled with hope, happiness, passion, and restlessness" (2).[42] Yet the play and its dramatic conflict are structurally disallowed to pursue the various possibilities faced by the young; they do not even address as a concrete problem society's growing inability to absorb or accommodate its young population. The choice of living either in a city or in a rural area is recast as a moral and ideological decision over which form of happiness to pursue and what political vision to identify with. Much poetic passion and

---

41. Quoted in Shi Tao, Xia Chun, and Shi Lianxing, "*Nianqing de yidai* daoyan sanren tan" (Conversation among three directors about *The young generation*), *Journal of Drama*, no. 176 (October 1963): 7. This connection to Liu Shaoqi may partly explain why the play was denounced during the Cultural Revolution when he was disgraced and driven from the presidency.

42. In the 1963 version, the time is instead described as full of "hope, vexation, passion and restlessness" (2). The minor change here is indicative of the general line of revision; the reading of the play is more uplifting, more heroic, and more idealistic as a result.

philosophical grandiosity is generated in the process, often rendering inexpressible the thorny details of a mundane situation. By the end of the play, for instance, Lin Yusheng agrees to return to his prospecting team, but we are never certain what will become of his relationship to Xia Qianru, who is apparently assigned to a different area. Instead, before the final curtain falls, Lin Lan, the spokesperson of the young generation, is to speak with the "utmost passion" and directly to the audience. At this point, the audience can no longer watch as spectators but must partake of the communal exhortation and share the same "hope, happiness, passion, and restlessness."

> Lin Lan: (*Walks to the front, facing the audience*) Good-bye, teachers! Classmates! Comrades! We are on our way, leaving you and heading to different posts. Like seeds spread over the land, we will take root there, germinate, blossom, and yield fruit. Good-bye! Dear comrades, we are on our way to create a beautiful future, with your expectations and blessings! (104)

The necessity of such a passionate life, as has been suggested, grows from resisting the bureaucratic rationalizations of political and social engineering. The massive transfer of educated youth to the countryside had the logistical purpose of managing unemployment in the urban area; it agreed with the general policy of developing streamlined socialist "producer cities" (instead of "consumer cities"), the point of which was still to enhance urban manageability.[43] Demographically and politically, this transfer carried out the strategy of populating the frontier regions with Han Chinese settlers. On a more visionary level, the relocation program was to contribute to the long-term goal of eliminating the entrenched disparity between the city and the countryside, although the result often seemed to add new strains to the relation between peasants and city dwellers.[44]

Given that central planning was the guiding principle and ideology underlying all such objectives, the source of spectacular youthful enthusiasm could not but be grand state rationality. The target of this manufac-

---

43. See R. J. R. Kirkby, *Urbanization in China: Town and Country in a Developing Economy, 1949–2000 A.D.* (New York: Columbia University Press, 1985), esp. 21–53, 103–33.

44. See Gardner, "Educated Youth and Urban-Rural Inequalities, 1958–66," 268–69.

tured passion, therefore, is to overcome apathy as much as to sublimate mundane details of life. While trying to first persuade Xia Qianru of the need to accept her job assignment, Xiao Jiye explains: "Of all the graduates, who doesn't have some practical difficulties? For instance, some may have a family problem; some may have an emotional entanglement; some may suffer from bad health; still some others may be sensitive to cold or heat, and so on. If everyone stresses only their own problems, what do you think will happen?" (46). Lin Yusheng's greatest offense, in the eyes of Xiao Jiye, is to put his own happiness "above the collective interest and outside state planning" (74). For this reason, Xiao Jiye himself must be projected as a hero whose last concern is his own physical pain or well-being. When faced with the possibility of losing a leg to cancer, he sees no alternative but staying at his job as a geologist. "Even if they really have to amputate it, I will return to the team on crutches. I may not climb mountains anymore, but I can stay in the flat area; I may not go outside anymore, but I can work in a tent. No matter what, I will work on the surveying team till the end of my life. . . ." (79).

Another instance of Xiao Jiye's poetic attitude toward life, this moment also reveals that a new work ethic is being promoted, and that the ordinary is reenchanted as an integral part of the glorious whole. If this political economy of passion exhibited on stage is run by the cultural department in the bureaucratic central planning, there is a parallel structure of symbolic rationality that oversees and resolves the dramatic conflict. The need to train a revolutionary young generation will acquire its symbolic value largely in terms of continuing a family tradition.

Family as the Symbolic Order

Three generations are represented in the play, and every character is related, either symbolically or biologically, as a member of one extended revolutionary family. The youngest generation—the third—includes not only all the main characters, but other students of the Geological Institute and high school graduates. The parents of Lin Yusheng and Lin Lan stand for the middle generation, here portrayed as a generation of revolutionary veterans or functionaries. Father Lin Jian, an invincible PLA general in the past, suggests a natural continuity between the task of socialist construction and the history of revolutionary war. Upon retiring from the army, he asked to work in agriculture but was instead appointed to be in charge of a large factory, a duty he now discharges with the diligence of a general. As we soon realize, his specific job bears little relevance, as long as he fulfills his position as a revolutionary father figure.[45] Mother Xia Shujuan represents the bureaucratic class that is usually referred to as "state cadre." Now in her mid-forties, she follows a routine work schedule and spends more time with the two children than her husband, who is always kept busy on the frontline and comes home only once in a while. In one stage production, the director decided to show Xia Shujuan as a sickly person in order to make her laxity toward Lin Yusheng more credible.[46] In the revised version, by contrast, she shows no signs of illness, but she still acts the indulgent mother who is also to learn a hard lesson in the course of the play.

While the anchoring role given to father Lin Jian may suggest a patriarchal inclination, the presence of Grandma Xiao seems to counterbalance that impression. As the only spokesperson of the first generation, Grandma Xiao, a retired worker, has an enormous investment in her parentless grandson, Xiao Jiye. With considerable self-control and dignity, she is the person to break the news to Jiye that he may lose his leg. To encourage the stricken young man, she sits him down and narrates the hardship she went through to raise him, her only grandchild, since 1936 when the little boy was one year old and his father was murdered by the Nationalist Guomindang. Incidentally, Jiye's father was her last son to die, and Jiye's mother is never mentioned (61). Because of her seniority and contribution, Grandma Xiao also commands great respect from the second generation. In the revised version of 1964, she directly intervenes and cautions Lin Jian to mind the goings-on in his family, complaining in particular that Xia Shujuan has been less than rigorous in educating the children (48–49). Through her concern about the well-being of the third generation, the task of training revolutionary successors is highlighted and put on the agenda.

What Grandma Xiao embodies on stage is a firm and gentle "revolutionary mother," a widely accepted honorific title for older women revolutionaries in China during the 1960s.[47] She bestows her maternal care

---

45. In an earlier version of the play, Lin Jian is still a general.
46. See Shi Tao, Xia Chun, and Shi Lianxing, "Conversation Among Three Directors," *Journal of Drama*, no. 176 (October 1963): 4–11.
47. After *The Young Generation* was produced in Beijing, a reporter from *Liter-

from the distance of a grandmother, which seems to enable her to put in perspective her love for the child. Gracefully aged and versed in folkloric wisdom, she has the greatest stake in ensuring that the revolutionary cause, now recounted as a family tradition, will be continued. In the play, Grandma Xiao is a generalized grandparent, whose gender does not lead to automatic questioning of patriarchy but on the contrary adds to it a benign and personable feature.[48] Of no small genealogical import is the fact that she is Xiao Jiye's paternal grandmother; hence, her surname Xiao, which has long replaced her own family name. At the same time, as a close next-door neighbor to the Lins, she participates in their family life as grandmother to both Lin Yusheng and Lin Lan. In a carefully arranged plot development, Lin Lan receives her first edification from Grandma Xiao at the conclusion of act 2. By the end of act 3, with little time lapsed since the previous act, Lin Lan is already making a solemn guarantee to her father, Lin Jian: "Do not worry, Father! We will march to the end along your road!" (84–85).

Lin Lan, as we have witnessed, is the more poetic of the two young people in the Lin family, although she is also more of a doctrinaire, as characterized by Lin Yusheng (10). She is quick to criticize her brother and even his girlfriend, and she would sooner share her thoughts with her father than seek support from her mother. While praised for personifying the "purity, bravery and high degree of self-disciplining possessed by young people raised by the Communist education,"[49] Lin Lan always listens to her father as the admiring daughter she is. She presents a continual semiotic and political taming, since the Yan'an era, of the woman who had been placed in a subject position by May Fourth liberal human-

---

ary Gazette interviewed some "old soldiers" (an army general, the vice-president of the national women's federation, and the deputy minister of geology) to reflect their appreciation of the play. Upon entering Mother Yang Zhihua's home, the reporter wrote, you would immediately feel that this was a "revolutionary family." Mother Yang (widow of the prominent Communist leader and theorist Qu Qiubai) particularly identified with Grandma Xiao in the play; the character onstage "expresses what we old people have in mind. We are just like her in life." See Fang Mao, "Laozhanshi tan *Nianqing de yidai*" (Old soldiers talk about *The young generation*), *Literary Gazette*, no. 311 (October 1963): 2–7.

48. Her role foreshadows what is to become a standard grandmother in the "model opera" *Red Lantern* of the Cultural Revolution.

49. Yao Wenyuan, "The Song of Youth in the Age of Socialist Revolution," *Literary Gazette*, no. 311 (October 1963): 14.

ism. A central trope for this process is precisely to change her role from that of a lover to a faithful daughter, often a daughter to the Party.[50] In concert with this identity makeover, Lin Lan must be free of attachments and have no romantic interests; her male friend Li Rongsheng needs to be younger and even childlike. Yet nowhere are the patriarchal values more readily affirmed than in the central action of the play, which amounts to a communal effort at rescuing Lin Yusheng the prodigal son, who finally comes to his senses and becomes aware of his obligations as family heir. His new consciousness acquires a general significance through revelations about his true identity, which also serve to convey the centrality of family structure to the symbolic order.

From all appearances, Lin Yusheng takes great pride in his distinguished family background. He confidently enjoys the prestige that comes with his father's prominence and he knows when to use his family's influence and connections to his own benefit. When Xiao Jiye warns him of sinking into the "bourgeois quagmire," all Yusheng needs to say is "Don't you scare me. I'm not from a bourgeois family" (75). In the earlier version, he promptly adds, "Please bear in mind that my family is a revolutionary family," to which Jiye will answer, "But that honor belongs to your parents."[51] This exchange, deleted from the 1964 edition, hints at the different social status between the Lins and the Xiaos: a cadre family versus a working class family. The modified version, however, prevents this divisive reading by giving Jiye's rebuttal a more magnanimous and more general appeal: "We are all revolutionary offspring. So we need to be all the more careful" (75). The subsequent revelation is not to contradict Jiye's statement here, for that would truly put in disarray a host of basic assumptions about the constitution of a revolutionary tradition. On the contrary, Yusheng is to be confirmed as a revolutionary descendant, except that he is not the biological son of Lin Jian and Xia Shujuan.

This brings us to the climax of the play, when Lin Yusheng tearfully reads the farewell letter that his mother wrote him, with her own blood,

---

50. See Meng Yue and Dai Jinhua, *Fuchu lishi dibiao: xiandai funü wenxue yanjiu* (Emerging from history: studies in modern women's literature) (Kaifeng: Henan renmin, 1989), 263–69. For another interesting interpretation, although from a different perspective, see C. T. Hsia, "Residual Femininity: Women in Chinese Communist Fiction," in *Chinese Communist Literature,* ed. Cyril Birch (New York: Praeger, 1963), 158–79.

51. *Scripts* (August 1963): 22.

moments before she was executed by "the enemy" for participating in a labor movement. This primal scene of sacrifice happened twenty-four years earlier, when Yusheng (in the earliest production his name meant "prison-born") was three days old. Since then, Lin Jian has taken care of the young boy, and he and Xia Shujuan decide to tell the truth only now because Yusheng, in Lin Jian's opinion, puts to shame more than the family by forging the medical report. "You have humiliated the working class. . . . You failed the Party's effort in raising you, failed your teachers' instructions. Worst of all, you let down your deceased parents!" (82) With everyone present duly shocked, Lin Jian produces the letter from a box and orders Yusheng to read it aloud. The stage is at this moment turned into an emotionalized history class by the public reading.

> Lin Yusheng: (*Reads aloud*) "My dear child:
>
> The executioner has raised his murderous knife. Our comrades are singing in an impassioned voice, and we are going to the execution ground very soon. From now on, you will never see your own parents.
>
> Dear child, I write this letter to you so that you will remember: your parents were both workers. . . . You may forget your father, you may forget your mother, but you may never forget that there are still class enemies in the world! You must fight for the noble ideals of communism! . . .
>
> Time is up. The doors are clanging! The executioner is here! Farewell, my dear child! We are leaving, but don't you forget your roots, not your roots . . ." (Toward the letter) Mother, my own mother! (*Hunches over on the table, crying*) (83)[52]

So much had to go into this document for it to be usable in the present context that its first version was twice as long, until one sensible PLA general in the audience commented that, realistically, the mother would not have sufficient time to pen an essay once the executioner was in sight.[53] Nonetheless, its overt constructedness did not seem to compromise its

---

52. Act 3 is translated by Kevin O'Connor and Constantine Tung, collected in *Literature of the People's Republic of China*, 629–41. For a full translation of the letter, see 639.

53. See Shi Tao, Xia Chun, and Shi Lianxing, "Conversation Among Three Directors," 6.

The Lyrical Age and Its Discontents **189**

emotional reverberations or ideological pertinence. It was even published in the national newspaper *Chinese Youth* so that readers could digest and memorize the text.[54] Within the play, the guilty conscience activated by the letter strikes not only Lin Yusheng, who soon after dashes into the timely thunderstorm that rages outside, but also Lin Jian the adoptive father. "My old comrades-in-arms! You sacrificed everything for the revolution, exchanging your blood and life for what we have today. But, what can I say . . . I let you down. I haven't brought him up as someone you'd hoped for" (83). In fact, everyone at the scene, except Lin Lan, has reason to feel ashamed: Xia Shujuan, the doting mother, falls silent; Xia Qianru, the compliant girlfriend, realizes what she must do. The pleading voice from the past loudly demands redemptive action.

The logic that fulfills itself in this climactic scene is deeply rooted in the notion of indebtedness, or even in a secularized version of original sin. Since the ultimate sacrifice was already made in an exchange, gratitude becomes the only payment that a later generation can offer to the revolutionary martyrs. That sacrifice instills a guilt-ridden self-conception in the young generation, and it requires a conformist relationship to the great deeds of the past. In this logic of symbolic exchange, forgetting the past constitutes an unspeakable betrayal and amounts to denying one's own origin and therefore one's identity. By contrast, the effort to keep alive a historical memory expresses the desire for continuity and for making the future comprehensible by connecting it, if not subjecting it, to the heroic past. A significant portion of the cultural-political energy in the young People's Republic was spent, as Dittmer observes, to satisfy the need of reminding the revolutionary Party of its charismatic origins and commitment.[55]

Yet even greater cultural specificity resides in the predominant family structure, through which the demand for gratitude as a form of ideological conformity is made in *The Young Generation*. The revelation of Lin Yusheng's true identity does not at all result in the collapse of his world or a reversal of fortune, such as a family secret, also revealed against the background of ominous thunder, would do in a classical tragedy by Cao Yu in the 1930s. Instead of bringing it to a crisis, the revelation fortifies the family by turning its symbolic composition into its own reason for

---

54. See *Chinese Youth* (5 October 1963).
55. Dittmer, *China's Continuous Revolution*, 25.

being and its strength. As the son to both his biological and adoptive parents, who represent the past and the present of the same cause, Yusheng is doubly obliged to continue the revolution as a family tradition. What the revelation and its subsequent effects illustrate, however, is not that the revolutionary cause is one family's business; rather, it has the life of a family enterprise, which can be sustained only by the continuing efforts of generations. This is certainly Lin Jian's understanding when, after Yusheng runs off to come to his senses in the drenching rain, he asks of his daughter, Lin Lan: "Our generation took great pains to seize political power and establish a proletarian family enterprise [*jiaye*].... How about our next generation? Will they all continue along our road to its end?" (84)

The composition of the Lin family makes intelligible a parallel between filial piety and the historical mission of the young generation. It also helps naturalize the family as the symbolic order of the new socialist society, which now identifies and positions its members in terms of family relations. What complicates this new symbolic order is that while it models itself after the extended family, it also discourages the natural family as the smallest and most exclusive social unit. Thus, the two recombined or artificial families in the play: the Xiaos and the Lins.[56] This type of heavily denaturalized revolutionary family would find its classical representation in the "model opera" *Hongdeng ji* (The red lantern), in which a family of three generations accommodates three separate surnames. This communal family also embodies an unmistakable utopian effort at creating a personable revolutionary society.

The flip side of this dominant order, however, is that anyone who does not belong in the socialized familial structure is viewed as a stranger or

---

56. In one of the earliest articles explicating the significance of *The Young Generation*, the author apparently noticed the importance of introducing a new concept and practice of kinship in the new socialist society, and he concluded that revolution is similar to a family enterprise and that family education was part of class education. "Family-based social relations are historically extinct in our real life, but traditional family and kinship concepts are far from eliminated. They are still part of the remaining feudalist ideology. For us today, children are not only the next generation of the family, but also of the revolution. Children and their parents are not only family members, but also comrades in the continual development of the revolutionary cause." See Wen Ping, "A Thought-provoking Theme: A Reading of the Play *The Young Generation*," *Journal of Drama*, no. 176 (August 1963): 24.

even an automatic suspect. Lin Lan's young friend Li Rongsheng, for example, is a problematic "social youth" until he meets Lin Jian, becomes domesticated, and addresses Xia Shujuan as "aunt" (*bomu*). While Lin Lan successfully introduces Li Rongsheng to her family, her brother Lin Yusheng never manages to bring home, or onstage, Young Wu, a dubious friend of bad influence and a different class origin.[57] In fact, friendship now has to be reinvented because it often presents a lateral association that undermines the family-centered vertical social structure.[58] Thanks to the new value of familiarity, Lin Yusheng's girlfriend, Xia Qianru, cannot be a total stranger but happens to be the niece of his foster mother. What the lyrical age envisions for itself is a society that does not need or acknowledge strangers. It is an enlarged family to which any unfamiliar element or presence evokes the horror of a quagmire, of invading virus and infectious diseases. Yet to those who accept and participate in the symbolic order, as Lin Yusheng describes with much gratitude before returning to the prospecting team, "our society is truly a big warm family. If someone falls, numerous comradely hands will reach out from all directions. Now all comrades have extended their hands to me. . . . Please wait and see" (101). The dramatic conflict is resolved only when he begins to heed his duty and indebtedness to the "big warm family."

Climax: The Ecstasy of Staged Life

The final scene of *The Young Generation* creates an arousing display of motion and youthful anticipation. Visionary stage directions suggest how to achieve the desired effect:

(One after another, trucks pass in the near background, carrying young people on their way to life; waves of passionate singing come through.)
    (People enthusiastically bid farewell to one another.)
        . . . . .

---

57. According to Lin Lan, Young Wu is a parasite who comes from a wealthy family and does not work (10). Apparently his family used to own a large business and now lives on interest since its property was nationalized in the mid-1950s.

58. For an earlier study of this topic, see Ezra F. Vogel, "From Friendship to Comradeship: The Change in Personal Relations in China," *China Quarterly*, no. 21 (January-March 1965): 46–60.

7. Stage design, *Nianqing de yidai* (The young generation) (1963). From *Xiji bao* (Journal of drama) (Beijing, November 1963).

> (The young people [onstage] wave good-bye to the audience; trucks continue to pass nearby; singing arises; further away trains are moving into the distance.) (104)

In the midst of this landscape of socialist modernization and a crescendo of commotion, Lin Lan the practicing poet delivers, "with utmost passion," an officious parting speech to her parents, Grandma Xiao, Brother Jiye, and, most important, the theater audience. Just as Lin Yusheng onstage is compelled to be grateful to a caring socialist society of a family, so the audience of "classmates and comrades" must participate in the communal salutation to the revolutionary youth. Here the desire to engage and educate the audience finds its most explicit expression. From the perspective of genre conventions, this ending serves to reinforce public space and launches the dramatic action beyond the limited area of the Lin family household (figure 7). One way to take stock of the political agenda of the play is indeed to see it as actively eliminating a viable living room drama.[59] A gradual disappearance of enclosed domestic space agrees well with the central ideological message that the play wants to convey. In one

---

59. See Raymond Williams, "Theatre as a Political Forum," in his *The Politics of Modernism: Against the New Conformists,* ed. with intro. by Tony Pinkney (London: Verso, 1989), 81–94, for a succinct analysis of the formal and intellectual crisis within the naturalist convention of focusing on the domestic bourgeois household in European drama at the turn of the century.

actual staging by the Beijing People's Art Theater, the set designer found it necessary to create a new environment for the final scene, where, with the help of a rotating stage, a panoramic view of the cityscape of Shanghai came to light and replaced the background of an encircling wall.[60]

The theatrical dynamic at the final moment is complex because it invites audience participation but deliberately precludes any possible interaction. By looking in the direction of the audience and addressing it as a collectivity, actors onstage are no longer part of a safely distanced spectacle for observation. On the contrary, they actively reach out and seek to elevate the audience, while dominating the interplay by prescribing audience reaction. This interpolating operation is consciously carried out throughout the play. In one director's rendering, when Lin Lan vows to continue the cause of her father's generation, instead of verbalizing her intention, she comes forward from the rear of the stage to join Grandma Xiao and her father. Once their visual dominance is established, "the three of them direct their excited, grave but earnest gaze toward the audience, and slowly move it up and beyond. . . ."[61] The same guiding gaze, in fact, does more than pin the audience in a morally and politically passive position. Since it is no longer a personalized look, it also ricochets, as it were, to impose self-examination on the actors themselves. The experience of playing Lin Lan both in the theater and on the screen, actress Cao Lei reported, "was not only two years of learning from her, but also two years of following the example of progressive people in real life and of studying advanced ideas."[62] At the Chinese Children's Art Theater, the director recounted, the entire staff assigned to produce *The Young Generation* was seized by a growing anxiety when they realized that they could not successfully enact the play unless they first developed "ideas and sentiments as well as qualities that are characteristic of our times."[63] For them, too,

---

60. See Liu Lu, "Tan *Nianqing de yidai* bujing sheji" (On the set design of *The young generation*), *Journal of Drama,* no. 171 (November 1963): 34–35. A different design, by the Chinese Children's Art Theater, combined the original two scenes and created one setting that relocates the site of action to a more public place—the intermediary area connecting the Lin and Xiao households. See Xu Xiaozhong, "Directorial Notes," *Journal of Drama,* no. 182 (February 1964): 38.

61. Xu Xiaozhong, "Directorial Notes," 38.

62. Cao Lei, "Zai he Lin Lan xiangchu de rizi li" (In the days spent with Lin Lan), *Dazhong dianying* (Popular cinema), nos. 296–97 (August-September 1965): 44.

63. See Xu Xiaozhong, "Directorial Notes," 39.

participation in the play was a training session, professional as well as ideological.

What we witness here is a telling instance of collectivized cultural production in the lyrical age. The theatrical dimension of *The Young Generation* revealed the centrality of the stage to the logic of the popular imagination of this visionary period. It was an age when the stage was expected to be a truthful mirror of life, and life itself was celebrated as a grand stage for purposeful action. Staging became the most expedient and most effective art form through which to enact national aspiration and generate revolutionary enthusiasm. Not surprisingly, it was at the height of this lyrical period that theater rapidly superseded the novel, cinema, and even poetry in its status as socialist mass culture.[64]

In a 1964 article, "Masters in Life, Masters on Stage," a well-known actress-cum-writer marveled at the continuity between contemporary life and the stage. A parade of metaphors helped Huang Zongying illustrate the importance of theater to the unfolding of a "socialist cultural revolution." The stage "is the fighting ground between new ideas and old forces; it is the platform for a singing contest to express communist ideals; it is the forum for a heated debate between the proletarian and the bourgeois world views; it is the fatal battleground of class struggle."[65] A literary theoretician also sought to explain, from a slightly different angle, the relevance of the "seething life" represented on stage during 1963–64:

> In this condition, drama is more than art work for people to appreciate, and theater is more than a place to entertain. These plays, because they profoundly reflect the revolutionary spirit of our time and portray the intense struggle in our historical period, become a mirror that helps people understand life in our times, a searchlight that illuminates the road for people to advance on, a textbook for life that guides people in how to engage in struggle.[66]

---

64. For an illuminating discussion of the obsession with the "stage" metaphor in modern Chinese political culture, see Joseph Levenson, *Revolution and Cosmopolitanism: The Western Stage and the Chinese Stages* (Berkeley: University of California Press, 1971).

65. Huang Zongying, "Shenghuo de zhuren, wutai de zhuren: dayan xiandai jumu suixiang" (Masters in life, masters on stage: thoughts on mass productions of modern drama), *Literary Gazette*, no. 314 (January 1964): 14–17.

66. Feng Mu, "Wutai shang feiteng de shenghuo: cong jinnian lai huaju chuangzuo

In one case, theater is viewed as restaging, although in a more intense dramatic form, the confrontations in real life; in another, the stage is called upon to project greater clarity onto reality. Both understandings emphasize the crystallizing function of public theater rather than its cathartic or entertaining aspects. The mass appeal of theater lies in the prevailing metaphor that "all the world is a stage," which encourages us all to dream of, or even participate in, a simplified and yet highly purposeful existence. It is the politicized theater that encapsulates a deep utopian desire for global transformation. For theater best expresses the impulse to sublimate life into an artistic experience; in the final analysis, it defies experiential time by staging a spatial and theatrical spectacle. The beauty of such theatrical spectacle is also the violence with which it recasts a mundane and normalized life. Hence, the arousing theatrics of all revolutionary enterprises. However, while ecstasy stimulated by staged life may ignite explosive youthful energy, the need to sustain such energy and passion will in the end present a sobering challenge, even the spectacle's undoing. If a staged spectacle lets us achieve a supreme joy at the expense of temporal duration, we also will seek, when a state of excitement leads to fatigue and pensiveness, comfort and self-reassurance through narratives, the quintessential art form of temporality. The resurgence of narrativity in the wake of theatricality, therefore, may be yet another sign of the arrival of a postrevolutionary age.

---

de chengjiu tanqi" (The seething life on stage: remarks on the achievements of theater in recent years), *Literary Gazette,* no. 315 (February 1964): 8.

6

Residual Modernism:
Narratives of the Self in the 1980s

The rhetoric of postmodernism, perhaps because it is largely amorphous and self-contradictory, holds a peculiar, almost uncanny, fascination for the cultural imaginary in China since the late 1980s. Its thematized trope of discontinuity seems to capture and ensure a general relief, a comforting sense of finally having left behind a nightmarish period of history, together with all the collective political aspirations and idealism that marked a tumultuous era of revolution. The celebrated postmodern playfulness and *difference* provide justification for a cynical detachment and at the same time promises various new forms of engagement in the field of discursive and representational practices. The persistent discrediting of notions such as "totality" and "teleology" that one finds in the postmodern theoretical discourse also serves to delegitimize the existing political reality of authoritarianism. Finally, postmodernism, with its ambiguous suggestion of historical periodization, readily meets the need of an emergent cultural logic when it at once conjoins a postrevolutionary (perhaps postsocialist as well) local space with a postmodern world (or simply the United States) and allows for a creative and enfranchising mockery of the revolutionary heritage. In this light, we can say it is the fairly uncertain feeling of being "post" rather than specifically "postmodern" that delivers some comfort as well as a new space for the imagination.

Postmodernism as Foreclosure

This conflation of a postrevolutionary ethos with postmodernist discourse has its additional historical relevance because of the introduction of a "socialist market economy." The peculiar synchronic juxtaposition of different modes of production (represented in such various forms of ownership as state-run, cooperative, joint-venture, and private single-household businesses) only adds to a general disorientation and skepticism. While the authoritarian political order in existence is continually challenged by a new social reality, the growing market economy also meets considerable resistance from the ideological holdover of a previous revolutionary age. Both socialism and capitalism, as two narrativizable historical choices, are questioned and discredited. This situation can be characterized as postmodern, as I have argued elsewhere, not only because it easily confirms the disappearance of all master narratives, but also because the term "postmodernism" best describes an intensified historical predicament where the persistence of modernity is perceived as such with dismaying clarity.[1] Expressive of a cultural logic that recognizes a peculiar situation where it is not possible either to resist or fully accept modernity, the postmodernist discourse in contemporary China thus becomes the symptom of a historic anxiety that is, nevertheless, foreclosed as such.

But the ironic turn of history is that postmodernism, because of the contradictions it indicates and articulates, invokes rather than cancels or supersedes modernism in this particular juncture. The unusual juxtaposition of different modes of production, in fact, seems to be precisely what Fredric Jameson thinks to be the typical condition of possibility for the emergence of a modernist aesthetics and politics in turn-of-the-century Europe. In commenting on the striking "coexistence of distinct moments of history" in Kafka's fiction—in particular, *The Trial*—Jameson observes that it is "the peculiar overlap of future and past, in this case, the resistance of archaic feudal structures to irresistible modernizing tendencies—of tendential organization and the residual survival of the not yet 'modern' in some other sense—that is the condition of possibility for high modernism as such." "What follows paradoxically as a consequence," Jameson continues, "is that in that case the postmodern must be characterized as a situation in which the survival, the residue, the holdover, the archaic, has finally been swept away without a trace. In the post-

---

1. See my essay "The Function of New Theory: What Does It Mean to Talk About Postmodernism in China?" in *Politics, Ideology and Literary Discourse in Modern China: Theoretical Interventions and Cultural Critique*, ed. Liu Kang and Xiaobing Tang (Durham, N.C.: Duke University Press, 1993), 279–98. For a more recent critique of postmodernist discourse in China, see Jing Wang, "The Pseudoproposition of 'Chinese Postmodernism': Ge Fei and the Experimental Showcase," in her *High Culture Fever: Politics, Aesthetics, and Ideology in Deng's China* (Berkeley: University of California Press, 1996), 233–60.

modern, then, the past itself has disappeared (along with the well-known 'sense of the past' or historicity and collective memory)."[2] This is, of course, a hypothetical consequence. Whether or not the triumph of the "postmodern" can be so thoroughgoing is very much open to debate, and, as Jameson suggests, to regard postmodernism as a complete and memory-free system would buy into the very ideology of the postmodernist celebration of the death of history. The residual traces of modernism in the postmodernist discourse are instead a constant and must be seen "in another light, less as anachronisms than as necessary failures that inscribe the particular postmodern project back into its context, while at the same time reopening the question of the modern itself for reexamination."[3] Those traces of modernism would only reveal the condition of modernity, of which the discourse of postmodernism is yet another ideological representation.

Clearly for Jameson the "residuality of the modern" can work as a powerful strategy to contextualize the postmodernist theoretical discourse. The notion of "residual modernism," it seems to me, can also be a very fruitful concept in discussing some contemporary Chinese literary production, especially the avant-garde fiction that is very often cheered as outright "postmodern." In discussing the "cultural challenge" posed by the experimental writings in the mid-1980s, for instance, critic Zhang Yiwu specifically uses the concept "postmodernist" to characterize the ideological and historical underpinnings of the new form of writing. Faced with the new challenges, "the two discourses of Reality and Modernity" that have sustained modern Chinese literature find themselves coming to a rapid demise. The narratives of the experimental fiction express a "postmodern" consciousness and "terminate in their own fashion the sacred tradition of May Fourth humanism, while at the same time making impossible the fantasy entertained by intellectuals about their values and positions."[4] But this "end of idealism" that the author believes to be the characteristic of "postmodernity" seems still to implicate much of the

---

2. Jameson, *Postmodernism, Or, The Cultural Logic of Late Capitalism* (Durham, N.C.: Duke University Press, 1991), 309. See "Notes Toward a Theory of the Modern" in "Secondary Elaborations" for a discussion of the relationship between modernity, modernization, and modernism, 302–13.

3. Jameson, *Postmodernism*, xvi.

4. Zhang Yiwu, "Lixiang zhuyi de zhongjie" (The end of idealism), *Beijing wenxue* (Beijing literature) (April 1989): 11.

modernist anxiety and despair. In fact, the narrator "I" of most experimental fiction he describes is identifiably a modernist hero: it is a narrator without a privileged position, having no control over events, and even less control over the ceaseless movement of language itself.

I shall not argue over who has a better definition of either "modernism" or "postmodernism" here, for both terms are constantly being redefined and expanded, anyway. What I intend to describe by the concept of "residual modernism" is not so much an outmoded literary production or some kind of revival as it is a conscious appropriation of a certain codified modernism. The creators of avant-garde fiction in late twentieth-century China are far removed, spatially and temporally, from the so-called high modernism of the West, and the conditions of possibility for either are also significantly different. Yet in the "residual modernism" that I discuss below there is an obvious appropriation of, if not careful subscription to, what Raymond Williams critically called the "ideology of modernism." This ideology expresses itself as a selective reading of modern European literature that applauds some writers over others "for their denaturalizing of language, their break with the allegedly prior view that language is either a clear, transparent glass or a mirror, and for making abruptly apparent in the very texture of their narratives the problematic status of the author and his authority."[5] For Williams, this ideological canonization of modernism has a close relationship to the conservative post-World War II settlement in the West and owes a great deal to a rapid depoliticizing appropriation of modernist techniques by consumer capitalism. With this development, modernism has lost its critical thrust along with its "anti-bourgeois stance."

But in residual modernism, this very "ideology of modernism" is restored its critical and oppositional potency, and its inner contradictions are revealed rather than concealed or smoothed out. Residual modernism in China, furthermore, appears to be not merely a transplantation of modernist techniques, but also a resumption of a modernist ethos and even modernist themes, only in much more intensified and self-conscious forms. This added intensity, however, is paradoxically what ultimately may lead to a postmodern foreclosure of anxiety, because it is an intensity experienced as already circumscribed and understood. In other words,

5. Raymond Williams, "When Was Modernism?" in his *The Politics of Modernism: Against the New Conformists,* ed. with intro. by Tony Pinkney (London: Verso, 1989), 33.

even if a classical modernist narrative (what Williams called an "intense, singular narrative of unsettlement, homelessness, solitude and impoverished independence") is restaged, it implicitly conveys a sense of relief. This relief is what I will call a postmodernist sensibility of residual modernism, or we can say that the unconscious of residual modernism strives for precisely such masochistic relief. In the avant-garde writings of the mid-1980s, especially in some narratives of the self by Yu Hua and Su Tong, we can certainly see this residual modernism at work.

The Problematic of Experience

Yu Hua's first major publication was "Shibasui chumen yuanxing" (On the road at age eighteen, 1987),[6] a short story about a young man who sets out to see and experience the real world. The young man, as the first person narrator, relates the events of one late afternoon when he was walking on a mountain road, "like a boat floating on the sea." He could not find an inn, and, as evening fell, he had to hitchhike, getting a ride on a truck that was heading in the same direction from which he had just come. The truck was carrying a load of apples, and when it broke down along the way, it was robbed and demolished by a crowd of peasants and children. The young man, too, was badly beaten while trying to stop the mob. A highly allegorical story, it is a narrative about initiation and reconciliation that adroitly blends obvious narrative elements of traditional bildungsroman, Kafkaesque absurdity with a sense of humor, and the theme of random yet methodical violence that would soon develop into one of the author's preoccupying motifs. Since the story is narrated as past personal experience, it also acquires a quietly detached tone that makes the events it describes all the more graphic and perplexing.

"On the Road at Age Eighteen" was immediately recognized as a sig-

---

6. Yu Hua, "Shibasui chumen yuanxing," *Beijing Literature* (January 1987); collected in Yu Hua, *Shibasui chumen yuanxing* (On the road at age eighteen) (Taipei: Yuanliu, 1990), 17–29. Although translations of passages in this chapter are my own, a complete English translation is available in Yu Hua, *The Past and the Punishments,* trans. Andrew F. Jones (Honolulu: University of Hawaii Press, 1996), 3–11. In the following discussion, references to page numbers are given in parentheses in the text, with the first number referring to the Yuanliu edition and the second to Jones's translation.

nificant literary work because it introduced, said the critics, a new mode of writing in contemporary Chinese literature. In his preface to Yu Hua's first collection, literary critic Li Tuo, who was directly responsible for the success of the young writer, observes that "Yu Hua's fiction completely shatters our age-old conventional understanding of the relationship between literature and reality, language and the objective world."[7] Following Roland Barthes's early defensive apology for literary modernism, Li Tuo gives Yu Hua and other young experimental writers a modernist reading and enthusiastically celebrates the belated arrival of a "writerly literature." This author-oriented literary production has "as its prior purpose to disrupt a given dominant language order, so as not only to problematize all existing literary and cultural codings but also to turn the act of writing into the exciting and risky process of creating a new universe." The emergence of this writerly literature, according to Li Tuo, formed an irresistible "avalanche" and signaled another "emancipation of language" that would contribute to a rewriting of modern Chinese literary history.[8]

Although he does not specifically use the term "modernist," Li Tuo shows an excitement over Yu Hua's fiction that comes largely from the recognition of a modernist politics of language at work. The critic is also sharply aware of a possible historical discrepancy. He points out that even if such a fascination with the newly discovered nonreferentiality and self-sufficiency of language has lost its freshness in the West, it is profoundly revolutionary in China. The "ideology of modernism" that Williams characterizes is thus ideologized once again, and its residual critical impulse reenergized and inscribed back. At this point it also becomes evident that beneath this obvious transferability of modernist techniques, "residual modernism" suggests a recognized recurrence of the condition of possibility that nurtured Western modernism in the first place. If, as Walter Benjamin argued, Baudelaire wrote for an age in which modern technologies of information brought about the "increasing atrophy of experience," and communicability of experience became a lost value, and if all of Proust's heroic literary efforts (by means of which the nineteenth century was finally made "ripe for memories") were concentrated on re-

---

7. Li Tuo, "Xu: xuebeng hechu?" (Preface: Where will the avalanche go?), *On the Road at Age Eighteen,* 9. Incidentally, this piece was originally published as a headline article in *Wenlun bao* (Journal of literary criticism) on 5 June 1989, one day after the Tiananmen incident.

8. Ibid., 10–12.

capturing past experience, modernism in the West then had as one of its obsessions the problem or impossibility of real experience.[9] Language was consequently problematized either because print mass media caused language to be devalued or because traditional linguistic habits had lost their relevance and impact. In other words, the modernist politics of language gained currency because a certain form of experience made it necessary to question language and reveal its unreliability to the extent that the writer had to construct his or her own world in and through language. Denaturalized language finally became symptomatic of an existing social order that was radically disintegrated and delegitimized.

If this is the case, Yu Hua's story offers a convenient point of departure for analyzing how a "residual modernism" helps to grasp a historical experience that constantly brings to crisis all given traditions and expectations. To assert that "On the Road at Age Eighteen" has a distinct modernist imagination is more than a theoretical conjecture, since at the time of its composition its author was enchanted by the writings of Kafka, which he had previously come across by chance.[10] As in the abstractly absurd world of K or the inarticulate Gregor of "Metamorphosis," the sequence of events Yu Hua's young hero experiences has a disturbing simplicity. Here, the narrative unfolds to belie a certain paradigm of experience and to parallel the emergence of a new self-consciousness. The force of the narrative lies in its problematizing the very category of experience. In the beginning, the protagonist, who is very proud of the few brownish hairs poking out on his chin, finds himself at home on the road by himself. "All the mountains and clouds. They reminded me of people I knew. So I called them aloud by their nicknames." As he looks for an inn for the night, he realizes that no one knows what lies ahead. They all tell him to "go over and have a look." The journey soon turns into a trying process from which the protagonist will have to emerge with a new self-conception and a new relationship to the outside world. The imaginary continuity between him and other people will break down and be displaced.

In a sense, the story can be read as a miniature of the bildungsroman

9. See Benjamin's essays on Baudelaire, Proust, and Leskov in *Illuminations,* trans. Harry Zohn, ed. with intro. by Hannah Arendt (New York.: Schochen Books, 1969), esp. 83–88, 157–65.

10. Zhu Wei, "Guanyu Yu Hua" (About Yu Hua), *On the Road at Age Eighteen,* 255.

in which the young hero or "youth," as Franco Moretti shows, sets off to experience and explore at once the two fundamentally constitutive aspects of modernity: mobility and interiority. Ever since *Wilhelm Meisters Wanderjahre,* "'apprenticeship' is no longer the slow and predictable progress towards one's father's work, but rather an uncertain exploration of social space, which the nineteenth century—through travel and adventure, wandering and getting lost, 'Boheme' and 'parvenir'—will underline countless times."[11] In Europe, the bildungsroman has been indeed a "symbolic form" of modernity, through which one of the constant contradictions of modern bourgeois culture—individual autonomy and social integration—is represented and given different articulations. The central character of the drama of the bildungsroman is invariably youth. Not surprisingly, in Chinese fiction of the late 1980s, especially in narratives by Su Tong and Yu Hua, critics have also noticed a strong "youth consciousness" that corresponds to a pervasive restlessness in society at large. "What is noteworthy is that this 'youth mentality' to a certain degree echoes a general mood in contemporary China. As the entire society slips out of paternalistic protection and unity, the sense of family is disappearing, and people are obliged to secure a position of their own. In addition, an intensified market economy starts to make society insensitive toward cultural values."[12]

The peculiarity about Yu Hua's story is that it is a narrative that forcibly brings together classical plots of the European bildungsroman that were developed over a good half of the nineteenth century through different political and social formations. In analyzing the ending of Balzac's *Lost Illusions* as a sample of the bildungsroman at its third dialectical stage, Moretti points out that, by this point, "the narrative of youth is no longer the symbolic form able to 'humanize' the social structure, as in *Wilhelm*

11. Franco Moretti, *The Way of the World: The Bildungsroman in European Culture* (London: Verso, 1987), 4. The introduction, "The *Bildungsroman* as Symbolic Form," is a succinct essay that deals not only with modernity but with the historical condition of modernism.

12. Wang Zheng and Xiao Hua, "Hubu de qingnian yishi: yu Su Tong youguan de huo wuguan de" (Complementary youth consciousness: things having or not having to do with Su Tong), *Dushu* (Reading) (July-August 1989): 103–04. This brief article is a brilliant study of the group of young writers represented by Su Tong and Yu Hua. The authors seem to go directly to the heart of the matter when they talk about a "youth consciousness" that reminds one of modernism (106).

Meister, nor, as in *The Red and the Black,* to question its cultural legitimacy. It only acts to magnify the indifferent and inhuman vigor of the modern world, which it reconstructs—as if it were an autopsy—from the wounds inflicted upon the individual."[13] In "On the Road at Age Eighteen," we witness, albeit metaphorically, all three of these distinct moments transformed and juxtaposed into one extremely seminal narrative by means of its rich symbolism. The "apprenticeship" motif appears at the very end of the story, as a moment of the past that has by now been fully disproved. The hero, after the utterly unintelligible "catastrophe," lies down inside the badly damaged truck and recalls one sunny, mild morning when his father prepared a red backpack for him and told him that he should get to know the outside world. "So I put the beautiful red backpack on my back. Father patted me once on the back of my head, just like patting a pony on its rump. At this I dashed out of my home with great joy and started to run happily, like a greatly excited horse" (29; 11). The presence of the father in the story is not so much recalled as it is undermined and reduced. Throughout the narrative, the oedipal attachment is strenuously repressed or simply forgotten (or are these two mental activities one and the same, anyway?) until the last moment when it returns only to be disavowed. The real world of experience is discontinuous with the "outside world" that the father evoked in the beginning, which is now carefully postponed to the last lines of the story. The figure of the father stands for a deceptive promise, a beautiful lie that has to be exposed as such. Recalling his father and that distant "sunny, mild morning" brings some comfort to the hero, either because he now knows that he, by reason of his own (psychological and physical) experience, has irrevocably entered the real world, or because he realizes the world of his father is no more than a fantasy. When the red backpack, prepared by the father and a strong symbol of the revolutionary heritage, is taken away effortlessly by the mysterious and faithless truck driver, the idealism of the father is debunked through the young hero's direct experience of betrayal and violence.[14]

13. Moretti, *The Way of the World,* 164.

14. The red backpack seems to be a favorite symbol of a bygone revolutionary age. In Su Tong's novella *Yijiu sansi nian de taowang* (Nineteen thirty-four escapes), the young protagonist in search of history also carries a red backpack. For an English translation, see Michael Duke, trans., *Raise the Red Lantern* (New York: William Morrow, 1993), 101–78.

If the red backpack embodies the ideological baggage of the father's generation, it also constitutes an identity of the young protagonist. When the backpack is taken away, for a moment he feels that he has nothing left. "It was completely dark by now, and there was absolutely no one around, except for the truck and myself, both every inch wounded" (28; 10). His experience of violence cuts short the course of development prescribed in the classical bildungsroman, where the individual is expected to be properly socialized at the conclusion of the narrative, either through a happy marriage or in the form of a fully mature personality. Violence now imposes upon the hero a new self-conception, a realization that between him and the world (in this case darkness and other people) there is an unsettling relationship of rupture and discontinuity. To resist violence, to stand against the objectifying power of betrayal and sheer force in the real world, the hero has to assert himself through discovering his own world, namely, his subjective interiority. "On the Road at Age Eighteen," therefore, is a parable about the painful birth of self-consciousness in a postrevolutionary era when all existing languages and meaning systems are shown to be incapable of explaining and containing individual experiences. Experience itself now needs restructuring.

The process through which the new self-consciousness appropriates interiority as its necessary form is closely mirrored and externalized in the unfortunate truck in the story that constantly breaks down. If the inn the hero initially looks for signifies a purposeful end (although simultaneously a very practical purpose), the truck that ends up taking him in the opposite direction completely displaces all notions of destination and necessity. It in fact introduces sheer contingency. "Although the truck was going to where I had just come from, I couldn't care less about direction. I needed an inn for now. Since there was no inn, I needed a truck, and the truck was right in front of me" (21; 4). Once the truck is repaired and he and the driver start enjoying each other's company, neither of them appears to care much about where they are going. "It now mattered little to us what lay ahead. As long as the truck was moving, we could always go over and have a look" (23; 6). At this point, the meaning and purpose of the journey is grasped (or lost?) in the process of traveling, and the moving truck is made home, both literally and metaphorically.

But this acquired carefreeness that is associated with the truck soon comes to an end when it once again breaks down. Then, in an oddly casual manner, the driver announces that the truck is beyond repair, and our young hero again has to worry about finding an inn. Yet what is to happen next makes irrelevant his brief enjoyment of mobility and his new understanding of purposefulness. Violence intervenes to short-circuit his potentially adventurous process of finding a home, and it forestalls the happy ending of a conventional bildungsroman narrative.[15] First, five people on bicycles with big baskets attached on either side come down a hill. When they discover a truckload of apples, they start unloading the truck. Taken aback, the young man steps over to stop the robbery and is punched in the nose, "blood gushing out like sad tears." Meanwhile, the truck driver appears indifferent to what is going on and takes pleasure in looking at the young man's broken nose. Then more people on bicycles arrive carrying big baskets, and finally even a hand tractor operator participates in this "catastrophe." The protagonist tries once more to confront the crowd and is beaten, kicked, and pelted with apples. "I didn't even have the strength to be angry. All I could do was watch this scene with growing indignation. I was angriest with the truck driver" (27; 9). The "catastrophe"[16] that he witnesses has a most ominous atmosphere about it. It is not merely a brutal violation of all social relations and institutions; it is also violence made absolute because of the absence of any significant articulation. Throughout the incident, not a single meaningful word is uttered except for the hero's angry and futile protests. Even the physical pain he sustains is mostly inflicted by the "numerous fists and feet" that apparently belong to no one particular person. Thus, the faceless crowd more than dispossesses the truck driver of his property; it deprives the event itself of meaning and intelligibility. A catastrophic experience such as this one becomes almost beyond rationalization when meaning is neither revealed nor enriched by means of violence, but, on the contrary, meaning is reduced or even canceled. Rather than suggest-

---

15. In commenting on the classical bildungsroman, Benjamin writes: "By integrating the social process with the development of a person, it bestows the most fragile justification on the order determining it. The legitimacy it provides stands in direct opposition to reality. Particularly in the *Bildungsroman,* it is this inadequacy that is actualized." From "The Storyteller, Reflections on the Works of Nikolai Leskov," *Illuminations,* 88. In this light, Yu Hua's refusal to represent such an integration suggests the recognized discontinuity between the social process and personal development.

16. It is significant that the phrase "*haojie*" is used here, a term that conventionally refers to the Cultural Revolution of the 1960s. At the lexical level, a certain historical referentiality is built into the narrative.

ing a liberating revolution, the robbery has the full implication of an inhuman war.[17] "I wanted to scream, but when I opened my mouth, no sound emerged" (26; 9).

When communication is violently suspended by an absence of reason or, shall we say, by civilized barbarism, and when violence reduces the human subject to his body and his body alone, the subject has to withdraw and observe the goings-on from a distrustful distance. It is a detached "gaze" that treats others as objects. The objectifying "gaze" that the young man now directs toward things and people around him has been forced upon him because he is the object of violence in the first place. "I saw the apples on the ground being picked up. . . . I saw them remove window panes from the truck. . . . I saw the ground being swept all clean. . . . All I could do was look, because I had no strength left even to be angry" (27; 9–10). Finally, he watches as the truck driver jumps onto the hand tractor, carrying the young man's red backpack, his sole possession. "I was hungry and cold, and I was left with nothing." Victimized as well as brutalized, the young man now sees his own condition mirrored in another victim, the demolished truck. Here we have some of the most gripping lines of the story:

> I sat there for a long time before I struggled to get up slowly. It was very hard for me because every move caused intense pain all over my body. Yet I still managed to get up. I limped over to the truck. It looked extremely miserable. It lay there with wounds all over it, and then I knew that I myself had wounds all over.
>
> It was completely dark by now, and there was absolutely no one around, except for the truck and myself, both every inch wounded. I looked at it with great sadness; it looked back at me with great sadness. I reached out to feel it. It was icy cold. (28; 10)

---

17. For Benjamin, catastrophic experience seems directly related to the increasing incommunicability of experience. In the wake of World War I, "was it not noticeable at the end of the war that men returned from the battlefield grown silent—not richer, but poorer in communicable experience? . . . For never has experience been contradicted more thoroughly than strategic experience by tactical warfare, economic experience by inflation, bodily experience by mechanical warfare, moral experience by those in power." From "The Storyteller," *Illuminations,* 84. We need to keep in mind that it was not until after World War I that modernism in the West gained its full swing and voiced an "age of anxiety."

In the damaged truck he sees not only the miserable consequence of violence, but also a shocking revelation. The truck provides a mirror image of his own wounded condition, and he is given a chance to see himself as a victim, as an object upon which senseless violence has been unleashed. In other words, in looking at the truck, the hero sees himself as others would see him and realizes his own susceptibility to being treated in the same manner as a truck can be. It is this awareness of his own objectifiability, of the revealed truth of his own vulnerability, that gives rise to a sympathetic identification between himself and the truck. At the same time, by locating in the silent truck an external symbol for his new self-conception, the young man at once acquires and articulates his subjectivity as a site of resistance against objectification. In the post-catastrophic moment, such a discourse of subjective interiority seems to supply a most consoling answer to the disturbing phenomena of human weakness and irrational violence, both revealed only at a historical moment of danger. It was in direct response to the horrifying spectacle of the great French Revolution, it seems necessary to recall, that Hegel developed his philosophy of subjectivity and the notion of *Innerlichkeit*. Both echoing Hegel's postrevolutionary reflection and condemning the "catastrophe" of the Cultural Revolution (1966–76), Liu Zaifu in the 1980s proposed to study a fulfilling "subjectivity of literature" in opposition to an institutionalized inhumanism.[18]

The metaphor of "subjectivity as a site of resistance against objectification" is a spatial one, and interiority, too, is conceivable only insofar as

---

18. See *Liu Zaifu lunwen xuan* (Selection of essays by Liu Zaifu) (Hong Kong: Dadi, 1986). I discuss this point in my essay on "The Function of New Theory." At the same moment that Liu Zaifu's theory was evoking vehement debates and controversy, narratives of the self became such a dominant phenomenon in literary production that some critics began feeling uneasy. See, for instance, Huang Hao, "Jiaose jinzhang: yige shuode taiduo tailei de 'wo'—xin shiqi diyi rencheng xiaoshuo de jiti pibei" (An intense role: An 'I' that is exhausted from speaking too much—collective fatigue of the first-person fiction in the new period," *Zuojia wenxue yuekan* (Writer's literary monthly), no. 253 (March 1990): 72–76. Huang Hao gives some interesting statistics in this article. Some 40 percent of contemporary fiction is narrated by an indefatigable "I." In this context, Lukács's accusation of a "carnival of interiorized fetishism" in Western modernism appears at once understandable and yet misleading. Both Huang Hao's critical essay and Lukács's general denunciation of modernism fail to comprehend a literary discourse that, while trying to overcome its historical condition, reveals some fundamental contradictions determining its own production.

it bears an oppositional relationship to that which constitutes exteriority. In the story we find precisely such a spatial restructuring. Realizing that he is getting icy cold, just like the truck, the young man gets inside the truck and lies down. "I smelled the gas that had come out. It smelled the same as the blood that had come out of my body. . . . I felt that even though the truck was wounded, its heart was still healthy and warm. I knew that my heart was also healthy and warm. I had been looking for an inn, and who would have thought that the inn should be here in you" (28–29; 10–11). The hero is finally home again, a home he finds and creates for himself and which now serves as a constant reminder—by means of its location and condition—of the absence of any social integration. He has set out hoping to know "the outside world" but ends up by knowing himself better. By finally identifying himself with the truck, which has replaced the inn, the young hero now possesses his own space and is enabled to articulate his redefined identity on the one hand and disown the mystifying heritage of his father on the other. His entire journey, therefore, comes through as a modernist voyage of self-discovery that is inseparable from a disintegrating world of experience.

More than a metaphor of the birth of subjectivity in Chinese fiction of the 1980s, "On the Road at Age Eighteen" also marks a turning point in Yu Hua's own development. From this moment on, it is observed, "Yu Hua recognized his new self from a previous obscurity, and his fiction acquired its own independent life for the first time."[19] This new identity that the author found for his fictional world is a productive one that expresses itself in continuous narrational experimentation and thematic variations. The subject matter of methodical cruelty and violence, by no means bereft of its historical reference and implicit social judgment, is masterfully developed and enriched in a series of stories best represented by "Xianshi yizhong" (One kind of reality). The critical interest in problematizing language and representation is pursued in narratives such as "Shishi ru yan" (This world of clouds), and a structurally perfect "Gudian aiqing" (Classical love) parodies traditional narrative patterns and cultural myths.[20]

19. Zhu Wei, "About Yu Hua," 256. See 256–66 for a summary of Yu Hua's writings from 1986 through 1988. Here, Zhu Wei believes that Yu Hua has finished a three-stage leap, a process of gradually discovering his own narrative voice and his own imagined world of absolute reality.

20. "Xianshi yizhong," "Shishi ru yan," and "Gudian aiqing," collected, respectively,

The central organizing principle of Yu Hua's writing nevertheless remains the same: an unrelenting critique of our everyday experience. Reviewing his own literary production in a 1989 preface to one of his collections, Yu Hua summarizes that his major intellectual concern has been to reveal a multidimensional and contradictory reality that remains obscured and simplified, not only by our everyday life and commonsensical order, but also by our language conventions. Thus, violence and catastrophe have their thematic value because they expose a chaotic reality that is the suppressed truth of our seemingly well-ordered existence. On the level of language, too, Yu Hua believes in constantly challenging common sense because the "indeterminate narrative language" sought by him focuses on concrete experience, whereas the "fixed language of the masses" only conveys judgment. "The language of the masses presents us with a world that is an incessant repetition. For that reason, my effort at finding a new language has as its aim to reveal to my friends and readers a world that has not yet been repeated."[21] The commonsensical world that Yu Hua wishes to derail and the fixed everyday language of the masses he finds so oppressive both belong to a sociohistorical reality against which the writer has to assert his identity with an increasing emphasis. The critical stance he takes against everyday life and the world of "ordinary administration" becomes available partly because of his self-conscious subscription to the aesthetics and political ideology in the modernist tradition of Kafka, Joyce, Robbe-Grillet, Faulkner, and Kawabata Yasunari.[22] In Yu Hua, we find one of the defining characteristics of "residual modernism": the ideology of modernism, as both a theoretical complex and a mode of literary production, now proves to be a fundamentally historicizing discourse because it reveals the condition of modernity and strips it of any possible euphoria. Through residual modernism, therefore, the modernist imperative for the New as well as the modernist fascination with the self are retrospectively shown to be deeply rooted in a recognized moment of incompleteness where all forms of social practice and existence

---

in Yu Hua's *On the Road at Age Eighteen* and *Shishi ru yan* (This world of clouds) (Taipei: Yuanliu, 1990).

21. "Zuozhe xu: xuwei de zuopin" (Preface by the author: hypocritical artworks), *This World of Clouds,* 16. One important aspect of residual modernism is its theoretical sophistication.

22. Yu Hua specifically mentions all these writers in the essay "Hypocritical Artworks" when he talks about the formal tradition of fiction. "Preface by the Author," 13.

suddenly exhibit a peculiar residuality because their contradictory juxtaposition makes coherent experience at once desirable and unattainable. If the high modernism of Kafka and his contemporaries is, in Jameson's words, "characterized by a situation of incomplete *modernization*,"[23] then in residual modernism the features and foreseeable consequences of the unfinished project of modernity are grasped simultaneously. This lack of ambiguity in historical vision will only make residual modernism all the more conscious of its own residuality as an oppositional presence.

The Unreal Urban Space

"On the Road at Age Eighteen" can be read as a metaphor for the genesis of residual modernism at a distinct historical moment of incomplete modernization. In this light, it becomes significant that different modes of transportation are carefully inscribed in the narrative. The truck, representing the most advanced technology in comparison with the bicycle and the hand tractor, is simply unable to fulfill its function and is systematically torn apart. The fate of the truck thus becomes emblematic of the antagonistic situation from which modernity struggles to emerge. It also resolutely dispels any nostalgic illusion about an idyllic premodern harmony. Thus, the violence, to which the truck as well as the protagonist are subjected, both symbolizes the crisis that such a coexistence is likely to incur and explains the agonizing necessity of residual modernism. This historicizing reading, however, does not make violence any more meaningful or acceptable to the individual; on the contrary, violence is revealed to be the precondition of meaning and to have its own history. This separation of a narrativizable collective movement from individual experience once again testifies to the defining condition of modernity.[24]

23. Jameson, *Postmodernism*, 310.
24. In another short story, "Siwang xüshu" (Narrative of death), Yu Hua further explores the historical significance of violence when the first-person narrator there tells of how "I," a truck driver, was murdered by a family of peasants with various farming instruments (a glittering scythe, a hoe, and a shovel) after an accident in which "I" killed their beautiful daughter. In the very end, with "my" body systematically pierced and cut up, "my blood ran about. My blood looked like the roots of a one-hundred-year-old tree that have surfaced above the ground. Then I died." In *On the Road at Age Eighteen*, 31–42.

Yet Yu Hua's persistent interest in violence as an expression of a historical moment of incompleteness unexpectedly brings him face-to-face with another aspect of modernity. Ordinary, everyday urban life is now examined in *Yijiubaliu nian* (1986; 1987), an epic-spirited novella about the disturbing reappearance of a violent past in the figure of a demented teacher. Taken from his family one night during the Cultural Revolution, and now a madman recognized by no one, the former teacher, now a ghost of violence, haunts a small, peaceful town and systematically inflicts on himself all the atrocious ancient forms of physical punishment that he used to study as a hobby. The novella *1986* is another highly symbolic story that treats violence as a disruptive return of the repressed. The town is crowded, inhabited by people who are eager to frequent movie theaters, cafés, and various product expos, the sole purpose of which, comments the narrator, "is to make people forget, to make people feel happy at this very moment." It is a postrevolutionary urban landscape where a mindless "they" count on fashions and consumption to help them leave behind a painful past.

> The catastrophe that occurred more than ten years ago now appears to be a mere fleeting cloud, and the slogans painted on the walls are completely covered up by repeated whitewashing. They see no trace of the past when they walk on the streets, they see only the present. Now there are lots of excited people walking on the streets, lots of bicyclists ringing their bells, and lots of cars blowing up lots of dust. Now there is a van with big speakers slowly moving along, the speakers loudly promoting birth control and advising people on how to avoid pregnancy. Now there is another similar van also slowly moving along, loudly reminding people of the misery caused by traffic accidents.[25]

Into this complacently regular and uneventful everyday life enters the story's protagonist, a limping madman who takes pleasure in stabbing, amputating, and castrating himself publicly in the street. More like a ghost from the past than a real human being, he is conveniently ignored and will finally realize that this world needs desperately to forget its past:

---

25. *Yijiubaliu nian* (1986) in *On the Road at Age Eighteen*, 57–58; 143. The second page number here refers to Andrew F. Jones's English translation of the novella in *The Past and the Punishments*, 132–80. The phrase for "catastrophe" here is again "haojie," the same as in "On the Road at Age Eighteen."

"He saw people walking around in the street over there. He looked at them as if looking at a stage from afar. They appeared on the stage, talked there and made all kinds of gestures. He was not among them; there was something in between. They were they, and he was he" (96; 175). The ghost of violence is eventually expelled and everyday life happily resumes its normal course.

Despite its explicitly accusatory message (the relationship between human cruelty and civilization is revealed as a given), the narrative about the return of the repressed identifies for the author another source of frustration—regulated and repressive everyday life. The significance of Yu Hua's *1986* lies in the fact that it depicts a peculiar postcatastrophic culture that strains to displace its revolutionary memory and desire by locating gratification, very often an impoverished kind, in the realm of consumption and mass culture (specifically represented in the novella by Marlboro cigarettes, Nestlé's Coffee, and romances by the Taiwanese writer Qiong Yao). While the Cultural Revolution as a massive social movement still haunts the sensitive writer with the enormous passion and horror that it generated, the complacency of a new consumer culture repels him and strikes him as unbearably boring. Thus, in another more complex and experimental novella, "Ciwen xiangei shaonü Yang Liu" (This story is dedicated to a girl named Yang Liu), the narrator, now a first-person "I," opens the carefully organized story with an ambivalent condemnation of "bourgeois" practicality: "For a long time, I had been living a bourgeois life. The place where I lived was called Smoke, and my apartment was a one-story house by the river. The structure of the house was an unimaginative rectangle, which suggested how simple and unambiguous my life was."[26]

The story, with parallel but intentionally disorienting repetition and heavy symbolism, tells how this "unimaginative" existence is first challenged by the complexity of real experience and then transformed by the insertion of an interiority that, symbolized by the image of the girl Yang Liu, can be at once libidinal desire and historical consciousness. The girl is both self and other, both imagination and memory, and her arrival at the "inner heart" of the narrator makes him restless because she exposes

26. *Ciwen xiangei shaonü Yang Liu* in *This World of Clouds*, 109. Translated as "This Story Is For Willow" by Denis C. Mair, it is collected in *China's Avant-Garde Fiction*, ed. Jing Wang (Durham, N.C.: Duke University Press, 1998), 114–46.

an "absence" in his life (123, 127). The girl appears when he, as usual, is roaming the streets aimlessly at night, looking at all the curtained windows, greatly perplexed by the inimical presence of other people. The urban landscape is deeply unsettling because "I," the narrator, is at once drawn to it and has to resist it. It is a space that becomes increasingly flat and homogeneous, from which history is in danger of disappearing once and for all.

This rising urban space irresistibly captures the imagination of Yu Hua and his generation and presents them with a troubling prospect. For them the new forms of experience made possible by the city are continually contradicted and made unreal by other spaces and times. It is a space that has to be constantly confronted and examined in terms of the rural and the historical; traces of both are ineradicable as a reminder of the situation of incomplete modernization. This characteristic skepticism toward city life is distinct not only in Yu Hua, but it is also readily recognizable in the writings of Ge Fei and Su Tong. In Ge Fei's stories, we witness a constant moving back and forth between two spaces—the country and the city. Most often it is this movement that creates tension and generates his narratives. As a result, the typical setting for his stories is some unspecified liminal site.[27] Tension between these two conflicting spaces also seems to permeate the fictional world of Su Tong, who, however, tries meticulously to keep them separate. Thus, on the one hand, he produces such notable works as *Yijiu sansi nian de taowang* (Nineteen thirty-four escapes) and *Qiqie chengqun* (Wives and concubines) which adroitly deal with historical events and interrogate our understanding of the past,[28] while, on the other hand, he continually expresses his anxiety about modern urban life in stories like "Pingjing ru shui" (As serene as still water) and "Nihao, yangfengren" (Hello, my beekeeper). These last

27. For an insightful discussion of Ge Fei's oeuvre, see Zhang Xudong's essay "Ge Fei yu dangdai wenxue zhong de jige muti" (Ge Fei and some main themes in contemporary literature), *Jintian* (Today), no. 2 (1990): 76–84. This essay's expanded English version appears in Xudong Zhang, *Chinese Modernism in the Era of Reforms: Cultural Fever, Avant-Garde Fiction, and the New Chinese Cinema* (Durham, N.C.: Duke University Press, 1997), 163–200.

28. Meng Yue's essay "Su Tong de 'jiashi' yu 'lishi' xiezuo" (The writing of 'family genealogy' and 'history' by Su Tong), in *Today*, no. 2 (1990): 84–93, offers an excellent analysis of this treatment of the past. See chap. 7, "The Mirror of History and History as Spectacle."

two stories are unmistakably set in a big city, and both are narratives told in the first-person. In them, we find a clearer and more self-conscious representation of the metropolitan space from the point of view of dissatisfied and rebellious youth. Here, one of the cultural forms of modernity will receive critical examination, and residual modernism finally confronts the space of the city. Once again, it becomes helpful to refer to Raymond Williams, who, in a memorable passage, described the modernist as a hero in revolt against the new experience of mass media in turn-of-the-century metropolitan cities:

> The experience of visual and linguistic strangeness, the broken narrative of the journey and its inevitable accompaniment of transient encounters with characters whose self-presentation was bafflingly unfamiliar, raised to the level of universal myth this intense, singular narrative of unsettlement, homelessness, solitude and impoverished independence: the lonely writer gazing down on the unknowable city from his shabby apartment.[29]

Narrating the Modern

Williams's depiction of an ideal-type modernist writer in either Paris or New York seems to be a perfect summary of the ethos in Su Tong's stories about the city. The subject matter of his "Hello, My Beekeeper" is youth and its conflict with the outside world, just as was the case in "On the Road at Age Eighteen." Different from the landscape of open nature in Yu Hua's short story (although it is a nature radically transformed through violence), the space in which Su Tong's young hero has his adventures is the city. But between these two stories there are striking structural similarities and narrational continuities. At the beginning of both stories is the moment of "me" entering a new space. The "I" that now moves, "just like a fish," into the city at a wintry dusk in Su Tong's story can nearly be taken as the "I" who left home and experienced a "catastrophe" on the road at age eighteen. By the end of "Hello, My Beekeeper" there is also a moment of relief when the young hero finds consolation in the fact that he belongs nowhere in particular and that his existence is already a purpose and a meaning in and of itself. In both narratives, mobility and

---

29. Williams, "When Was Modernism?" 34.

interiority are in a sense put on trial and finally affirmed as valuable aspects of the experience of the modern. "Things are always like this. You constantly have to leave one place for another. You can't think of another way of living. I have to determine my next destination while on the train. I will never go home, because I've sworn not to."[30]

"Hello, My Beekeeper" is about a young college dropout's adventures in a big, rapidly modernizing city. The fictive city Nanjin that he approaches at the beginning of the story is the ninth of a series of cities that he has visited, intending to study each of them for his project in a new discipline of "urban studies." On his way to the city he encounters a mysterious middle-aged beekeeper in a dreamlike field of wildflowers who tells him to stay in a certain Peace Hotel in Nanjin and wait for the beekeeper's return. Preoccupied by the beekeeper's promise, the young man turns his stay in the city into a prolonged Kafkaesque search, during which he experiences a wide spectrum of "transient encounters," such as a hapless sexual incident, prostitution, the criminal underground, death, even romance. The Peace Hotel provides a perfect site for novelistic narration, an ideal meeting place for all sorts of characters (including a disgruntled "old revolutionary" complaining of inadequate housing, a fundraiser for a literary journal whose business card bears four unrelated titles, and a wealthy Cantonese caught with a prostitute who subsequently buys himself out of trouble), while the city as a whole constitutes an enormous impersonal space that the protagonist explores as a Baudelairian *flâneur* ("My profession was to ramble through all the f——ing cities"), which he maps and remaps through his experience and movement. Life in the city turns out to be such a disintegrative experience that he soon realizes the need to constantly construct a new identity for himself. Yet his initial fascination is a feeling of freedom.

> I was now used to roaming the streets, which seemed to be a major method of investigating the city. I put my hands in the warmth-deprived pockets of my coat and strolled aimlessly along the streets, seeing myself reflected in shop windows and transformed into a member of this city. My serious face and leisurely pace had lost all the characteristics of my small hometown. The result of this transformation I called urbanization, which meant success in fleeing my family. (27)

30. "Nihao, yangfengren," *Beijing Literature* (April 1988): 36. In the following discussion, references to page numbers are given in parentheses in the text.

A major attraction of the city for this young drifter is its offering of a different social landscape from the small town that he finds extremely "boring and eventless" and where his older brother suffers from severe depression. The "silly-looking" small town is a part of the young man's identity that he desperately wants to shed, as if "out of habit." The city also frustrates him, even makes him lonely, but it is never boring, and it always exceeds his expectations. Thus, his experience in the city becomes preferable not because of all the pitiful individuals he encounters, but because of the very possibility of meeting them in the first place. This new experience of the self—as a nameless observer of a big-city crowd—now generates and defines the narrative and at the same time is critically questioned.

Here we see a significant wedge driven between the narrative form of "Hello, My Beekeeper" and its express content or plot. The plot of the story is the young man's persistent waiting and searching for the absent beekeeper. The search constitutes a meaningful event for the young man, because to some extent it organizes his experience of the city. The beekeeper, whose laughter reminds the narrator of his depressed brother and who attracts him with a "weird superhuman aura" (23), belongs neither to the small town nor to the big city. He embodies harmony with Nature (he travels to wherever the flowers are), and his unconventional lifestyle expresses an aura of authenticity that is absent from life in both the small town and the city. He is referred to simply as "Beekeeper," which in Chinese sounds like "One who cultivates craziness." If we take the small town as the place of traditional, premodern repetitiveness and drudgery (where the hero's father manually stirs a huge vat of green-blue dye day after day) and the city as a disorienting field of modern dynamism and discontinuity, the beekeeper's world of naturalness then exposes either space as an impossible site for authentic and integrated experience.

Yet the space inhabited by the beekeeper is an imagined one that is invoked as a critique of both stifling stagnation and rapid urbanization. It is again an interiorized space where the self is able to enjoy its fulfillment, just as Nature is still imagined to possess a utopian wholesomeness. Obviously, the traceless beekeeper and his fantasy land belong to a form of experience that is valuable because it is already recognized as absent. Just as with the discourse of subjectivity, the utopian impulse embodied by the beekeeper reveals the ideological engagement of residual modernism in a historical moment of incomplete modernization. (In this light, I would think it misleading to accentuate a "postmodernist" profile in Su Tong.)[31] The young hero's search for the beekeeper, therefore, becomes a symbolic act of escape that, nevertheless, constitutes his identity. His obsession with the search, shared by the young first-person narrator of *Nineteen Thirty-four Escapes,* finally leads to a dramatic episode in which a fast-talking girl expresses her love and tells him that he himself is a romantic beekeeper. Afterward, he has a dream that can be read as an expression of the utopian longing of residual modernism.

> I dreamt the beekeeper was walking forward and I was following him. We were crossing a field of purple flowers in the spring, while an ox-drawn cart loaded with bee hives was creaking by on the dirt road. . . . I found the place the beekeeper led me through very familiar, but I had no way to tell where it was. It looked like the outskirts of the town of Nijiang, or my small hometown. It also looked like nowhere but a distant new world of mystery. (34–35)

When the protagonist voices his conflicting feelings about the countryside, he articulates an essential ambivalence in residual modernism. As an ideologized discourse about the condensed experience of modernity, residual modernism is profoundly ambivalent about the process of modernization because it is recognized as at the same time necessary and repressive, emancipatory and dystopian. Residual modernism is a discourse that is acutely aware of its contradictory impulses. "You cannot imagine how intensely I felt both ambivalent and empty. You cannot understand the contradiction I felt because I hated the country village [*xiangcun*] as much as I was moved by pastoral scenery [*xiangye*]" (23).

If, however, the hero's search for identity is the explicit purpose and organizing plot of "Hello, My Beekeeper," the process of the search, namely his experience in the city, assumes a narrative form that reveals further ambiguities. The process becomes significant and even enjoyable insofar as it is a form of experience that generates incessant narration. The whole sequence of events in the story is organized not so much by a temporal progression as by the young man's continuous spatial movement across the city. Along a horizontal plane of juxtaposition are numerous

---

31. See Wang Zheng and Xiao Hua, "Complementary Youth Consciousness," 107. Here they raise the concept of "postmodernism" as a possible category for understanding this group of young writers.

episodes and mini-narratives that are independent and discontinuous of each other. So the three inserted subtitles for three different series of narratives in the text (Peace Hotel Guests Number 1, 2, and 3) serve to break as much as produce the illusion of a coherent narration. Each series, in addition, begins with the same question, supposedly addressed to the new hotel guest by the narrator: "Have you seen a beekeeper?" Each time the narrator "I" is either misunderstood or simply ignored. What follows is invariably digression and interruption, fragmented experience that refuses to lend itself to any focused communication or storytelling. Here we can view the thematic plot of the story, namely the hero's determined search for identity, as what Benjamin described as the "shock defense" that strenuously tries to fend off various stimuli from life in the city and keeps the integrity of a narratable experience. It is, however, those stimuli, those uncontrollable and fleeting digressions and interruptions, that move the narrative forward and become what is lived through. The form of the narrative reflects the impossibility of achieving meaningful experience, together with all its linkages and complexities.

Thus, the narrative form assumed by the young man's futile search corresponds to the structure of his consciousness to the extent that it repeats the frustrated effort to organize his experiences in a modern metropolis. Since city life turns out to be most susceptible to narration—in Balzac's Paris of early capitalism, there was an irrepressible need for what Franco Moretti calls "sheer narration"[32]—the narrator feels his self-identity at once threatened by and given a certain form in this explosive narrativity. On the one hand, he has to contain this sheer narration by subjecting it to a framework of intelligibility, but on the other it is through narration, through recounting other guests' stories, that he realizes his own value and identity—his difference from others. In a sense, narration now occurs not so much to communicate experience as to present itself as a divergent form of experience that still needs further organizing. It becomes a self-propelled mechanism that the narrator as a subject has to halt in order to form not merely a possible relation with the world but also a self-definition. Thus, the narrative form of "Hello, My Beekeeper" has its own historical significance because its irresistible and disruptive energy is symptomatic of the difficult situation that the agitated modern subject confronts.

32. Moretti, *The Way of the World*, 146.

The sheer narration that the young man wishes to contain and resist is best represented by newspapers, in which he finds not only an overabundance of unrelated happenings, but also a devaluation of experience itself. Coincidentally, the mysterious beekeeper inscribes his directions for the young man on a piece of newspaper (the *Nanjin Evening News*), thus forcing the young man to read the clipping over and over again in the hope of finding some revelation. There he finds a fragmented sentence about a court decision in a theft case, a fatal accident, and a report about an AIDS patient (23–24). This newspaper clipping appears early in the narrative, preceding the young man's actual encounter with the city. Thus, the three unrelated events that are juxtaposed randomly (in the format of a newspaper) predetermine the form of his experience in the city and have a paradigmatic value for his own narrative. The dominant pattern of urban life, in other words, is revealed in the story to be that of a torn newspaper, with fragmented narratives that have neither beginnings nor endings. (In Su Tong's "As Serene as Still Water," we find an episode composed entirely of newspaper headlines, ranging from complaints about unequal opportunities for young people, to secrets of longevity to the arrest of a certain burglar-murderer.) Toward the end, another clipping from the *Nanjin Evening News* is mysteriously delivered to the young man's hotel room with a message from the beekeeper. It is an indecipherable message consisting of a drawing and a poem, neither of them making much sense. But still it is a message in the beekeeper's familiar tadpole-shaped handwriting, and it is determinedly not narration. The message negates the newspaper and gathers its force from the fact that it is inscribed over the narration that saturates modern urban life. The significance of these two messages handwritten on a piece of newspaper is parallel to that of the beekeeper himself. Together, they call forth an imaginative eccentricity that comments on the shrinkage of experience in modernity.

While the strategy with which to confront this new explosive narrativity is to stubbornly pose the same question, "Have you seen a beekeeper?" the embattled subject also has to imagine a gratifying "new world of mystery" to transcend the immediate environment. On two separate but related levels, the first-person narrator experiences these two critical impulses: on the level of the narrative, he organizes his stories to show their irrelevance to his thematic inquiry (or rather the very relevancy of his search for meaning), and on the level of content he depicts the city as a dystopian space devoid of genuine experience. The modernizing city is shown to generate narration but not genuine narrative. The "sensation of the modern age may be had," Benjamin concludes his discussion of Baudelaire's vision of Paris in the nineteenth century, at a dear price: "the disintegration of the aura in the experience of the shock." Baudelaire is the first poet to have understood and portrayed modernity in his poetic imagination, because he has given "the weight of an experience" to something lived through from moment to moment, thus consenting to the disintegration of the aura.[33] For Baudelaire, a narratable and potentially complete experience was irreparably disconnected from the immediate and often involuntary sensation that one continuously had when mingling with the city crowd. In Su Tong's narratives of the city we also find such a disconnection. The sensation of the modern age, as in Baudelaire, is enjoyed with great apprehension, and the aura that breathes historical authenticity remains a utopian vision rather than a complete dissipation. The utopian moment in residual modernism, in other words, is a historical necessity precisely because the incompleteness of a historical process is fully grasped, and, more importantly, its inevitable completion is perceived as being in need of critical demystification.

This brings us back to the question of history, which directs our attention to the content of the narrative. "Content" here should not be regarded as an enfeebled category; rather, it corresponds to the historical significance of the narrative form. In a sense the content even attempts to explain and narrativize the emergence of sheer narration itself. At first glance, the modernizing city seems to have blotted out history completely. Absent from both the urban space and its symbol—the newspaper world of shock value—is any trace of the previous revolutionary era, except for one moment when the young hero, upon first entering the city, comes across a used shoe lying on the road at an intersection. It is a Liberation shoe that was popular in the early 1970s, now all by itself, yet not without some arrogance (21). After that, the lonely shoe never reappears. Its subsequent disappearance suggests the extent to which memory of a revolutionary past has been successfully erased. It also dramatizes the bankruptcy of a revolutionary heritage that the young hero finds useless and impossible to identify with. Yet its presence as a spectral reality

---

33. Benjamin, "On Some Motifs in Baudelaire," *Illuminations*, 194.

greatly arouses the young man's curiosity, and he decides to study the abandoned shoe as the first "strange phenomenon" of the city.

Each of the three Peace Hotel guests whom the protagonist meets subsequently represents a distinct historical moment, and together they contribute to a narrative continuity. The "old revolutionary," who fought both the Japanese and the Nationalists, still carries wounds from wartime but now finds himself unfairly ignored. He travels to the city to file complaints and seek justice. His presence, although nearly anachronistic, bitterly accuses a revolutionary tradition of shamelessly betraying its individual participants. The fund-raiser, on the other hand, carries a business portfolio laden with six different identification cards and is desperately searching for a new profession. Not having physical wounds from a war, he is also without any real identity because he is one of those functionaries of the previous regime who are now dislocated by a new social reality. In contrast to this meticulous and timid cadre-turned-businessman, the parvenu Cantonese understands how money works and takes pride in his new wealth. A conspicuous consumer of new status-symbol goods (Pepsi, Kent cigarettes, and French perfume), he is a contemporary of the narrator and represents the emergent organizing principle of city life—monetary exchange. He is most disagreeable to the young hero because of his mercantile vulgarity and hedonistic self-indulgence. He also caricatures a moment that has completely suppressed the revolutionary past.

These three Peace Hotel guests, with none of whom the young hero can readily identify, combine to announce the ineluctable arrival of a postrevolutionary age, in which both memory and forgetting appear equally disturbing, because both enable the narrator to recognize a tremendous discontinuity. Thus, his only strategy, or his search for self-identity, has to be an act of escape, an affirmation of his freedom not to be engaged, a solitary *freedom from*. Therefore, we see him constantly on the run. He runs from a friendship that becomes exploitative, from an institution that helps people find jobs, and even from possible romance. Finally, the young man has to run from the city itself.

"Hello, My Beekeeper" is one of the first and most successful narratives in Chinese literature of the 1980s to approach the city as a growing field of cultural and experiential disconnections. The tension between the narrative form and the ideological content suggests the intensity of that discontinuity. The experience of restless youth and its final escape seem to imply a suspicion of the emerging urban culture. The young hero in the end finds it necessary to keep moving. But there is no nostalgia for either the revolutionary past or life in a boring small town, even though we may detect some disquieting resemblance between the deserted Liberation shoe at the beginning and the lonely young man who stands by the street watching people hurrying home. "It was the last winter day of 1986, on a street in one city" (36). This one-line paragraph describes an oppositional loneliness that is interiorized and remains self-consciously on the margin. Both the young man who is determined not to reconcile himself to the city and the recalcitrant Liberation shoe are suddenly revealed to be symbols of separate residual moments. But it is impossible to invoke the Liberation shoe and what it stands for as a demystifying force precisely because of its lack of interiority. In the increasingly oppressive modernizing urban landscape, youth has to be in possession of both mobility and interiority in order not to vanish or be consumed altogether.

Here we find the relevance of the concept of "residual modernism." Yu Hua and Su Tong are representative residual modernists because for them incomplete modernization demands a creative recycling of the ideology of modernism in order for this historical moment to be representable and represented critically. Through the lenses of modernism, they reexamine the renewed onset of the modern, both its myths and demystifications. This resorting to modernism as canonized techniques and codified ideology hardly suggests an impoverished imagination or inadequate historical consciousness on the part of the practitioners of residual modernism. On the contrary, by means of a resituated recycling, residual modernists show an even firmer grasp of the enduring dilemmas and contradictions that underlie the condition of modernity. They also succeed in retroactively revealing that European modernism itself was a discourse of spectrality in the first place. In other words, modernism became an available ideology precisely at the moment when historical experience in Europe was fraught with residual forms and possibilities (even the Future uncannily appeared reminiscent of a past imagination). Residual modernism therefore is a more intense and, if possible, purer modernism. This greater intensity that defines residual modernism does not necessarily mean that it will surpass modernism in its ingenuity or achievement. Rather, it indicates the persistence of an agonizing incompleteness. It also highlights the contradiction of a historical moment in which modernity, while still struggling to emerge, is already perceived to be a positively residual, if not archaic, form of experience. At a time when postmodernism is believed to have bidden a final farewell to the anxiety of the modern, the vitality of residual modernism forces us to again confront modernity and all its unresolved complexities.

7

The Mirror of History and History as Spectacle: Reflections on Xiao Ye and Su Tong

Thus the life of someone whose existence has somewhat preceded our own encloses in its particularity the very tension of History, its division. History is hysterical: it is constituted only if we consider it, only if we look at it—and in order to look at it, we must be excluded from it.
—Roland Barthes, *Camera Lucida*

The two novellas I wish to discuss here—Xiao Ye's *Ganlan zhen 1944* (The town of Olive in 1944) (1989)[1] and Su Tong's *Yijiu sansi nian de taowang* (Nineteen thirty-four escapes) (1987)[2]—share something in common more than is suggested by their two similar titles. In both, a specific year locates a historical moment in the past, and the two different moments of history invoked here both precede the experience of the two respective authors. For Xiao Ye (Hsiao Yeh) (1951-), the prolific and popular Taiwan novelist and scriptwriter (*Kongbu fenzi* [The terrorizer], 1988), the year 1944 is just as remote and unapproachable as the year 1934 is to Su Tong (1963-), who began publishing in the late 1980s in China and has produced a series of stories about the bygone generation of his parents and grandparents. As the first-person narrator in Xiao Ye's story tells us, "1994 was the Republican year 33. I was not yet born then; my parents had not even met each other" (208). The same awareness of the unbridge-

---

1. Xiao Ye, *Ganlan zhen 1944*, collected in his *Wudi haixing* (Legless starfish) (Taipei: Yuanliu, 1989), 207–33.

2. Su Tong, *Yijiu sansi nian de taowang*, collected in his *Qiqie chengqun* (Wives and concubines) (Taipei: Yuanliu, 1990), 13–78. Translations of passages in this chapter are my own. For a complete English translation, which I consulted, see Michael Duke, trans., *Raise the Red Lantern* (New York: William Morrow, 1993), 101–78. In the following discussion, references to page numbers are given in parentheses, with the first number referring to the Chinese edition and the second to Duke's translation.

able distance from a particular historical moment is articulated with equal force by Su Tong's first-person narrator in *Nineteen Thirty-four Escapes:* "For a period of time my history book was covered with the year 1934. The year 1934 radiated strong shafts of purple light that circumscribed my thinking. It was a remote past moment that did not exist anymore, and it remained true for me like the circles of an ancient tree. I could sit upon it and regard the events and changes that took place in 1934" (18; 105).

The affinity between these two stories goes beyond their similar titles. Both stories have a first-person narrator who contemplates history with determination and looks back at the past hoping to recapture or even relive what took place before his own arrival. Both narrators express a strong nostalgia that is only mitigated by the constant invocation of distinct, almost filmic, images of past events. In fact, visual images here seem to be the dominant mode of knowing, and the spectacle of history the central means by which the narrator satisfies his longing for meaning and self-identity. To visualize history, to imagine it as if gazing at a spectacle—this is the precise starting point of Xiao Ye's *The Town of Olive in 1944*.

It is of interest to observe at the outset that Xiao Ye wrote the story under discussion in the emotionally agitating summer of 1989. It was a time when, in the author's words, "everyone was involved in a historical torrent without knowing it." The only thing he found feasible and appropriate to do was to write short stories frantically so as to gain some distance and put things in perspective. That summer proved to be very productive for him. As the author comments in his preface to the collection of stories that came out in 1989, *The Town of Olive in 1944* is "about all of one writer's possible imaginations of a single remote Chinese town in a time before his birth, and the subsequent bankruptcy of those imaginations" (7). The story tells of how one Taiwanese scriptwriter, Gao Tian, is invited to collaborate with one well-known Japanese filmmaker, Mr. Suzuki, in a joint film project about the Sino-Japanese conflict in southwestern China during World War II. While writing the script for such a film, which is expected to satisfy both the Taiwanese and Japanese markets, the writer runs into tremendous difficulties. The stressful situation in which he finds himself not only indicates the complexity of factors involved in the process of film production, such as commercial concerns and ideological constraints, but also points to the impossibility of reliving history as it was actually lived, or, to put it otherwise, of representing history as such.

The main plot of the story is a search for historical truth, an effort to re-create historical reality. While the Japanese director has personal experience of the Sino-Japanese war, the Taiwan-born Chinese scriptwriter, who is the "I" narrator of the story, is far removed from the war, both in terms of time and space. "For me, the town of Olive is merely a geographical name one finds on a Chinese map, and I am using this name totally out of convenience. Since I have no knowledge whatsoever of this town, its population, size, or customs, the town appears to me just as remote and unfamiliar as any other nameless towns in Europe or Africa" (207). Yet it is in this town that the writer decides to stage his story and imagine what the war was like back in 1944. The very obscurity of the town gives him much more freedom and space in imagining and reproducing the past. "The reason I chose the town of Olive, which is close to Tengchong, as the locus for my story was that there were very few records available about it. I could have the most space for fiction, elaboration, and imagination" (209).

The marginal space occupied by the town of Olive provides an ideal site for Gao Tian the writer to retrieve a marginal history, a different memory and representation of a major war in the past. The original conception of the film is geared more toward commercial success, with a star-studded cast and a big budget. Some very weak pacifism also is pumped into the script, less to raise serious questions about the war than to be ideologically fashionable. Because it is initially proposed by the Japanese, the first draft presents the story from a Japanese perspective, depicting how a platoon of Japanese soldiers heroically defended one of the last military strongholds to the very end. Although the Japanese director Suzuki (whose continual eating throughout the story makes the reader suspect a morbid and compulsive appetite for whatever is consumable) claims to be a pacifist, the Taiwanese scriptwriter finds it uninteresting to tell yet another all-too-familiar war story. His immediate objection is that the plot too much resembles conventional Chinese films in which one sees similar depictions of the heroic deaths of Chinese soldiers. What he now wishes to resist is the master narrative of either victory or defeat. Instead, he wants to tell the story of the war from a different perspective. "I decided to put aside the original story. . . . I found another perspective, another standpoint, not that of the Japanese, nor that of the Chinese, but instead the viewpoint of the ethnic minorities who live in the border area of Yunnan. I wanted to look at the war from their perspective"

(214). From this viewpoint, which allows him to combine spatial marginality and ethnic minorities, he will more effectively reexamine historical experience as well as its representation. This strategy for ideological critique readily reminds us of the Fifth Generation films in China, such as *Daoma zei* (The horse thief), *Liechang Zhasa* (On the hunting ground), and, to a certain extent, *Huang tudi* (The yellow earth). Gao Tian's desire to evoke such a historical possibility goes beyond aesthetic estrangement and directly mirrors a growing indigenous consciousness in Taiwan since the mid-1980s. The nativist drive for self-determination in Taiwan, as in all national myths of origins, consists in retrieving a local history that gives the present a differentiated and unique identity.

So "looking at the war" in this context acquires two distinct but related meanings: one is to try to experience or remember the war differently; another is to represent the war from this particular angle, to create new images and spectacles; for, after all, the joint project is to make a movie, to produce a visual representation of the war. "To look at the war" now demands that this part of history be examined from a distance and yet in a creative engagement. Only through this active look or gaze will a piece of past history be recovered and brought back to memory with any relevance to present concerns and desires. In other words, history is indeed invoked as a mirror, but it is a mirror that does not necessarily reflect or verify certain truth, as traditional historical writings and wisdom would try to suggest. On the contrary, it is a mirror in the sense that every person who looks at history will invariably also see his or her own image and self. Representation of the past always mirrors present engagement, anxiety, and longings. Thus, the scriptwriter's decision to approach the war from the perspective of ethnic minorities serves at least two purposes simultaneously. It is a challenge to the commercialized film industry and a critique of the ideology of chauvinistic nationalism. At this point, it is all the more relevant that this story is about the making of a film. It becomes clear how much ideological weight the production of visual imagery carries, especially in our scopophiliac modern culture where a carefully constructed image often provokes critical reflection as much as it may pass as the enduring truth of a past moment. The scriptwriter's self-imposed critical mission, therefore, is to revolt against those predetermined and preprocessed images, to make visible a history that has been either obscured or underrepresented. To see history this way has yet another significance. It is not only to show a part of history that has not been represented so far, that is, to see history differently, but also to see concrete images, to restore its facticity to the historical moment in all of its details and contingencies, in all of its visual richness and depth.

The story then proceeds to tell how Gao Tian the hardworking writer tries to "see" the war from his particular viewpoint. This heroic endeavor excites him and causes his final disappointment, because what he strives for is precisely the impossible, namely, reliving instead of representing a forgotten history. Yet it is the impossible prospect of reliving history that greatly attracts the writer and inspires his imagination. After much research into the customs and rituals of the ethnic minorities with whom he is now genuinely fascinated, the writer forms a story line and can see that "one after another the characters begin surfacing." In rapid succession, a whole cast of characters present themselves, almost surreally, in the writer's vision, most of them defined by their function in the movie: a pacifist Japanese medical lieutenant, a returned Chinese student with his Japanese wife, an unyielding village master, a traitor, etc. But with all these characters, the writer still does not know how to unfold the story because he has not found the right image or the right moment that speaks to him. This frustration marks the first stage of Gao Tian's effort at retrieving a different history, at which point he is still very much within the narrative's framework. Narrative itself now becomes a debilitating device because something about the war defies narration. The writer is so obsessed with thinking up some interesting story that he has nightmares which mostly consist of haunting images of emptiness and silence. One way or another, narration falls into the given pattern, and the writer finds this susceptibility to an easy and unchallenged story line deeply unsettling.

Narrative, or rather the seduction of narration, now blocks rather than leads to the writer's grasp of history. The need to tell a coherent story becomes an obstacle to his approaching history or even communicating with it. As long as he cares about telling a story, Gao Tian finds himself far removed from the historical moment that he wants to experience and endow with an image. One way or another, he realizes, he is brought back to speak to the market and satisfy the consumers' appetite for either sensation or comfort. At this point, the writer decides to make a trip to Japan and eventually to Hiroshima. While in the still disturbingly barren Hiroshima, he finds nothing, he nonetheless is constantly haunted by the famous filmic image from *Hiroshima, mon amour:* a naked couple silently making love against the background of the debris of the first atomic bomb. This image, together with the calm and flat male voice of the film ("Tu n'ai *rien* vu à Hiroshima. Rien"), suddenly reveals to the writer something uncanny about the war and the impossibility of telling a true story about it. "I finally understood this line, because I came to Hiroshima" (220). An intense visual image illustrates an up-till-now enigmatic utterance regarding the impossibility of seeing anything. This connection comes as a profound revelation, and Gao Tian decides to turn away from narration and let himself really see and imagine.

Visual imagination thus seems to be the only way to approach the totality of historical experience, or at least to metonymically make apparent the irretrievable and unrepresentable whole. The real, in other words, is made conceivable through the intervention of a critical imaginary. Historical consciousness becomes more a space-oriented vision than a time-oriented narrative. Conjured images of the town of Olive and reconstructed scenes from a certain past moment now bear much more revelation than does a narrative that has to organize time and the sequences of events. "What is the town of Olive like? It is close by the River of Longchuan, but then do people living there have to depend on the river for their livelihood? Can one sail a boat on the river? I try to make this town become active and alive, without necessarily being true to reality" (224).

In his effort to revive the town of Olive, so as to approach truth rather than reality, the scriptwriter turns to filmic images and presents life in the town as if it were watched through a horizontally moving camera. What we have, then, is a colorful picture of everyday life and a sense of uncontrollable simultaneity. All the things that the writer now makes us see happen at the same time, and we feel that instead of observing life in this small town from a remote historical distance, all of a sudden we are brought face-to-face with those who are walking down the streets and through the boisterous and pleasantly distracting street fair. Here, we have a description that is no longer the same as what Lukács once denounced as naturalistic and devoid of any critical judgment. Rather, literary description, carried out here in the mode of cinematography, suggests a drive to go beyond the linguistic medium and invites us to visualize, even when its content appears to be incoherent and disorienting. Images now become a preferred method by which the vitality and truthfulness of a historical moment are brought back.

It is interesting to observe how this filmic representation is realized in the text. In order to evoke visual images or a cinematic vision, the text has to call into place the subject of a viewer. "If you happen to be at a street fair, you will see. . . ." The "you" here is the observer, either the reader or, more probably, a potential moviegoer. What you will see is not a complete action or a contrivedly revealing dramatic situation. On the contrary, you will see concrete objects and colors that make up the reality of everyday life in this remote frontier town. ". . . You will see, in the glaring sunshine, those shining steel knives, silver jewelry for women, tapestry and embroidered silk. Some Chinese merchants sell matches, salt, cosmetics, imported goods, snow peas, and green peppers; Baiyi peddlers sell rice, homemade cloth, bamboo products, sweet potatoes, and mung beans; finally some Gawas sell herb medicine, pumpkins, areca nuts, and even firewood" (224). This detailed listing of goods on sale at the fair does not exactly recall a Balzacian moment of almost breathtakingly close and relevatory description or, for that matter, any realistic representation in the classical sense. Rather, in this one brief paragraph, we move rapidly and are forced to see an abundance of objects, glittering details that swarm up and fill our vision, each demanding some attention. In other words, it is like following a camera and steadily glancing over a panoramic shot of the site. We see the process, and we see ourselves approaching a specific moment in history with all its irreducible reality, even though this reality might be imaginary.

Then, in a series of sentences, our overview of the situation assumes a different pace, and it becomes more like watching a movie. The camera, after rolling over the fair as background, now further zooms in on two kids playing in the marketplace.

> Kala and Luosi are also in the crowd. Kala is just reaching to catch a dragonfly that is resting on a decoration made from a cow horn when the dragonfly appears to be startled and takes off.
>
> It turns out that a jeep and a military truck with a full load of Japanese soldiers are speeding by. Inside the jeep sits a Japanese officer.
>
> With the villagers running in all directions, the guards hasten to salute the jeep and the truck.

>   Outside a Buddhist temple somewhere in the town hangs a sign that reads "Headquarters of Military Guard in the Town of Olive."
>   At this point we get to see better the temple and some other architecture. (224–25)

Instead of a narrative sequence, visuality now dominates and introduces a different mode of experience. Visual representation provides a much more immediate access to a past context of lived experience, the totality of which is at once presumed and broken into multiple continuous and discontinuous moments. As a result, Gao Tian feels much more confident and at home with his project. "The town of Olive acquired a much better image in my imagination. . . . Olive was no longer a geographical term, nor a black dot one finds on the map. The entire town became active in my imagination. There were people living in town, there were things happening, and the war was going to reach it" (225–26).

Not surprisingly, we witness a nostalgia expressing itself in the writer's effort to imagine the past. But this is a cult of image that has a different significance than what Fredric Jameson once described as "the cult of the glossy image" that one usually encounters in so-called "nostalgia films and texts." The "unimaginably intense delicacy of hue" to which the audience is exposed in contemporary Hollywood film, according to Jameson, is precisely what makes the filmic image inauthentic and pastiche. "From time to time such sheer beauty can seem obscene, the ultimate form of the consumption of streamlined commodities—a transformation of our senses into the mail-order houses of the spirit, some ultimate packaging of Nature in cellophane of a type that any elegant shop might well wish to carry in its window."[3] What Jameson points to is the insatiable consumption of images in the postmodernist "society of the spectacle." In such a culture, content, an enfeebled category, is often confused with form—or, rather, it is superseded by form. Image means and becomes everything. However, the predominance of or even obsession with images is not exactly an escape from history in the case of the Taiwanese scriptwriter, who only wishes to write about a past war differently. Even though he can vividly imagine a past moment and is indeed writing for a film production, images alone are not enough; or, conversely, they contain too much and appear too overwhelming and unfathomable. The content of

---

3. Fredric Jameson, *Signatures of the Visible* (New York: Routledge, 1990), 85.

The Mirror of History **233**

his images is purposely charged and made much more complex. At least they are not prepackaged enough to make the censors happy. After a preliminary review, the censors and some critics insist that the content of the film, as Gao Tian presents it, is not quite correct and therefore ideologically unacceptable. They do not see how a Chinese can write such a detached and neutral film script about that bloody war. Their final conclusion leads them to question the identity of the scriptwriter: "This script does not read like it was written by a Chinese, but rather by a person from a third, neutral country, outside both China and Japan. After all, aren't you a Chinese? A Chinese has to have a Chinese position and perspective . . ." (230).

Gao Tian's effort to see and imagine history finally leads to a fundamental question about his own self-identity. Those pointed questions about his national allegiance underscore his growing awareness of himself as a Taiwanese freed from an obsession with China. The mirror of history once again turns out to be indispensable for any conception of self or subjectivity. This theme seems to have a parallel development in Su Tong, especially in the story we will explore in a moment. But first, we need to comment further on the intriguing relationship between images and narrative or content. In *The Town of Olive in 1944,* vivid and concrete images are charged with the difficult, if not impossible, task of retrieving the lost dimensions of history. Images not only suddenly expose the reduction and violence that an apparently coherent and consistent narrative might do to history; they also acquire a life of their own, an aesthetic energy as well as historical vitality. To wipe out or suppress these images, therefore, is the same as to deny that history was once actually lived and experienced, not as part of some meaningful grand narrative, but precisely as that contingent and precarious process of life. Also, images of the past are shown to be able to reveal the distance between past and present. The unbridgeable gap between a past moment and the present is repeatedly underscored through these images, because unlike a narrative ready for consumption, a real and tangible image of a particular history will in the final analysis remind us of nothing but the removedness or pastness of that moment.[4] Images by their very reality or truthfulness tell the truth of

---

4. In talking about photography, Roland Barthes also emphasizes the unbridgeable distance between an image and its referent: "What the Photograph reproduces to infinity has occurred only once: the Photograph mechanically repeats what could never

their radical otherness. To see, in this context, to indulge in visual imagination, is then to recognize history as difference and at the same time to pose a question about the viewer, the subject who imagines and gazes at history. Thus, the final frustrated utterance of the writer: "What on earth was the town of Olive like? What on earth took place in the year 1944?" (232). The whole process of his trying to imagine the town of Olive has to be at the same time a journey of self-discovery and a confrontation with a different other.

This frustration may bring in the notion of the sublime, the felt presence of the unrepresentable. Gao Tian's anguished utterance reveals that history is indeed that sublime moment of human experience because its presence is everywhere, although it can never be retrieved either experientially or even representationally. The ideological function of seeing therefore becomes clear insofar as the immanent presence of history is brought home and highlighted. The historical vision here is not reminiscent of the certainty and lack of ambiguity that a contemplative Cartesian subject is supposed to have enjoyed in one of the "scopic regimes of modernity."[5] On the contrary, it articulates the frustration of a time when, with an overabundance of images and photographic reproductions, history is still grasped as that which surrounds us without being representable. No wonder, then, that the first-person narrator in Su Tong's novella *Nineteen Thirty-four Escapes* should have uttered a similar question with the same anxiety: "Nineteen thirty-four. Do you know? Nineteen thirty-four was a year of disaster" (18; 105).

Since Xiao Ye's story is about the production of images—namely, the germination of a regional imagination in excess of nationalist discourse in writing the script for a film—the primacy of visuality in his narrative should hardly come as a surprise. But in Su Tong's narrative of a fictional familial genealogy we also find the same drive for a concrete, almost tangible image of the past. As critic Meng Yue points out, in Su Tong's writings, especially in his historical narratives, there is very nearly an imperative for the reader to see, to visualize the past. Between empty year numbers and the fictive world that the writer creates there is a constant

---

be repeated existentially." See his *Camera Lucida: Reflections on Photography* (New York: Hill and Wang, 1981), 4.

5. See Martin Jay, "Scopic Regimes of Modernity" in *Vision and Visuality,* ed. Hal Foster (Seattle: Bay Press, 1988), 3–23.

gaze that is requested by the narrator and which makes a meaningful connection between these two different realms. "As a result, phrases like 'I see,' 'you see,' 'he sees,' and other imperatives in the text demanding you to look become a unique narrative mechanism in his series about the 'Maple-poplar Village.' They also constitute an unusual narrative strategy in contemporary fiction."[6] Meng Yue calls our attention to a key feature of Su Tong's writings and links this feature with an ideological commitment on the writer's part. The very gaze of the narrator, or the action of looking back at history, is more often staged for the purpose of getting people's attention so that the observer himself can be looked at as such. The gaze is directed so as to be looked at and gazed upon. "[The narrator] tells not only of 'the story of his ancestors,' but also of his own gaze, other people's gaze, and his gaze at other people's gaze."[7]

The historicizing gaze that Meng Yue finds fascinating in Su Tong is particularly relevant and instrumental in *Nineteen Thirty-four Escapes*. A complex and seminal story, this novella can be studied from a great variety of critical readings and approaches, but it is indeed revealing to examine the evocation of vision and visuality in the narrative. What we will find is perhaps more than a confrontation with history, even a rethinking of the ultimate meaning or possibility of knowing history. As Meng Yue suggests, the seeing of history represented in Su Tong's stories in fact points to the very unknowability of the past, and at the same time it arouses our desire to see and know.

In *Nineteen Thirty-four Escapes,* Su Tong tells a story of the gradual but no less violent disintegration and dispersal of a family in rural southeastern China in the 1930s. It is also a story about the difficult and painful transition from country to city, from the values of traditional community to the energy as well as fluidity of urban life. A prodigiously reproductive Grandmother Jiang, six of whose seven children die off during the course of the story, is the heroine. She is also the object of the narrator's gaze at the beginning of the narrative. The narrator is unmistakably identified as a young man in late twentieth-century China who seems obsessed with the past of his father and grandfather. A young man who grows increasingly uncomfortable in the city, the narrator "I" is more and more

---

6. Meng Yue, "Su Tong de 'jiashi' yu 'lishi' xiezuo" (The writing of "family genealogy" and "history" by Su Tong), *Jintian* (Today), no. 2 (1990): 86–87.

7. Ibid., 87.

convinced that his rural family, or the generation of his grandparents, had lived a glorious life in history. In comparison with their life experience, he finds his own existence shamefully pale and trivial. His desire to recall the past, to see how his relatives had lived and loved, therefore, is first aroused by his dissatisfaction with his own life in the present. His anxiety to escape from the normalcy of the present expresses a sense of loss and dislocation that one will find in some of Su Tong's other stories, notably his stories about contemporary cities in China, such as "As Serene as Water" and "Hello, My Beekeeper."[8] In this sense, Su Tong's narrator here represents a generation that grew up during the traumatic Cultural Revolution, without necessarily experiencing the trauma, and which now finds itself at a loss in a monstrous and rapidly modernizing urban landscape.

Thus, history is invoked first as a fantasy that somehow unflatteringly mirrors an uneventful and routinized present. For this reason, whenever the past is represented, Su Tong's narrative always describes it with the richest color and imagination possible. "The year 1934 radiated strong shafts of purple light that circumscribed my thinking." At the same time that Su Tong and his generation feel they have been denied access to the past, they also realize that history may well be their only means of challenging the dominant ideology of everyday life. The contrast between a rich history and a monotonous present is most persistent throughout Su Tong's historical narratives. His nostalgia is so self-indulgent and oriented toward sensuous details that critics have even noticed, with approbation, an "effeminate sensibility" in Su Tong's perpetual regard of the past.[9] (The same nostalgic longing for a past glory is also apparent in the Taiwan writer Lin Yaode's epic-spirited novel *1947—Gaosha baihe* [1947— Lilium formosanum],[10] where we can find almost the same fascination with condensed and striking images that are treated as if retrieved from the collective unconscious.)

A retrospective gaze with such intellectual and libidinal investment invariably produces a central image or spectacle that captures the subject's fantasy about the past. In *The Town of Olive in 1944,* we have seen a dra-

8. See chap. 6, "Residual Modernism: Narratives of the Self in the 1980s."
9. See Wang Zheng and Xiao Hua, "Hubu de qingnian yishi: yu Su Tong youguan de huo wuguan de" (Complementary youth consciousness: things having or not having to do with Su Tong), *Dushu* (Reading) (July-August 1989): 103–04.
10. Lin Yaode (Lin Yao-te), *1947 Gaosha baihe* (Taipei: Unitas, 1990).

matic moment when a historical past "surfaces" just as if from a deep body of water. In *Nineteen Thirty-four Escapes,* we once again encounter the same "surfacing." First regarding the year 1934 as an ancient tree and then assimilating himself as part of it, the narrator succeeds in seeing "Grandmother Jiang surface from history" (18; 105). Such a surfacing, a coming into being, demands an image of its own:

> The Woman Jiang stands motionless on her lanky legs, as if nailed to a patch of chilly and muddy rice field. That is a picture of early spring and a country woman. Her cheekbones protruding, Jiang's face is covered with mud. She lowers her head to listen to the sound made by the baby in her belly. She feels herself as a barren hill, where men cut down everything and then plant sons and daughters like trees, one after another. She listens to the baby's sound as if listening to the wind blowing against her, blowing against a barren hill. (19; 105–06)

The entire history of that diaspora in 1934 is encoded in and derived from this image of Grandmother Jiang standing in the rice paddy listening to her unborn baby. It is first a projection, a spectacular image called forth by the narrator, through his intense gazing at the year 1934 as an enigmatic object. In this spectacle we are told not only that Grandmother Jiang is once again pregnant, but subsequently we also are brought to see this country woman from another angle, namely, through the binoculars of the rich farmer Chen Wenzhi. A perverse voyeur, Chen Wenzhi hides on top of his black-bricked mansion and observes men and women toiling and copulating in the open field. "The background remains the brownish yellow hill in the northeastern part of Maple-poplar Village, with the black-bricked mansion on the hill. Grandmother Jiang and my father thus stood against the historical spectacle of fifty-odd years ago" (29; 119).

This spectacle is only one stimulant that excites the narrator's "fantastically beautiful imagination." In contrast to this primal moment of "surfacing," other things have "sunk" into the bottomless pit of history, one of which being the wooden house in the city where Grandfather Chen Baonian ran his bamboo shop and determinedly uprooted himself from the rural country for good (24; 113). Indeed, only images of people seem to remain accessible. "Among my relatives of the past, the First Dog-brat of the Chen family, with the image of a young boy who collects animal droppings, attracts my attention in the familial genealogy" (25; 113).

Almost every character that appears in the story, or, rather, every member of the family now recalled, has a distinct image. Phoenix, "the most beautiful woman" of the Chen family, for instance, is now remembered as a "spot of purple light." Fifty years after her mysterious death, "I try to capture that spot of purple light in my familial genealogy that was my grand-aunt. Even if Phoenix were a beautiful firefly that hurriedly passed in front of me, how could I capture the purple light she emits?" (31; 122). Another woman, Huanzi, whose presence in this reconstructed family history is as indelible as her once fashionable blue cotton overcoat, also possesses her own particular image. A lover and concubine of Grandfather Chen Baonian, the petite Huanzi was pregnant in the winter of 1934 and was taken back to the village to give birth. We are presented with the moment of the tense encounter between Grandmother Jiang and Huanzi on a chilly winter morning. "My Grandmother Jiang stood by the door and watched the little woman Huanzi walking on the snow and approaching the ancestral home of the Chen family. The blue cotton overcoat of Huanzi radiated a strong blue light against the snow on the ground, and it hurt Jiang's eyes. The first conversation between these two women fifty years ago now distinctly comes to me and into my ears" (68; 166). Here we first get a chance to see the situation, from the perspective of Grandmother Jiang, who receives the woman from the city with an understandable hostility. Only after a luminous image that makes the characters identifiable and distinct do we have a chance to hear their greetings and conversation. Visual images of the past precede any other memories, as well as our understanding and interpretation.

This predominance of visual spectacle in fact constitutes the basic narrative structure of the story *Nineteen Thirty-four Escapes*. Again and again we are brought to see rich and concrete "spectacles" of a past moment. At the very beginning, we are told, "if you now go and push open the door of my father's house, you will only see my father and my mother. My other six relatives are not at home now. They are still wandering around like black fish out there" (17; 103). They are absent, and the entire endeavor of telling the story of the "diaspora" is to bring them back home, to make them the narrator's companions, imaginary yet most satisfying. Thus, to see is not only to overcome their absence; it also reveals this very absence and recognizes it as that which makes narration both necessary and possible. The retrieved images we see or are brought to see point to a lack that constitutes our own experience. Again, history and images of history are constructed as a mirror in which the narrator has a chance to see himself as if seen by others and regarded from the other end of history.

The desire to see that underlies and organizes the entire narrative forces us to ask questions about the narrator as an engaged and transformed subject. We are constantly made aware that the narrator is in fact seeing and imagining with us. He makes us see things as he imagines them. He also reminds us continually that neither he nor we know that particular year, 1934, at all.

> To me the winter of 1934 appears to be so strange. I have no idea how to describe my forefathers who were active in my family history in that winter. I was told that my grandfather Chen Baonian also carried his son Dog-brat outdoors for some sunshine. Then he would be watching, together with Dog-brat, the small woman Huanzi putting up clothes to dry. What was it like for these three people to look at each other with her blue dress hanging between them? What was it like for the sun of the 1934 winter to shine over these three people? Do I know? (66; 164)

What is unknowable and irretrievable is the immediate lived experience of a past moment. Although the narrator knows the ending to the scene he depicts here—that Dog-brat was going to die and Huanzi would be sent off to the country to give birth to her illegitimate child—he no longer can know how it was at that particular moment in the winter of 1934 with all of its experiential irreducibility. Throughout the story he continually expresses his anxiety over the impossibility of reliving the past, of actually seeing and feeling the same as his forefathers once did.

Indeed, the fascination with history that now possesses the young man in the 1980s is precisely this awareness of an unbridgeable gap between his own present and the history that has led up to it. His desire to see and imagine the past is not at all dampened by his knowledge of the gap between him and that past. On the contrary, this very unknowability gives him more space for imagination and a chance for him to confront the past. It is through this seeing, this rich imagination, that he will have a chance both to (re)possess a history for himself and to find his own identity. The seeing here is as much a projection as an introjection, through which the narrator fashions an image of himself and implicates himself into the historical narrative. What the narrator of *Nineteen Thirty-four Escapes* faces is a mirror of history that does not necessarily reveal some truth about or message from the past. Rather, it is a mirror in which the narrator wishes to find his self-identity and construct his own subjectivity. The mirror of history, once again, is the mirror in which he finds a self-image, a distanced but full reflection of and on his own existence.

The mirror of history in his narrative constitutes the narrator's own self-consciousness in that it looks back and reflects. The exchange of gazes between the narrator and what he narrates is the most striking feature of the story. We not only have a first-person narrator, an "I" who recounts his effort at retrieving his family history, but we also have the reader addressed directly as "you." Characters in the story are imagined with such intensity that they constantly look back at both the reader and the narrator, and silently but with eloquence they address a collective "we/us" of the present. Between this looking back and forth, between a vividly colored vision of the past and the pale and empty present, the narrator asserts himself and proclaims a new image and identity. At one moment of his search for the past, he comes to the town that used to be known for its bamboo products. His "gaze" grows like an "extended ivy" that embraces the road and passers-by (23; 111–12). However, at the same time, he feels watched.

> I fancy that I see the small attic of the Chen bamboo shop in the old town known for its bamboo products, where Dog-brat and his friend Little Blind used to live. The window of the attic would give out a weak red glow at night; it was a red light from their eyes. You will be touched when you look up at the attic, you will see people on top of people. They are peeping at us from an attic that no longer exists; they are floating in the empty sky of 1934. (62; 159–60)

The tension between the past and the present is here transformed into an exchange of gazes. In this imaginary exchange, the narrator realizes that he is at once an observer of history and a participant in it. He no longer possesses a complete identity; on the contrary, he needs to look back and confront the past. This exchange establishes his identity and at the same time challenges the reality of his own moment. History, in other words, is here invoked to create a Brechtian estrangement that historicizes the present and reveals its boundedness or incompleteness. The imaginary gaze from the past functions as the mirror that is indispensable for the formation of the subject. In this reflecting mirror of history, "the subject finds or recognizes itself through an image which simultaneously alienates it, and hence, potentially, confronts it."[11]

The subplot of the story is, then, a tale of search, the narrator's search for a history of his family and for a self-identity. In the beginning there is a moment when he realizes that his shadow at night in the city looks weird. He is disturbed because he is reminded of a person on the run. By the end, when he has told the story of diaspora, he turns around to have another look at his shadow and believes he is now ready to walk through the city at night. "If you open the window, you will see my shadow projected onto the city, floating and rising. But who will be able to tell what a shadow that is?" (78; 178). The final question is about identity, the narrator's identity in the wake of the narrative. In the mirror of history, the young man finds his own identity, or rather, finds his own identity problematized and complicated. And he seems satisfied.

Let us come back to the story one more time. The whole story derives from the desire to see—to see how "my Grandmother Jiang" on one spring day more than fifty years ago stood in the rice paddy and listened to the baby stirring in her body. Here is a cinematic structure of implicated visual relations. First, we see her standing at the center of our vision; then our view is elevated, and we see the background. On the yellow hill is a black-bricked building. Its presence is constantly felt by Grandmother Jiang because, we are told, the rich farmer Chen Wenzhi is watching her with a pair of Japanese binoculars. Thus, a whole visual field is introduced, and a power relationship is inscribed into the picture. So is history injected into that almost idyllic picture of a pregnant country woman planting rice in an open field. It would be interesting to examine the politics of vision in terms of sexual difference constructed and represented here, but I would like to look further into the relationship between visuality and narrative explored in the text.

The primacy of visuality that we witness in Su Tong's narratives of history registers a different experience of images than what we would find in a postmodern "society of the spectacle," even different from the context in which Xiao Ye ponders the meaning of seeing the past differently. In a postmodern culture where images and visual experience become the

---

11. Jacqueline Rose, "The Imaginary," in her *Sexuality in the Field of Vision* (London: Verso, 1986), 174.

dominant mode of knowledge and perception, the glossy and perfect photographic images, either of a reconstructed past or of contemporary life, in fact indicate a "crisis of historicity" because those hyperreal and depthless images flatten and reduce, rather than reinforce, the historical distance or "aura" that we need to sense about past events. What disappears or becomes unimaginable is precisely that whole lived context of past experience. A hyperreal image blocks and displaces rather than registers a moment of history.[12] But in Su Tong's narrative we find something else. Here, our starting point is an imagined spectacle of the past, with all its lived concreteness and rich coloration. But this will not be where the narrator stops. First compelling the reader to see, to be reconciled with this image, the narrator moves on to contextualize the spectacle and charges it with raw human passion and innermost desires. In other words, the spectacle now becomes both the starting point and the end product of a historical imagination.

The purposes served by such a narrative strategy are multiple, as Meng Yue in her essay has reminded us. But besides the determined function of resisting an ideological suppression of history, the emphasis on visuality is also symptomatic of a poverty of images in general, especially images of the recent past, in post-Cultural Revolution China. Su Tong's narrative is effective and powerful because the images that he constructs of the past are both different from the conventional and institutionalized perception of the past (here it is the 1930s) and, at the same time, fantastically realistic and intimate. In a political culture that constantly erases differences in history as well as images of the past, Su Tong's story opens a new visual field and gives rise to fresh imagination. Images or imaginations of a past that is different become an enormously effective way to reappropriate history and revive that which threatens to disappear forever.

The reappropriation of history is the common theme shared by *Nineteen Thirty-four Escapes* and *The Town of Olive in 1944*. The desire for reappropriation stems from the realization that history is in constant danger of being subjugated to one master narrative. The richness and im-

---

12. For a critique of the postmodern consumption of depthless images, see Jameson's "Postmodernism, Or, The Cultural Logic of Late Capitalism," collected as the first chapter in his book of the same name (Durham, N.C.: Duke University Press, 1990), esp. 8–9. Also, Jean Baudrillard's discussion of "simulacra and simulations" is helpful. See *Jean Baudrillard: Selected Writings,* ed. with introduction by Mark Poster (Stanford, Calif.: Stanford University Press, 1988).

mediacy that an image promises seem to be the best reason to go back to history. Thus, the history-hungry narrator in Su Tong's story experiences the hallucination of seeing his relatives continually emerge from the past. "I feel that I see Grandmother Jiang carry my father on her back and run about in the bitter wind and rain of 1934. The saw-shaped scar on her forehead glowed. A picture of my grandmother, the pond of the dead, and the lush purslane repeatedly flashes in front of my eyes, but I cannot imagine the unusual suffering my grandmother experienced by the pond of the dead" (55; 151). This image, just as many other images that the narrator continues to see, is by itself, as the narrator realizes, "a specific historical content" (59; 156). To retrace that historical meaning, he has to reconstruct an entire story and make the spectacular image speak and give forth all of its deeply embedded secrets and revelations. To see, to understand the historical spectacle finally leads to a rewriting of history, and, in this particular case, to a "spectacularization" of history.

Finally, as if by accident, this rich imagination of history that we witness is achieved without any photographic images. At one point, the narrator expresses his ambivalent feelings toward the absence of any pictures that would have allowed him better access to the past. "Huanzi and Phoenix were the two most beautiful women in my family. It is a pity that neither left behind a picture, and as a result I have no means to decide whether they really looked like each other that much" (71; 169). The interesting point here is that the regret felt by the young man is not that he cannot tell whether they were really beautiful or how beautiful they were. Instead, he is saddened because he cannot tell whether they were like each other. It remains uncontested that they were beautiful, just as that particular history is always exciting and spectacular. Photographic images could have helped not because they may determine truth or falsehood, but because they would have let us see better.

The cultural significance of Su Tong's narratives of spectacular history is manifold. It first indicates a general cultural crisis in which official, mainstream historiography is continually challenged. This effort at rewriting and retrieving history is reflected in some other notable writers such as Mo Yan and Liu Heng, in whose work we can find a shared fondness for historical spectacle. The spectacularization of history also points to a recognized need in postrevolutionary Chinese culture to search for a new identity, a new self-consciousness that can claim a different history than what has been instituted in the past forty years or so. In his *Nineteen*

Thirty-four Escapes, Su Tong best captures this critical impulse and opens up new possibilities of looking into the mirror of history. In many aspects, Xiao Ye's writings have a comparable function, especially his stories about historical experience such as "Qiangbao" (Violence), and "Women de Heilong jiang a" (Our Black Dragon River). In *The Town of Olive in 1944,* the search for a new self-identity is further complicated by the fact that the novella is staged against a transnational and multicultural background. (Another perfect example of the same trend will be Lin Yaode's novel *1947—Lilium formosanum,* mentioned above.) Although Xiao Ye's narrative is structurally simpler, the ideological message appears to be much more complex and self-conscious than that in Su Tong. This, of course, is not a moment to make any value judgment, but one cannot help but feel that Xiao Ye's desperate attempt to find a minoritized perspective on a grand historical narrative has to reflect a new *collective* self-consciousness and self-image that was coming of age in Taiwan in the last quarter of the twentieth century, whereas Su Tong's historical nostalgia gathers its potency and relevancy precisely from an *individualized* gaze that he stubbornly directs upon our past. Yet both writers find their inspiration in conjuring up and letting themselves be absorbed in a fantastic historical spectacle.

8

In Search of the Real City:
Cinematic Representations of Beijing and
the Politics of Vision

Potentially, the city is in itself the powerful symbol of a complex society. If visually well set forth, it can also have strong expressive meaning.
—Kevin Lynch, *The Image of the City*

That the city of Beijing presents a perfect spatial embodiment of a traditional culture caught in the maelstrom of rapid and condensed modernization is readily observable, even to a passing tourist. "Beijing is a microcosm of China," so an up-to-date pocket travel book informs its readers and potential travelers. "It combines village and metropolis, Western-style modernization and Chinese tradition, new-fashioned pomp with old-fashioned modesty. It is a showcase of China's policy for reform and opening up to the West."[1] Another contemporary guidebook (from the "Travel Survival Kit" series) gives more in-depth information: "All cities in China are equal, but some are more equal than others. Beijing has the best of everything in China bar the weather: the best food, the best hotels, the best transport, the best temples. But its vast squares and boulevards, its cavernous monoliths and its huge numbers of tourists are likely to leave you cold. It is a weird city—traces of its former character may be found down the back alleys where things are a bit more to human scale."[2]

Indeed, probably no visitor to Beijing in the 1990s would fail to notice the weird, sometimes mind-boggling character of this sprawling urban center that is becoming increasingly similar to Los Angeles. It is one of the oldest cities in the world, and yet compressed sites or islands of its

---

1. Don J. Cohn, *A Guide to Beijing* (Lincolnwood, Ill.: Passport Books, 1992), 12.
2. Joe Cummings et al., *A Travel Survival Kit: China,* 3rd ed. (Berkeley: Lonely Planet, 1991), 485.

imperial past are now barely visible under the veil of brownish smog and against the ragged backdrop of masses of prefabricated, international-style apartment buildings or more recent all-glass high-rises. Its broad and often dishearteningly straight, but increasingly jammed and billboarded boulevards, while still stridently reminding you of the scale and aspiration of a recent collective project and central planning, are continually humanized and made lively by an unstoppable flow of millions of bicyclists. If you decide to move across the city, either on foot or by any means of transportation, you will soon find yourself experiencing starkly different sections and neighborhoods (in terms of the appearance of their residents, architectural style, spatial arrangement, and noise level), which, as in almost any other large city in the world, exist side-by-side and form silent commentary on one another. This "synchronicity of the nonsynchronous," as Ernst Bloch's useful phrase describes it, finds its expression in another space-related human experience, namely, the multiple means of transportation on Beijing's streets, from pedicabs, to overcrowded buses, to the latest Lexus.

Of this uneven but changing cityscape, we find timely and fascinating representations in Chinese cinema since the late 1980s, for which the dynamics and social, if also libidinal, energy of the modern city have become a much-explored theme and created a new film genre. The one particular sequence of images and soundtrack I have in mind is the opening collage in *Wanzhu* (Troubleshooters, dir. Mi Jiashan, 1988). The film's location is emphatically contemporary Beijing. Two enormous characters for the title of the film are projected onto three re-created primitive masks; they are accompanied by a soundtrack that captures a vocal fragment from some traditional opera or storytelling, shifts to a shrill siren that drowns out the narrating voice, and then records some boisterous marketplace where voices shouting out the names of popular magazines can be distinguished. But this brief temporalized sequence of sound effects is only the preface to an explosive juxtaposition of often fragmented but nonetheless spectacular images of the city. Through a zoom lens, the spectacle of traffic congestion is brought much closer, and minimal depth of field underscores a compressed urban spatiotemporal regime; unsteady and fast-moving shots of glass buildings (unmistakable signs of contemporaneity), with twisted reflections of other high-rises and construction cranes, suggest the spatial fragmentation with which an awestruck observer is forced to become reconciled. Then, quickly, the camera is directed back at the hustling and bustling streets where it presents a series of incomplete, unrelated snapshots of crawling vehicles, expressionless old women, hordes of bicyclists, country girls gathering at a labor market, a frowning youth with a punk haircut—all horizontal images of an expanding metropolis from the perspective of an apparently disoriented subject. Over this collage of urban spectacles, contemporary Chinese rock and roll (clearly reminiscent of early Bruce Springsteen) is introduced to make direct commentary:

> I once dreamed about life in a modern city,
> But I don't know how to express my present feeling;
> Buildings here are getting taller and taller every day,
> But my days here are not that great.[3]

In fact, 1988 saw the production of a series of films on the subject of contemporary city life, at least four of them based on novels or novellas by the popular Beijing writer Wang Shuo. Hence, 1988 has been dubbed "the year of Wang Shuo" in Chinese cinema.[4] These films about the city, mostly directed by members of the Fifth Generation,[5] form a distinct genre and indicate a different intellectual concern and cultural criticism than in earlier Fifth Generation experiments or, indeed, in the tradition of New China cinema. By New China cinema, I mean the state-supported film industry that came into being with the founding of the People's Republic in 1949. Its brief and frequently interrupted course of development notwithstanding, New China cinema is mass-oriented and generally identified with a formulaic socialist realist aesthetic, "a didactic fusion," as one critic puts it, "of classic Hollywood filmmaking and Soviet Stalin-

---

3. The lyrics go on like this: With a friend I always kill some time in a bar, / While the tape player repeats all the hit songs. / You think one way and you talk one way, / Because everyone wears a toy-like mask. / What should I say?

4. These four films are *Wanzhu, Lunhui* (dir. Huang Jianxin), *Da chuanqi* (dir. Ye Daying), and *Yiban shi haishui, yiban shi huoyan* (dir. Xia Gang).

5. Two other city films that came out in 1988 are *Yaogun qingnian* and *Fengkuang de daijia*, directed, respectively, by Tian Zhuangzhuang (*Daoma zei*, 1986) and Zhou Xiaowen (*Zuihou de fengkuang*, 1987), two well-established Fifth Generation filmmakers. In 1987, at least two films by directors of the Fifth Generation were also about the contemporary cityscape: *Gei kafei jiadian tang* (dir. Sun Zhou) and *Taiyang yu* (dir. Zhang Zeming).

ist style."[6] The preferred subject matter for this determinedly revolutionary popular cinema is collective heroism and socialist construction, while its audience is often imagined to be a politically engaged nation instead of sentimental urban dwellers. Consequently, the experiential city fades as a pertinent cinematic theme or field, and the well-lit imagery of contemporary life found in New China cinema invariably comes from either an industrial construction site or the countryside undergoing profound transformations. Even the revolutionary past, when it is projected in New China cinema, is systematically romanticized and made to adhere to the current representational hierarchies. Against this staid tradition of "revolutionary realism combined with revolutionary romanticism," the Fifth Generation of filmmakers introduced a fresh cinematic language and vision in the mid-1980s by bringing into focus a remote and obscure location, temporal as well as spatial, that bespeaks a different and yet concrete reality of depth. What enabled their breakthrough was clearly a modernist aesthetics and avant-gardist challenge against didactic mass cinema.[7] Hence, the initial defamiliarizing impact of *Huang tudi* (The yellow earth, dir. Chen Kaige, 1984), *Daoma zei* (The horse thief, dir. Tian Zhuangzhuang, 1986), and *Hong gaoliang* (Red sorghum, dir. Zhang Yimou, 1988), all now considered classics of Fifth Generation filmmaking.

In the new genre of city films that attracted members of the self-consciously innovative Fifth Generation, a central symbiosis is suggested between the experience of discontented youth and a vast, disorienting

6. For analyses of some representative film texts from the New China cinema tradition, see Chris Berry, "Sexual Difference and the Viewing Subject in *Li Shuangshuang* and *The In-Laws*," in *Perspectives on Chinese Cinema*, ed. Chris Berry (London: British Film Institute, 1991), 30–39; Ma Junxiang, "*Shanghai guniang*: geming nüxing ji 'guankan' wenti" (*The girl from Shanghai*: revolutionary women and the question of "viewing"), in *Zai jiedu: dazhong wenyi yu yishi xingtai* (Rereading: the people's literature and art movement and ideology), ed. Tang Xiaobing (Hong Kong: Oxford University Press, 1993), 127–46.

7. For a genealogical account of the origin of the Fifth Generation and its modernist politics, see Xudong Zhang, *Chinese Modernism in the Era of Reforms: Cultural Fever, Avant-Garde Fiction, and the New Chinese Cinema* (Durham, N.C.: Duke University Press, 1997), 215–31. See also, for instance, the statement by one of the leading members of the Fifth Generation in the interview "A Director Who Is Trying to Change the Audience: A Chat with Young Director Tian Zhuangzhuang," conducted by Yang Ping, in *Perspectives on Chinese Cinema*, 127–30.

urban space that invariably provides a symbolic replication of the complexity of contemporary sociopolitical life caught in the maelstrom of modernization. Against the spatial complexity of the city, youth, while celebrated as a concentrated expression of the cultural dynamics of modernity, is nonetheless frequently depicted on the screen as a disillusioning experience of foreclosed mobility, repressed libidinal energy, and entrenched filial obligation and duties. For instance, in *Troubleshooters,* we see how three young men struggle without much success to run their own service company, whose daily operation and customers bring to the surface the frustrations and crises deeply embedded in contemporary society. A significant development in the film is that once the story line begins and we are witnessing the nitty-gritty of the company's business, the city no longer appears as a spectacle to marvel at. Instead, the urban landscape recedes, as it were, into the distance and turns simultaneously into an untranscendable historical condition and an experiential immediacy that together smother any coherent perception. Put differently, the city becomes both an all-encompassing cultural construct and an inescapable natural environment, one reinforcing the other. By the end of the film, it is clear that the filmmaker has persistently refused to present the city as promising a possible perceptual totalization; contrary to the opening collage, the final, slow-rolling shot of people lining up to seek help at the revamped service company conveys a reconciliation, on the part of a besieged and reflective subject, with ordinariness as well as situatedness. The city by now irretrievably recedes into the distance and becomes a grandiose myth no longer relevant to the daily lives of its inhabitants. It is now a labyrinthine complex without a coherent pattern, or what Kevin Lynch once promoted as the "legibility" and "imageability" of the cityscape.

However, this film genre, with its critical message about "the estranging city and a paralyzed subject,"[8] did not reach its thematic and cinematic perfection until 1989, when Xie Fei completed *Benming nian* (Black snow), a sober portrayal of ordinary life in Beijing executed with a film-noir sensibility. It may appear coincidental that an outstanding member of the Fourth Generation (here the term refers to the group of Chinese filmmakers who were systematically trained from the late 1950s to early

---

8. Peng Wen, "*Benming nian:* mosheng de chengshi yu tanhuan de zhuti" (*Black snow:* the estranging city and a paralyzed subject), *Dianying yishu* (Film art), no. 212 (1990): 41.

1960s and reached their professional maturity only in the late 1970s because of the disruption of the Cultural Revolution) had to come in to realize the potential of the new genre, for the directors in this transitional generation of directors are often viewed by critics as forever negotiating for their own artistic identity. Compared to the more cosmopolitan Fifth Generation, they appear as "reluctant, awkward pursuers of the novel and embarrassing believers in cheap humanism and historicism."[9] As the proud, however abused, offspring of New China cinema, they now find themselves, by default, inheriting a battered establishment, and yet they cannot afford to dissociate themselves either emotionally or intellectually from what shapes and defines them. This character profile of the Fourth Generation is closely borne out by another intriguing city film, *Beijing nizao* (Good morning, Beijing, 1990), directed by Zhang Nuanxin (*Sha Ou* [Sha Ou], 1981; *Qingchun ji* [Sacrificed youth], 1986). Given their professional training and familiarity with socialist realism, Fourth Generation directors have a strong sense of social responsibility and usually feel more at home dealing with the rural landscape or the contrast between the city and the countryside. Indeed, members of this generation are the ones who made some of the most successful and realistic films about rural China in the 1980s, such as *Rensheng* (Life, 1984) and *Laojing* (Old well, 1987) by Wu Tianming, and *Yeshan* (In the wild mountains, 1985) by Yan Xueshu.

Fully accepting his identity as a Fourth Generation director, Xie Fei nevertheless from the beginning exhibited a spiritual affinity with the younger generation. From his earlier, emotionally charged *Women de tianye* (Our wide fields, 1983) to *Xiangnü Xiaoxiao* (The girl from Hunan, 1986), which echoed the ethos of critical cultural root-seeking, Xie Fei established himself as the most sensitive filmmaker of his generation. In *Black Snow,* he not only redirects his own philosophical thinking, but also introduces a new intellectual tension into the city-film genre. As the film critic Peng Wen observes, while city films by the Fifth Generation express a hidden desire to identify with and belong to the new urban culture, "in *Black Snow,* 'the city' is obviously presented as an estranging and hostile space, to cope with which the filmmaker recommends resistance and disengagement."[10] Still, there is enough continuity to read Xie

---

9. Xudong Zhang, *Chinese Modernism,* 223.
10. Peng Wen, "*Black Snow,*" 42.

Fei's intervention as an extension of the general interest in the city. It is mostly a thematic continuity, an increasingly critical examination of an emergent urban culture. "From *Troubleshooters* to *Black Snow*," as another film critic remarks, "Chinese cinema has reached a universal subject matter in world cinema, namely, the experience of anomie and disorientation in a commodity society, also known as the age of market economy."[11] In this light, *Black Snow* deserves a closer look, especially from the perspective of how the city now figures in the everyday experience of unfulfilled youth.[12]

Depth and Social Criticism

While reviewing films about Rome by Vittorio De Sica in postwar Italy, Pierre Sorlin sees the filmmaker as someone who experimented with two different groups of images of the city. In the neorealist cinema of the 1950s, filmmakers "were aware of the blossoming of urban areas and tried to express, cinematically, the complex relationships between old town centers and new outskirts. After 1965 or so, other cinematographers were no longer able to tell, or see, what towns were, and [they] created a blurred image of cities."[13] This blurred vision, according to Sorlin, was first articulated in De Sica's *The Roof* (1956), in which "the strong system which associated the center and outskirts, presented as complementary entities, vanished, and the picture of towns began to lose focus."[14] Subsequently, images of open and formless shantytowns came in to diffuse the neorealist effort that, through cinematic projection, had sought to make

11. Wei Xiaolin, "*Benming nian* de renzhi jiazhi" (The cognitive value of *Black snow*), *Film Art,* no. 212 (1990): 51.

12. In a 1984 essay, Xie Fei emphasized the importance of representing daily life. Commenting on Raizman's *A Personal Life* (1983), Xie Fei wrote: "No significant events, heated dramatic conflicts, and unusual techniques are used. On the contrary, it vividly depicts a variety of characters, touches profound social problems and philosophies, and is obviously a contemporary product." See Xie Fei, "My View of the Concept of Film," trans. Hou Jianping, in *Chinese Film Theory: A Guide to the New Era,* ed. George S. Semsel et al., trans. Hou Jianping et al. (New York: Praeger, 1990), 79.

13. Pierre Sorlin, *European Cinemas, European Societies, 1939–1990* (London: Routledge, 1991), 135.

14. Ibid., 126–27.

sense of an expanding urban landscape and the intricate human lives embedded in it. One classic moment of such neorealist clarity can be found in De Sica's *The Bicycle Thief* (1948), where "extreme depth of field shots accentuate Ricci's isolation: when he searches the thief's home for traces of his stolen bicycle, for example, we see in the background most clearly a neighbor closing her window, as if to cut off all possibility of communication between Ricci and the thief's neighbors."[15]

The loss of such all-encompassing visual clarity in the wake of neorealist cinema, suggests Sorlin, registered a new perception of the European city, a historical moment in which "filmmakers ceased to view cities as potential works of art."[16] Thus, the gradual disappearance of neorealism may point to a general disavowal of allegorical totalization on the one hand and of active social engagement on the other. It may even signal the arrival of a postmodern urban life, for which the source of excitement is no longer the visionary modern city or a neorealist "aspiration to change the world."[17] If this fundamentally moral commitment underlies all forms of the realist ideology, one crucial difference between neorealism and socialist realism may be no other than the former's fascination with, and critical exploration of, the anonymous and multidimensional modernizing city. Socialist realist cinema, at least its Chinese variant, is identifiable insofar as the city on a human scale is disallowed. "The Chinese version of what the Italians called 'neorealism' had been a feature of the 'golden age' of Chinese cinema in the late 1940s," remarks Paul Clark, but it was superseded by socialist realism in the 1950s. As a result, "the urban tragicomedies and social melodramas of the late 1940s were replaced by socialist melodramas set in either urban workplaces or the countryside."[18] In the 1980s, with socialist realism falling into disrepute, the city and its cinematic possibilities returned to the Chinese screen with considerable vengeance.

15. Bondanella, *Italian Cinema from Neorealism to the Present* (New York: Unger, 1983), 60.

16. Sorlin, *European Cinemas*, 136.

17. After making clear the relationship between the classical realist ideology of the nineteenth century and neorealism, Millicent Marcus, in his *Italian Film in the Light of Neorealism* (Princeton, N.J.: Princeton University Press, 1986) observes that neorealism in Italian cinema expressed an "immediate postwar optimism about the attempt to shape political reality according to a moral idea" (28).

18. Paul Clark, "Two Hundred Flowers on China's Screens," in *Perspectives on Chinese Cinema*, 40–61.

What I wish to accomplish through a close reading of *Black Snow* and *Good Morning, Beijing,* is to show that the return of the city in late twentieth-century Chinese cinema once again highlights questions of realism and social engagement. These two starkly different cinematic representations of the city of Beijing articulate separate visions of reality and politics. While in *Black Snow* our view is constantly immobilized by close-ups and focal lighting, *Good Morning, Beijing* moves us with a gratifying story and fluid cinematography. The city in *Good Morning, Beijing,* which may be provisionally described as "neorealist" in style, is amply narratable and eventually comes together as an allegorical social space. In *Black Snow,* however, through the prevalent use of limited field-depth cinematography, Xie Fei focuses our gaze on an embattled individual by keeping his surroundings in a shadowy blur that effectively blocks the city from ever emerging as a graspable totality.

The dramatic tracking shot at the beginning of *Black Snow* immediately sets the chromatic tone and visual structure of the film and establishes itself as an exemplary moment in a conceivable Beijing noir. Hearing first a passing train and then solitary but heavy footsteps, we realize that we are in a dimly lit subway station and following someone, presumably toward the exit. Then the credits begin to roll, and the hand-held camera films to the rhythm of someone walking. Soon we see stairways leading to the ground and a street scene. The person in front of us and at the center of the screen, in the light of the exit, shoulders a stuffed knapsack and wears a bulky coat. Yet the looming, open space is hardly inspiring because the narrow strip of a wintry sky is an impenetrable gray, and a few ghostly bystanders all appear to be uniformly blue or of a nondescript monochrome. As the man (we can assume that by now, judging from his build and the gender-specific hat he is wearing) is about to fully emerge from the subway, the camera quickly shifts, and we see him again, from a slightly downward angle, in some narrow and tortuous lane, which is hopelessly cut short by another train hissing by at the top of the screen. It is a virtual shantytown, void of any human presence at the moment. Then the man walks through a gate, and the camera is noticeably lowered so that the lane becomes even more oppressive and suffocating. There are still no human beings in sight, and the overcrowded space is dominated by an official radio voice announcing first some prohibitive policy and then a train disaster. The impersonal voice fades away as we turn a corner, and an old man's sickly cough, together with a baby's impatient cry, becomes more irrepressible, punctuated only by the sound of flowing tap water. After yet another unexpected turn, we hear a fragment of softened pop rock that seems to float listlessly, and when we are sufficiently lost in this directionless space, the man is suddenly stopped by a fence, and at the same time the camera comes to a standstill.

But the man quickly pushes open the fence and walks up to a shanty that shows no signs of life. While he struggles with his key in the lock and eventually has to break through the door, a compassionate female voice, probably from a radio next door, gradually replaces the news broadcast and, in the elegant style of the traditional art of storytelling (*pingshu*), either narrates a distant event or proffers a reflective commentary. In fact, this formulaic but mysteriously soothing voice will remain as the predominant background sound, as if supplying a slightly sorrowful historical commentary on present conditions, during the sequence in which the man enters the room, bumps into a few ill-placed objects, examines the disorderly surroundings, and finally takes off his hat and gloves. Only at this moment do we get our first frontal view of him, a sturdy young man in his mid-twenties. Apparently he knows this place, for very soon he finds himself a cigarette buried in a drawer and, while searching for matches, catches sight of a framed picture. He picks up the frame, gazes into it, and blows hard at the dust gathered on it. At this moment, the alarmed voice of an old woman comes from off the screen: "Who is it? Is it Quanzi?"

Li Huiquan is the name of the young man, the hero of the film. He has just returned home after spending about a year in prison, during which time his mother has died. Now he finds himself back in a desolate room, all alone, jobless, and facing the task of starting his life anew. Based on a psychological novel by Liu Heng, the plot of the film is about how hard, and eventually impossible, it is for Li Huiquan the ex-convict to assimilate himself back into society and lead a normal life. Unable to get a job at the factory where his mother used to work, which is now officially declared bankrupt, Li Huiquan decides to rely on himself and sets up a stall at a street market to sell shoes and clothes. After a slow start, his business grows steadily; in the meanwhile, he gets to know Zhao Yaqiu, an aspiring singer performing part-time in a bar. At the bar, he also meets Cui Yongli, a shrewd, self-made broker who profits from clandestine and apparently illegal business deals. While Cui Yongli supplies quantities of popular fashion goods (mostly lingerie), Li Huiquan occasionally escorts Zhao Yaqiu home after her work. With her charming innocence she seems to restore in him a sense of being respected and even needed. Subsequently, she becomes the object of his libidinal desire. Yet he cannot bring himself to express his tender feelings toward the trusting young girl; instead, he resorts to masturbation at night. At the same time, partly thanks to Cui Yongli's brokering, Zhao Yaqiu becomes relatively successful and grows increasingly indifferent to the young man whom she once obviously admired. Then Li Huiquan's former accomplice and prison mate, Chazi, descends one night from the skylight window, hungry as a wolf after being on the run from the law for about two weeks. Chazi's sudden return devastatingly reminds Huiquan of his own solitary existence, which makes his advice that Chazi turn himself in ring hollow. Finally, the fact that Chazi, ruthlessly disowned by his own family, has to run away from him and for his life, together with the knowledge that Zhao Yaqiu has become her agent's mistress, crushes Li Huiquan's fragile world. He badly beats up Cui Yongli, and, in a desperate last effort, he presents the now glamorous Zhao Yaqiu with a gold necklace. His offer is politely turned down, and after aimlessly roaming into a park at night Li Huiquan is robbed and then fatally stabbed by two teenagers. In the film's last shot, we are given a prolonged look downward at his bent body lying among waste paper and garbage on the floor of a deserted open-air theater, which, according to director Xie Fei, constitutes his authorial comment on the vacuity of a purposeless existence.[19]

The senseless death at the end certainly appears to attach an anticlimactic conclusion to the narrative. Yet it symbolically brings to completion the film's critical reflection on the limits and anxieties of city life. A full circle of hermeneutical meaning is thus achieved in terms of both narrative and cinematography. As Peng Wen remarks, the unfolding of the story adopts the pattern of a classical linear narrative, and from Li Huiquan's return (new life) to his death there is a "complete closure."[20] This narrative closure is reinforced by a visual as well as auditory imagery that at the very end recalls the film's beginning. Here is again a prolonged and uninterrupted tracking shot of the young man, his back turned to us and his footsteps echoing hollowly. The movement of the camera suggests unsteady steps, while the muffled and unreal background noise and

---

19. Xie Fei, "'Di sidai' de zhengming" (The proof of the "fourth generation"), *Film Art,* no. 212 (1990): 23–24.
20. Peng Wen, "*Black Snow,*" 43.

laughter of a dispersing theater crowd do not divert our attention from the dying hero. The image of the public and the public space itself both fall out of focus and become a grotesque blur. Li Huiquan finally collapses in the empty theater. Through such structural symmetry, this last moment of arriving at his death and his return in the film's beginning powerfully complement each other, the result being a disturbing transgression of given categories and myths about city life. If, at the beginning, Li Huiquan's coming home can be viewed as returning to an interior hopelessly under surveillance (suggested by the harsh radio voice), the ending represents a final disconnection between the public and the private, the environment and its perception by the individual. Only at the moment of his random death, in a deserted public space, does Li Huiquan voicelessly and yet in vain express his individuality and with desperation expose the underlying current of loneliness.

Both critics and the filmmaker himself have remarked on the strong tendency of intellectualizing, obviously in the humanist tradition, throughout *Black Snow*.[21] The whole style of the film, from its predominant melancholy, grayish-blue tone to the virtual absence of external music, reflects the meditative commentary of a sympathetic intellectual. I wish to argue, however, that it is this philosophical interest in the existential condition of an individual in the modern city that leads to the blurring of the city itself, which has the cinematographic effect of keeping the viewer and, by extension, the subject on the screen from gaining a commanding perspective on the urban environment and its relationships. The concerned gaze that the film directs upon the subject and his immediate surroundings is so intense that the rest of the city has to be kept at a distance and as an incomprehensible background. In other words, for the anxiety of the individual subject to be experienced as such, the connection between him and the city must be revealed as nonexistent, and his anguish shown as that of one incapable of identifying himself with the

---

21. See, for instance, Chen Xiaoming, "Daode zijiu: lishi zhouxin de duanlie" (Moral self-salvation: the breaking of a historical axis), *Film Art,* no. 215 (1990): 105. While describing the difference between *Black Snow* and his earlier films, Xie Fei emphasizes his philosophical beliefs. "Surely there was some change in my conception, but in my artistic creation, I as always held dear my ideals, and stayed with my value judgment as far as the true, the good, and the beautiful versus the false, the evil, and the ugly in our life experiences are concerned." See Xie, "The Proof of the 'Fourth Generation,'" 20.

environment from which he nonetheless cannot escape. "But let the mishap of disorientation once occur," Kevin Lynch writes when emphasizing the importance of keeping the city an imageable environment, "and the sense of anxiety and even terror that accompanies it reveals to us how closely it is linked to our sense of balance and well-being."[22]

At this point, we may identify a modernist aesthetics of depth in the film *Black Snow*. Such an aesthetics is usually articulated with a self-conscious, if not ideological, exploration of favorite high modernist themes of interiority, anxiety, experiential authenticity, and frustrated desire. This "inward turn" that we will discuss in relation to Li Huiquan's experience, however, does not carry the same "politicality" or utopian desire that Fredric Jameson sees underlying the alleged subjectivism in the classics of Western modernism. "Modernism's introspective probing of the deeper impulses of consciousness, and even of the unconscious itself," proposes Jameson, "was always accompanied by a Utopian sense of the impending transformation or transfiguration of the 'self' in question."[23] The anxiety that Xie Fei portrays in his film, while clearly echoing a modernist introspective probing, is generated less by a blocked utopian excitement about transforming the self or society than by a profound uncertainty over the very content of such a transformation. It is a postutopian anxiety, in that the interiority explored here resides not so much in some meaningful transitional linkage between tradition and modernity as in a nonspace rejected by, and excluded from, both the past and the future. In the interior space encircling Li Huiquan, while memory or nostalgia offers hardly any comfort, the future is disclaimed with equal dismay. It is the grim reality of a cagelike present that renders anxiety as the experience of inescapability and claustrophobia.

Let us return again to the opening shot to further examine the aesthetics of depth in the film as a whole. One reading of that seemingly endless walk along a tortuous lane in a shantytown is that it suggests the difficult path through which one arrives at the present. It is a metaphor of living through twisted history itself. "If the gray experience of walking belongs to history," the literary critic Chen Xiaoming comments, "then the shabby house as the 'present tense' of the narrative is joined with the

22. Kevin Lynch, *The Image of the City* (Cambridge, Mass.: Technology Press, 1960), 4.
23. Fredric Jameson, *Postmodernism, Or, The Cultural Logic of Late Capitalism* (Durham, N.C.: Duke University Press, 1991), 312.

'now' of the character. This small house therefore becomes the starting point for Li Huiquan's self-renewal; it also indicates the end of past history. As a closed space of existence for an individual and a 'present' that must separate itself from its own history, this house has to resist the outside world as much as society."[24] Indeed, what Li Huiquan does here is walk away from the city, from any form of collectivity, and into his own interior space. As he moves into the depths of the shantytown, the camera begins to descend from an encompassing view of the site down to a close tracking shot of the hero. Very soon, we are brought so close to the person walking in front of us that we can no longer have the initial, although momentary, coherent perception of the environs. Our understanding of the situation becomes firmly meshed with Li Huiquan's vision, which quickly turns out to be partial and unmediated.[25] While the sorry images of an overcrowded shantytown evoke poverty as the poignant critique of a failed social project, the failure of the current situation is ultimately presented—by means of camera angles and an evocative soundtrack—as a dead-end entrapment. The only escape seems to be Li Huiquan's home or his private room, but this much-needed interior holds for the young man a memory both too painful and too broken to be of any redemptive value for the present.

This spatial tension, in which depth is embraced out of despair, gives rise to an existential anxiety and at the same time endows that anxiety with social criticism. It also generates two related kinds of visual imagery. The city, when it appears at all, is reduced to fleeting images of empty streets, noisy traffic, dimly lit back alleys, and pale, cold streetlights. All of these images irrepressibly suggest Li Huiquan's unease with the public dimension of the city and even his fear of it. In contrast, the interior into which the individual subject now retreats is continually interrupted and revealed to be vulnerable. Within this second group of images, we

24. Chen Xiaoming, "Moral Self-Salvation," 103.

25. The "inward turn" or psychologization of experience that I relate here with the aesthetics of depth can also be observed in the original novel, which opens with Li Huiquan's return to his home and a wintry present. Here is Howard Goldblatt's translation of the first sentences: "A fat white guy was squatting in the yard. Li Huiquan, his knapsack slung over his shoulder, noticed the frosty grin as soon as he walked through the gate, so he walked over and wiped it off. Chunks of coal for eyes, a chili-pepper nose, a wastebasket hat—the same stuff he used as a kid." Liu Heng, *Black Snow*, trans. Howard Goldblatt (New York: Atlantic Monthly Press, 1993), 3.

8. Film poster, *Benming nian* (Black snow) (1989). Courtesy of Zhongguo dianying ziliao guan, Beijing.

can further distinguish two distinct clusters. One consists of those midrange shots of Li Huiquan in his home. Here, the camera always remains at the hero's eye level, and, through a zoom lens, as the director Xie Fei later reminds us, the character is shown in much sharper focus than his surroundings so as to intensify his psychological isolation.[26] Also, invariably, a top light intrudes, which, like the neighbor's loud radio and TV, reinforces a sense of both antisociality and voyeuristic surveillance.[27]

The other cluster of representations of the interior occurs in the bar (another favorite symbol of modern city life that I comment on below) where close-ups of a pensive Li Huiquan, usually in the dark but sometimes under a direct top light, are frequently crosscut with luminous and intensely colorful images of the singer Zhao Yaqiu (figure 8). The interi-

26. Xie Fie, "The Proof of the 'Fourth Generation,'" 26.
27. See Liu Shuyong, "Zaoxing zuowei yuyan: qianlun *Benming nian* de yongguang chuli" (Imaging as language: on the lighting technique in *Black snow*), *Dangdai dianying* (Contemporary cinema), no. 35 (April 1990): 87–91.

ority experienced in this situation is of a more emotional nature and is contrasted to the fluidity and vacuity of popular music as a pliable form. The visual proximity of a desiring subject to the object of desire actually underlines the unbridgeable gap between them and forms a disturbing imagery of an emotional and communicational blockage. The profound irony is that commodified art now supplies the expression and appropriates the content of the subject's inmost memory and desire.

If Li Huiquan's ultimate despair is partly attributable to his inability or unwillingness to accept the cruel fact that Zhao Yaqiu is, after all, a popular performer who has to prostitute style for marketability, truthfulness for a universally appropriable external form, his own political identity—or, rather, a blatant lack thereof—constitutes his tragic character. An ex-convict for the crime of aggravated assault, and now the owner of a fashion stall, Li Huiquan finds himself an automatic misfit in a society where a highly moralistic political culture still dominates, while economic activity outside the public sector inevitably smacks of (or rather thrives on) amorality and even illegality (as embodied by the broker Cui Yongli). One defining feature of the dominant political culture is its refusal to recognize the complexity of everyday life, in particular its quotidian ordinariness and mundane needs and passions. Because the crime he committed and the punishment he consequently received appear to be so utterly "petty" in the sense that neither can be explained away by some political misfortune or injustice and thereby rehabilitated and turned into a source of honor, Li Huiquan is at once identified as a dismissable outsider and an invisible member of society. His explosive anger at Chazi's parents, who disown their criminal son so as to be accepted by society at large, directly articulates his frustrated protest against a tightly knit and dehumanizing social fabric. A stunning representation of Li Huiquan's social invisibility comes at the end, when, in that fateful evening in the park, he drags his wounded body through a complacently indifferent crowd. By now a thematic connection is established between Li Huiquan's ambiguous political identity, or the difficulty of narrating his life story, and the blurring or perceived illegibility of the city on which I commented. The unapproachable city, from which Li Huiquan wishes desperately to disengage himself, becomes the gigantic symbol of a social failure.

Urban Relationships Reconnected

The historical significance of *Black Snow* in contemporary Chinese cinema lies in the fact that, better and more focally than other films of the same genre, it presents the city as a social issue and makes visible the deep anxiety it simultaneously generates and suppresses. Private interior space is masterfully shown to be both a necessary shelter and an inescapable entrapment, while realistic images of stark poverty and disrepair quietly depict a demoralized collective imagination. The psychological depth, together with the libidinal frustration, of the individual is sympathetically explored and turned into a metaphor for the anxious, embattled subject of a peculiar historical moment—before a repressive political order ceases to demand homogeneity from members of society, a vibrant market economy sets in to instill anonymity and indifference. If the political reality is embodied in the gloomy urban landscape (predominantly the oppressive shantytown), new and rampant commercialism finds its perfect figuration in the attractive but heartless singer Zhao Yaqiu. The final death of the hero, therefore, while suggesting a strong social criticism, also drives home the impossibility of dissipating individual anxiety through any overarching myth or rationalization, which in recent Chinese history has shifted from an egalitarian vision of socialist paradise to the ideology of economic development and prosperity.

To further understand the politics of such a postutopian anxiety, we should turn to *Good Morning, Beijing*, a noticeably different filmic representation of contemporary life in that city. Here, in contrast to a blurred image of the city, we see a continual mapping of the sprawling cityscape; instead of an aesthetics of depth as social criticism, we find a persistent temporalization of space, linking different parts of the city through narratable, individual experiences. In her preproduction exposition of the film's theme, director Zhang Nuanxin made it clear that *Good Morning, Beijing* would pursue an "expressive, documentary" style to truthfully reflect the flow of daily life, with a sense of humor and light comedy. The soundtrack would be mostly live recording, and the color a shade of pleasantly harmonious gray. Set in a contemporary Beijing awash in the "great wave of the market economy," this film would follow everyday events in the life of a group of young people, but in reality mirror the contemporary social theme of "reform and opening up." It should also convey a refreshing broadmindedness—"everyone's pursuit has its rationality and every attitude to life should be given its due understanding." The director decided to use the title *Good Morning, Beijing* "because this film will present a snapshot of millions of Beijing citizens, depicting the life of those ordinary people quietly working in the most basic strata of our society."[28] Consciously or not, Zhang Nuanxin envisioned her movie largely in terms of a neorealist style of filmmaking, central to which are semidocumentary techniques and social concerns.[29]

This preproduction statement, however, should not limit our reading of the film too much because it was a document intended to secure the film its official approval and funding (in post-1989 China). Still it does strike the keynote for this public-oriented representation of life in Beijing. The plot of *Good Morning, Beijing* may appear complex at first glance. It centers on a young woman, Ai Hong, who works as a bus conductor, and it follows her successive relationships with three young men: first, her co-worker Wang Lang, then the bus driver Zou Yongqiang, and finally the currently unemployed but new-fashioned and imaginative Keke. She eventually marries Keke and with him starts a private business. Because Wang Lang has no definable character of his own, Ai Hong's departure from him is relatively easy to explain, but her break with Zou Yongqiang, a caring, honest young man who somehow lacks the courage to imagine a different life for them, causes her much soul-searching (figure 9). Her liaisons with and movement among these three very different young people have an obviously allegorical importance. They repeat, as one critic suggests, a classic narrative format in which the female character, by her departure, either symbolizes negation of an outmoded or objectionable way of life, or, through her acquiescence or eventual return,

---

28. Zhang Nuanxin, "*Beijing nizao* de daoyan chanshu" (The director's thematic exposition of *Good morning, Beijing*), *Contemporary Cinema*, no. 39 (December 1990): 53–54.

29. Acknowledging the formidable difficulty in generalizing about neorealism, Millicent Marcus nonetheless offers a useful description of what constitutes its basic style and techniques. "The rules governing neorealist practice would include location shooting, lengthy takes, unobtrusive editing, natural lighting, a predominance of medium and long shots, respect for the continuity of time and space, use of contemporary, true-to-life subjects, an uncontrived, open-ended plot, working-class protagonists, a non-professional cast, dialogue in the vernacular, active viewer involvement, and implied social criticism" (Marcus, *Italian Cinema*, 22).

9. Film still, *Beijing nizao* (Good morning, Beijing) (1990). Courtesy of Zhongguo dianying ziliao guan, Beijing.

represents affirmation of a certain value system or accepted ideology.[30] In such a narrative tradition, women are made to express rather than create value. The value system to which Ai Hong subscribes in the end is therefore an emergent one associated with the market, which specifically calls for desirable character qualities such as energy, independence, and adventurousness. In the film, Keke, who at first pretends to be an overseas Chinese and wears a Harvard T-shirt, personifies such a new spirit, and his enthusiasm and modern lifestyle will help him win Ai Hong away from a reticent and much-inhibited Zou Yongqiang.

Indeed, the economy of passion in *Good Morning, Beijing* makes it a narrative that explicitly participates in an ongoing and large-scale cul-

30. Zhang Wei, "Nüxing de guishu yu lishi qianyi: *Beijing nizao* de yuyanxing chanshi" (The position of the woman and historical transformation: an allegorical interpretation of *Good morning, Beijing*), *Contemporary Cinema*, no. 39 (December 1990): 55–56. One needs to note here that this reading is heavily influenced by Laura Mulvey's critical analysis of classic Hollywood narrative cinema.

tural revolution through which habits, mentalities, and social structures will all be systematically transformed so as to legitimate the market as an important organizing principle of society. It is also a narrative about social discontent and its mitigation through the introduction of desire.[31] Desire becomes a positive social value in the film, not only in that it expresses a putatively collective vision of a different *Lebenswelt*, but also, perhaps more crucially, because it sets free the energies and imaginations of individuals. The engendering of this emancipatory desire is narrated and at the same time explained in Ai Hong's departure from Zou Yongqiang and her subsequent fascination with Keke, who appears to move in a more mobile space with unmistakable signs of modernity (taxis, nightclubs, Western-style grocery stores, and general sociability). (The social content of such a desire can be gauged from the fact that, although this can be read as a conventional triangular love story, "love" is never pronounced as of major significance in the plot's unfolding. On the contrary, Ai Hong's affair and eventual marriage with Keke, an odd twist, are auxiliary means for her to discover and assert her own new identity.) As a direct opposite to Keke, Zou Yongqiang belongs to a conformist world in which filial duty and respect for his superior combine to demand from him gratitude and, at the same time, provide him with a sense of security. He lives with his parents in an overcrowded Beijing courtyard where his mother has to continually cut short his only expression of individuality (playing the traditional Chinese violin and later the guitar) out of consideration for the neighbors. Unlike Keke, he shops in a featureless department store, and he expresses his affection for Ai Hong by buying her a practical skirt, whereas Keke enchants her with a Walkman and a tape of American rock and roll.

Thus, these two rivals for Ai Hong's affection are highly symbolic figures, each representing a separate social reality and cultural logic. Yet the residual and the emergent conditions of existence, if we wish to so understand the symbolism here, are engaged in a rhetoric of compromise and tolerance. The ideological emphasis placed on compromise renders untenable a facile dichotomy of tradition versus modernity that seems to suggest itself here as an interpretative framework. On the contrary, this rhetoric of compromise enables the film to sympathetically portray Zou

31. It is interesting to note that in its subtitled English-language version, the film is given a much more suggestive title, *Budding Desires*.

Yongqiang's frustration, the grave social-historical (dis)content of which is now effectively displaced as momentary personal misfortune. As director Zhang Nuanxin puts it, even though he cannot, primarily emotionally, identify with the dominant Zeitgeist of the market, Zou Yongqiang maintains his decency and worthiness and continues to work and contribute to society.[32] At the same time, Keke is transformed in the process from a conspicuous consumer of urban culture back into a productive member of society. The film's concluding sequence brings together all the major characters in a dramatic moment when Ai Hong, now an apparently successful self-employed businesswoman, and her husband get onto the bus that Zou Yongqiang still drives and on which Wang Lang still works as a conductor. After a brief and polite exchange of greetings, Zou Yongqiang turns around and starts the bus. Slowly, the camera pulls back to show all four very different young people aboard the same bus peacefully moving along a sunny street in Beijing.

This comforting moment of rapprochement, we are told by a subtitle on the screen, arrives one year after the main action of the film. In this rich final image, the element of time is as important as the central message about the ineluctable coexistence of different modes of production. Time here signifies change, progress, and a healing process as well. Time also becomes identified with the future, or rather with some utopian projections from the present. Actually, even at the beginning of the film, where we are shown Ai Hong still in bed one early morning, time as a major factor is introduced emphatically when the ticking alarm clock goes off. It is time for the young bus conductor to go to work, and the whole interior space is thus redefined and forced open by a universal clock time. Unlike *Black Snow,* where time is subjectivized and locked into a depressing present, *Good Morning, Beijing* is a film about the multiple and contradictory temporal flows in the space of the enormous city. Spatial structures, locations, and relations now acquire a temporal, historical significance to the extent that we can speak of a socially produced "spatiality" which, according to Edward Soja, "like society itself, exists in both substantial forms (concrete spatialities) and as a set of relations between individuals and groups, an 'embodiment' and medium of social life itself."[33] Through

32. Zhang Nuanxin, "The Director's Thematic Exposition," 54.
33. Edward W. Soja, *Postmodern Geographies: The Reassertion of Space in Critical Social Theory* (London: Verso, 1989), 120.

the narrative of the film, the uneven and multidimensional spatial relations are mapped and reconnected, and the city of Beijing is brought together as an imaginable totality, as a fascinating collection of images of various social realities that simultaneously exist and interact.

So a central plot in *Good Morning, Beijing* is the movement from the initial spatiotemporal structure of a confining domestic interior (underlined by the close-up shot of a cage with an impatient bird chirping in it) to an open cityscape that is emphatically contemporary and modernizing. Of particular interest in the opening sequence is a stark "crudeness" of the interior space—crude surfaces as well as crude conditions of existence. In this cramped room we realize that life has to be reduced to its bare necessities; it is an enclosed space kept flat and public by the absence of any refinement or the possibility of privacy. It becomes a most efficient extension of the workplace because "home" now stands less for separation from work than for a direct reproduction of labor. When at home, Ai Hong, as we see later, also has the task of taking care of her invalid grandpa. She readies coal for heating, fixes the exhaust pipe with the help of Zou Yongqiang, and, in the same room where her grandpa lies in bed year round, she prepares porridge for him and washes her hands in a basin next to the window. The same embarrassing experience of scarcity is even more pointedly represented at Zou Yongqiang's home, where, in his parents' makeshift bedroom, the whole family eats supper and watches TV while the father soaks his feet in a basin of warm water. At the end of dinner the son's duty is to take the basin, walk through a dark hallway, and drain the water into a public sink located in the courtyard.

In isolation, such images of impoverishment and severely constrained conditions of existence would not necessarily mean social criticism or cultural commentary. On the contrary, scarce and overcrowded domestic space would only appear "natural" or "realistic" enough, since some public places to which the camera brings us (such as the bus company headquarters, the police station, and the hospital) have surfaces and structures no less shabby and perfunctory. A Third World condition—here the term is used strictly to refer to generalized inadequate living conditions and a preindustrial, underdeveloped socioeconomic infrastructure—can hardly be grasped as such unless defamiliarized by images of, or references to, a different, more advanced stage of modernization. In *Good Morning, Beijing*, as we will see momentarily, the Third Worldness of the city is candidly acknowledged, together with its explicitly anticipated changeover.

It is extremely significant, however, that the Third World condition presented by the film carries with it not so much mere self-loathing (would that be politically incorrect?) or self-glorification (would that be politically correct?) as an almost restless utopian desire for self-transformation. In this sense, the film as a Third World production is also conscientiously for a Third World audience, insofar as an undesirable present condition of existence is both represented as an immediate collective reality and historicized as some fast-vanishing remnant of a better future.[34]

Consequently, the series of images that reveals an impoverished everyday life acquires its historical content when it is juxtaposed with a different sequence, a different set of spatiotemporal structures. We may even argue that history, or a historical understanding of contemporary Beijing, becomes accessible precisely when this juxtaposition of different spatial realities and relationships is employed as a strategy of characterizing an incomplete, in-progress present condition. One way to describe this spatial coexistence or simultaneity could be the architectural notion of "a collage city," where "disparate objects (are) held together by various means" to form a composite presence.[35] In the film, the city of Beijing does become fragmented into a collage of various sites, rhythms, and intensities, but the movements through the city of the characters, in particular Ai Hong, reconnect all these obviously discontinuous moments. Thus, there is still the possibility of narrating one's story in the city, of presenting a spatial experience in temporal terms. As an apt symbol of collective practice, the moving bus, where much of the movie's action takes place, provides an ideal vehicle for linking up different parts and

---

34. There is another group of films in contemporary Chinese cinema whose cultural "Third Worldness" is marketed primarily to First World film audiences. Films by Zhang Yimou (*Ju Dou*, 1990; *Raise the Red Lantern*, 1992) seem to be favorite samples of this group.

35. Colin Rowe and Fred Koetter, *Collage City* (Cambridge, Mass.: MIT Press, 1978), 139–40. I would like to point out that Rowe and Koetter's vision of a "collage city" expresses a typical postmodernist sensibility and ideology. "Collage city" is offered as a solution to the anxiety generated by both utopia and tradition: "because collage is a method deriving its virtue from its irony, because it seems to be a technique for using things and simultaneously disbelieving in them, it is also a strategy which can allow utopia to be dealt with as image, to be dealt with in *fragments* without our having to accept it *in toto,* which is further to suggest that collage could even be a strategy which, by supporting the utopian illusion of changelessness and finality, might even fuel a reality of change, motion, action and history" (149).

functions of Beijing. From here we see images of Beijing as a political center (Tiananmen Square), a rapidly modernizing metropolis (all-glass high-rises), and an overpopulated Third World city (business districts and shopping streets). In a sense, the moving bus serves as a clever self-reflection on the rolling camera and our viewing experience.

It is, however, Ai Hong's experiences as an individual subject who strives to change her own historical situation that endow the city with a humanizing narratability and a spatiotemporal coherence. We first see her get up early in the morning, run through the empty lane of the neighborhood, and hop onto Wang Lang's bicycle to go to work. Working on the bus is a demanding job, but she gets to meet and observe people. (Here, the bus is also a substitute for modern city streets, bound to be occupied by what Walter Benjamin once called an "amorphous crowd of passers-by.")[36] One day her friend Ziyun comes onto the bus and proudly tells her that she now works as a typist for a joint-venture company. At her invitation, Ai Hong decides to pay her friend a visit and subsequently finds herself inside a business office on the sixteenth floor of a guarded building. This is one of those standardized, new international-style offices (polyester carpet, air-conditioning, and low ceilings), equipped with word processors, contemporary furniture, and a coffeemaker. The most astonishing feature of this claustrophobic office, when we recall Ai Hong's home as well as her workplace, are the smooth white walls and shiny objects. The glass coffee table quietly reflects, the sofa extends a comfortably curvaceous line, and the steel sink gives forth a hygienic silver glare. This interior space is totally alien to Ai Hong, and at first she appears intimidated. The polished surface not only outlines a new form of labor no longer associated with bodily discomfort or endurance, but it also suggests a simplification of social relationships to those of an impersonal "cash nexus." Rather fittingly, in this seemingly depthless space, Ziyun, with her own experience, calmly illustrates to her awestruck friend some fundamental aspects of modern urban life: contingency and mobility.[37]

This modern office space can also be taken as an instance of the post-

---

36. Walter Benjamin, *Illuminations*, trans. Harry Zohn (New York: Schocken Books, 1969), 165.

37. While putting on makeup in the office lavatory, Ziyun tells Ai Hong that even though her salary is handsome, she has no job security; then, when asked about her boyfriend, she replies that they split up because "it was too demanding for both of us."

10. Film still, *Beijing nizao* (Good morning, Beijing) (1990). Courtesy of Zhongguo dianying ziliao guan, Beijing.

modern "relief" that a world of smooth objects may promote.[38] If it has a shattering effect on Ai Hong because it exposes as "premodern" or "yet-to-be-modernized" the shabbiness of her own world, it also initiates a readjustment of her relation to the city. Her eyes are suddenly opened, as it were, and she is able to experience and perceive the city as an enormous spatiotemporal structure that energetically produces a wide range of social realities and personal identities. In the following sequences, we see Ai Hong enjoy Korean food at a fancy restaurant with Zou Yongqiang and a friend of his; we see her wander into an upper-grade grocery store and find herself followed by an admirer who introduces himself as Keke (figure 10). Soon, she and Keke go to a nightclub where he performs with passionate emotion and dedicates a song to her. At the end of that evening, he takes her home in a taxi. Finally, as a high point of their romantic affair, and also to divert Ai Hong from her work, Keke suggests that they leave the city and go on a vacation. This series of concrete and very often discontinuous spatialities demands that Ai Hong constantly map and re-

38. See Jameson, *Postmodernism*, 313–15.

map the city in order to achieve a coherent perception of both herself and her environment. Indeed, instead of being incapacitated by this new spatial multiplication, Ai Hong insists on keeping the city a legible human space by heroically redesigning herself and rewriting her own story. Her narrative therefore presupposes the possibility of becoming, and it is this conviction that supports a profound optimism about social change and self-transformation, personal as well as collective. In this light, the brief trip that Ai Hong and Keke make to some historical site (now a popular tourist attraction) away from Beijing becomes a significant move. It reintroduces historical time as the untranscendable horizon of experience, and it localizes—albeit in its absence—the city as a reality with reachable limits.

Our reading therefore suggests that the spatiotemporal structure underlying the narrative of *Good Morning, Beijing* remains resolutely accessible to representation, in spite of all apparent conflicts and disjunctures. Ai Hong's story can be read as a narrative of the birth of urban individualism and self-consciousness, and her spatial movement in the city at once reveals and reconnects the complexity of social structures and relations, whether public or private, emergent or residual. Not surprisingly, the cinematic images we witness here are eventually controlled and organized by the subject, rather than the other way around. Unlike in postmodern cinema, where representation, according to David Harvey's persuasive analysis, runs into crisis because of a pervasive "time-space compression" engendered by a late capitalism of flexible accumulation,[39] *Good Morning, Beijing*, as a visual representation, is still fascinated by the seemingly infinite possibilities and frontiers promised by a modernizing metropolis. If one dominant theme of postmodern cinema, as Harvey shows through his readings of *Blade Runner* and *Wings of Desire* (respectively about Los Angeles and Berlin), is an impossible conflict "between people living on different time scales, and seeing and experiencing the world very differently as a result,"[40] what we find in this particular Chinese film is rather a "neorealist" arranging of urban relations and a utopian resolution of conflicts arising from city life. By continually moving its characters across the uneven urban landscape, *Good Morning, Beijing* evokes the city itself as an intimate participant that quietly justifies their

39. Harvey, *The Condition of Postmodernity: An Enquiry into the Origins of Cultural Change* (Cambridge, Mass.: Blackwell, 1989), 322.
40. Ibid., 313.

endeavors and aspirations. It is a film that refuses to let close-up images of the city blur its organizational logic and multiple functions, or to allow the city to disappear as a mappable totality. Its general visual clarity, enhanced by continual shots with great depth of field, mirrors the filmmaker's effort to influence and shape our understanding of the changing city.

By way of conclusion, I wish to bring together and compare the different political visions in *Black Snow* and *Good Morning, Beijing*. Both films feature a pivotal scene in a lively nightclub. In *Black Snow,* Li Huiquan as a member of the audience is painstakingly separated from the solo singer, both visually and emotionally. But when Ai Hong and Keke in *Good Morning, Beijing* go to a bar with live music, Keke joins the band and asks to participate. He sings and dedicates to Ai Hong a popular song by rock star Cui Jian, which Ai Hong will also learn to sing, even though she appears to be at a loss when hearing the song for the first time. The interpretation that I would propose, if only too schematically, is that these two different moments express two approaches to the city that are at odds with each other. If we characterize the politics of *Black Snow* as a refusal and contemplation by means of a modernist aesthetics of depth, the rhetoric of compromise in *Good Morning, Beijing* necessarily valorizes cultural and political participation, which in turn articulates the legitimating ideology of a growing market economy. Whereas the market economy arrives to present an open city to Ai Hong and her contemporaries, some deep (well-nigh instinctive) suspicion of the market triggers Li Huiquan's anxious, and to a large extent forced, retreat to interiority. In one case, neorealist techniques are used to rationalize the modernization project, while in the other a hypertrophy of modernist subjectivity emits uncompromising social criticism. Herein lies the cognitive value of *Black Snow,* which may be realized only with critical reflection on the part of the viewer.

These two significantly contradistinct political visions and cinematic languages hardly escaped the notice of the Chinese audience when *Black Snow* and *Good Morning, Beijing* were released in 1989 and 1990, respectively. They were quickly recognized as representative works of the rising city cinema. While *Black Snow* enjoyed the rare distinction of winning both domestic and international honors (Best Picture at the Thirteenth National Hundred Flowers Awards and the Silver Bear Prize at the Berlin Film Festival), *Good Morning, Beijing* was a remarkable box-office success. Quoting Cesare Zavattini, the theorist of Italian neorealist cinema, an enthusiastic commentator commended the second film for truthfully capturing contemporary everyday life in the ancient capital city and in the process revealing a deeper historical meaning.[41] At the same time, the critical recognition of *Black Snow* caused considerable uneasiness among mainstream critics and media. A brief essay in *Popular Cinema*, appearing next to Lei Da's endorsement of *Good Morning, Beijing*, sought to explain why the Hundred Flowers Award won by *Black Snow* did not mean that the film is flawless. In fact, the essayist denounced the film as deeply flawed because, in spite of its artistic achievements, "it does not find (or does not want to find) a new worldview and a new character that new social forces, who represent a new mode of social production, ought to possess."[42] It would be an involved task to unpack the loaded discourse and ideological stances here. Suffice it to say that at stake are some profoundly unresolved questions about artistic and social forms, about representation and engagement, all of which these two films succeed in bringing to the fore by evoking separate intellectual and aesthetic traditions. If our analysis of their indebtedness to either modernism or neorealism shows both films to be an ideological intervention, it should also be clear that we cannot dismiss one on the account of the other. Rather, these two films should be viewed together, and perhaps between them we will begin to approach the impossible urban reality signified by Beijing.

41. See Lei Da, "Dangda dushi fengjing xian: tan yingpian *Beijing nizao*" (Contemporary urban landscape: about the film *Good morning, Beijing*), *Dazhong dianying* (Popular cinema), no. 450 (December 1990): 4–5.

42. See Zheng Shu, "Xie zai *Benming nian* huojiang zhihou" (Afterthoughts on *Black snow* winning the award), *Popular Cinema*, no. 450 (December 1990): 5.

9

New Urban Culture and the Anxiety of Everyday Life in Late-Twentieth-Century China

There is no question that in contemporary China a market economy is finally prevailing, and with irresistible force is penetrating into every fiber of social life, fueling an explosive capitalist Great Leap Forward thus far unmatched in modern Chinese history. No question, either, that a post-socialist consumerism has, as Theodor Adorno would say, turned the commodity form into an ideology of its own and even skillfully capitalized on the bygone revolutionary age and its passionate utopianism. It is not surprising at all, for instance, to see middle-aged "budding tycoons . . . dining on peasant fare like cornmeal cakes and rice gruel in one of several new Beijing restaurants serving Cultural Revolution (CR) cuisine."[1] Retro-Maoist cuisine aside, those ingenious ideas to cash in on the one-hundredth anniversary of Mao Zedong's birth, whether officially endorsed or not, serve as yet another good case in point. When such robust commercialism and entrepreneurialism eventually make inroads into the traditionally ideological front of the socialist regime, namely, the realm of centralized cultural production, we hear an almost audible sigh of relief, a not-so-quiet celebration of the demise of overpoliticization and the end of Ideology. The market is welcomed in general by writers and artists alike as a liberating agency, and the implied personal autonomy, perhaps more than artistic freedom, greatly excites the imagination of generations of state-employed "cultural workers," who have been frustrated by a "velvet prison" for too long.[2] Already, even from afar, we witness a "young

---

1. See *Newsweek,* 10 January 1994, 8. Zhu Kunnian, the owner of a husk-strewn CR-style restaurant, is quoted here as saying: "We're not nostalgic for Mao, per se. We're nostalgic for our youth." See also Catherine Sampson, "Retro Maoist Cuisine Is a Hit in China," *Wall Street Journal,* 2 February 1994, A14.

2. For instance, in an interview, Chen Jiangong, an established Beijing writer, argues that the speed at which literature and art enter the market has been unsatisfyingly slow. "No doubt that the market is a strange thing to us, and writers and publishers need to be more imaginative in this aspect." See Yan Xinjiu, "Zhongguo zuojia kan shi-

and restless" literary production that bears only the faintest resemblance to the moralism and heroism glossing the works from the age of socialist realism.³ Instead, "shock value" is quickly recognized and cherished as an effective marketing strategy. At the same time, the great divide between so-called popular or mass culture and serious or elite culture is resurfacing, and together they highlight features of a culture that, as a whole, is openly entangled with the desires and frustrations provoked by rapid modernization.

The complexity of the situation can hardly be understood simply in terms of the marketization of a centrally planned economy in general and ideologically controlled cultural production in particular. The staggering demand for mass cultural products and kitsch also seems to stem from more sources than the direct lure of consumerism. One way to gauge the transformation is to realize the extent to which the city has arrived to occupy the center stage in cultural orientation and the social imaginary. The way for the current economic boom was first paved by the "household responsibility system" in agriculture (implemented in the late 1970s) and was boosted by large-scale absorption of foreign and transnational investment capital in the "special economic zones" along the coastal area. But it is the emergence and flourishing of what economists and social engineers call "village and township enterprises" that have probably effected the most profound impact on the country's social and geographical landscape. Acting both as trading posts and locations of export-oriented light industry, hundreds of thousands of such enterprises help to channel an enormous surplus labor force from the countryside into the market as well as into the industrial sector. As a result, "agricultural diversification and rural enterprises have reduced the urban-rural gap," even though, as

---

chang" (Chinese writers converse on the market), *Zhongguo qingnian* (Chinese youth) (February 1993): 4. All ten writers interviewed, among them Liu Heng, Wang Zengqi, and Wang Meng, believe that the market mechanism provides a new opportunity for literature and art (4–7). The term "velvet prison" comes from the Hungarian writer Miklós Haraszti, *The Velvet Prison: Artists Under Socialism*, trans. Katalin and Stephen Landesmann, with the help of Steve Wasserman (New York: Basic Books, 1987).

3. See Howard Goldblatt's book review, "The Young and the Restless," *Los Angeles Times*, Sunday, 5 September 1993. In these young writers, such as Liu Heng, Su Tong, and Mo Yan, Goldblatt observes a "common thread of misanthropy" and an "emphasis on skewed family relations and anti-Confucian behavior, which includes incest, rape, murder, voyeurism and more."

a bitter result, "total regional disparity throughout China has probably widened."[4]

As one Chinese commentator has argued in favor of this development, world historical experience has shown that the modernization project invariably involves marketization, industrialization, and urbanization; and recent Chinese history has also demonstrated the necessity of making a final transition from the country to the city, from the rural to the urban.[5] Indeed, this new wave of massive urbanization comes as a direct reversal of the official policies of the socialist period, the ethos of which in hindsight appears to have been persistently resistant to the "dissociation of sensibility" accompanying modernization. During the 1960s and 1970s the ideologically sanctioned method of overcoming the difference between town and country, for instance, was to suppress nonfarm employment or deurbanize society as a whole. A deeply entrenched agrarian tradition helped to justify an essentially antiurban policy of modernization without urbanization, for urbanism was more often than not identified and condemned as the embodiment of evil modern capitalism.[6] The alternative vision of a Third World modernity saw itself in terms of self-reliance, strategic industrialization, and a negation of market forces, international as well as domestic. The socialist cities, at least in theory, "should become Spartan and productive places with full employment, secure jobs with a range of fringe benefits, minimal income and life style

---

4. Sen-dou Chang and R. Yin-Wang Kwok, "The Urbanization of Rural China," in R. Yin-Wang Kwok et al., eds., *Chinese Urban Reform: What Model Now?* (Armonk, N.Y.: M. E. Sharpe, 1990), 151.

5. For a semiofficial statement, see Gou Shi, "Jiakuai nongcun chengshihua jincheng" (Speed up the urbanization of the countryside), *Zhongguo jingji tizhi gaige* (China's economic system reform), no. 95 (November 1993): 46. For a comprehensive case study, see Yia-Ling Liu, "Reform from Below: The Private Economy and Local Politics in the Rural Industrialization of Wenzhou," *China Quarterly* 130 (June 1992): 293–316.

6. See, for instance, essays collected in Victor F. S. Sit, ed., *Chinese Cities: The Growth of the Metropolis Since 1949* (Oxford: Oxford University Press, 1985). In his introduction, Sit lists a few articles of interest here: L. J. C. Ma, "Counterurbanization and Rural Development: The Strategy of Hsia-Hsiang," *Current Scene* 15:889 (1979): 1–11; A. Koshizawa, "China's Urban Planning: Towards Development Without Urbanization," *Developing Economies* (1978): 3–33; C. P. Cell, "Deurbanization of China: The Urban Contradiction," *Bulletin of Concerned Asian Scholars* 11, no. 1 (1979): 62–72.

differences, an end to conspicuous consumption and lavish spending, and with decent consumption standards for all."[7] Consequently, postsocialist urbanization means not merely a physical transformation of the previously rural landscape but also the institution of social values, such as mobility, privacy, and diversity, that are associated with life in the modern city. The consumer city, in place of the discredited model of producer cities, reasserts itself as the dominant center of a new political economy and should offer us a clue to the logic of Chinese culture in the age of global capitalism.

This emergent urban culture, as can be expected, exhibits many recognizable features, if not caricatures, of modern metropolises in the West. In this sense, a sprawling city such as Guangzhou or Shanghai grows to be more and more part of the global, standardized geography of modernization.[8] As in many other parts of the world, high-rises have erupted here, standing for financial capacity and stability, often with a transnational connection, and beltways have been hastily extended to ease traffic congestion and push the sound and the fury of the city beyond the given boundary. With heavy smog hanging as a permanent backdrop, streetside billboards and advertisements stylistically reminiscent of the Cultural Revolution's visual regime neatly block the view and aggressively demand consumers' attention; leisure time for the city dweller quickly turns into a busy search for entertainment and diversion. As evening falls, loud and color-splashing karaoke bars dutifully supply sentiment and expression to the fashionable and adventurous, and the milling crowd, as in all big cities, takes pride in being indifferent and anonymous. Nevertheless, a faceless AM or FM talk-radio host will reach out to comfort lonely souls and will assume, with enthusiasm, the time-honored role of a matchmaker in the middle of the night. McDonald's or Pizza Hut may add a welcome cosmopolitan flavor to daily staple food, whereas home-grown

---

7. Martin King Whyte and William L. Parish, *Urban Life in Contemporary China* (Chicago: University of Chicago Press, 1984), 16. Whyte and Parish's book is a comprehensive study of the structure and content of city life during the socialist period.

8. I wish to emphasize that contemporary Chinese urban culture can and should be subjected to the same classic scrutiny and creative analyses that we find in the writings of Georg Simmel, Emile Durkheim, Walter Benjamin, Kevin Lynch, and Raymond Williams. Their critical insights into the modern city and its culture will prove to be an indispensable basis for any credible urban studies in contemporary China.

TV sitcoms—in ever-greater doses and punctuated by imposing commercials—adroitly spice up an otherwise increasingly routine and eventless life.

A more ominous view of such reckless urbanization, in the opinion of a *Newsweek* reporter, is the arrival of "nightmare cities," overstretched by the growing number of ethnic peasant ghettos—"virtual Chinatowns in China." With "tidal waves of humanity" rolling from the vast inland to the more prosperous coastal cities, "China will be presented with vast breeding grounds of urban unrest."[9] This dark vision undoubtedly calls our attention to the stark reality of city life in China, a brewing area for new forms of class, gender, and ethnic conflicts. But the very monstrosity of "nightmare cities" also bespeaks, even if negatively, the fact that the city has moved onto the center stage of contemporary Chinese cultural and political life. "A terrible beauty," as William Butler Yeats would say, is once again being born.

To all appearances, everyday urban life as normalcy now seems successfully instituted; for good reason, this is celebrated as a genuine cultural revolution in late twentieth-century China. Interestingly enough, this normalcy, which comes in the wake of a massive socialist experiment, can be readily theorized as well as rationalized through Marxian terminology. It is not at all difficult, for instance, for the general social discourse to grasp that the market is the operating logic behind everyday urban life. The Janus face of the market, both a liberating "angel" and a destructive "devil," is very much accepted as a necessary reality principle. Thus, an article that appropriately appears in the "Think Tank for the Coming Century" section in *Chinese Youth,* a popular magazine published by the League of Communist Youth, asserts: "The market economy is an 'angel,' because it transforms the world into a colorful place; it is also a 'devil' because it puts existing values and social order in complete disarray. In the words of Karl Marx, this means a revolution in the realms of politics, consciousness, spirit, and morality."[10] According to the article's author, the market economy will introduce a complete renewal of Chinese society in terms of its social organization. With the market as a leveling

9. George Wehrfritz, "Nightmare Cities," *Newsweek,* 26 December 1994, 106–08.

10. Xu Weixin, "Shichang jingji jiang shi Zhongguo shehui quanmian gengxin" (The market economy will completely renew Chinese society), *Chinese Youth* (August 1993): 22.

mechanism, the individual will be freed from total dependence on and control by the work unit, and the work unit in turn will itself be released from the rigid bureaucratic hierarchy. Another desirable consequence is that social life will be less politicized because society at large will become pluralized and politics will cease to provide the only meaningful content. Chinese society as a whole, concludes the author, is bidding farewell to a past in which politics dominated all details of everyday life. The new era of "open and plural development," propelled by the market, will usher in a younger, more energetic, and more colorful society.[11]

As optimistic an assessment as that may be, the article nonetheless brings to our attention a central feature of twentieth-century Chinese revolutionary culture, and, at the same time, it sheds light on the making of contemporary urban culture. The author describes the social reality that the new market economy will help to dismantle as either the "traditional socialist system" or simply the "traditional system." This traditional social organization valorizes communality, hierarchy, and ideological homogeneity, all of which contribute to an impoverishment of everyday life. This impoverishment takes the form of moralizing feelings, social relations, and quotidian routines; it is thus an impoverishment paradoxically sustained by an immense richness in political meanings and consequentialities. The ultimate injunction of this mode of social life is stated in a slogan popular during the radical 1960s: "Make a revolution in the depths of your soul."[12] With such an imperative for ethical politics, everyday life is not without its excitement or content; on the contrary, it is nothing but ritualized content, and it can be full of pious passion and longings. With ideology or political identity as its sole content or depth, everyday life is organized, rendered meaningful, and effectively reduced in form. This constitutes what Agnes Heller, following George Lukács, has described as an "emergence" from everyday life through homogenization, more specifically a "moral homogenization," the criteria of which are "concentration on the given objective, subordination to it

---

11. Ibid., 22–23. Xu's conclusion concurs with Gordon White's well-documented analysis that the spread of market relations has effectively "created the basis of, and context for, new forms of sociopolitical participation and organization, to varying degrees independent of and/or in opposition to the Party/state." See White, *Riding the Tiger: The Politics of Economic Reform in Post-Mao China* (Stanford, Calif.: Stanford University Press, 1993), 217.

12. In Chinese, the slogan usually goes "Linghun shenchu nao geming."

of everyday activities, even their partial or total suspension."[13] Although Heller acknowledges that "everyday life could not be reproduced without the heterogeneous human activities," she, as much as Lukács, emphasizes the process of homogenization as collective creation or re-creation for the "objectivation" of human "species-essentiality."[14] Put differently, the heterogeneous forms of everyday life can be transcended or emerged from only when they are endowed with the content of homogenized social relations and pursuits.

A collective desire to resist the inertia of everyday life was an integral part of the grand socialist movement in modern China. Moreover, the same desire, which Agnes Heller characterizes as the "necessity of philosophy" after religion, has been universally experienced in the age of modernity. After all, modernization arrives only when instrumental reason secures a desacralization of the human as well as the natural world and when a secular ordinary life is affirmed to be equally providential and indispensable to human identity. The humanist culture of modernity, according to Charles Taylor, affirms the full human life "in terms of labour and production, on one hand, and marriage and family life on the other."[15] Against such massive democratization or cultural leveling, various modernisms, conservative or radical, arise in protest and "in the search for sources which can restore depth, richness, and meaning to life."[16] The modernist aspiration of writers like T. S. Eliot or D. H. Lawrence, observes Taylor, "is usually made more urgent by the sense that our modern fragmented, instrumentalist society has narrowed and impoverished our lives."[17] To emerge from this secularized everyday life, to transform *the ordinary life* into *the good life,* therefore, is as much a modernist desire as a critique of modernity. This antimodern and yet modernist rejection of everyday life seems to be a deeply embedded impulse of the revolutionary culture in modern China, which often expresses itself in the Maoist utopian longing for a full and complete life. The success of

13. Agnes Heller, *Everyday Life,* trans. G. L. Campbell (London: Routledge & Kegan Paul, 1984), 87.
14. See ibid., 56–59.
15. Charles Taylor, "Part III: The Affirmation of Ordinary Life," in *Sources of the Self: The Making of the Modern Identity* (Cambridge, Mass.: Harvard University Press, 1989), 213.
16. Ibid., 495.
17. Ibid., 490.

such a politics of utopia, however, can perhaps be measured only in its failure, in its negation by late twentieth-century consumerism and mass culture, which, I wish to argue, in fact helps to retroactively release the utopian potency of a revolutionary tradition. "In terms of political positions and ideologies," as Fredric Jameson comments on the failed radical traditions in literature and culture, "all the radical positions of the past are flawed, precisely because they failed. . . . What they achieved, however, was something rather different from achieved positivity; they demonstrated, for their own time and culture, the *impossibility* of imagining Utopia."[18]

To demonstrate that a deep utopian impulse of the Chinese revolutionary culture is to overcome ordinary everyday life would be a complex process, and it probably could be achieved only negatively, namely, through an examination of *signifying absences*. The four general developments that Charles Taylor believes to have contributed to the culture of modernity, for example, could be a useful point of departure in a cultural studies approach: the new valuation of commerce, the rise of the novel, the changing understanding of marriage and the family, and the new importance of sentiment.[19] We would likely find in the revolutionary tradition a systematic suppression or reorientation of these activities that would have helped to affirm and define a secular everyday life. A persisting paradox here is that the fuller life envisioned by Maoist social engineering reflects both an essentially agrarian imagination and a fascination with modern industrial power, both an egalitarian commitment to social harmony and an almost aristocratic refusal of the mundane and the physical.

From such a vision of the good life, which valorizes completeness and transcendence, is derived an aesthetics of scale rather than of detail, for immediacy and particularity would only swamp any effort to overcome the daily routine. This in part explains why artwork from the revolutionary period is dominantly perspectival and panoramic.[20] In *New Look of*

---

18. Fredric Jameson, "Immanence and Nominalism in Postmodern Theoretical Discourse," in *Postmodernism, Or, the Cultural Logic of Late Capitalism* (Durham, N.C.: Duke University Press, 1991), 208–09. See also in the same volume Jameson's discussion of artist Robert Gober's work in "Utopianism After the End of Utopia," 154–80. My line of reading here is deeply indebted to Jameson's "Marxian positive hermeneutic," even though I may be simplifying some of his ideas.

19. See Taylor, *Sources of the Self*, 285–302.

20. Ellen Johnston Laing, in her *The Winking Owl: Art in the People's Republic of*

New Urban Culture 281

11. Peasant painting, *New Look of a Village* (1974). From *Peasant Paintings from Huhsien County* (Peking: Foreign Languages Press, 1974).

a Village (1974) (figure 11), a representative Huxian (Huhsien) County peasant painting from the heyday of the socialist revolution, we see the way that a politicized public space has endowed labor with global signifi-

China (Berkeley: University of California Press, 1988), traces the political history of art during the radical 1960s. "[Other] landscapes done during this period," she observes, "are also vast panoramic vistas, and their subjects are usually, if not the already established themes based on revolutionary history, then clearly delineated motifs of socialist triumphs in public projects: bridges, busy ports, dams, reforestation" (78).

12. Peasant painting, *The Whole Family Studies the Communiqué* (1974). From *Peasant Paintings from Huhsien County* (Peking: Foreign Languages Press, 1974).

cance. The continuity of spatial structure neatly defers gratification and yet keeps in perspective the consummating *promesse de bonheur* (promise of happiness). In a similar spirit, *The Whole Family Studies the Communiqué* (1974) (figure 12) presents the extended family as a political unit and projects a domestic interior that is open and public, simple but productive, and ultimately centered on the communal as well as spiritual act of reading. In these stylized images of happiness, the political economy of the sign forcefully distributes the socialist ideals of equality, use value, self-reliance, and homogenized social relations. It is by no accident, moreover, that these socialist realist representations of rural life were acclaimed as emblematic of "the socialist new culture" at the time.[21] As mentioned, the ruralization policies, or the "development without

21. In the foreword to the English edition of *Peasant Paintings from Huhsien County* (Peking: Foreign Languages Press, 1974), the government compilers laud the peasant artists as "masters of the socialist new culture." Moreover, "they have set a pattern for developing fine arts as a spare-time activity in rural areas and become a model for professional artists."

urbanization" model, of the 1960s and 1970s could be seen as a collective effort to ensure an organic and connected life that threatens to unravel in the urban landscape. These Huxian County peasant paintings, which enjoyed considerable popularity and official sponsorship in the mid-1970s, best capture an age for which *la sociabilité villageoise* (village harmony) was the norm and the ideal form of life.²²

In fact, we have to understand this particular art form, together with many other signifying practices from that period (such as the "revolutionary model theater," public squares, and massive parades), as constituting a revolutionary mass culture. It is a mass culture that emphasizes content over form, use value over exchange value, participatory communal action over heterogeneous everyday life. Hence, such a mass culture is profoundly romantic in its form and utopian in its vision; it is necessarily didactic rather than entertaining, production-oriented rather than consumption-oriented. The historical relevance of this specific mass culture, especially its utopian vision, however, may become all the more recognizable and even compelling only when it is negated as a hegemonic, practiced social order. Only in absentia does this revolutionary mass culture reveal itself to have been a heroic effort to overcome a deep anxiety over everyday life, often at the cost of impoverishing it. When everyday life is affirmed and accepted as the new hegemony, when commodification arrives to put a price tag on human relations and even on private sentiments, participatory communal action may offer itself as an oppositional discourse and expose a vacuity underlying the myriad of commodity forms. The persistent nostalgia for Mao and his era in late twentieth-century China is a good sign of the collective anxiety that the market economy has given rise to.²³ But it cannot be concluded that this postrevolutionary culture is without its consolation or even its utopian appeal. In fact, a direct function of the rising consumerism is to contain

22. The phrase *la sociabilité villageoise* is from historian Jean-Pierre Gutton's book *La sociabilité villageoise dans l'ancienne France: solidarités et voisinages du XIIe au XVIIIe siècle* (Paris: Hachette, 1979).

23. Sociologist Wang Yanzhong also points out that "Mao Zedong fever" reflects a popular longing for the charismatic leader in an age of growing institutionalization. See Zhang Zhanbing and Song Yifu, *Zhongguo: Mao Zedong re* (China: Mao Zedong fever) (Taiyuan: Beiyue wenyi, 1991), 275–76, 280–81. One of the good things about this popular sentiment, according to the authors of the book, is that it will call attention to issues such as inflation, social security, justice, and a communal spirit (284–85).

and dissolve the anxiety of everyday life, to translate collective concerns into consumer desires, by which means even the revolutionary past may be made profitable.

Thus, the transitional quality of late twentieth-century Chinese culture can be observed as two related social discourses: an anxious affirmation of ordinary life and a continuous negotiation with the utopian impulse to reject everyday life. This transition, part of the long revolution toward modernity, is readily observable as the tension between the city and the country. As has been pointed out, urbanization has certainly shifted the focus of the social imaginary, but the country still refuses to disappear, and frequently it flashes back, so to speak, to throw an unsettling light on the urban landscape. While an apparently amorphous urban everyday life becomes the norm and an alienating institution, rustic simplicity and authenticity seem to possess a greater peculiar attraction. In this light, just as there can be a revolutionary mass culture, so there is bound to be another mass culture that observes the logic of the reproduction of everyday life. Whereas the revolutionary mass culture needs to project a life that is wholesome but abstract, the new urban culture has to present a secular existence that, routine though it may be, is full of concrete expectations and fulfillments.

At this juncture it is useful to examine some contemporary literary works in order to appreciate the emergent and contested urban consciousness, with the aim of determining whether the works in question belong to mass culture or high literature. A good case in point is the 1993 novella *Shenghuo wuzui* (Life is not a crime) by a young writer, He Dun. This story, a loosely organized first-person narrative about a young man's various efforts to make money on his own in the inland city of Changsha, may be paradigmatic of the narratable experience of a whole genuinely postrevolutionary generation of urban youth. The world in which the young man finds himself is one of entrepreneurial adventure, prostitution, violence, organized crime, commodities, and quick money. As in his other novella, *Wo bu xiangshi* (I don't care), He Dun hurriedly narrates in a factual, indifferent tone of understanding, but with no compassion, moments and sensations in the hero's busy, directionless life. The series of events is barely coherent, and its multiplicity seems to be the only narratable content of the young man's experience. The story begins with a brief ritual of initiation, a moment at which the hero, He Fu, then an impoverished high school teacher, is invited to enter the symbolic space of the narrative—a domestic space pointedly exhibiting its contemporaneity through an ostentatious display of objects, commodities, and details. One afternoon in May, He Fu and his wife, Zhu Li, decide to pay a visit to an old friend of his, who now runs a department store and self-consciously belongs to the new managerial class.

> When I, having made love with Zhu Li around noon, walked into Qu Gang's apartment and saw how luxuriously furnished it was, I felt reasonably calm. Qu Gang owned an apartment with four rooms, one of them used as the living room. The surrounding walls were decorated with pink enameled tiles, a chandelier hung from the ceiling, and the floor was covered with inlaid parquet. There was a nicely crafted, snow-white composite dresser, on which stood an imposing 28″ Toshiba color TV. Next to it was a video machine; further down stood an American-made Sherwood stereo system. After my wife and I had settled down in the elegant sheepskin sofa, my wife said: "Your sofa is so comfortable to sit in." "Imported from Italy," Qu Gang replied, throwing over to me a "555" cigarette. "Cost me about ten grand. It better be comfortable to sit in." "That much money?" Zhu Li felt the sofa. "That was too expensive." Qu Gang smirked without comment, "Do you guys want coffee or tea?" [24]

This initial moment is pivotal to the story in that it introduces desire, or, more exactly, it gives concrete, physical shape and expression to a desire for self-transformation. The material world becomes a prominent index not so much of vulgarity as of an enviable spiritual resilience. The same moment also offers a redefinition of everyday life, of domestic existence as graspable through various tangible forms—in this case, expensive consumer goods. This stuffed showroom will not be entered again, but it provides meaning and image to the space in which He Fu, the aspiring consumer/entrepreneur, wishes to participate. (At this point, however, he feels embarrassed to even talk about money because he has to save every penny in order to purchase a color TV.)

Before rushing ahead to condemn this unabashed consumerism, we need to realize that it probably has its origin in a not-so-distant past when consumption was maximally suppressed from the reproduction of everyday life. Almost directly, this commodity fetishism comes as a rebellion

---

24. *Shenghuo wuzui* (Life is not a crime), in *Shouhuo* (Harvest), no. 99 (1993): 25; *Wo bu xiangshi* (I don't care), in *Shanghai wenxue* (Shanghai literature), no. 192 (September 1993): 4–41.

against, or an overcompensation for, the utopian life depicted in an artwork such as *The Whole Family Studies the Communiqué*. In the wake of such a clearly defined and community-oriented form of life, in which spiritual elevation was the predominant need, there is a striking lack of perspective in He Dun's story about the bestirring life in late twentieth-century Changsha. The narrator, moreover, consistently refuses to impose moral judgment or even indicate indignation. As the story rapidly unfolds, the day-to-day events, frustrations, and expectations that befall him and fellow city dwellers keep his attention riveted, and the city in which he moves never emerges as a totalizable spatiality. Only toward the very end of the story do we find a pause and a moment of doubt. And this occurs when another old friend, like a specter from the unspeakable past, returns to question He Fu's increasingly complacent daily life. Very tellingly, this friend is an artist who lives in the distant frontier of Xinjiang and finds himself not welcomed while visiting Hunan, his place of birth. In the story, the artist serves to pose a fundamental question about value, which He Fu, with a lot of sarcasm, dismisses as metaphysical and pointless. But when the artist friend leaves in disappointment early the next morning, the hero feels the warm flow of an old friendship and becomes guilt-stricken. Then rain starts pouring down outside: "Several times I made up my mind to go out, but lacked the courage to walk in a thunderstorm. I gazed at the heavy rain that would possibly never stop and said to myself: 'This world really makes people suffer.' As soon as I said this, it dawned on me that all those things—about which I had been too excited to fall asleep normally in the past few months, and which could be described as forming a beautiful blueprint—had all of a sudden turned into a pile of broken tiles."[25] This is where the narrative ends, and we leave the hero with the pouring rain, pondering over the transcendental meaning of the world.

Despite a final, reflective moment like this one (perhaps an "epiphany"?), *Life Is Not a Crime* resolutely subscribes to the urban space it depicts. It is a paradigmatic narrative of the city because it is motivated by a fascination with the apparently infinite possibilities of form that a city now allows. This "guilt-free life" is a fragmented but concrete existence, the moral content of which is realized in action rather than in contemplation. The fact that the idealistic artist appears unexpectedly, only at

---

25. He Dun, *Life Is Not a Crime*, 53.

the end of the story, calls our attention to a spectrality about his being. Perhaps he is a residual modernist bent on revealing the incompleteness of life in modernity. Even though this artist figure disappears altogether from He Dun's later work, his fleeting presence here reveals a fundamental lack. His lonely departure also suggests that the pursuit of a full life is now a personal commitment and has to be conducted at the margin, far away from the crowded urban landscape.

If what He Dun chooses to depict is the heterogeneous "stuff" of everyday urban life, the satisfaction of which is frequently achieved through objects and commodities, then Wang Anyi, an established and prolific contemporary writer, presents an intriguing examination of urban sensibility and emotional life. What I have in mind is her novella *Xianggang de qing yu ai* (Love and sentiment in Hong Kong), a piece of writing that bears an uncanny resemblance to Zhang Ailing's (Eileen Chang's) story from roughly fifty years earlier, *Qingcheng zhi lian* (Love in a fallen city). Critically acclaimed for having a strong "future look," Wang Anyi's contemporary story tells of an affair in Hong Kong between an aging but wealthy Chinese-American businessman and his crass and practical mistress, who is an immigrant from Shanghai and now desperately wants to go to the United States. The tale begins as yet another affair based on an exchange of favors, and it ends with the woman heading for Australia several years later, leaving behind an older Lao Wei, who, in her absence, finds himself more than ever attached to the city of Hong Kong. In an associational and even nostalgic style, Wang Anyi patiently explores all aspects of the question of "how the bustling and prosperous metropolis participates in the emotional life of people."[26] The story is equally a rich and complex narrative about Hong Kong, the spectacular city that may strike one at first as a "great encounter, a miraculous coming together,"[27] but eventually reveals its many depths and dimensions over time. For the protagonists in the story, Hong Kong is a city of both past and future, a transit stopover that nonetheless indiscriminately shelters homeless souls and even nurtures attachment and love. The fact that Lao Wei and his mistress, Fengjia, are no longer young and are perhaps much too practical also indicates a mature approach to the city, what Raymond Wil-

26. See the "Editor's Words" section at the front of *Shanghai Literature,* no. 191 (August 1993), in which Wang's story appears.

27. Wang Anyi, *Xianggang de qing he ai* (Love and sentiment in Hong Kong), in *Shanghai Literature,* no. 191 (August 1993): 4.

liams calls the perspective of "an adult experience."[28] For the author of the story, too, Hong Kong, as a completely urbanized space, presents an enormous field of multiple new possibilities and expectations, a whole new civilization that stands in need of comprehending, representing, and probably evaluating.[29]

Yet, just as in *Life Is Not a Crime,* the narrative of *Love and Sentiment in Hong Kong* is a careful withholding of moral judgment or criticism. Instead, it continuously marvels at the protean shape possessed by the contemporary city and the endless variations—in lived space as well as in the human heart—that the city constantly provokes. With deliberate slowness, the narrative moves us through a series of spatial structures that are emphatically urban: courteous service but impersonal hotel rooms, private and yet uniform apartments in a twenty-story building, and new but empty homes waiting to be furnished with a personal touch. It assembles into a colorful picture such activities as shopping, dining, riding the double-decker bus, pursuing domestic pleasures, and engaging in small talk on the phone. In the eyes of the narrator, Hong Kong is no less than the city of all cities. Just as every detail of leisurely urban life offers instant satisfaction and is savored with deliberate pleasure, so every moment is charged with ambiguities and open to interpretation. For instance, taking a double-decker bus to go home, Lao Wei and Fengjia look out to enjoy the busy street scenes, in particular those apartment windows seemingly within arm's reach. "These windows reveal the most sincere, most practical ways of sustaining life; these are ways that will remain unchanged forever, as permanently as rivers flowing and the sun and

---

28. At the beginning of his *The Country and the City* (New York: Oxford University Press, 1973), Williams writes in a personal tone: "I have felt also the chaos of the metro and the traffic jam; the monotony of the ranks of houses; the aching press of strange crowds. But this is not an experience at all, not an adult experience, until it has come to include also the dynamic movement, in these centres of settled and often magnificent achievement" (5).

29. This is not to say that the city has not appeared in Wang Anyi's work until this moment. Based in Shanghai, Wang Anyi is probably one of the very few contemporary Chinese writers who take the city as a serious subject of their writings. In a short essay, "Nanren he nüren, nüren he chengshi" (Men and women, women and the city), written in 1986, she already theorized on the freedom and opportunity that the city may present to women. For her, the city represented a welcome break with the agrarian tradition in which only men could have excelled. See Wang Anyi, *Huangshan zhi lian* (Love on a barren mountain) (Hong Kong: South China Press, 1988), 243–48.

the moon revolving. They belong in the same category as the sky and the ocean beyond the lights in Hong Kong, as the rocks standing in the sea water. They are the solid foundation of the marvelous spectacle of Hong Kong. Here you find the most ordinary life, as ordinary as the intriguing spectacle of Hong Kong can be."[30] Against this backdrop of heterogeneous coexistence, human experience is described as anything but uneventful. Here, the narrator is greatly fascinated by the new modality that Hong Kong promises to human sensibility.

> In such a hot and humid evening, you never know how many stories are strolling along the streets, pausing and moving hesitantly. Some of them just have a beginning, some of them are coming to an end, and some others are right in the middle. This is why evenings in Hong Kong are full of turns and suspense. These are the least quiet and peaceful evenings, with numerous comedies and tragedies unfolding at the same time . . . . [The drama of Hong Kong] offers you excitement that cannot be total, and despair that will never be complete. *It promises you a last ray of hope when everything turns out to be a disappointment; it also adds a broken piece when you finally possess everything.* Yet no matter what, the story of Hong Kong will never come to an end. There will always be instruments playing in the theater of Hong Kong, and there will never be a dying out of the lights in Hong Kong. (Emphasis added)[31]

These observations by themselves may not be profound or original, and some of them already have been made—for instance, in Zhang Ailing's stories about Hong Kong and Shanghai in the 1940s[32]—but in the context of contemporary Chinese social discourse, the Hong Kong that Wang Anyi narrates here is undoubtedly a purposeful metaphor for a cultural choice. As a geographical embodiment of the social imaginary, Hong Kong indeed stands as a city of the future. It offers itself as an ideal instance of the heterotopian urban life that the Chinese postrevolutionary culture seems anxious to understand and eventually to acquire.

Most noticeably, therefore, the broken but concrete life stories that

---

30. Wang, *Love and Sentiment in Hong Kong*, 10.
31. Ibid., 15.
32. For an insightful analysis of the sense of "incompleteness" and modernity in Zhang Ailing's fiction, see Meng Yue, "Zhongguo wenxue 'xiandai xing' yu Zhang Ailing" (The modernity of Chinese literature and Zhang Ailing), *Jintian* (Today), no. 3 (1992): 176–92.

Wang Anyi tells us here are hardly affected by either collective consciousness or political aspirations. There is barely any reference to recent history. However, this does not necessarily mean that there is no shared vision of the future. The peculiarity of Hong Kong, as portrayed in Wang Anyi's narrative, is that it is completely postindustrial and urbanized. This is perhaps where the writer sees the relevance of Hong Kong as a paradigmatic space for an approaching future. On the one hand, the city of Hong Kong appears to be an enormous postmodern shopping mall, where everything is for sale and all anxieties can be shopped away; on the other hand, the city is full of human drama because, ceaselessly, "it throws an inclusive party by inviting all kinds of loneliness, and arranges a grand reunion by bringing together all moments of solitude."[33] The story of Lao Wei and Fengjia and their use and understanding of each other should ultimately be read as a defense of the richness of a mundane urban life. In her novella, Wang Anyi anticipates a major cultural transformation in contemporary China as much as He Dun does in his fragmented stories about the city of Changsha. Both writers grasp the city as central to a postrevolutionary reality, and, in doing so, they make representable an age in which the emergent hegemony is no longer Ideology or Collectivity, but rather everyday life. Also in this sense, they blend mass culture and high literature and directly participate in the making of a new urban culture, the historical function of which is to help absorb the shock of urbanization and ultimately to legitimate modernity.

By way of conclusion, I would like to briefly discuss three very different artworks to highlight some of the points made earlier. These three paintings may be described in terms of genre: political poster, commercial billboard, and autonomous art; they also can be defined in terms of their style: socialist realism, capitalist realism,[34] and neoimpressionism. By putting them together in a collage, however, I wish, first, to visually demonstrate a historical development and second, to point to three elements of late twentieth-century Chinese culture. Clearly, *The Motor's Roar* (1974) (figure 13) records an idealist era in which industrial as well as agricultural productivity acquires an ideological value and serves as a means of social homogenization. This pursuit of meaning is

33. Wang, *Love and Sentiment in Hong Kong*, 15.
34. Michael Schudson has used this term to describe the ideology of American advertising art. See his *Advertising, the Uneasy Persuasion: Its Dubious Impact on American Society* (New York: Basic Books, 1984), 214–18.

13 and 14. Peasant paintings, *(above) The Motor's Roar* (1974) and *(left) Old Party Secretary* (1974). Both from *Peasant Paintings from Huhsien County* (Peking: Foreign Languages Press, 1974).

292   *Chinese Modern*

15. Photograph, *Bringing You the Colors of the World, Giordano*, by Xiaobing Tang (1993).

strongly indicated by the conspicuous presence of a newspaper and a red book, which endows this life form with a spiritual content and eventual transcendence (see figure 14). The peasant of the Socialist New Era, however, does not occupy center stage but happily embodies instrumentality and directs our attention away from himself. This reification becomes more striking when we meet the warm and engaging gaze of the urban consumer in *Bringing You the Colors of the World, Giordano* (1993) (figure 15, color plate 1: following page 290). The subject of the dramatically fulfilling fantasy world must dominate our view because the mirror image functions by infiltrating our self-conception and consciousness. This world of the self-assured consumer is just as unreal and utopian as that of the self-abnegating producer, even though they suggest very different means of transforming the world. In this light, both socialist realism and capitalist realism are utopian art forms designed to alleviate the anxiety of everyday life and to help their respective viewers cope with the secular condition of modernity. The gray standardized office building against which this billboard is erected first seems to justify the need for such a fantasy and then quietly belies it.

New Urban Culture 293

16. Oil, *Dream Girl,* by Qiu Tao (1985). From *Beyond the Open Door: Contemporary Paintings from the People's Republic of China,* ed. Richard E. Strassberg and Waldemar A. Nielson (Pasadena: Pacific Asia Museum, 1987).

Finally, *Dream Girl* (1985) (figure 16, color plate 2: following page 290) by Qiu Tao presents itself as a revelatory act of intervention as well as a critique of the politics of utopia. One possible reading is to see a case of "sentimental confection which doubtless reflects westernized fantasies of romance common to the younger urban generation."[35] But when placed next to the other two paintings, the sullen face and greenish skin of the "dream girl," in sharp contrast to the bright and dancing red, seem to

35. Richard E. Strassberg, "The Opening Door of Contemporary Chinese Painting," in *Beyond the Open Door: Contemporary Paintings from the People's Republic of China,* ed. Richard E. Strassberg and Waldemar A. Nielsen (Pasadena, Calif.: Pacific Asia Museum, 1987), 15–16.

suggest a forced recognition, or acceptance, of some unromantic reality or truth. The colorful dress can barely support or hold together a cold, despondent body, and this is where the inertia of everyday life erupts. Instead of transferring or diverting the anxiety of everyday life, *Dream Girl* exposes it to our view and presents no less than a dystopian reality. This makes the painting a faithful extension of the critical spirit in Western modernism and gives it a political thrust. Yet because of its autonomous stance, it is fundamentally a deconstructive art form and remains opposed to the mass cultures represented by the other two images.

The situation that needs careful consideration now, however, is that the two uplifting images are more mass-oriented and positive precisely because they contain a utopian element. Whereas one image points to a moral being as the means to emerge from everyday life, the other, also as a compensation, substitutes consumer needs for global desires. In both images, the viewer is invited to participate in a promised good life, in one out of a moral imperative, in the other through imaginary identification. The fact that one of them was officially endorsed in 1974, and the other was publicly displayed in the streets of Guangzhou in 1993, is a telling indication of the extent of the cultural transformation in late twentieth-century China. What is more interesting is to read these two images as indices of two different cultural logics and visions of history: organic and transcendence-immanent rural life vs. incomplete but detail-centered urban existence. These two life forms are ultimately ideological efforts to overcome the anxiety of everyday life—which is also the bottom line of modernity.

Excursion II

Decorating Culture: Notes on Interior Design, Interiority, and Interiorization

"Inconspicuous consumption," observes Pilar Viladas, the architecture and home design critic for the *New York Times Magazine,* characterizes a prevailing aesthetics of simplicity in American home furnishings and decorations during the 1990s. "Rather than putting their money on display, people seem to be investing in a quieter brand of luxury, based on comfort and quality."[1] As if disclosing a new discovery, the design and style industry reveres as its motto "less is more," and a far-reaching movement away from the "overdesign" of the 1980s toward the Ordinary, according to Henry Urbach, a contributing editor at *Interior Design* magazine, is driven by the yearning for a simple and familiar life. "The Ordinary has gained momentum in recent years as a kind of compensation for, or reaction against, the extraordinary changes affecting our everyday lives. No place seems safe, least of all the home, where privacy and tranquillity cannot be taken for granted."[2]

The current reaffirmation of a private and unpretentious home may be an expected pendular swing of the fashion world; it may even have its psychological origins, as Urbach suggests, in the American ambivalence toward "showing off wealth"; and it may be the eventual, gadget-weary homecoming of a much publicized postmodernism, which has fully revealed itself as an ideology of everyday life in the postindustrial sector of global capitalism. Whatever the readings, interior design erects an intriguing sign system that indexes the individual psyche as well as the collective one. In material forms and relations, it stages a certain conception of home—a given notion of belonging and selfhood. Interior design— even innocuously selecting and arranging furniture in an apartment—

---

1. "Inconspicuous Consumption," *New York Times Magazine,* Part 2, "Home Design," 13 April 1997, 25.

2. "Hide the Money!" *New York Times Magazine,* Part 2, "Home Design," 13 April 1997, 8–10.

bears witness to our personality and imagination. In short, it offers one form for externalizing our inner life or interiority.

I examine in this excursion the transformative relationship between interior design and interiority in the context of late twentieth-century Chinese culture. The interior design promoted in the China of the 1990s is anything but inconspicuous, standing in spectacular contrast to and negation of the austere simplicity of the "socialist modern" during the 1960s and 1970s. Through reading a seminal narrative intimately and contextually, I trace the mutations of interiority from an overdetermined concept of protest to its co-optation by a nascent sign consciousness in the realm of popular culture. The same literary text lets us examine the discursive legitimation of and strategies for interiorization, a process that both instills and answers psychic and institutional needs for a rapidly modernizing economy.

Deliberate Display and a Fast Life

Toward the end of his much acclaimed novella *Didi nihao* (Hello, my younger brother, 1993),[3] He Dun, an energetic literary newcomer based in the provincial capital Changsha, arranges for the hero of his story to enjoy a meaningful moment of peace and contentment. Throughout the narrative, Deng Heping, his period-specific given name meaning "peace," is referred to as "my younger brother" and is continuously cast in the awkward role of a rebellious and estranged family member. Disrespectful of his orthodox, revolutionary father and showing great ingenuity in capitalist entrepreneurship, Heping embodies a post-Cultural Revolution generation that, reaching its adulthood in the early 1980s, appears both familiar and yet ominously uncontainable in Chinese society in the 1990s. The novella begins in 1988, when Heping is twenty-six and definitely beyond his formative years. In that year, because of a series of misdeeds, one of which is impregnating his nineteen-year-old girlfriend, Heping finally manages to enrage "my father" to such a degree that he is permanently barred from visiting his parents' apartment. Incidentally, as the narrator coolly comments, "my father," at the same promising age

---

3. Collected in He Dun, *Shenghuo wuzui* (Life is not a crime) (Beijing: Huayi, 1995), 278–360. Further page references to this story are given in parentheses in the text.

of twenty-six, had expelled his own landowning father when he led a brigade of Communist guerrillas and ransacked the estate in 1948.

As the dense and fast-paced narrative winds to a sudden halt, we reach the wet December of 1992 and realize that "my younger brother" has apparently "made it." In hurriedly following the protagonist around, we quickly get absorbed in, even fascinated by, his world of objects, desire, money, and action. The novella, together with He Dun's other fictional narratives about contemporary Changsha, indeed offers a raw account of the widespread capitalist drive that has become a concrete passion for this generation of Chinese urban youth. Through all the rough and often sordid ups-and-downs in his fortunes and emotional life, Heping emerges as a self-made and self-confident hero, inspiring as much envy as admiration from the narrator, his ambivalent but ultimately sympathetic older brother. Even the young man's physique undergoes a significant metamorphosis in the process of assiduous self-fashioning. Gone are the two diseases, fistula and hyperthyroidism, that put him at a disadvantage when he was also a constant annoyance to his parents and superiors. Radiating a robust glow, he now proudly rides an expensive Honda motorcycle and is preparing for a second marriage. The woman he loves and whom he will marry on New Year's day of 1993 was the neglected but beautiful wife of Heping's one-time boss, a local Mafia leader who made his wealth through heroin trafficking and was eventually arrested and condemned. Since Dandan, a successful hairdresser, is now visibly pregnant, they need to get the wedding ceremony out of the way soon. Heping, however, is busier than ever, because he retails materials for building decoration, and 1992 happens to be a year when the entire nation, the reserved narrator chronicles, is consumed by a craze in "real estate, construction, gas and water-heater installation" (354). To take full advantage of the new fad in home improvement, Heping has to leave his wife-to-be behind and shuttle nonstop, usually by truck, between Changsha and Guangzhou, scrambling for supplies that are now in great shortage. One afternoon, after another bumpy trip, he comes back exhausted, only to find his one-bedroom apartment totally transformed.

> Younger Brother languidly pushed open the door and was taken aback. The living room was completely redecorated. What used to be soft green walls were now covered with crimson red wallpaper with brick designs on it; overhead a soft red drop-ceiling of plywood was added. The original panel-

ing of chestnut-colored plywood was now replaced with the same material in pink. "She moved her Red Hair Salon here," Younger Brother muttered to himself. The four walls of the bedroom, from bottom to top, were all covered with ash boards, and the floor was parqueted in a basket weave pattern. The furniture was now a luxuriant deluxe set, of a pleasant maroon color. The old white composite set was nowhere to be found. "She knows how to spend money," Younger Brother threw himself onto the bed and marveled. "But this is pretty comfy." (355–56)

This newly decorated interior space that Heping enters comes as both a surprise and a reassurance. Everything he sees is new and unfamiliar, but together they win his recognition, almost instantaneously, and are accepted as his own possessions. He immediately claims this showroom as his home by throwing himself onto the comfortable bed. Although Dandan is not there to greet him, the meticulous design loudly bespeaks her presence. In fact, her absence conveniently allows him to closely examine their new home and to absorb her anticipation for their future life together. Through her choice of objects, materials, and design, Dandan creates a private and concrete space that mirrors their private and concrete desires. It is also at this moment that Heping, the intrepid small-business owner, fully experiences, as if stepping outside himself, the seductive power of consumption and translates the home interior surrounding him into a sign of his social success. Hence, his appreciative comment to Dandan when he wakes up hours later: "This feels just like staying in a four-star hotel" (356).

In fact, throughout the story, Heping is consistently studied as a conspicuous consumer, for whom consumption is more of a practiced ideology than a satisfaction of whimsical needs. He readily embraces what Jean Baudrillard describes as the "system of objects" and, with great proficiency, commands the sign language of commodities.[4] He and his cohorts demonstrate an instinctive grasp of the status symbolism associated with brand names, foreign products, and luxury items. While the cigarettes he smokes evolve from domestic to American brands, his footwear also progresses from generic "pointy and shiny black shoes" to "Italian-made crocodile skin shoes," which he is quick to show off by putting his

---

4. Jean Baudrillard, "Sign Function and Class Logic," in his *For a Critique of the Political Economy of the Sign*, trans. with introduction by Charles Levin (St. Louis: Telos Press, 1981), 29.

feet on a table as a means of convincing his friends of his ambition. When the business of his Hongtai Decoration Materials store flourishes, bringing in a net profit of 700,000 yuan (equivalent to US $85,900), he rewards himself by upgrading his motorcycle from a Chinese-made Nanfang to a Royal Honda, and he makes a point of visiting all of his friends and acquaintances on this handsome machine equipped with twin tailpipes. Yet nothing as deeply and completely gratifies him as the new domestic setting that he finds at home. For this is effectively the first time that, instead of demonstrating to others what he likes and can afford, he gets to view his own wealth and accomplishment splendidly displayed for his consumption alone. In a sense, he is now invited to read the sign of his own success rather than parade it around as an invidious distinction.

Deliberate display is what this particular scene of interior renovation brings to the foreground. It is also the intended effect of such detailed description. For both the character in the story and the related narrator, the pleasure derived from registering those ornamental details is irrepressible and functions as a driving force behind the narrative. An obsession with the ornament, of which Heping is a professional promoter, penetrates the fictional world, both its form and content. Not only does the story's young hero gradually learn how to distinguish himself through costly designer attire, but the narrator also continually relies on naming various objects and spelling out prices in order to make his representation realistic. Meticulous care is taken in the narrative to specify, often in an offhand fashion, whether a fountain pen is from the United States or a bicycle is just an ordinary domestic Phoenix. The reality effect of novelistic discourse now relies on recognizing the differentiating function that commodities are called upon to serve as everyday objects. All commodities, indeed, participate in an ingenious "social discourse of objects" that contributes to what Baudrillard once described as a general "mechanism of discrimination and prestige."[5] According to the French sociologist, reflecting on the logic of rising consumerism in post–World War II Euro-America, there always exists a "political economy of the sign," in which commodities or objects are consumed not so much for their utility or use value, as for their explicit sign value. Parallel to the signifying operation of all languages, the sign value of objects enforces a logic of differentiation and establishes, through display and conspicuous

5. Ibid., 30.

consumption, a distinctive hierarchy of taste, status, and identity. "Signs, like commodities, are at once use value and exchange value. The social hierarchies, the invidious differences, the privileges of caste and culture which they support, are accounted as profit, as personal satisfaction, and lived as 'need' (need of social value-generation to which corresponds the 'utility' of differential signs and their 'consumption')."[6] Human needs, Baudrillard further observes, are never a natural experience or objective perception, but they always have an ideological genesis from above and in the privileged. In fact, needs are necessarily constructed to provide the alibi or self-evident rationale for any given stage of "consummative mobilization,"[7] which proves to be a central legitimizing process of the late capitalist mode of production.

The extent of such a consummative mobilization is abundantly testified to in He Dun's city narratives. Moreover, the very mode of his storytelling is obviously implicated in the commodification of literature, mirroring the reorganization of literary production and consumption by the logic of the market. In his exposé-style depiction of an ill-defined zone of emerging capitalism, a subtle legitimation of this desublimated reality seems to be at work everywhere, either in a tale of individual success and failure or through the discourse of desire and needs. This may explain why He Dun's writings are greeted with great enthusiasm by commentators who see the vitality generated by materialist pursuits as a better alternative to ideological coercion or purity. With the sudden arrival of this literary black horse around 1993, it became possible to announce a new direction in literary development. For in his determined immersion in contemporary life, He Dun has apparently rid himself of the compulsion to either negotiate with or poke fun at a formative revolutionary prehistory and memory. No longer do we constantly run into the irreverent deconstruction of the past that was once the main appeal of Wang Shuo's loquacious narratives based on a "hooligan culture."[8] Also far removed from He Dun's creative concern is the imperative of experimen-

---

6. Baudrillard, "For a General Theory," in his *For a Critique of the Political Economy of the Sign*, 125.

7. See Baudrillard, "Beyond Use Value," in his *For a Critique of the Political Economy of the Sign*, 130–42.

8. See Geremie Barmé, "Wang Shuo and *Liumang* ('Hooligan') Culture," *Australian Journal of Chinese Affairs*, no. 28 (July 1992): 23–58.

tation, thematic as well as technical, that propelled a college-educated group of young writers, such as Su Tong, Yu Hua, and Ge Fei, to international recognition in the second half of the 1980s. What the bearded writer from Changsha has to offer, if we adopt a useful phrase from the editors at *Shanghai Literature,* a trendsetting journal that helped bring He Dun onto the national scene, is *xin shimin xiaoshuo,* a "new fiction of city dwellers," or, better yet, a "fiction of the emerging urban bourgeoisie."[9]

For one critic, Chen Xiaoming, He Dun's matter-of-fact narratives of an uneven and pragmatic cityscape provide an apt metaphor for contemporary mainstream culture. In them there is a pulsing desire to "capture the external shape of contemporary life, to plunge into this life on its own terms, so as to be freed, in the process, from the Enlightenment nightmare long bedeviling literature."[10] Such hyperbolic approbation obviously reveals as much about Chen's own agenda as the narratives he is describing. While trying to give a historical profile to a "belated generation" that has come of age in the 1990s, Chen Xiaoming has devoted many of his recent writings to the cause of rejecting, with a markedly postmodernist rhetoric of playfulness and populism, what he and his comrades believe to be the elitist and moralistic tradition of modern Chinese literary discourse.[11] In his view, the "Enlightenment nightmare," a nightmare that must be escaped, demands from the creative writer too rigid a moral obligation to educate the masses and to participate in a collective cause.

9. The notion of "xin shimin xiaoshuo" (new fiction of city dwellers) first appears in "Bianzhe de hua" (Notes from the editors), *Shanghai wenxue* (Shanghai literature), no. 202 (July 1994): 1. Two issues later, the same journal (no. 204 [September 1994]: 80) announced a literary contest held by itself and *Foshan wenyi* (Foshan literature and arts), based in Guangdong. "New fiction of city dwellers" was the theme of this nationwide competition, although the focus fell on Shanghai and Guangdong. According to the editors, the "emergence of the city and an urban class is most concentrated and obvious" in these two areas, which now play a leading role in the development of a market economy. This "new fiction of city dwellers" seems to point to a newer literary interest than the "fiction with a cultural concern" (wenhua guanhuai xiaoshuo) that *Shanghai Literature* was actively promoting earlier in 1994.

10. Chen Xiaoming, "Jianyao pingjie" (Brief commentary [on He Dun's *Life Is Not a Crime*]), in *Zhongguo chengshi xiaoshuo jingxuan* (Anthology of Chinese urban fiction), ed. Chen Xiaoming (Lanzhou: Gansu renmin, 1994), 304.

11. See, for instance, Chen Xiaoming's preface to He Dun's *Life Is Not a Crime* (Beijing: Huayi, 1995), "Wanshengdai yu jiushi niandai wenxue liuxiang" (The belated generation and the literary trends in the '90s), 1–9.

In contemporary China, which Chen tactfully characterizes as still largely at the stage of primitive accumulation in a "socialist market economy," the role of the writer needs to be modified. The new writer is urged to denounce, together with a heroic avant-garde pose and commitment, all notions of depth, allegory, and originality. Instead of seeking access to a great myth, a master language, or historical totality, the new writing needs to fully explore existential immediacy, the world of ephemera, and a centerless and fluid culture. It ought to be an externalized writing that amounts to a pleasurable performance. He Dun's fiction, according to Chen Xiaoming, best represents this emerging literary sensibility in that, by proffering "spectacles of desire" as both its content and form, his narrative incidentally becomes a reassuring mirror for "an age without interiority." Evoking Roland Barthes's notion of the pleasure of the text, Chen even suggests that such desirous fiction actually fulfills a legitimate purpose that should be served by adult reading materials.

> Life in this age already has no interiority. People are obsessed with elevating themselves from poverty, and are continually incited by the prospect of instant riches. Writers of the "belated generation" have a firm grasp on such tendencies of our time. Without any polishing or ornamentation, they put in front of us the chaotic and vibrant conditions of such a life, presenting a swift, indiscriminate flux of phenomena. Their method of directly representing the appearances of life serves to highlight the rawness of a coarse and vulgar reality.[12]

The verdict that there is no longer interiority in an unreflective writing and, by extension, urban culture comes into this context hardly as a negative assessment. On the contrary, Chen celebrates this absence as a form of emancipation, as a generative break with "traditional or classical discourses." Such an assertion enables Chen to describe and embrace a historical condition in which, as Marx would say, "all that is solid melts into air." The implicit logic of his post-Enlightenment vision is that only when unhampered by moral scruples or concerns with values and truths can a society allow itself to be truly secularized and absorbed in the ephemeral rather than the eternal or fundamental. Only when driven by desire will the individual be enabled to act as an individual, and resolute action will become a positive value in and of itself. By virtue of reproducing,

12. Ibid., 6.

through explosive narrativity, the rhythm and effect of such down-to-earth bustling, He Dun's fiction, suggests Chen, works as both a demonstration of and a testimony to the demise of an inhibiting interiority. In other words, a new round of consummative mobilization has rendered superfluous all notions of integrity, conscience, spirituality, and, finally, self-reflection.

The Marketing of Interiority

It would be a rewarding project to reconstruct a genealogy of the concept of "interiority" in the intellectual debates of contemporary China. With its unmistakable Hegelian inflection, the idea of "interiority" was a correlative to the much-contested notion of "subjectivity" that Liu Zaifu determinedly advanced in the early 1980s.[13] One of the reasons for the controversy over "subjectivity," in addition to its potent political implications in a still harsh culture of collectivist uniformity, was the amorphousness and subsequent theoretical versatility of the term itself. Even in "the master grammarian of the subject" Liu Zaifu's own writings,[14] and his remarkable efforts notwithstanding, the definition of "subjectivity" never achieves a degree of clarity that is promised. The inevitable result is that one vague term by default becomes the designator of a complex of ideas, agendas, and intellectual sources. Nonetheless, Liu Zaifu does supply a historical analysis to explain the necessity of subjectivity in literary discourse and, in the end, to justify the use of the term itself. His central goal being to protest a political instrumentalization of literature and, ultimately, of human subjects, Liu Zaifu repeatedly advocates "subjectivity" as "not only a function of subjective consciousness but also the entire

13. See my "The Function of New Theory: What Does It Mean to Talk About Postmodernism in China?" in *Politics, Ideology, and Literary Discourse in Modern China: Theoretical Interventions and Cultural Critique,* ed. Liu Kang and Xiaobing Tang (Durham, N.C.: Duke University Press, 1993), 278–99; Jing Wang, "Romancing the Subject: Utopian Moments in the Chinese Aesthetics of the 1980s," in her *High Culture Fever: Politics, Aesthetics, and Ideology in Deng's China* (Berkeley: University of California Press, 1996), 195–232; see also the Chinese collection of essays on the topic, *Wenxue zhutixing lunzheng ji* (Collection of essays on literary subjectivity) (Beijing: Hongqi, 1986).

14. This honorific title comes from Jing Wang, "Romancing the Subject," 201.

essence of the Subject's existence." Its higher level is "what has become capable of resisting the forces of consciousness, symbols, and culture."[15] The "transcendent character" of literature will not be revealed until literary creation becomes positively an exercise of subjectivity, because "on a deeper, more fundamental level [the literary world] symbolizes the free spirit of humans, rooted in the Subject's formation of value based on its own need."[16] At this juncture, the "need" that the Subject experiences or perceives obviously is more of a spiritual and intellectual nature than the concrete consumer desires that bestir the characters in He Dun's mapping of Changsha. And the frequently impenetrable elaboration on "subjectivity" is intended to erect a protective shield against a volatile and dehumanizing force, often under the grandiose name of historical change or progress.

If the discourse of subjectivity, inspired by belief in a humanist universality, once served as a veiled plea for positive creative as well as political freedom, then interiority could be viewed as a defense of negative freedom, the right to resist by escaping and turning inward. Both concepts, in agreement with the Enlightenment tradition of antidespotism, affirm human liberty through the possibility of a reflective, critical consciousness. The liberating impact of Wang Meng's use of the interior monologue device in the early 1980s is a good case in point.[17] This supposedly modernistic literary technique reintroduced an inner voice and individual consciousness that had been systematically disallowed in the socialist realist tradition. It helped shift the focus of literary representation from an omniscient view of collective action to a contemplative view of personal experiences. For a later group of experimental writers, too, interiority has been a favorite trope, and the exploration of a painful, almost mystical sensitivity of the body and mind, such as we see in Yu Hua, often constitutes the discovery of a site of resistance by a helpless individual confronted with a sweeping catastrophe or violence.[18] The Chinese postrevolutionary tale of subjectivity, as Jing Wang comments pointedly, "is

---

15. Liu Zaifu, "The Subjectivity of Literature Revisited," trans. Mary Scoggin, in *Politics, Ideology, and Literary Discourse in Modern China*, 57–58.

16. Ibid., 68.

17. See William Tay, "Wang Meng, Stream-of-Consciousness, and the Controversy Over Modernism," *Modern Chinese Literature* 1.1 (Spring 1984): 7–21.

18. See chap. 6, "Residual Modernism: Narratives of the Self in the 1980s."

a story of resistance and conflict, a story about insurgent, albeit self-deceptive, strategies of *depoliticization* and *interiorization* that theorists and writers adopted to position themselves against the autocratic Father at home."[19] Only in hindsight and from afar, however, would such strategies appear to be unbearably romantic and even self-deceptive. In its historical context, the inward turn or withdrawal to the subjective interior was rather a desperate effort at defeating total despair.

Is this the interiority that, evoked only a decade ago as an indispensable humanizing experience of individual freedom and self-consciousness, is now pronounced dead and buried? When the critic Chen Xiaoming marvels at the vibrancy of a contemporary world that has allegedly shed its interiority, is he also suggesting that the concept of interiority is part of the "Enlightenment nightmare" and needs to be exorcised? The answer seems to be obvious, given the almost delirious fascination that a portable postmodern antihumanism excites in him. In his eagerness to latch onto an intellectual trend, Chen readily surrenders to the compulsion to generate signs, following a Baudrillardian political economy, for their sign exchange value. At the same time, he is perhaps blinded by the glare to which he is attracted. The indiscriminate collection of terms and neologisms that stud his prose, from "postcolonial characteristics" to "post-Oriental perspective" to "anti-allegorical strategy," makes us wonder how much he is describing his own writing technique when he exhorts young authors: "One will have enough to support a fictive narrative as long as one manufactures some spectacles of desire with a viewing value."[20] It is the oversight in his insight, however, that reveals Chen to be sadly limited by his own absorption into appearances or arousing visions.

A central example is the discussion of interiority. The dialectical development of such a concept seems to escape Chen when, in a sweeping abandonment of all related notions such as depth and the contemplative subject, interiority is declared to be not only unnecessary, but also *impossible*. The "swift, indiscriminate flux of phenomena" is so irresistible that anyone who wishes to have access to the truth and reality of life in the 1990s cannot afford to step aside and reflect. Facing a contempo-

19. Wang, "Romancing the Subject," 197–98 (original emphasis).

20. The same statement appears in his prefaces to *Anthology of Chinese Urban Fiction* (18) and to *Life Is Not a Crime* (6). The two pieces are dated 5 October 1994 and 20 March 1994, although they contain many identical paragraphs.

rary world that happily "gallops forward," "no one can grasp its essence, or touch its spirit and soul."²¹ While hastiness is certainly the defining style of He Dun's narratives, in all his stories about restless young people in Changsha, or what Chen calls "urban nomads without a job," there is always a deliberate pause, a ritualistic instance of entering an interior space. In *Life Is Not a Crime,* this initiation takes place early in the plot and serves to introduce desire and aspiration into the first-person narrator. An old friend's ostentatiously decorated living room, which the hero visits for the first time and observes in quiet amazement, begins to instill in him a deep dissatisfaction with his own life. A new self-image emerges and is associated with a concrete interior space.²² At the very end of another structurally similar novella, *Wo bu xiangshi* (I don't care), the central character, Damao, goes to visit his grieving girlfriend in her tiny apartment. He comforts her gently and whispers into her ear what he envisions for their future together, until his words make "her entire body as passionate as horses running wild in the grassland."²³ Toward the end of *Hello, My Younger Brother,* Heping returns home to find the interior of his domicile transformed, as if miraculously. The significance of these separate moments may point to an emergent form of interiority, which is closely related to a new sense of private interior space and eventually to the necessary mechanism of interiorization. We now turn to the historical condition of such a connection.

It is no accident that Heping in *Hello, My Younger Brother* should end up being a retailer of decoration materials and find this business enormously profitable. Soon after he is banished from his parents' home, which consists of a modestly furnished four-bedroom apartment allotted in accordance with the father's official position, Heping voluntarily quits his miserable job as a high school teacher and begins his illustrious business career as a petty street peddler of smuggled cigarettes. At this stage, transaction takes a primitive form and financial compensation is minuscule, but independence and purposefulness provide enough thrill for him to persevere. Then, thanks to the connections that Dandan makes for him, Heping becomes the manager of a nightclub and starts to mar-

21. Chen, preface to *Life Is Not a Crime,* 4.
22. See chap. 9, "New Urban Culture and the Anxiety of Everyday Life in Late Twentieth-Century China."
23. See He Dun, *Wo bu xiangshi* (I don't care), in his *Life Is Not a Crime,* 276–77.

ket, with instinctive adroitness, popular entertainment that caters to a new demand for culturally acceptable intimacy and private sentiments. One failed marriage and some hostile situations later, Heping loses his nightclub and, true to his resilient mind and body, quickly finds himself engaged in a more lucrative trade—supplying prefab materials for a city that is suddenly possessed by the need for both exterior and interior decoration.

"Nineteen ninety-two was a year of decoration craze in the city of Changsha," the narrator of *Hello, My Younger Brother* describes with considerable ambivalence. "Many shops were torn down beyond recognition, but overnight they would all be decorated absolutely anew. As if caught in a fierce competition, one store after another rushed to have itself remodeled. Some big department stores may just have had a facelift in the first half of the year, but soon they would break everything into pieces and start all over" (354). Such extensive and rapid restyling no doubt affects the appearance of and life in the city; it helps set off a new visual regime and sign system that directly contribute to the urban spectacle of desire. Tellingly enough, the shops and department stores are most ready to undergo such cosmetic renovation, to present themselves at the cutting edge of the latest fashion, and, ultimately, to package their commodities with an external and ostentatious sign of modernity. Heping's flourishing business, therefore, can be taken as an index to a culture that demonstrates a new sign-consciousness, one for which the production of difference through sign exchange becomes an instrumental operation. Sign exchange, suggests Baudrillard, is no less than the central logic of a consumer society's political economy.[24]

The enticing spectacle generated by a pervasive consummative mobilization turns out to be, not unlike the neon signs in a busy shopping

---

24. In "The Ideological Genesis of Needs," Baudrillard argues that "consumption does not arise from an objective need of the consumer, a final intention of the subject towards the object; rather, there is social production, in a system of exchange, of a material of differences, a code of significations and invidious (*statuaire*) values. The functionality of goods and individual needs only follows on this, adjusting itself to, rationalizing, and in the same stroke repressing these fundamental structural mechanisms." See his *For a Critique of the Political Economy of the Sign*, 75. For a lucid discussion of Baudrillard's development of Marx's analysis of the capitalist mode of production, see Douglas Kellner, *Jean Baudrillard: From Marxism to Postmodernism and Beyond* (Stanford, Calif.: Stanford University Press, 1989), esp. 19–25.

district, an illusion of differentiation that colorfully decorates the stark reality of commodity exchange based on the principle of equivalence. The art of design and decoration, therefore, is the quintessential enterprise that at once advertises and disguises the truth of a consumer culture. It is mass production coupled with mass consumption, observes Penny Sparke in her history of design and culture in the twentieth century, that puts "design in the centre of the picture as it is design that provides the variation that is so essential to modern society."[25] With the alchemy of design, an industrial product is transformed into a deliberate object that signifies its invested difference and, consequently, systematic meaning. It is Bauhaus, the pioneer school of modern industrial design in the 1920s, that, in the words of Baudrillard again, "institutes this universal semantization of the environment in which everything becomes the object of a calculus of function and of signification. Total functionality, total semiurgy."[26] When it penetrates into the domestic interior and incorporates personal space into sign exchange, design encounters a situation where commodified difference is dramatized even further: the home interior has to signify a private domain as such, both to its occupant(s) and to a conceivable public. In comparison with the exterior decoration that makes over shop windows, buildings, or the city as a whole, interior design is compelled to address an individual rather than a projected crowd, to speak a more intimate *parole* with accented variations. It is only logical, then, to anticipate that interior design, as a business and generator of sign value, will cash in on personal preferences, encourage hobbies and idiosyncrasies, and profit from the notion of multiple identities. At the same time, interior design, by instilling a sign-consciousness in our most private and personal sphere, serves to acculturate us to the system of sign-objects—namely, to interiorize the political economy of the sign. At this point, the discourse of interiority gathers not only a legitimizing impetus from the market but also a concreteness that promises to atomize and undermine the metaphysical dimension of the interior. Instead of articulating a spiritual or psychic structure of depth, interiority may now describe a new frontier market for customized products of sorts.

This transmutation of a charged intellectual concept can be best exam-

25. Penny Sparke, *An Introduction to Design and Culture in the Twentieth Century* (London: Allen and Unwin, 1986), xxii.
26. Baudrillard, "Design and Environment," *For a Critique of the Political Economy of the Sign,* 185.

ined in the widespread interest in interior design in contemporary China. Partly as the result of the new housing policy that requires residents to purchase their apartments from their respective work units, and partly because of the gradual opening of a real estate market, urban Chinese now view their dwellings as their most significant investment. The idea of owning your own "dream home," as the *New York Times* reported, finally catches on—at least in Shanghai, "the nation's most affluent and modern-minded city."[27] After more than a quarter-century during which the idea of a private home was systematically erased and interior design was an alien concept, city dwellers now invest a great deal of money and time in decorating and remodeling what they can claim as their own living space. Privatization in this area necessarily gives rise to an awareness among homeowners different from an aesthetics of austerity bred by publicly subsidized, and therefore standard and communal, housing projects. In Shanghai in 1996, for instance, residents reportedly spent an average of 10,000 yuan (about US $1,230) for modernizing the bathroom alone in a given household, even though a typical bathroom is no larger than four square meters. Zhan Musi in *Shanghai Pictorial* finds this new trend one that is worth encouraging. "Being the most private space in everyday life, bathrooms are where people can relax, examine and refresh themselves. We should create an elegant and pleasing atmosphere in a place from which a good mood begins."[28] Although in the initial stages of the new housing policy, apartment owners, perhaps out of habit, may have followed the same format in home improvement, very soon it became clear that individuality and uniqueness were crucial elements of interior design.

Another indicator of the popular interest in home improvement is the growing demand for calendars that reproduce large and high-quality glossy prints of "modern living," a genre that came into vogue only in the 1990s. All of these imposingly gorgeous pictures appear to be taken directly from either an Ethan Allen catalogue or *Country Living* magazine (figures 17 and 18). Alongside these fancy images are more specific and better organized instruction manuals or catalogues that also sell in large

27. Seth Faison, "For Sale at Last in China: Dream Homes, but No Sink," *New York Times,* 3 September 1998, B1, B9.

28. See *Shanghai huabao* (Shanghai pictorial), no. 2 (1996): 18–19. Incidentally, the reporter's name, "Zhan Musi," is the accepted Chinese transliteration of the English first name "James."

17. *(above)* Photograph, "Xiandai jushi" (Calendar: modern living) (1997). Courtesy of Shanghai huabao chubanshe. 18. *(below)* Photograph, "Jia/Home" (Calendar) (1997). Courtesy of Jiansu meishu chubanshe.

quantities. One book among numerous such publications, published by China Trade Press, bears the suggestive title: *Fengyu zhong de lüdao—xiandai jiaju* (Safe haven in a storm—modern living). Although its collection of designs and styles is not at all outstanding, the editor's comments are offered in an embellished literary style, and his preface, titled "Home," reads as a perfect example of how effortlessly a cluster of once politically sensitive ideas, such as "individuality," "self-expression," "privacy," and "interiority," can be grafted onto a commercial advertisement targeted at the new managerial class.

> In modern society, the connotation of "home" can no longer be restricted to a protective shelter. For people who are trying to adapt to the rapid pace of contemporary life, it has become a pursuit and a desire to create a cozy and sweet home, a home that also fully reveals their individual personality. Economic growth and the emergence of new cities now give you the opportunity to approach or even arrive at such a goal. Once you hold in your hand the key to your new home, you should turn your long-cherished dreams into reality, as if you were painting on a pure white canvas, with every stroke of the brush conveying your talent in design and your cultivation.
>
> After a long day of hard work, when you leave far behind the madding clamor of society, when you return to your own home and find there a soothing environment with its refreshing and graceful design, you will feel the gentle caress of such an elegant atmosphere. Without being aware of it, you will be naturally relieved of all the anxiety pent up inside you. You will achieve relaxation with your loved ones in the harmony of such a "love nest." . . .
>
> Everyone can be a designer. How about you?[29]

Collected in this brief text is such a miscellany of claims, assumptions, and stylistic registers that to fully decode it we will have to embark on an extensive cultural study, especially when we place such an articulation back in its own historical moment. In the present context, this type of writing is worth noting because of the sense of travesty it evokes. Only a decade ago, the creative freedom of the human subject, together with the depth of his or her inner world, was the enlightenment cause be-

---

29. Lin Gang, ed., *Fengyu zhong de lüdao—xiandai jiaju* (Safe haven in a storm—modern living) (Beijing: Zhongguo shangye, 1995), n.p.

hind Liu Zaifu's famously abstract theory of subjectivity and his thesis on the composite nature of characters. Now, acknowledgment of similar demands is aggressively made in an emerging consumer culture that must regiment a work-versus-leisure division in order to jump-start and sustain its economic development. If interiority, for the humanist discourse of the 1980s, was a global concept with which to protest and resist political repression and homogenization, then, in the consumer culture of the 1990s, all inner yearnings and visions are increasingly channeled to their external expression in concrete sign-objects. The humanist fascination with interiority, in other words, secretly and only in failure aspires to a wholesome existence, to an artistic transformation of the outside world; its commercial parody, however, serves to substitute specific consumer needs for any transcendental desire. It is therefore hardly "an age without interiority," but a time when people's lives will have to be systematically interiorized and interiority imaginatively engineered and expanded so as to create more fantasies and more needs. On an even grimmer note, this is hardly a moment where one can gleefully denounce the "Enlightenment nightmare." Rather, the contemporary development forms part of the "dialectic of Enlightenment," for a voracious consumer culture may have been prepared—paradoxically and in the first place—by lofty, contemplative humanist ideals.[30]

Toward an Injured Form of Interiority

Nonetheless, we may and probably have to regard Lin Gang's brief preface as containing a faintly utopian vision and an implicit critique of "the rapid pace of contemporary life" that exacts a tremendous human price. The anxiety that needs release at the end of the day has everything to do

30. This is, of course, the central argument of Max Horkheimer and Theodor Adorno in *Dialectic of Enlightenment*. In a more immediate case, Liu Zaifu's writings in defense of economic reform, for example the volume *Gaobie geming: huiwang ershi shiji Zhongguo* (Farewell to revolution: review of twentieth-century China) (Hong Kong: Cosmos, 1995), coauthored by Li Zehou and Liu, may suggest that the humanist cause of Enlightenment does not oppose general modernization. On the contrary, it is part of the cultural revolution that heralds the arrival of a mass society, although the gratification-oriented consumer hardly resembles the free and self-expressive Subject envisioned by the theoreticians of modern subjectivity.

with reclaiming one's own mind and body from normalized stress. Interior design, as it is advocated here, only dramatizes the discontinuity between alienating work and creative freedom, and interiority, now evoked in a specific form, persists to remind the individual subject of how fragmented and limited his or her life may be. It is not surprising, therefore, to see how closely the generic description in the preface corresponds to the experience of Deng Heping, the successful owner of Hongtai Decoration Materials store in He Dun's novella. Upon his return to "a soothing environment with its refreshing and graceful design," as we have seen, Heping feels he is entitled to some relaxation with his beloved Dandan "in the harmony of such a 'love nest.'" The newly designed interior not only expresses Dandan's artistic nature but also awakens Heping's own imagination and creative impulse. When he finally notices the two framed still lifes put up by Dandan, Heping decides that he will find a poster of the sea to decorate the wall, because he likes the open ocean better.

A consistent gender-based division of labor, as well as of value, defines the role of Dandan, who appears to inspire a more spiritual need in Heping. It is of great significance that while Heping is absorbed in running the store, Dandan chooses to re-create their own private home. This plot arrangement reinforces the symbolic meaning in the story of Dandan, whose complex character is first indicated by the soulful and melancholy cello that she plays. (By contrast, Heping's failed first marriage was with an up-and-coming movie actress.) What Heping returns to find, on this happy occasion, is therefore more than a comfortable home; it also promises a fulfilling private world that will only add depth and content to his existence. A new experience of interiority, engendered by the expressive interior design, seems to be within his grasp. This becomes the most utopian moment in the narrative because it signals a final reconciliation, a complementary union that will elevate the relationship between Heping and Dandan to a new height.

What complicates the situation greatly, however, is that He Dun's narratives refuse to stop at a triumphant moment where the hero may be seduced into believing that the world of his creation answers to his aspiration. A symbolic crumbling always follows. There is always a pause, a suspension of normal goings-on, or even an absurd death, that puts in disarray all splendid displays of success, material as well as spiritual. Within his narratives of fast urban life, a specter of the unconsoled is created to haunt the city landscape. In the particular story that we have been examining, a traffic accident kills Dandan and the three-month-old fetus inside her. This occurs the day following Heping's coming home and, as the narrative makes clear, before the night of passionate lovemaking that she promises him. The much-anticipated evening would have made the remodeled apartment really a part of his intimate being, an extension of his interior world. As it is now, the new home interior stands only as a reminder of the porcelain fragility of the world of objects; more ominously, the death of the unborn child hints at the impossibility for a potentially gratifying everyday life or relationship to reproduce itself. The symbolism of having Dandan thrown off Heping's powerful motorcycle and crushed to death is too strong to ignore. This scene of devastation reaffirms, in a cruel fashion, the need for an interior space to cushion the impact of the outside world. Until this instant, Heping shows little concern with his world of fast and fragmented experience, and even less interest in the generally unanswerable questions of causality and meaning. In her gruesome death, Dandan is transformed, literally and figuratively, from an inspiring designer of home interiors into the announcer of an injured form of interiority. The last sentence of the novella reverberates to the primal, haunting scream uttered by Dandan, and it is her voice that penetrates deep into Heping's entire being. "It was no longer a human cry, but the cracking sound of glass. For a long time, it hovered over the intersection, humming and parading like a phalanx of spotty-legged mosquitoes. One of those mosquitoes quickly took hold of my younger brother's ear, and fastened itself, like a thumb nail, onto his eardrum, permanently . . ." (360).[31]

The productive question to be asked about He Dun's fast-paced narratives, therefore, is not what alternative there is in an age of no interiority, but what function interiority, now recommended as spiritual resilience at a moment of worldly crisis or breakdown, is called upon to

---

31. This final scene of death and articulation brings to mind observations that Theodor Adorno once made on the "dialectic of interiority" and the paradox of expression in modern art in his *Aesthetic Theory*. "Authentic art is familiar with expressionless expression, a kind of crying without tears," Adorno writes. "Granted, the subject cannot and must not speak the language of immediacy. But it can and does continue to articulate itself through things in their alienated and disfigured form" (Trans. C. Lenhardt, ed. Gretel Adorno and Rolf Tiedemann [London: Routledge & Kegan Paul, 1984]: 171–72.)

serve. It is by far much thornier to determine, for instance, whether or not those instances of putting one's faith and strength to the test actually interrogate the interiorization of consumer needs. Do the evocations of a transcendental longing at the end actually add to the legitimacy of massive consummative mobilization? Put differently, the question may have to be: What if interiority is served as an *alibi* in a culture that of necessity decorates and accessorizes everything for recognition? Or, conversely, does the injured form of interiority that Dandan articulates in her death reveal a fundamental structure of interiority—its success in failure? Of greater theoretical relevance could be a general question about the astonishing speed in which "interiority," as a central value and practice of Euro-American modernity, gets recycled and appropriated, for all intents and purposes, in late twentieth-century Chinese culture. Is this a necessary process before the notion becomes once again exhausted and ripe for historical inquiry; what does the rapidity of its transmutation entail insofar as a legitimating narrative of modern capitalist cultural logic is concerned? Does it suggest that ours is still part of the moment when interiority and its corollaries are conjured globally only to undermine their pertinence?

10

Melancholy Against the Grain: Approaching Postmodernity in Wang Anyi's Tales of Sorrow

A postmodern challenge, Julia Kristeva remarks at the end of her 1987 book, *Black Sun: Depression and Melancholia,* now confronts the "world of unsettling, infectious ill-being" that Marguerite Duras so determinedly creates in her fiction. Underlying the novelist's imagination is a silence or nothingness that insists on being spoken as the ultimate expression of suffering and that often "carries us to the dangerous, furthermost bounds of our psychic life." Yet, what the irreverent postmodern abandon finds in a Durasian malady of grief, Kristeva laments, is "only one moment of the *narrative synthesis* capable of sweeping along in its complex whirlwind philosophical meditations as well as erotic protections or entertaining pleasures. The postmodern is closer to the human comedy than to the abyssal discontent." Postmodernity erects an "artifice of seeming" and offers the "heartrending distraction of parody," both of which promise to act as antidepressants for a literary obsession with the illness of modernity.[1]

At this point, Kristeva, the renowned semiotician of desire, seems to suggest that a modernist seriousness and a postmodernist parody form successive phases of the "eternal return of historical and intellectual cycles."[2] This pattern of recurrence, however, is not so much a temporal process as a temperamental one, through which our experience in and of historical time becomes affected and eventually representable. "Thus moods are *inscriptions*," she declares earlier in the book. "They lead us toward a modality of significance that . . . insures the preconditions for (or manifests the disintegration of) the imaginary and the symbolic."[3]

---

1. Julia Kristeva, *Black Sun: Depression and Melancholia,* trans. Leon S. Roudiez (New York: Columbia University Press, 1989), 258–59.
2. Ibid., 259.
3. Ibid., 22.

Relying on this thesis, Kristeva is able to conclude her somber study of melancholia and literature on a reassuring note: "Does not the wonderment of psychic life after all stem from those alternations of protections and downfalls, smiles and tears, sunshine and melancholia?"[4] The challenge of the postmodern, therefore, lies not necessarily in the threat that the malady of grief would be rendered passé and obsolete at one stroke but rather in recognizing the dialectics, the dynamic alternations that bring forth a postmodern lightheartedness in the first place. It is the capacity of our inner emotional existence that is being put to the test.

In fact, this is the stated motivation for Kristeva's journey into the dark interior of depression and melancholia. At the beginning of *Black Sun*, she writes, "For those who are racked by melancholia, writing about it would have meaning only if writing sprang out of that very melancholia. I am trying to address an abyss of sorrow, a noncommunicable grief." Her first question is then a direct inquiry about the origins of her ravaging melancholia: "Where does this black sun come from?"[5] The main body of the book, in which she reads not only clinical cases of feminine depression but also literary texts by Dostoyevsky and Duras, therefore registers a double movement. It records Kristeva's broad effort to reinterpret melancholia from a psycholinguistic perspective; yet it is also a text that answers her own "glaring and inescapable" depression. Her writing about melancholia combats her devitalized existence by helping her name and dissect the abyssal and unnamable suffering that overpowers her. In other words, hers is a self-reflective text, produced with a narrator's full knowledge of the postmodern challenge to come at the end.

"The easily spotted triggers of my despair"

The immediate reason why the Kristeva of *Black Sun* is introduced here in a chapter purportedly about Wang Anyi, the prominent contemporary Chinese writer, is that both writers at one point describe a similar onset of unspeakable sorrow. The accounts of their encounters with melancholy reveal a shared logic, although Kristeva's musings have the appearance of either psychoanalysis or literary theory, and Wang Anyi's narration is

4. Ibid., 259.
5. Ibid., 3.

strictly fictional. In addition, while what Kristeva studies includes clinical melancholia, Wang Anyi's literary works deal mostly with melancholy as a subjective mood.[6] Nonetheless, more substantive reasons for making this initial comparison will become obvious in this discussion of some of Wang Anyi's more recent stories, which may be called "tales of sorrow," as suggested by the writer herself in *Shangxin Taipingyang* (Sadness for the Pacific). The most vital linkage, on an abstract level, may lie in the similar response that both writers choose to mount to the postmodern challenge, namely, a melancholy subjectivity.

To begin answering her own question about the origins of melancholia, Kristeva ponders a series of possibilities. "The wound I have just suffered, some setback or other in my love life or my profession, some sorrow or bereavement affecting my relationship with close relatives—such are often the easily spotted triggers of my despair." As if this list is not enough, she goes on to enumerate a second, more severe group of likely causes: "a betrayal, a fatal illness, some accident or handicap that abruptly wrests me away from what seemed to me the normal category of normal people.... What more could I mention? An infinite number of misfortunes weighs us down every day."[7]

When the confessional, presumably male, first-person narrator in Wang Anyi's 1990 novella, *Our Uncle's Story*, announces his decision to tell a story, he apparently suffers from a setback in his love life and experiences the consequent interruption of everyday normalcy. His sudden discovery, which comes to him one day as a result of some "extremely personal incident," is an unsettling insight about himself: "I've always thought that I was a happy child, but now I realize I am actually not." This new realization dawns on him as an "elegant sadness," which prompts his desire to tell a story.[8] Yet this young writer-narrator does not wish to disclose the personal affair that triggers his new self-conception because it has something to do with love and sentiment. His therapeutic device, then, is to

---

6. For a discussion of the changing implications of these related terms, see Jennifer Radden, "Melancholy and Melancholia," in *Pathologies of the Modern Self: Postmodern Studies on Narcissism, Schizophrenia, and Depression*, ed. David Michael Levin (New York: New York University Press, 1987), 231–50.

7. Kristeva, *Black Sun*, 3–4.

8. Wang Anyi, *Shushu de gushi* (Our uncle's story), collected in her *Xianggang de qing yu ai* (Love and sentiment in Hong Kong) (Beijing: Zuojia, 1996), 2. Page references to this work are given in the text as *Shushu*.

tell a story about another, more established writer, whom the narrator refers to as "our uncle" and whose awkward fate in the whirlwind of contemporary life gives rise to great ambivalence on the part of the narrator. This ambivalence is so intense that, toward the end, the storyteller concedes that this is the first story that has ever had such a personal impact on him. All of his previous stories deal solely with other people and involve less investment. The uncle's life story, however, parallels the narrator's own "personal incident," which appears utterly trivial and frivolous when compared to the grand drama of the uncle's life tale. Nevertheless, the narrator feels that his recent experience allows him a better psychological interpretation of the events in the uncle's life. Therefore, he is compelled to tell this story, and his conclusions are: "The outcome of our uncle's story is that he will no longer be happy. After I finish telling the story of our uncle, I will never tell a happy story again" (*Shushu*, 77).

In the end, we never find out what the "extremely personal incident" is that causes the narration of an unhappy story, although numerous hints are planted that "an individual inflicted an acutely painful experience" on the narrator (*Shushu*, 23). Nor do we get a closer look at the narrator himself, except for a broad-brush, intellectual portrait of a young, fashionable, self-confident writer (of the same age as Wang Anyi herself) who is now stricken by an elegant sadness and absorbed in sober introspection. Yet the narrator's temperament, poignant comments, and reflections frame the entire story, which proves to be as much a narrative about the political and erotic vicissitudes in the uncle's life as it is an analytical account of the historical constitution of the narrator's own melancholic mood. His altered perspective on reality and on his profession affects him to such a degree that he has no other story to tell but this fateful one. "Put differently, if I do not finish telling this story, I will not be able to tell any other stories. What's more, I am astonished by the fact that I should have already told so many stories before this one; all of those stories would have a different appearance if they were to be told after this one" (*Shushu*, 1–2).

What we see emerging from the beginning of his narrative is the almost standard structure of metafiction, in which a potentially infinite mirror game of writing a story about story writing is set to unfold. Yet the refreshing spin of *Our Uncle's Story*, according to literary critics, comes from the productive tension that Wang Anyi maintains between the two levels of narration. Instead of ossifying the metafictional operation into a stiff technique or purpose, she adroitly keeps the encasing narration itself open to interpretation. For this reason, Wang Anyi's story is considered more successful than other works in contemporary experimental fiction.[9] For the critic Li Jiefei, the writing of *Our Uncle's Story* marks a definite turning point in the novelist's conception of the art of storytelling. It ushers in a new logic of literary creation, the premise of which is no longer referential experience or reality but the independent technique of crafting fiction. This transformation makes Wang Anyi a pioneering "novelistic technician," whose later stories should therefore be taken as part of a larger myth-creating project.[10]

While it is highly debatable whether, in the 1990s, one could label Wang Anyi as a freshly converted and purist "technician" bent on conjuring up a mythic world of her own, there is little doubt that *Our Uncle's Story* initiated a new mode of writing for the writer herself. It is a narrative, in the writer's own words, that contains her "most fully developed emotions and thoughts in a long time." The writing of this story brought Wang Anyi back into her "own personal experiential world" and compelled her to dissect something that is deep in her and painful to look at. Yet she had to compose this story because, in hope of lessening her "solitude and loneliness," she needed to share the pain of confronting the most sensitive and also the most sacred part of her world and her being.[11] After the critical success of *Our Uncle's Story,* Wang Anyi continued her well-known productivity and still excelled at putting together intriguing stories buttressed by realistic character sketches.[12] More and more, how-

9. See the comments made by Zhang Xinying and Gao Yuanbao in Chen Sihe, Wang Anyi, Gao Yuanbao, Zhang Xinying, and Yan Feng, "Dangjin wenxue chuangzuo zhong de 'qing' yu 'zhong'—wenxue duihua lu" (The "light" and "heavy" in contemporary literary works: dialogues on literature), *Dangdai zuojia pinglun* (Review of contemporary writers), no. 5 (1993): 14–23, esp. 17–18.

10. Li Jiefei, "Wang Anyi de xin shenhua—yige lilun tantao" (Wang Anyi's new mythology: a theoretical investigation), *Review of Contemporary Writers,* no. 5 (1993): 4–8.

11. Quoted in Chen Sihe, "Bijin shijimo de xiaoshuo" (Fiction close to the fin de siècle), collected in Wang Xiaoming, ed. *Ershi shiji Zhongguo wenxue shilun* (Essays on twentieth-century Chinese literary history) (Shanghai: Dongfang chuban zhongxin, 1997), 3:444–45.

12. Of this group of Wang Anyi's narratives collected in *Love and Sentiment in Hong Kong,* "'Wenge' yishi" (Anecdotes from the "Cultural revolution") and "Beitong zhi di" (The land of sorrow) are perhaps the most representative, 425–501, 124–59.

ever, her writings seem concentrated on capturing and gauging a mood, a persistent sentiment or emotional state that, because of its profoundly ambivalent nature, becomes intensified rather than diffused through narration. A central pathos is maintained and developed into an expressive affect, such as longing, sorrow, and nostalgia. *Wutuobang shipian* (The utopian chapters, 1991), for example, is an evidently autobiographical narrative about longing as itself an authentic passion that promises a perfect happiness, and that is in itself a comfort and an ideal.[13] In *Xianggang de qing yu ai* (Love and sentiment in Hong Kong, 1993), Wang Anyi's novella about the possibilities for emotional attachment in a consumerist metropolis, constant grief for the present as already past underlies an uneventful world.[14] Readily observable in these narratives is a reflective sorrow and mournfulness.

In retrospect, the narrator of *Our Uncle's Story* is telling a prophetic truth about Wang Anyi's writings when he declares that no more happy narratives will follow it. Or he happens to be the mouthpiece through which the author verbalizes her own melancholic mood. More revealing is the writer-narrator's observation that many of his earlier stories would have a different outlook if they were told now. This proves to be the case with Wang Anyi's critically acclaimed novella *Sadness for the Pacific* (1993), which is an imaginative rewriting of an earlier, much simpler short story. What motivates the rewriting, as the new title indicates, is an irresolvable sadness, a global desolation that, as I will show, lies at the heart of Wang Anyi's melancholy imagination. But before we examine *Sadness for the Pacific,* let us return to *Our Uncle's Story* for clues about the origins of a disconsolate period. The trigger of ensuing unhappiness may well be the sudden crumbling of a presumed reality.

"And yet we have no courage to live a deep life"

All things considered, *Our Uncle's Story* is among the few truly complex and challenging works in late twentieth-century Chinese literature. It is a profoundly unsettling story in which the author methodically under-

13. See Wang Anyi, *Wutuobang shipian* (The utopian chapters), collected in *Love and Sentiment in Hong Kong*, 257–304.
14. See my discussion of this novella in chap. 9.

mines established narrative paradigms, mocks aesthetic pretensions, and offers biting criticisms of ideological constructs. An occasional satirical tone aside, it is also a full-fledged allegory about the inescapable burden of one's own past, about suffering as constitutive of an individual's self-consciousness. Its circular structure of a double narrative, moreover, enables a parodic commentary on a society that rapidly outpaces itself and, in the process, yields little legitimacy to any hyperextended narratives of historical progress. We can even say this felicitous, irony-driven form effects the same "heartrending distraction of parody" that Julia Kristeva detects in a postmodern playfulness.[15] What comes through is indeed a heartbreaking ambivalence, directed toward a disorienting age that disavows genuine passion or heroic possibilities. Largely for this reason, the critic Chen Sihe believes that *Our Uncle's Story* ushered in a new reflective mode of writing for Chinese fiction of the 1990s, which, at the end of a long and turbulent century, exhibits both general despair and spiritual resilience.[16]

The story of "our uncle" is a tragicomic one, inextricably interwoven with the course of political and cultural life in China during the second half of the twentieth century. The nameless uncle, explains the narrator, is not a relative or even a friend, but rather a representative of the older generation whose members were put into political exile as subversive "rightists" in the late 1950s, only to return to center stage as triumphant heroes of society some twenty years later. This generation's wasted youth and talents have been the subject of numerous movies, memoirs, and stories, including the uncle's own successful writings, widely assumed to be autobiographical. As a result of his story about the suffering of a young rightist, the uncle wins instant fame, becomes a full-time writer employed by the state, and is relocated from the remote village where he has lived in exile to the provincial capital. This is where we find the uncle at the beginning of the narrative. In a matter-of-fact tone, the narrator undoes the popular image of rightists as romantic young men who invariably bade tearful farewells to their loves and, in eternal darkness, embarked on cold,

---

15. According to Linda Hutcheon, the theoretician of postmodern poetics, parody is a central trope of postmodern fiction and art, because, "through a double process of installing and ironizing, parody signals how present representations come from past ones and what ideological consequences derive from both continuity and difference." See her *Politics of Postmodernism* (London: Routledge, 1989), 93–117.

16. See Chen Sihe, "Fiction Close to the Fin de Siècle," 444.

snowy journeys to the forsaken western frontier. The truth is that the uncle was too young to fall in love then and was quietly sent home to his obscure native town rather than to remote Qinghai. He was first assigned to menial labor at the local school and later started teaching. Only after he had developed a following as a writer, quips the narrator, did tales of his trek to Qinghai get concocted and circulated.

From the outset, the uncle's story is told to debunk recent cultural myths and to reveal the gap between representation and lived experiences. When he describes the uncle's marriage to one of his students, for instance, the narrator realizes that a wide range of narrative conventions for romances exist for such an event.

> Many inspiring tales can be spun about a female student from a small town falling in love with her teacher, who happens to be from the city and an ex-rightist. There is the love relationship between a simple person of nature and a cultured person of society; there is the attachment between a free person and an exile, just as in the story of a Decembrist of old Russia and his wife; there is also the attraction between a person from an entrenched family and a rootless stranger. With these three relationships blended together, one can probe deep into human nature and capture a broad social background, bringing together a specific reality and a permanent humanity. Such a story our uncle did write, in fact more than once. (*Shushu*, 8)

Eventually, all of these elements seem to find their way into the uncle's stories and combine to make the misery of his youth appear soulful, heroically tragic, even sublime, a suffering that becomes an object of envy to the younger generation. The task of demythologization that the narrator sets himself, therefore, has to start with recounting the uncle's life in the small town. It is, in fact, an uneventful life, although two key events take place during the spring following the uncle's marriage. The first event is the birth of their son, Dabao, which disappoints the uncle deeply because he wishes them to have a daughter. The second incident, rather "petty and frivolous," happens one spring evening. Accused of frolicking with one of his current students and subjected to brutal communal humiliation, the uncle has to be rescued by his wife, who then turns the tables by verbally attacking the younger woman in public for three long days and nights.

This demoralizing incident, according to the narrator, provides a credible motive for the development of the uncle's story, even though it may be altogether fabrication. Perhaps the uncle never talks or writes about what actually happened, the narrator further speculates, because the incident would compromise the heroic narratives of his noble suffering. But this sordid affair has the effect of "nailing suffering into one's body," of rendering anguish into a memory of complicity (*Shushu*, 11). It does not help the husband love his wife any better either, for that would be yet another hackneyed story. Instead, the narrator sees the growing resentment that the uncle harbors against his protective wife and the binding institution of marriage. "He felt that marriage did not lessen the humiliation and misery inflicted upon him, as it was supposed to. On the contrary, it intensified the humiliation and misery by giving it a lasting shell, now impossible to forget" (*Shushu*, 23). To numb his faculty of memory, the uncle indulges in sensual pleasures, starts drinking and smoking, beats his wife during the day, and demands sexual favors at night. He readily banishes his own soul and perseveres in an instinctual existence "like an animal" (*Shushu*, 26). Suicide as protest or for the sake of personal integrity is the remotest idea from his deadened mind.

Through his testimonial narratives in the wake of the discredited Cultural Revolution, however, the uncle manages to turn his personal ignominy into noble political suffering. He now reconstructs his life in a fictional world, where "all past experiences can be amended, the beautiful and the sublime preserved, the ugly and the base completely eliminated, and the destroyed given a new life" (*Shushu*, 28). His desire to shed his former self provides the psychological motivation for his seminal story, in which a young rightist departs this dismal world by inhaling poisonous gas. Symbolically, "our uncle's new life began with the death of a young rightist" (*Shushu*, 29). Not surprisingly, according to the narrator, the same need to forget a painful past lies behind the uncle's widely publicized divorce, although the public tends to believe that another woman is the direct cause. At this point, the narrator details the uncle's romantic adventures after he moves to the city as an intellectual celebrity. First, he regularly visits an older woman for platonic consolation and summons a young one, about the age of his imaginary daughter, for more physical satisfaction. Then, in an effort to convince himself of his unflagging vitality, he sets out to conquer even younger women, easily winning them over with his paternal charm and rich experience. One inevitable exception, the narrator infers, occurs when the uncle visits Germany with a delegation of Chinese writers and mistakenly concludes that his attractive blonde interpreter must welcome his amorous groping.

The blunt slap on the face that the uncle receives from the German woman, as the narrator continually reminds us, is mandated by his own logical inference. He has to rely on conjectures and reasonings in order to lead his story to its known ending, which is the uncle's final insight into his own unhappy fate. This reconstruction, therefore, becomes an opportunity that allows the narrator to compare and comment on two succeeding generations of writers. The term *generation* in the text now connotes undeniable cultural and psychological differentiations. While his analysis of the uncle's generation is penetrating but sympathetic, his assessment of his own generation conveys as much self-content as self-doubt. It is at this juncture that the narrator directly participates in the story and voices his ambivalence toward a contemporary world where either generation's self-image often turns into a burlesque.

In the narrator's summary, the main distinction between these two generations of writers is that the older one already has its belief system in place when its normal course of life is derailed, whereas the younger generation encounters great social transformation before it has time to form any coherent ideals or worldviews. A constant source of anxiety for the uncle's generation, therefore, is whether to accept or reject a new idea or reality. Driven by the need for a systematic faith, this generation always seeks meaning and causality among things; with classical romanticism as its cultivated aesthetic sensibility, it is perpetually perplexed by the divergence between reason and emotion. "When [our uncle] lost one faith he had to look for another; when he accepted one principle of action he had to enthrone it as faith and then went on to witness yet another war for the same throne" (*Shushu,* 51). The younger generation, however, appears to have completely rid itself of any global romantic aspirations and possesses the prerequisites for playing pragmatic games, albeit under nihilistic pretenses.

> We grew up in an age of cultural desolation, and then came into a most open time. One hundred years' worth of ideas, the most sophisticated as well as the crudest, from the end of the last century to the present, rushed in to swamp us overnight. What we ended up picking had much to do with

our endowments and luck, but on the surface, we gave the impression of being innovative from day to day, always leading the newest trend of our time....

The latest philosophy urged us to believe in the significance of the moment, telling us that history is made up of instants and that every instant is real. All we need do is enjoy to the fullest the pleasure and revelation of the moment. (*Shushu*, 29, 62)

These contrastive profiles bring into view two antithetical generations, and their difference is pointedly projected as one between an older, depth-obsessed modernist and a younger, postmodernized cosmopolitan. In neither case does the metafictional structure of *Our Uncle's Story* allow the narrator to invest a stable, positive value.[17] While the postmodernist playfulness precludes any genuine passion or commitment, the grave modernist faith is revealed to be a compensatory myth. To adopt Julia Kristeva's characterization, the young generation misses an abyssal "winter of discontent," but the vain and all-too-human uncle can hardly resist the seduction of a shimmering postmodern "artifice of seeming" either. In a hurry to postmodernize himself, the uncle rushes through two conceptual thresholds and plunges himself into the contemporary whirlwind, mistaking the shrinking of experience for new discoveries. "At first, fiction was for him an imaginary world in which our uncle could satisfy certain psychological needs of his; now it was reality that was transformed into a fictitious world, which supplied evidence and material for his novels." Inhabiting a real world that he took as a mere extension of his fiction, the uncle "no longer worried that an ordinary life could harm him and consequently showed greater than usual readiness to be vulgar" (*Shushu*, 48).

What undercuts this postmodern elusiveness and dismantles the artifice of seeming in *Our Uncle's Story* is the return of the repressed past, not necessarily through the memory of a redemptive mission, but rather in the form of its unspeakable failure. Forgotten pain returns when Dabao, the

---

17. This absence of positive terms, a necessary condition for signification according to Saussurian structural linguistics, apparently causes discomfort in one commentator, who complains that the novella fails to provide a positive, uplifting attitude toward life. See Yan Shu, "'Shushu' de kunhe—tan *Shushu de gushi*" (The confusion of "our uncle": on *Our uncle's story*), *Zuoping yu zhengming* (Works and controversies), no. 128 (August 1991): 79–80.

uncle's frail and inarticulate son, shows up one day as an adult stranger and asks his father to find him an office job in the city. The father's resentment of his own past leads to an icy indifference, which quickly breeds a murderous hatred in the son. In the end, wielding a kitchen knife, Dabao steals into his father's bedroom, only to be overpowered by his outraged and stronger father. The father wins the battle, but sees in his opponent's despicable face a reflection of himself. In the pathetic weeping of the beaten, he cannot but hear his own life story bitterly recounted. "Overnight, our uncle's hair turned completely gray. He realized that he was not to be happy anymore" (*Shushu*, 75).

Thus, the uncle's victory is also his defeat. The final scene of the tragicomedy of his life, which the young narrator and his associates appreciate as if it were directly from a Shakespearean play, restages his life as inescapable suffering. He is now compelled to mourn the virtual death of his own son, whom he regards with a classical psychoanalytic ambivalence of love and hatred. Grief for the loss of a loved person or the loss of some abstraction, according to Freud, may be the cause for both mourning and melancholia. "The loss of a love-object," furthermore, "constitutes an excellent opportunity for the ambivalence in love-relationships to make itself felt and come to the fore." A Freudian explanation of melancholia depicts a mental economy wherein "countless single conflicts in which love and hate wrestle together are fought for the object."[18] The loss of his child is precisely such a traumatic experience that foregrounds the uncle's ambivalence toward the failure of his life, which becomes the origin of his sorrow and his melancholy grasp of truth. The same ambivalence also affects the narrator, who, through an "extremely personal incident," comes to the same revelation as the uncle in his grander drama. The failure of history, as the narrator now realizes, is ultimately a failure of human will, because enormous pain comes from living in historical truth. It is this revelation that puts in critical perspective his own postmodernist predilections: "We always seek depth and detest shallowness, and yet we have no courage to live a deep life. A deep life is too serious and too momentous for us; we simply cannot stand it" (*Shushu*, 77).

18. Sigmund Freud, "Mourning and Melancholia," *Collected Papers* (New York: Basic Books, 1959), 4:161, 168.

"The same sharp sorrow suddenly arose from the vast ocean"

To draw a not entirely improbable comparison, *Our Uncle's Story,* in Wang Anyi's literary imagination, may occupy the same position that *The Origin of the German Play of Mourning* does in Walter Benjamin's historical thinking. In his study of the seventeenth-century baroque *Trauerspiel* as a historical structure of feeling, Benjamin develops his messianic hermeneutics and asserts that a theory of *Trauer* can be secured only "in the description of the world which emerges under the gaze of the melancholic."[19] By reconstructing this mournful gaze, in the words of Max Pensky, Benjamin delineates a "melancholy subjectivity" that dialectically unifies insight and despair and thrives on a symbiotic connection between a contemplative subject and the desacralized world of objects.[20] Central to this form of critical subjectivity is the resurrected notion of "heroic melancholy," to which I will return at the end of this chapter. With the completion of *Our Uncle's Story,* Wang Anyi seems to have discovered a passage to historical depth by way of sadness or melancholy. The unhappy tales that have ensued are intensely subjective and are often centered on intriguing anamnestic images. If *Our Uncle's Story* offers a self-conscious narrative of the origin of her melancholy writing, in her 1993 novella, *Sadness for the Pacific,* Wang Anyi gives a global expression to melancholy subjectivity through revisiting a family history of sadness.

Sadness for the Pacific is not so much a story about the genesis of melancholia as it is an emotional exploration, set against a contemporary landscape of postmodernity, of the melancholy truth of the passion incited by modernity. It has the structure of retracing a family tree over time and space, and the first-person narrator, who now seeks to empathize with her ancestors, participates in the narrative by projecting a subjective mood of sorrow over past events and retrieved memories. Nostalgia, as both the motivation for, and the mode of, historical remembrance, grips the narrator, and her journey into the past becomes an encounter with varying degrees and occasions of the same lament and mourning. The melancholy

19. Walter Benjamin, *Origin of the German Play of Mourning,* quoted in Max Pensky, *Melancholy Dialectics: Walter Benjamin and the Play of Mourning* (Amherst: University of Massachusetts Press, 1993), 90.

20. Pensky, *Melancholy Dialectics,* 107; see chap. 2, "*Trauerspiel* and Melancholy Subjectivity," 60–107.

mood, as Kristeva would say, is inscribed here as the originary language, as the modality of significance that precedes any meaningful articulation. In the text, this melancholy is specifically associated with a contemplating individual who is stricken by the sublime eternity of a vast ocean.

At the beginning of the story, we find the narrator aboard a ship in the sun-scorched Strait of Malacca on her way to the Malaysian island city of Binang. This ancient passageway brings to her mind the adventures of Zheng He, the Chinese navigator of the fifteenth century who sailed the same reflecting waters; the surrounding tropical geography excites in her no small curiosity either, with its exotic names suggesting a strange mixture of exuberance and desolation. This initial free association already sets up the structure of the narrative as one of a contemporary traveler's looking for signs of historical depth and relevance. As her destination arises on the distant horizon, she suddenly realizes that her father must have had the same view half a century ago when he and his theater group were approaching Binang. Such an imaginary identification with her father transfers the narrator back to the past and enlivens that earlier moment with a tangible immediacy. With the apparition of her father as a young boy hovering over herself and the Pacific Ocean, the narrator enters a space of spectrality in which the past as ghost always returns for a revelatory first time.[21]

> Back then, my father was nineteen years old, obsessed with theater and national salvation. He had followed the opera troupe from Singapore, traveled across the Malay Peninsula, and was going to Binang as the final stop. All the way, the group sang songs dedicated to the cause of fighting the Japanese. It was also the mid-summer season of southern monsoons, and the tropical sun had tanned my father dark as coal. A sun-burned teenager in short pants appeared in my view. With his appearance, a sharp sorrow unexpectedly arose from inside me. The same sharp sorrow suddenly arose from the vast ocean, expanding and penetrating. Even the sun turned into a source of excruciating pain.[22]

---

21. The notion of the specter as "repetition *and* first time" comes from Jacques Derrida, *Specters of Marx: The State of the Debt, the Work of Mourning, & the New International,* trans. Peggy Kamuf (New York: Routledge, 1994), which, among other things, offers a complex discussion of the relationship between spectrality and mourning and is profoundly pertinent to our investigation of contemporary melancholy.

22. Wang Anyi, *Shangxin Taipingyang* (Sadness for the Pacific), collected in her *Love*

This visceral experience of sadness in the middle of a timeless ocean strikes a keynote, and the rest of the narrative flows as if in an unstoppable search for the connection between this intense sorrow and the vivid image of an inspired teenage boy, who, as "my father," stands for an ineluctable destiny. Encoded in the anamnestic image is also the narrator's origin and sense of belonging, which she now must know. In order to fully account for this image and its inexplicable, but enveloping, melancholy, the narrator will have to relive time and space as lived by the bygone generations of her family. This root-seeking search will lead her southward through the Pacific as she retraces her forefathers' footsteps over Southeast Asia and through Singapore's gradual emergence as an independent modern nation. In the end, a melancholy perspective on the rootlessness of humanity on a global scale takes hold. The solidity of dry land dissolves, and the ocean asserts itself as the ultimate background and limit to human existence: "A world map shows us that even continents are drifting islands.... The ocean may well be the last home for humanity, the dead end of human migration. Herein lies all the sadness for the Pacific" (*Shangxin,* 383).

The hypertrophy of melancholy subjectivity in *Sadness for the Pacific* is most striking when we compare this 1993 narrative with Wang Anyi's 1985 short story "My Origins." The earlier account is also given from the perspective of a first-person narrator (whose name is Wang Anyi, no less), but in a markedly realistic style, and is broken into two separate components: the first about her search for her mother's old Hangzhou home; the second focused on her father's family overseas, mostly on the amused observations of her cousin, who is visiting from Singapore in the early 1980s.[23] This second part records many significant details that will reappear in the later, longer story—for example, the colorful confetti at the outset of the father's voyage to mainland China when he was twenty-one,

---

and Sentiment in Hong Kong, 306. Page references to this work are given in the text as *Shangxin.* The phrase I translate as "sharp sorrow" is *shangtong,* which conveys both a physical sensation and a mental state, evoking what Freud described as *Schmerzunlust* in his essay on "Mourning and Melancholia."

23. Wang Anyi, "Wo de laili" (My origins), in her *Xiao baozhuang* (Baotown) (Shanghai: Shanghai wenyi, 1986), 100–130. Wang Anyi has another loving portrait of her father in the essay "Huashuo fuqin Wang Xiaoping" (About my father Wang Xiaoping), collected in her *Pugongying* (Dandelions) (Shanghai: Shanghai wenyi, 1988), 78–86.

and his not knowing how to use a blanket efficiently on arriving in a chilly Shanghai. However, no clear picture of either family emerges; the best that the confused narrator can visualize about her great-grandmother is a tiny boat drifting into the misty ocean. Everything about that ancient Fujianese woman "was too unspeakably vague, remote, and strange for me to feel related to it," sighs the narrator. More news about her relatives across the ocean started coming in later, "but because of the barrier of language and the lapse of time, or for other reasons, I always felt alienated from them. As a result, I was convinced I had a muddled origin."[24] Nonetheless, she regards herself as being as Chinese as everyone else around her, although the question of her true historical origin remains, especially after her Singaporean cousin sends over a photograph of the tomb where her grandparents and great-grandmother are buried. This question proved to be so haunting in reality that Wang Anyi felt compelled to confront it again in a two-part book with the scholarly-sounding title *Patrilineal and Matrilineal Myths*, in which *Sadness for the Pacific* constitutes the first, patrilineal part.[25]

The pathos of the 1993 "patrilineal myth" seems to have drawn on two narrative modes that best define Chinese literature of the 1980s. One is the earlier and widely influential movement of cultural root seeking, which helped establish an anthropological concept of tradition and naturalistic vitality as critical antidotes to turbulent state politics as well as to the ills of modernization. The other development, loosely called either experimental or even avant-garde, is one in which writers such as Mo Yan and Su Tong, by pursuing family genealogy as a personal and often redemptive project, push further the same intellectual and emotional concern with historical representation that underlies root-seeking literature. To these literary movements Wang Anyi has been an attentive and contributing contemporary.[26] In *Our Uncle's Story*, the narrator makes a point

24. Wang Anyi, "Wo de laili," 121–22.
25. See Wang Anyi, *Fuxi yu muxi de shenhua* (Patrilineal and matrilineal myths) (Hangzhou: Zhejiang wenyi, 1994). Both parts of this volume, *Sadness for the Pacific* and *Jishi yu xugou* (Records and fiction), were first published separately in the journal *Shouhuo* (Harvest) in 1993. An unabridged version of *Records and Fiction* was also published as an independent novel in 1993.
26. Wang Anyi's 1985 story "Baotown" (its English version collected in *Baotown*, trans. Martha Avery [New York: Penguin, 1989]), for example, is often regarded as a representative work in the mode of critical root seeking.

of presenting the root-seeking movement as an intellectual watershed between the uncle's generation and that of younger, more cosmopolitan writers (*Shushu,* 38–39). On another occasion, Wang Anyi singles out Su Tong's novella *Nineteen Thirty-four Escapes* (1988) as a pivotal text in the experiment of fictionalizing family genealogy. The title alone is fascinating enough, she writes, for the word "escape" already evokes a concrete mode of existence and suggests a perennial human condition of fleeing flood, war, and famine.[27] This fascination with desperate flight leads Wang Anyi to rediscover her family genealogy in light of the turn-of-the-century Chinese diaspora over the South Pacific. A broadened cultural geography in her narrative consequently helps reveal the historicity of such formations as the nation-state and national identity.

In *Sadness for the Pacific,* however, it is the stark discrepancy, from a contemporary perspective, between this perennial human restlessness and individual heroic efforts that seizes the narrator and engulfs her in a global melancholy. A woeful sense of loss and inconsequentiality, if not outright futility, now filters her vision of the youthful enthusiasm of her father's generation. At the same time, what renders her sorrow so visceral and indivertible is an anxiety over the absence of comparable passion in her own life and the bustling world she inhabits. To compensate for this perceived lack, the narrating subject indulges in intense nostalgia, which, by widening the gap between a vividly remembered past world and an increasingly standardized present life, serves to defamiliarize the present as having failed its own historical potentials. Such is the dialectical structure of the discourse of melancholy, which underlies the narrator's awestruck gaze at her father's specter over the Pacific Ocean and her prolonged stay in front of her ancestors' grave, now overgrown by robust tropical vegetation.

Moved by the imagined scene from her father's idealistic youth, the narrator looks back at herself and realizes that in her origins "there were actually traces of the tropics" (*Shangxin,* 306). Now finding herself in Singapore for the first time at age thirty-seven, she discovers that a tropical island demonstrates its history through a changing human physiognomy. There, old people, wearing the grave expression of a tightly knit frown,

---

27. See Wang Anyi, *Jishi yu xugou—chuangzao shijie fangfa zhi yizhong* (Records and fiction: one method of creating the world) (Beijing: Renmin wenxue, 1993), 413. Chap. 9 (pp. 367–413) of this obviously autobiographical novel may be read as a self-analysis of Wang Anyi's literary career.

all appear dark, angular, and achingly doleful. "Young people, however, have grown paler thanks to the incubation of modern air-conditioning. They no longer bear a regional distinction in their facial features and instead appear increasingly internationalized." Walking down the quiet side streets in Chinatown, the narrator sees in every old person the shadow of her own wearied and sorrow-laden grandparents. Although their pictures have always been in the family photo album, she never really recognizes them until she visits their grave, which is the first thing she does after arriving in Singapore. On approaching the cemetery, she feels her growing grief being compounded by the brutal heat. "An endless sorrow welled up inside me, and I wondered, how could the dead rest in peace in such sweltering heat?" Etched in the tombstone is a picture of her grandparents, looking as plaintive as ever. She also finds her own name engraved in the stone. "Not until then did I realize the fateful connection between myself and the old couple permanently asleep underneath the ground. I felt a deep pain for them, one that bound our hearts and bodies together" (*Shangxin,* 307).

Later, the narrator will observe that in her search for family roots in this "cosmopolitan nation-state" that too quickly buries its past, she reaps only two things: the oppressive heat and a deep sorrow (*Shangxin,* 330). The clean and orderly city streets offer no consolation, nor do the impressive high-rises. The constant tropical temperature allows her to relate to her grandparents and to fathom what they must have endured when they, as first-generation immigrants, fought various hardships and each other in their struggle to settle in this new land. It also lends itself to a textured background against which the narrator can picture her father's unhappy childhood. In days dominated by the same tropical heat, a reticent, sunburned child would watch the ocean all by himself, nurturing his first fantasies about the mainland. "A sad child gazing into the sea: this was a melancholy, heartbreaking picture" (*Shangxin,* 316).

Nonetheless, her father is now recalled as a most representative modern youth. Born a full century after the British East India Company merchant Sir Stamford Raffles first landed in Singapore in 1819, as the narrator continues to infer from the historical context, her father comes of age in a time still charged by the revolutionary ethos of May Fourth literature. As an impressionable boy, he must have paid his homage to Yu Dafu, the outspoken sufferer of modern romantic melancholy, who came to Singapore in 1940 and excited the imaginations of many an aspiring literary youth.[28] Based on an imaginary meeting between her father and Yu Dafu, the narrator goes on to portray a young generation of ethnic Chinese who, influenced by May Fourth liberal humanism, consciously practiced a modern way of living, longed for the mainland as their spiritual homeland, and readily identified with the cause of national salvation during the Japanese invasion of China. What the narrator reassembles, from the unfamiliar tropical landscape, is the same central bildungsroman of the generation of Chinese who, as the spiritual offspring of the May Fourth era, turned into the revolutionaries of the 1940s. It has the universal modern plot of an individual actively seeking to participate in a greater national historical enterprise. Her father's passionate longing for the mainland is first expressed as the indefatigable enthusiasm with which he joins the Malay Chinese theater troupe and its tour of the peninsula to promote the cause of the Resistance. Eventually, it will lead him to Shanghai and, after many self-doubts and trepidations, to the Communist base in southern Jiangsu. By then, he has consciously overcome his initial uneasiness with a crude communal life and matures into a "true soldier" (*Shangxin*, 371). He welcomes and enjoys the trip to the barren hinterland as a peaceful return to the warm interior of a maternal body.

At the same moment her father penetrates the mainland and claims his Chinese identity, her second uncle and his comrades are mobilizing to defend Singapore against the Japanese, who cross the Johor Strait on 8 February 1942. Such striking synchronicity of two distinct moments is the narrator's basic compositional strategy, by means of which she manages to include numerous historical figures, events, anecdotes, and legends as integral to her family history. From British colonialism to Lee Kuan-yew's successful rule in postcolonial Singapore, from the modern rubber industry to the worldwide Great Depression, from the course of World War II to the Comintern's determination to prevent the Japanese from attacking the Soviet Union, her multifocal narrative explores the tension between textbook knowledge on the one hand and concrete images and personal stories on the other. The ever-deepening gap between a concep-

28. Here is one instance, out of several in the text, where the need for melancholy imagination is satisfied at the expense of historical accuracy. The narrative suggests that his meeting with Yu Dafu inspired the father to join the opera troupe in 1938, but historically Yu Dafu did not land in Singapore until 1940. See *Sadness for the Pacific*, 317–18.

tual history and anamnestic concentrations makes unavoidable the question of historical failure and success, which proves to be a determining question for a melancholy subjectivity.

Of all the characters and family members, Second Uncle is portrayed with the greatest love and empathy. While Father deserts his parents to devote his life to drama and revolution, First Uncle is an avid gambler, who in his old age turns out to be a good citizen of contemporary Singapore, with the pride of "a well-mannered child brought up by Lee Kuan-yew." Unlike his two older, self-absorbed brothers, the youngest brother, Second Uncle, "an unusually tender and kind boy," is much more grounded, sensitive, and compassionate toward the people around him (*Shangxin*, 331). He may share a similar abstract longing for the mainland, but he never leaves Singapore to pursue another path to self-realization. The narrator imagines his body to be slender and nimble, almost effeminate, and his soul to be that of a resolute hero. He quietly joins the Resistance during the war and, at age eighteen, is tortured to death by the Japanese police. After his death, "his soul soared into the sky and looked down. Only then did he find his island so gorgeously green that it made his heart ache. Floating in its radiant translucence, the island drifted with the ocean waves. At this he broke into tears" (*Shangxin*, 383). Both Father and Second Uncle, in contrast to Lee Kuan-yew, the most prominent Singaporean of the same generation, are "hot-blooded and passionate" young men, and both are vulnerable to a "drifting sensation" that is inseparable from their life on a small island (*Shangxin*, 333–34). Father, in the end, returns to the mainland to escape that anxiety over rootlessness and successfully integrates himself into the maternal body of collective history. The pragmatic Lee Kuan-yew, with no idealistic pretensions, institutes a postcolonial order and helps "produce a new people" on the island for the modern world (*Shangxin*, 377). Almost paradoxically, as the narrator comments, "the day when Singapore finally gained independence was also the moment when my father was exiled for real" (*Shangxin*, 378). For as a romantic revolutionary and determined expatriate, Father can no longer claim any affinity to his rapidly modernizing country of birth.

Such personalized perspectives give the narrator a chance to ponder the implications of a Singaporean-style prosperity. Ambivalence once again surfaces when she realizes that the stern rationalization necessary for Lee Kuan-yew's success, which seems to underline the contemporary horizon of expectation, has little room for her father's idealistic passion and aspirations.[29] Keenly aware of a cityscape shaped by global capital and culture, she finds herself haunted by thoughts of Second Uncle, whose untimely death creates a permanent lack and source of sadness for generations in the family. His memory, just like the granite war memorial, casts a gray, melancholy shadow over the present routine and insists on outlining history as a sorry experience of fragments and incompleteness. By inserting itself to prevent the present from coalescing into a seamless contemporaneity, this shadow comes alive as a haunting spirit that embodies other visions.

> The war memorial was a building endowed with the richest sentiment in this cosmopolitan nation-state. It projected a gentle and sorrowful shadow in front of us; it was the one consolation that I could find on this island, offering solace for the sadness that Second Uncle caused my grandparents. I left the war memorial and walked toward the bustling and colorful Bugis Street. Underneath my footsteps was a city street that was built over the ruins of the past two hundred years. The sun was shining. Who knows how many shadows and images were flying in the luminous sunlight, crisscrossing, up and down, and through my body and soul. All I could do was to approach and try to comfort my second uncle in the formless and weightless air. This caused such a bone-crushing ache! (*Shangxin*, 330)

"Les mélancolies historiques, les sympathies à travers siècles"

In *Sadness for the Pacific* the narrator's immense sorrow over a past moment that is at once intimate and yet unapproachable originates in the end in a simultaneous longing for, and fear of, the genuine passion that she witnesses in the youth of her father and Second Uncle. This conflict translates into a deep historical ambivalence, which, expressed in the form

---

29. In this light, Wang Anyi's text can be read as a complex response to the growing desire, among Chinese theoreticians as well as policymakers, to emulate the Singapore model of modernization, which is promoted as an effective combination of the Confucian tradition and modern Western technologies, although it also is obvious that Singapore does not enter the story because of an established analysis on the writer's part. To fully grasp the global concern of the narrative, we need to accept that Singapore, as part of the postmodern transnational landscape, signifies modernity at large.

of melancholy subjectivity, is in fact a complex response to another mass reaction to utopian visions. Her melancholy occurs at a moment when the modern project of collectively determining human destiny seems to be universally disavowed and when capital claims a global hegemony. Yet "haunting belongs to the structure of every hegemony."[30] Amid the spreading postmodern euphoria, melancholy alone reveals negativity as indispensable to dialectical truth. When the high tide of entrepreneurial individualism rises across the land to sweep away egalitarian conformity, so reflects Wang Anyi in 1993, there ought to be solitary souls whose reaction is more contemplative than instinctive or spontaneous. Now is the time for writers to understand that "the independence we so desperately fought for does not entirely consist in happiness. Suffering is its essence."[31]

It may be helpful to recall that we began our discussion of Wang Anyi's writing of melancholy by way of Kristeva's description of the ravaging effect of melancholia. To the crushing experience of melancholic depression, Kristeva writes, "I owe a supreme, metaphysical lucidity. . . . My pain is the hidden side of my philosophy, its mute sister."[32] What Kristeva goes on to state in semiotic terms, along with her feminist concerns, is largely the European Renaissance concept of a "heroic melancholy," which views the moody temperament as a blessed curse, a humoral source of insight and creativity.[33] A consistent fascination accompanies the symptomatology of melancholia and depression from Hippocratic times to the twentieth century, although each historical age has offered a different etiology. Throughout the centuries, especially in the wake of great social upheaval, continual heroic encounters with melancholia have generated different legends, memories, and images.[34] More often than not, the melancholy figure emerges as the mournful and profound individual,

---

30. Derrida, *Specters of Marx*, 37.

31. Wang Anyi, "Kexi bushi nongchaoren" (Sorry, but we are not surfers), *Review of Contemporary Writers*, no. 5 (1993): 27–28.

32. Kristeva, *Black Sun*, 3–4.

33. This notion in its most concentrated form was developed by Marsilio Ficino (1433–99), a Florentine humanist, who in turn took the idea from the Greek text *Problemata Physica* (attributed to Aristotle). See Stanley W. Jackson, *Melancholia and Depression: From Hippocratic Times to Modern Times* (New Haven, Conn.: Yale University Press, 1986), 100–101.

34. See Jackson, *Melancholia and Depression*, 29–246.

bitter but compassionate, endowed with an artist's sensitivity and imagination. For with the onset of melancholia—not unlike the liminal experience of madness—insight and darkness are fused together, and the afflicted individual gains access to the ultimate truth only to compound his or her incapacitating sadness and pain. This brings about such an intensely private suffering that any effort to ease it through externalization is bound to result in ever greater despair. Hence, the "abyss of sorrow," the "noncommunicable grief," that constitutes Kristeva's melancholia.

The ideal of *melancolia illa heroica* proved instrumental to Walter Benjamin in his study of the baroque *Trauerspiel*. In Baudelaire, he again would find its perfect embodiment for Europe's modernizing nineteenth century. Through its heroic form, as Max Pensky points out when explicating Benjamin's "melancholy dialectics," the discourse of melancholy secures "the truest and most powerful historical image of its dialectical structure."[35] If such a discourse yields a dialectic of the emotive and the cognitive, heroic melancholy then strives to elevate this affective experience to a new form of subjectivity, albeit a precarious one. What helps keep this heightened subjectivity grounded and expressive, consequently, is bound to be melancholy as content rather than as form. Underneath Duras's inconsolable grief, explains Kristeva, lies the modern, silencing "malady of death" violently exposed by Auschwitz and Hiroshima, which now "informs our most concealed inner recesses."[36] Similarly, at the heart of Baudelaire's poetic rage lies the very inability to experience. The lyrical poet in the age of commodity capitalism, in the words of Benjamin, holds in his hands only "the scattered fragments of genuine historical experience. . . . To his horror, the melancholy man sees the earth revert to a mere state of nature. No breath of prehistory surrounds it: there is no aura."[37] It is this loss of aura, just as it is the loss of voice in the case of Duras, that dialectically marks Baudelaire's melancholy vision with historical specificity.

Historical melancholy, as I have tried to show here, is the origin and content of Wang Anyi's more recent tales of sorrow. It expresses the profound ambivalence that the writer, conscious of the approaching end of

---

35. Max Pensky, *Melancholy Dialectics*, 32.

36. Kristeva, *Black Sun*, 221.

37. Walter Benjamin, "On Some Motifs in Baudelaire," in his *Illuminations*, trans. Harry Zohn (New York: Schocken Books, 1968), 183–84.

a century, sustains toward the course of twentieth-century Chinese history, in particular its human dimension. Utopian longings, generated by grand historical visions that are brought into focus at moments of collective action, inevitably turn into traumatic experiences for the individual, but the rapid dissipation of idealistic passion in a postrevolutionary contemporary world also seems vastly depressing. The loss of genuine excitement, therefore, becomes the historical moment in which Wang Anyi, through a discourse of melancholy, examines the dialectics of success and failure. This structure of feeling generates the central plot of her late genealogical "myths": a melancholic individual in the contemporary world trying to recall and reconcile herself with historical failures as human triumphs.

For this reason, my claim that Wang Anyi's recent fiction articulates a "postmodern melancholy" does not mean that melancholy itself becomes a postmodernist sentiment. Rather, it acknowledges the postmodern condition that Wang Anyi's melancholic writings critically reveal and even interrupt. We may go so far as to conclude that her melancholy, in which the longing for a modern longing causes the deepest sorrow and ambivalence, gathers its historical content and relevance only in an age that deems itself "post" and beyond all ideologies of the modern. In other words, Wang Anyi's postmodern melancholy may be read as a critique of a transnational postmodernism that, in the words of Ross Chambers, is nonmelancholic, "a kind of modernism without its pathos of lack."[38] Melancholy against the grain: this may explain why in Chinese literature at the end of the twentieth century there is an increasingly pronounced mood of sorrow, particularly among a new generation of women writers.[39] This latest development raises complicated issues of gender, aesthetics, and subjectivity that ought to be engaged at greater

38. See Ross Chambers, *The Writing of Melancholy: Modes of Opposition in Early French Modernism,* trans. Mary Seidman Trouille (Chicago: University of Chicago Press, 1993), 208.

39. For instance, in 1996 issues of *Review of Contemporary Writers,* we find the following essays: Xie Youshun, "Youshang er bu juewang de xiezuo—wo du Chi Zijian de xiaoshuo" (A writing that is melancholy but not despairing: my reading of Chi Zijian's fiction) (no. 1: 66–71) and Meng Fanhua, "Youyu de huangyuan: nüxing piaopo de xinlu mishi—Chen Ran xiaoshuo de yizhong jiedu" (Melancholy wilderness—the psychological history of female homelessness: an interpretation of Chen Ran's fiction) (no. 3: 57–62).

length. It also adds renewed urgency to a famous question, posed by Gustave Flaubert in 1853, about historical necessity: "Whence come these fits of historical melancholia, these affinities from century to century, etc.?"[40] To begin answering this inquiry, we will have to enter the mournful and searching gaze that a melancholic directs at the world.

40. Quoted in Chambers, *The Writing of Melancholy,* vii.

AFTERWORD

Thus the mournful and searching gaze that we recognize in the last chapter brings a reflective, if necessarily open-ended, closure to this study, and we find ourselves at the conclusion of a long and eventful twentieth century. We also find ourselves on the threshold of a new millennium that is steadily losing its auratic abstractness and appears far more familiar and banal than once anticipated or fantasized. In a deflated sense of the expression, we live in an age where the future is already now.

To better survey the melancholy subject's field of vision as delineated by Wang Anyi and her late twentieth-century contemporaries, we may recall the utopian millenarianism of Liang Qichao, the most ardent reformist thinker of late Qing China. His exuberant "Ode to Young China," penned at the dawning of the twentieth century, for instance, conjures up a fantastic vision of grandeur and climaxes in apostrophizing "My beautiful young China that is as eternal as heaven; my magnificent Chinese youth who are as bountiful as the land."[1] This stirring essay, together with Liang's many other passionate writings, affirms a redemptive future through "as much an invocation of a promising new age as a celebration of the global imaginary into which China as a youthful new nation is about to enter."[2] The future, for Liang and his generation of Chinese, was envisioned to be radically different from their present, and yet it would have to be delivered through present action. Such a supremely confident "Young China" consciousness or optimistic anticipation has been instrumental in shaping twentieth-century Chinese political and cultural life, and it has been called upon to legitimize various ideologies and movements as modern and/or revolutionary. Even repressive political regimes would find it useful to resort to the myth of an imminent glorious national renewal; conversely, nationalism as a legitimation mechanism has frequently given rise to authoritarianism and a politics of sublimation, both of which exacted disciplinary uniformity and enor-

1. Liang Qichao, "Shaonian Zhongguo shuo" (Ode to young China), *Yinbingshi heji-wenji* (Collected writings from the ice-drinker's studio: collected essays) (Shanghai: China Books, 1936), 5:12.
2. Xiaobing Tang, *Global Space and the Nationalist Discourse of Modernity: The Historical Thinking of Liang Qichao* (Stanford, Calif.: Stanford University Press, 1996), 37.

mous human sacrifices. The passion and trauma caused by a century of war and revolution becomes, by the 1990s, the object of an ambivalent, painfully self-conscious gaze in Wang Anyi's "tales of sorrow." A positive, global longing is at once disavowed and longed for, and her tender attention to the personal and the quotidian arises inextricably with a sense of loss and incompleteness. The same melancholic and pensive search is evident in Chen Ran's fiction about contemporary urban life, precisely because she insists on removing "the Chinese female subject from the overarching concern with any kind of determining meaning—revolutionary passion, humanistic love, lust for the new and different—outside of what she can gain from her own daily life."[3]

Herein lies yet another possible way of conceptualizing the passage from the modern to the postmodern. The heroic project of social transformation and engineering goes awry, and everyday life reemerges as an inescapable continuity. The "overarching concern" that is now displaced or debunked seems to be telltale of the operational logic of modernization, and of a utopian modernity in general. Yet any such neat narrative of modernity yielding to its antithetical other in postmodernity may itself betray the same impulse of constructing a rational explanation or seamless horizon of intelligibility. A more dialectical and historically sensitive approach derives from the notion of spectrality, by which we see the present as continually haunted and disturbed by ghosts of the past. The specter of past passions and sentiments, as Derrida observes, will always return for a revelatory first time. If modernity was famously haunted by the nightmare of history from which the modern subject desperately tried to awaken, postmodernity becomes conceivable when a once self-reassured modern vision metamorphoses into a ghostly, even shameful, afterimage. From this perspective, historical movement appears not so much as a temporal flow as an ever-expanding space of spectrality. This is how we may begin to theorize Wang Anyi's postmodern melancholy; this is also why it is crucial to revisit Liang Qichao's "Ode to Young China" as we try to fully comprehend Wang Anyi's musings on adulthood as inevitable adulteration.

Yet at this point an empirical question of method may present itself. How can we be certain that Wang Anyi's sorrowful narratives speak to

3. Wendy Larson, "Women and the Discourse of Desire in Postrevolutionary China: The Awkward Postmodernism of Chen Ran," *boundary 2* 24.3 (Fall 1997): 223.

Liang Qichao's inspirational essay from almost a hundred years ago? May it not be a happy coincidence that by juxtaposing these two vastly different writers and their different genres of writing (fiction versus polemical essays), we confirm an implicit narrative embedded in this study of modern Chinese literature and culture? A more blunt question may be posed: What is the criterion of selection for *Chinese Modern* as a whole? What justifies our moving from Wu Jianren's ambivalent *Sea of Regret* to Ding Ling's ultimately romantic Shanghai narratives to the residual modernism of the 1980s?

A direct answer to these questions has two parts. First, as a matter of truism, all criteria of selection are, in the final analysis, arbitrary and ought to be viewed on their own systemic terms; second, this particular collection of texts is determined by the larger narrative logic and structure of *Chinese Modern*. Together, the literary and visual materials that I examined in the preceding pages bring forth a conceptual coherence in my rethinking of China's twentieth century. They all deepen, to varying degrees, my appreciation for a central dialectics in terms of which competing claims for or against being modern become intelligible and can be related to one another. At the same time, these texts, by virtue of their different genres and effects, demonstrate a historical multiplicity or nonsynchronic synchronicity that is at the core of Chinese modernity. There is no pretension here to deal exclusively with masterpieces or high aesthetic achievements. On the contrary, through what I call an "intimate reading," I show how canonical, popular, marginal, or even ephemeral texts can all begin to reveal and comment on their own making, on the one hand, and a persistent condition of production, which is generalized here as the Chinese modern, on the other.

I would, however, resist labeling *Chinese Modern* as an instance of what has been described as literary historiography in the mode of an indiscriminate postmodern encyclopedia, where "its explanations of past happenings are piecemeal, may be inconsistent with each other, and are admitted to be inadequate."[4] For obvious reasons, or rather absences, I would not characterize this study as forming a narrative history either. Granted that its indirect narrative bears witness to subjective investment and even commitment, each chapter nonetheless enters a past moment

---

4. David Perkins, *Is Literary History Possible?* (Baltimore: Johns Hopkins University Press, 1992), 60.

and places it in the context of its own genealogies, articulations, and intersections. As I indicate in the Introduction, it may be impossible for any one narrative history of twentieth-century China to register all the moments recollected in *Chinese Modern,* if only because this book traces more than one imaginative trajectory and deliberately traverses an uneven terrain of signification.

A more complicated response to the question of how this book is put together will have to return to the conceptual coherence or operative dialectics that I believe underlies it. For only through such a conceptual framework will the juxtaposition of Wang Anyi and Liang Qichao become revelatory, and the earlier readings of interior design and the tubercular body, for instance, be meaningfully undertaken. This is where it is crucial to insist on approaching twentieth-century Chinese literature and, by extension, cultural formations as a dynamic totality, as an interactive, interconnected whole. For it may quickly become insufficient to repeat that the dialectics of the heroic and the quotidian demand that we read texts from various sources, high, low, and in between. It may also be misleading to suggest that the method here is ultimately one of logical induction, or that it boils down to stating a governing Zeitgeist in the now suspect Hegelian fashion. While we derive considerable satisfaction from reading specific texts intimately and creatively, it is just as crucial for us to always keep in sight their overlapping contexts and to open our texts to the elemental forces of history. This involves more than being sensitive to the text-context interaction, because the question is how to gain access to the—by definition—disembodied contexts and to conceptualize the intruding presence of history. Put differently, how do we understand history as both abstract and concrete, both imagined and lived, both external and internal?

Such an inquiry into historical hermeneutics no doubt leads in many directions and to many answers; it certainly complicates the process even more when we realize that there could be different constructions or interpretations of the more specific concept of twentieth-century Chinese literature. Not only may Chinese literature's content, meaning, and logic be variously construed, but even its coverage, reference, or legitimacy may be seriously negotiated and contested. In the mid-1980s several rising literary critics in China proposed, for a pathbreaking first time, that twentieth-century Chinese literature be grasped "as an indivisible and organic totality." They viewed the development of this body of literature as an ongoing process of transformation, through which traditional literature gives way to modern literature, Chinese literature merges into "world literature," modern national consciousness enters literary expression, new literary genres and forms emerge and eventually establish themselves. Their strong "totality consciousness" (zhengti yishi), they explain, would enable them, in literary studies and historiography, to achieve historical depth, intervene in the present, and anticipate the future.[5] As pronounced as their totality consciousness is a mission consciousness, for at the time they obviously viewed it their historical task—after the dogmatic aberration of the intervening socialist period—to integrate contemporary Chinese literature of the reformist "New Era" back into the more open-minded and innovative May Fourth tradition. The legitimating discourse for this conception of "twentieth-century Chinese literature," therefore, was modernization and cosmopolitanism.[6]

In contrast to this commanding narrative of a multiple rational unfolding, the more recent *Literature of China in the Twentieth Century* by Bonnie S. McDougall and Kam Louie adopts an intrinsic approach to literary history while acknowledging changes in literature both as an artistic practice and as a social institution. In hopes of representing and explaining the inner dynamics of literary production in twentieth-century China, the authors of this informative history focus on the three major genres: fiction, drama, and poetry. The continual interaction among these literary forms and their coeval unevenness provide the organizational structure of a historicizing narrative. Thus, the ascendance and political prominence of one particular genre over the other two, such as poetry during the May Fourth period and drama during the Cultural Revolution, shed light on the general background of the given historical moment. Attention to this mobile triad logically leads McDougall and

---

5. Huang Ziping, Chen Pingyuan, Qian Liqun, "Lun 'ershi shiji Zhongguo wenxue'" (On "twentieth-century Chinese literature"), originally published in *Wenxue pinglun* (Literary review), 1995, collected in Wang Xiaoming, ed., *Ershi shiji Zhongguo wenxue shilun* (Essays on twentieth-century Chinese literary history), vol. 1 (Shanghai: Dongfang chuban zhongxin, 1997), 1–20.

6. As if in response to this initial proposal, when he published a much more systematic book elaborating a necessary totalizing approach, Chen Sihe would emphatically describe "twentieth-century Chinese literature as an open totality." See his *Zhongguo xin wenxue zhengti guan* (A comprehensive review of Chinese new literature) (Taipei: Yeqiang chubanshe, 1990), esp. 1–22.

Louie to divide twentieth-century Chinese literature, ostensibly from 1900 to 1989, "into three major periods on the basis of changes within the structure of the literary canon."[7] Although in the end the authors also affirm that literature produced in twentieth-century China is undoubtedly part of world literature, they apparently arrive at the conclusion by a different path than that outlined by the Chinese critics in the mid-1980s. The totality of twentieth-century Chinese literature, in other words, contains meanings and revelations that are contingent upon the context or discursive tradition in which this body of literature is configured.[8]

The authors of *Literature of China in the Twentieth Century* obviously are aware of a further complication in examining this literature as a whole. Since midcentury, they note, "the development of literature in Taiwan, Hong Kong, and Overseas Chinese communities took separate routes." Consequently, they decide to leave these "largely independent literatures" out of their presentation of "the literature of China."[9] By limiting their scope to mainland China, McDougall and Louie make their history much more manageable and coherent, but at the same time they effectively subject this literary history to the geopolitical stipulations of the modern nation-state. While historiographical expediency may call for such a clear demarcation, the invigorating ambiguity of "twentieth-century Chinese literature" stems from the fact that, when taken as an interconnected whole, this body of literature will always force us to critically reconsider our assumptions about what constitutes the identity of modern China.

---

7. Bonnie S. McDougall and Kam Louie, *The Literature of China in the Twentieth Century* (New York: Columbia University Press, 1997), 8. In historical hindsight, we may question whether the stirring events in the spring of 1989 constituted such a significant discontinuity as is suggested by *The Literature of China,* in which the authors designate "1966–1989" as one continuous, although eventful, period.

8. For instance, in the afterword for his *The City in Modern Chinese Literature and Film: Configurations of Space, Time, and Gender* (Stanford, Calif.: Stanford University Press, 1996), Yingjin Zhang suggests succinctly that the evolving tension between the city and the country forms a central theme around which successive periods and various elements of modern Chinese literary history can be examined (pp. 261–68). David Der-wei Wang, in his *Fin-de-siècle Splendor: Repressed Modernities of Late Qing Fiction, 1849–1911* (Stanford, Calif.: Stanford University Press, 1997), offers a rather different perspective on modern Chinese literature when he brings literary productions in China, Taiwan, and Hong Kong at the end of the twentieth century into a historical dialogue with the last fin-de-siècle.

9. McDougall and Louie, *The Literature of China,* 9.

The concept of "Taiwan literature" and its relationship to the literature of China, in fact, are fascinating topics to ponder and investigate. To deny any relationship between these two entities is itself to postulate a relationship; to pit one against the other amounts to a more radical alternative; to see them as evolving from a common cultural heritage and absorbed in the same maelstrom of modernity points to yet another way of making sense of these two separate developments. The third approach, which I adopt in my comparative reading of Su Tong and Xiao Ye, is for me a productive one and promises a great field for future research. The history and vitality of Taiwan and Hong Kong literatures in the twentieth century, I would argue, make an ever more compelling case that by "modern Chinese literature" we understand not a narrow nation-state institution (in the modern Japanese tradition of *kokubungaku*), nor just one geopolitically bounded literary production, but rather a vast literature written in modern Chinese and interacting with long and uneven literary and cultural traditions—regional as much as national. Just as "Taiwan literature" is a legitimate concept denoting literature produced in Taiwan, so "Chinese literature" should be usefully broadened to mean "Zhongwen wenxue" (literature in Chinese) and replace a narrowing "Zhongguo wenxue" (literature of China, or even, of the Chinese nation-state).[10]

Untidy but inevitable complications, as much as various methods of configuration, in the study of twentieth-century Chinese literature finally bring home one central point. Our reading and understanding of this body of literature must be an open-ended interpretive project. The "totality of twentieth-century Chinese literature" is a concept that is open to continuous construction and contestation. Yet it is an indispensable construct insofar as each and every instance of interpreting a specific text in this tradition bespeaks, either explicitly or implicitly, a certain conception or evaluation of its entirety. At this point, our belief in democracy and the principle of tolerance may convince us that all methods and readings have their inalienable right, if not always intellectual merit. Ultimately, however, it also becomes irrefutable that different conceptions of twentieth-century Chinese literature and its inner dynamics highlight different ideological visions of Chinese modernity. Such highlighting constitutes the epistemological advantage of entertaining the notion

10. See my article "On the Concept of Taiwan Literature," *Modern China* 25.4 (October 1999): 379–422.

of totality; it should also encourage us to go on and seek a more explanatory critical language and analytical model through which to understand various totalizing methods and ideologies themselves. Needless to say, this is not at all the central task undertaken in *Chinese Modern;* I nonetheless hope that the book's underlying conception and interpretations will make a modest contribution to an incipient study of twentieth-century Chinese literature and culture as one dynamic and interconnected whole. Only when viewed in its entirety will the extraordinarily rich and tortuous history of twentieth-century Chinese literature and culture reveal its dialectical meaning and enable the literary and cultural critic to "continue to pass judgment on the abstract quality of life in the present, and to keep alive the idea of a concrete future."[11] On this account, *Chinese Modern* is written for the past century as well as for the new, postmillenarian one.

11. This quotation is taken from the last section of Fredric Jameson's *Marxism and Form*, where he defines the tasks of a dialectical criticism. In the contemporary world of late capitalism, according to Jameson, it is no longer possible to find the older realistic cultural works that Lukács examined and where reality and its interpretation are built together. The traditional symbiosis of the fact and commentary on the fact is now rendered asunder, and "the literary fact, like the other objects that make up our social reality, cries out for commentary, for interpretation, for decipherment, for diagnosis." Yet all other disciplines seem to have failed to offer a viable approach to this problem. "It therefore falls to literary criticism to continue to compare the inside and the outside, existence and history, to continue to pass judgment on the abstract quality of life in the present, and to keep alive the idea of a concrete future." See *Marxism and Form: Twentieth-Century Dialectical Theories of Literature* (Princeton, N.J.: Princeton University Press, 1971), 416.

GLOSSARY

This is a selected list of Chinese names, titles, and terms.

A Ying 阿英
baihua 白话
Ba Jin 巴金
Bashi ri huanyou ji 八十日环游记
Beijing nizao 北京你早
Beitong zhi di 悲恸之地
Benming nian 本命年
bomu 伯母
Cao Xueqin 曹雪芹
Cao Yu 曹禺
cheng 诚
Chen Kaige 陈凯歌
Chen Pingyuan 陈平原
Chen Ran 陈染
Chen Sihe 陈思和
Chen Xiaoming 陈晓明
Chen Yun 陈耘
chinian 痴念
chixiang 痴想
Ciwen xiangei shaonü Yang Liu 此文献给少女杨柳
Cui Jian 崔健
Da chuanqi 大喘气
Dai Jinhua 戴锦华
Daoma zei 盗马贼
Daqing 大庆
Da youren 答友人
Dazhai 大寨
Di Baoxian (Pengdeng ge) 狄保贤(平等阁)

Didi nihao　弟弟你好

Ding Ling　丁玲

e'ren　恶人

Ershi nian mudu zhi guai xianzhuang　二十年目睹之怪现状

feng　疯

Fengkuang de daijia　疯狂的代价

Feng Menglong　冯梦龙

Fengyu zhong de lüdao—xiandai jiaju　风雨中的绿岛－现代家居

fengzi　疯子

Fu Lin　符霖

Fuxi yu muxi de shenhua　父系与母系的神话

Ganlan zhen 1944　橄榄镇1944

Gaozu　高祖

Ge Fei　格非

Gei kafei jia dian tang　给咖啡加点糖

Gudian aiqing　古典爱情

guguo　故国

guli　故里

Guomindang　国民党

Guo Moruo　郭沫若

Guo Zhenyi　郭箴义

gutu　故土

Guxiang　故乡

guyuan　故园

Haitian duxiaozi　海天独啸子

Hanye　寒夜

hao　好

haoren　好人

He Dun　何顿

Henhai　恨海

Hongdeng ji　红灯记

Hong gaoliang　红高粱

Honglou meng　红楼梦

huaju 话剧

Huangshan zhi lian 荒山之恋

Huang tudi 黄土地

Huang Zongying 黄宗英

huixiang 回乡

Hu Shi 胡适

Hu Yepin 胡也频

Jia 家

Jiang Guanyun 蒋观云

Jiang Qing 江青

Jiating wenti 家庭问题

jiaye 家业

jiefu 节妇

Jie hu hui 劫余灰

jingcheng 精诚

Jinggang shan 井冈山

Jingwei 精卫

Jingwei shi 精卫石

Jin Songcen 金松岑

Jishi yu xugou 纪实与虚构

Ju Dou 菊豆

kang 炕

Kongbu fenzi 恐怖分子

kuang 狂

Kuangren riji 狂人日记

lai 来

laohaoren 老好人

Laojing 老井

Lei Da 雷达

Liang Qichao 梁启超

Liaozhai zhiyi 聊斋志异

Liechang Zhasa 猎场扎撒

Li Jiefei 李洁非

Lin Gang　林刚
Lin Shu　林纾
Lin Yaode　林耀德
Li Tuo　李陀
Liu Bang　刘邦
Liu Heng　刘恒
Liu Shaoqi　刘少奇
Liu Zaifu　刘再复
Li Yang　李扬
Lunhui　轮回
Lu Xun　鲁迅
Mao Dun　茅盾
Mao Zedong　毛泽东
Mengke　梦珂
Meng Yue　孟悦
Mi Jiashan　米家山
Mo Yan　莫言
Nahan　呐喊
Nianqing de yidai　年轻的一代
Nihao yangfengren　你好养蜂人
nikeng　泥坑
1947 Gaosha baihe　1947高砂百合
Nüwa　女娲
Nüwa shi　女娲石
Peng Wen　彭文
Pingjing ru shui　平静如水
pingmin　平民
pingshu　评书
Pu Songling　蒲松龄
Qiangbao　强暴
Qianwan buyao wangji　千万不要忘记
qing　情
Qing bian　情变

Qingcheng zhi lian　倾城之恋
Qingchun ji　青春祭
qing jiao　情教
qing ji cheng chi　情极成痴
Qingshi leilüe　情史类略
Qin hai shi　禽海石
Qiong Yao　琼瑶
Qiqie chengqun　妻妾成群
Qiu Jin　秋瑾
Qiyuan　憩园
qu　去
Rensheng　人生
Ri　日
Shafei nüshi de riji　莎菲女士的日记
shangshan xiaxiang　上山下乡
Shangxin Taipingyang　伤心太平洋
Sha Ou　沙鸥
Shenghuo wuzui　生活无罪
Shi ji　史记
Shi jing　诗经
Shi Nai'an　施耐庵
Shishi ru yan　世事如烟
Shitou ji　石头记
Shui　水
shuqing shidai　抒情时代
Shushu de gushi　叔叔的故事
Sima Qian　司马迁
Su Tong　苏童
tanci　弹词
Tang Sheng　唐生
Tan Sitong　谭嗣同
Wang Anyi　王安忆
Wang Guowei　王国维

Wang Meng 王蒙

Wang Shuo 王朔

Wanzhu 顽主

wenqing 文情

Wo bu xiangshi 我不想事

Women de Heilong jiang a 我们的黑龙江啊

Women de tianye 我们的田野

Wu Jianren 吴趼人

Wu Tianming 吴天明

Wutuobang shipian 乌托邦诗篇

Xianggang de qing yu ai 香港的情与爱

Xiangnü Xiaoxiao 湘女潇潇

xiangtu wenxue 乡土文学

Xianshi yizhong 现实一种

xiaoshuo 小说

xiao tiandi 小天地

Xiao Ye 小野

Xie Fei 谢飞

xieqing xiaoshuo 写情小说

Xinmin congbao 新民丛报

Xin qingnian 新青年

xin shimin xiaoshuo 新市民小说

Xin xiaoshuo 新小说

yanqing xiaoshuo 言情小说

Yao Wenyuan 姚文元

Yeshan 野山

Yijiu sanling nian chun Shanghai 一九三零年春上海

Yijiu sansi nian de taowang 一九三四年的逃亡

yu 欲

Yuanye 原野

Yu Dafu 郁达夫

Yueyue xiaoshuo 月月小说

Yu Hua 余华

Zhang Ailing　张爱玲

Zhang Minquan　张民权

Zhang Nuanxin　张暖昕

Zhang Yiwu　张颐武

Zhongguo qingnian　中国青年

Zhongguo xiaoshuo shi　中国小说史

Zhou Guisheng　周桂笙

Zhu ni jiankang　祝你健康

Zisha　自杀

Ziye　子夜

SELECTED BIBLIOGRAPHY

Only those books directly quoted from or referred to in the preceding pages are included in this bibliography. Journal titles and individual essays are not listed.

A Ying. *Gengzi shibian wenxue ji* (Anthology of literature about the 1900 incident). Beijing: Zhonghua shuju, 1959.

———. *Wan Qing xiaoshuo shi* (History of late Qing fiction). Beijing: Dongfang, 1996.

———. *Xiaoshuo santan* (The third collection of essays on fiction). Shanghai: Shanghai guji, 1979.

Adorno, Theodor W. *Aesthetic Theory.* Translated by C. Lenhardt. Edited by Gretel Adorno and Rolf Tiedemann. London: Routledge & Kegan Paul, 1984.

Althusser, Louis. *Lenin and Philosophy and Other Essays.* Translated by Ben Brewster. New York: Monthly Review Press, 1971.

Anderson, Marston. *The Limits of Realism: Chinese Fiction in the Revolutionary Period.* Berkeley: University of California Press, 1990.

Ba Jin. *Ba Jin quanji* (The complete works of Ba Jin). Beijing: Renmin wenxue, 1986–93.

———. *Ba Jin wenji* (Collected works of Ba Jin). Beijing: Renmin wenxue, 1962.

———. *Cold Nights, a Novel by Ba Jin.* Translated by Nathan K. Mao and Liu Ts'un-yan. Hong Kong: Chinese University Press, 1978.

———. *Chuangzuo huiyi lu* (Reminiscences about my writing). Hong Kong: Joint Publishing, 1981.

———. *Family.* Translated by Sidney Shapiro. New York: Doubleday, 1972.

———. *Xiaoren xiaoshi* (Little people and little things). Shanghai: Wenhua shenghuo, 1945.

Barlowe, Tani, and Gary J. Bjorge, eds. *I Myself Am a Woman: Selected Writings of Ding Ling.* Boston: Beacon Press, 1989.

Barthes, Roland. *Camera Lucida: Reflections on Photography.* New York: Hill and Wang, 1981.

———. *S/Z.* Translated by Richard Miller. New York: Hill and Wang, 1974.

———. *Writing Degree Zero.* Translated by Annette Lavers and Colin Smith. New York: Noonday-Farrar, 1968.

Baudrillard, Jean. *For a Critique of the Political Economy of the Sign.* Translated with an introduction by Charles Levin. St. Louis: Telos Press, 1981.

———. *Jean Baudrillard: Selected Writings.* Edited with an introduction by Mark Poster. Stanford, Calif.: Stanford University Press, 1988.

Baum, Richard, and F. C. Teiwes. *Ssu-ch'ing: The Socialist Education Movement of 1962–1966*. Berkeley, Calif.: Center for Chinese Studies, 1968.

Benjamin, Walter. *Illuminations*. Translated by Harry Zohn. Edited with an introduction by Hannah Arendt. New York: Schocken Books, 1969.

Berman, Marshall. *All That Is Solid Melts into Air: The Experience of Modernity*. New York: Penguin, 1988.

Berry, Chris, ed. *Perspectives on Chinese Cinema*. London: British Film Institute, 1991.

Birch, Cyril, ed. *Chinese Communist Literature*. New York: Praeger, 1963.

Calinescu, Marei. *Five Faces of Modernity: Modernism, Avant-Garde, Decadence, Kitsch, Postmodernism*. Durham, N.C.: Duke University Press, 1987.

Chambers, Ross. *The Writing of Melancholy: Modes of Opposition in Early French Modernism*. Translated by Mary Seidman Trouille. Chicago: University of Chicago Press, 1993.

Chan, Anita. *Children of Mao: Personality Development and Political Activism in the Red Guard Generation*. Seattle: University of Washington Press, 1985.

Charney, Leo, and Vanessa Schwartz, eds. *Cinema and the Invention of Modern Life*. Berkeley: University of California Press, 1995.

Chen Bohai and Yuan Jin, eds. *Shanghai jindai wenxue shi* (History of modern Shanghai literature). Shanghai: Shanghai renmin, 1993.

Chen Pingyuan. *Ershi shiji Zhongguo xiaoshuo shi: di yi juan 1897–1916* (History of twentieth-century Chinese fiction: volume one, 1897–1916). Beijing: Peking University Press, 1989.

———. *Xiaoshuo shi: lilun yu shijian* (History of the novel: theory and practice). Beijing: Peking University Press, 1993.

———. *Zhongguo xiaoshuo xushi moshi de zhuanbian* (The transformation of the narrative pattern in Chinese fiction). Shanghai: Shanghai renmin, 1988.

Chen Sihe. *Zhongguo xin wenxue zhengti guan* (A comprehensive review of Chinese new literature). Taipei: Yeqiang chubanshe, 1990.

Chen Xiaoming, ed. *Zhongguo chengshi xiaoshuo jingxuan* (Anthology of Chinese urban fiction). Lanzhou: Gansu renmin, 1994.

Chen, Yu-shih. *Realism and Allegory in the Early Fiction of Mao Tun*. Bloomington: Indiana University Press, 1986.

Chen Yun, Zhang Lihui, and Xu Jingxian. *Nianqing de yidai* (The young generation). Beijing: Zhongguo xiju, 1964.

Chow, Rey. *Woman and Chinese Modernity: The Politics of Reading Between West and East*. Minneapolis: University of Minnesota Press, 1991.

Cong Shen. *Qianwan buyao wangji* (Never forget). Beijing: Zhongguo xiju, 1964.

Deleuze, Gilles. *Coldness and Cruelty*. In *Masochism: "Coldness and Cruelty" by Gilles Deleuze and "Venus in Furs" by Leopold von Sacher-Masoch*. Translated by Jean McNeil. New York: Zone Books, 1989.

Deng Jiuping and Yu Haiying, eds. *Tiandong cao: yi guxiang* (Chinese asparagus: remembrances of the native land). Beijing: Zhongguo duiwai fanyi, 1995.

Denton, Kirk A., ed. *Modern Chinese Literary Thought: Writings on Literature, 1893–1945*. Stanford, Calif.: Stanford University Press, 1996.

Derrida, Jacques. *Of Grammatology*. Translated by Gayatri C. Spivak. Baltimore: Johns Hopkins University Press, 1974.

———. *Positions*. Translated by Alan Bass. Chicago: University of Chicago Press, 1981.

———. *Specters of Marx: The State of the Debt, the Work of Mourning, and the New International*. Translated by Peggy Kamuf. New York: Routledge, 1994.

Ding Ling. *Ding Ling daibiaozuo* (Representative works by Ding Ling). Edited by Jiao Shangzhi and Liu Chunsheng. Zhengzhou: Henan renmin, 1988.

———. *Ding Ling wenji* (Collected works of Ding Ling). Shanghai: Yiwen shudian, 1936.

Dittmer, Lowell. *China's Continuous Revolution: The Post-Liberation Epoch, 1949–1981*. Berkeley: University of California Press, 1987.

Doleželová-Velingerová, Milena, ed. *The Chinese Novel at the Turn of the Century*. Toronto: University of Toronto Press, 1980.

Duke, Michael S., ed. *Modern Chinese Women Writers: Critical Appraisals*. New York: M. E. Sharpe, 1989.

Eagleton, Terry. *Against the Grain: Essays, 1975–1985*. London: Verso, 1986.

Feng Menglong. *Qingshi leilüe* (A classified history of passion). Edited by Zou Xuemin. Changsha: Yuelu shushe, 1984.

Ferguson, Priscilla Parkhurst. *Paris as Revolution: Writing the Nineteenth-Century City*. Berkeley: University of California Press, 1994.

Feuerwerker, Yi-tsi Mei. *Ding Ling's Fiction: Ideology and Narrative in Modern Chinese Literature*. Cambridge, Mass.: Harvard University Press, 1982.

Foster, Hal, ed. *Vision and Visuality*. Seattle: Bay Press, 1988.

Foucault, Michel. *Discipline and Punish: The Birth of the Prison*. Translated by Alan Sheridan. New York: Vintage, 1979.

———. *History of Sexuality, Vol. I: An Introduction*. New York: Vintage, 1980.

———. *Madness and Civilization: A History of Insanity in the Age of Reason*. Translated by Richard Howard. New York: Vintage, 1973.

Freud, Sigmund. *Civilization and Its Discontents*. Translated by James Strachey. New York: Norton, 1961.

———. *Collected Papers*. New York: Basic Books, 1959.

———. *Freud: On War, Sex, and Neurosis*. New York: Arts and Sciences Press, 1947.

———. *Inhibitions, Symptoms, and Anxiety*. Revised and edited by James Strachey. New York: Norton, 1989.

——. *Sexuality and the Psychology of Love.* Edited with introduction by Philip Rieff. New York: Collier Books, 1963.
——. *The Standard Edition of the Complete Psychological Works of Sigmund Freud.* 24 vols. Translated by James Strachey. London: Hogarth Press, 1961.
Gerstlacher, Anna, Ruth Keen, Wolfgang Kubin, Margit Miosga, and Jenny Schon, eds. *Woman and Literature in China.* Bochum: Brockmeyer, 1985.
Gilman, Sander. *Franz Kafka: The Jewish Patient.* New York: Routledge, 1995.
Gipoulon, Catherine, trans. *Pierre de l'oiseau Jingwei: Qiu Jin, femme et révolutionnaire en Chine au XIXe siècle.* Paris: des femmes, 1976.
Guo Zhenyi. *Zhongguo xiaoshuo shi* (History of Chinese fiction). Changsha: Commercial Press, 1939.
Habermas, Jürgen. *The Philosophical Discourse of Modernity: Twelve Lectures.* Translated by Frederick Lawrence. Cambridge, Mass.: MIT Press, 1987.
Hanan, Patrick, trans. *The Sea of Regret: Two Turn-of-the-Century Chinese Romantic Novels.* Honolulu: University of Hawaii Press, 1995.
Harvey, David. *The Condition of Postmodernity: An Enquiry into the Origins of Cultural Change.* Cambridge, Mass.: Blackwell, 1989.
Hawkes, David, trans. *The Story of the Stone: A Chinese Novel by Cao Xueqin in Five Volumes.* London: Penguin, 1973.
He Dun. *Shenghuo wuzui* (Life is not a crime). Beijing: Huayi, 1995.
Heller, Agnes. *Everyday Life.* Translated by G. L. Campbell. London: Routledge & Kegan Paul, 1984.
Horkheimer, Max, and Theodor W. Adorno. *Dialectic of Enlightenment.* Translated by John Cumming. New York: Seabury Press, 1972.
Hsia, C. T. *A History of Modern Chinese Fiction, 1917–1957.* New Haven, Conn.: Yale University Press, 1961.
Hsia, Tsi-an. *The Gate of Darkness: Studies on the Leftist Literary Movement in China.* Seattle: University of Washington Press, 1968.
Hsü, Kai-yu, and Ting Wang, eds. *Literature of the People's Republic of China.* Bloomington: Indiana University Press, 1980.
Hu Shi [Hu Shih]. *Hu Shi wencun* (Selected works of Hu Shi). Taipei: Yuandong, 1971.
Hu Wanchun and Fu Chaowu. *Jiating wenti* (Family problem). Shanghai: Shanghai wenhua, 1964.
Huang Lin. *Jindai wenxue piping shi* (History of modern literary criticism). Shanghai: Shanghai guji, 1993.
Hutcheon, Linda. *The Politics of Postmodernism.* London: Routledge, 1989.
Jackson, Stanley W. *Melancholia and Depression: From Hippocratic Times to Modern Times.* New Haven, Conn.: Yale University Press, 1986.
Jameson, Fredric. *Marxism and Form: Twentieth-Century Dialectical Theories of Literature.* Princeton, N.J.: Princeton University Press, 1971.

———. *The Political Unconscious: Narrative as a Socially Symbolic Act.* Ithaca, N.Y.: Cornell University Press, 1981.
———. *Postmodernism, or, The Cultural Logic of Late Capitalism.* Durham, N.C.: Duke University Press, 1991.
———. *Signatures of the Visible.* New York: Routledge, 1990.
Jia Zhifang, Tang Jinhai, Zhang Xiaoyun, and Chen Sihe, eds. *Ba Jin zuopin pinglun ji* (Essays on Ba Jin's works). Beijing: Zhongguo wenlian, 1985.
Jian Yizhi, Chen Erdong, Zhao Shaoliang, and Wang Xiaochuan, eds. *Zhongguo jindai wenlun xuan* (Selections from early modern Chinese literary criticism). Beijing: Renmin wenxue, 1962.
Karatani Kojin. *Origins of Modern Japanese Literature.* Edited and translated by Brett de Bary. Durham, N.C.: Duke University Press, 1993.
Kirkby, R. J. R. *Urbanization in China: Town and Country in a Developing Economy, 1949–2000 A.D.* New York: Columbia University Press, 1985.
Kristeva, Julia. *Black Sun: Depression and Melancholia.* Translated by Leon S. Roudiez. New York: Columbia University Press, 1989.
———. *The Kristeva Reader.* Edited by Toril Moi. New York: Columbia University Press, 1986.
Kwok, R. Yin-Wang, et al., eds. *Chinese Urban Reform: What Model Now?* Armonk, N.Y.: M. E. Sharpe, 1990.
Lacan, Jacques. *Écrits: A Selection.* Translated by Alan Sheridan. New York: Norton, 1977.
———. *The Four Fundamental Concepts of Psycho-Analysis.* Edited by Jacques-Alan Miller. Translated by Alan Sheridan. New York: Norton, 1977.
Laing, Ellen Johnston. *The Winking Owl: Art in the People's Republic of China.* Berkeley: University of California Press, 1988.
Lang, Olga. *Pa Chin and His Writings: Chinese Youth Between the Two Revolutions.* Cambridge, Mass.: Harvard University Press, 1967.
Lau, Joseph S. M., C. T. Hsia, and Leo Ou-fan Lee, eds. *Modern Chinese Stories and Novellas, 1919–1949.* New York: Columbia University Press, 1981.
Lee, Leo Ou-fan. *The Romantic Generation of Modern Chinese Writers.* Cambridge, Mass.: Harvard University Press, 1973.
———. *Voices from the Iron House: A Study of Lu Xun.* Bloomington: Indiana University Press, 1987.
———, ed. *Lu Xun and His Legacy.* Berkeley: University of California Press, 1980.
Levenson, Joseph R. *Revolution and Cosmopolitanism: The Western Stage and the Chinese Stages.* Berkeley: University of California Press, 1971.
Levin, David Michael, ed. *Pathologies of the Modern Self: Postmodern Studies on Narcissism, Schizophrenia, and Depression.* New York: New York University Press, 1987.

Lewis, John Wilson, ed. *The City in Communist China*. Stanford, Calif.: Stanford University Press, 1971.

Li Cunguang, ed. *Ba Jin yanjiu ziliao* (Research materials on Ba Jin). Fuzhou: Haixia wenyi, 1985.

Li, Wai-yee. *Enchantment and Disenchantment: Love and Illusion in Chinese Literature*. Princeton, N.J.: Princeton University Press, 1993.

Li Yang. *Kangzheng suming zhi lu: shehui zhuyi xianshi zhuyi (1942–1976) yanjiu* (The path of resisting destiny: a study of socialist realism [1942–1976]). Changchun: Shidai wenyi, 1993.

Li Zehou. *Zhongguo jindai sixiangshi lun* (Essays on modern Chinese intellectual history). Taipei: Fengyun shidai, 1990.

——— and Liu Zaifu. *Gaobie geming: huiwang ershi shiji Zhongguo* (Farewell to revolution: review of twentieth-century China). Hong Kong: Cosmos, 1995.

Li Zongying and Zhang Mengyang, eds. *Liushi nianlai Lu Xun yanjiu lunwen xuan* (Selected essays of Lu Xun studies in the past sixty years). 2 vols. Beijing: Zhongguo shehui kexue, 1982.

Liang Qichao. *Yinbingshi heji-wenji* (Collected writings from the ice-drinker's studio: collected essays). Shanghai: China Books, 1936.

Lin Gang, ed. *Fengyu zhong de lüdao—xiandai jiaju* (Safe haven in a storm—modern living). Beijing: Zhongguo shangye, 1995.

Lin Yaode [Lin Yao-te]. *1947 Gaosha baihe* (1947—Lilium formosanum). Taipei: Unitas, 1990.

Lin Yü-sheng. *The Crisis of Chinese Consciousness: Radical Antitraditionalism in the May Fourth Era*. Madison: University of Wisconsin Press, 1979.

Link, E. Perry, Jr. *Mandarin Ducks and Butterflies: Popular Fiction in Early Twentieth-Century Chinese Cities*. Berkeley: University of California Press, 1981.

Liu Heng. *Black Snow*. Translated by Howard Goldblatt. New York: Atlantic Monthly Press, 1993.

Liu, Kang, and Xiaobing Tang, eds. *Politics, Ideology, and Literary Discourse in Modern China: Theoretical Interventions and Cultural Critique*. Durham, N.C.: Duke University Press, 1993.

Liu, Lydia H. *Translingual Practice: Literature, National Culture, and Translated Modernity—China, 1900–1937*. Stanford, Calif.: Stanford University Press, 1995.

Liu Zaifu. *Liu Zaifu lunwen xuan* (Selection of essays by Liu Zaifu). Hong Kong: Dadi, 1986.

Lu Xun [Lu Hsün]. *A Brief History of Chinese Fiction*. Translated by Yang Hsien-yi and Gladys Yang. Peking: Foreign Languages Press, 1959.

———. *Lu Xun quanji* (The complete works of Lu Xun). Beijing: Renmin wenxue, 1981.

———. *Lu Xun: "Diary of a Madman" and Other Stories*. Translated by William A. Lyell. Honolulu: University of Hawaii Press, 1990.

———. *Silent China: Selected Writings of Lu Xun.* Edited and translated by Gladys Yang. London: Oxford University Press, 1973.
———. *Zhongguo xiaoshuo shilüe* (A brief history of Chinese fiction). Beijing: Beixin shuju, 1937.
Lukács, Georg. *Realism in Our Time: Literature and Class Struggle.* Translated by John Mander and Necke Mander. New York: Torchbooks-Harper, 1964.
Lyell, William A. *Lu Hsün's Vision of Reality.* Berkeley: University of California Press, 1976.
Lynch, Kevin. *The Image of the City.* Cambridge, Mass.: Technology Press, 1960.
McDougall, Bonnie S., and Kam Louie, *The Literature of China in the Twentieth Century.* New York: Columbia University Press, 1997.
Malmqvist, Goran, ed. *Modern Chinese Literature and Its Social Context.* Nobel Symposium (32). Stockholm, 1977.
Mao Dun. *Midnight.* Translated by Hsu Meng-hsiung and A. C. Barnes. Peking: Foreign Languages Press, 1957.
———. *Yexiangwei* (The wild roses). Shanghai: Dajiang shupu, 1929.
———. *Ziye* (Midnight). Beijing: Renmin wenxue, 1988.
Mao Zedong. *Ten More Poems of Mao Tse-tung.* Hong Kong: Eastern Horizon Press, 1967.
Meng Yue and Dai Jinhua. *Fuchu lishi dibiao: xiandai funü wenxue yanjiu* (Emerging from history: studies in modern women's literature). Zhengzhou: Henan renmin, 1989.
Mi Hedu. *Hongweibing zhe yidai* (The red guard generation). Hong Kong: Joint Publishing, 1993.
Moretti, Franco, *The Way of the World: The Bildungsroman in European Culture.* London: Verso, 1987.
Mowry, Hua-yuan Li. *Chinese Love Stories from the "Ch'ing-shih."* Hamden, Conn.: Archon Books, 1983.
Mulvey, Laura. *Visual and Other Pleasures.* Bloomington: Indiana University Press, 1989.
Newton, Judith, and Deborah Rosenfelt. *Feminist Criticism and Social Change: Sex, Class and Race in Literature and Culture.* New York: Methuen, 1985.
Nietzsche, Friedrich. *On the Genealogy of Morals.* Translated by Walter Kaufman and R. J. Hollingdale. New York: Vintage, 1968.
Outram, Dorinda. *The Body and the French Revolution: Sex, Class, and Political Culture.* New Haven, Conn.: Yale University Press, 1989.
Peasant Paintings from Huhsien County. Beijing: Foreign Languages Press, 1974.
Pensky, Max. *Melancholy Dialectics: Walter Benjamin and the Play of Mourning.* Amherst: University of Massachusetts Press, 1993.
Perkins, David. *Is Literary History Possible?* Baltimore: Johns Hopkins University Press, 1992.

Průšek, Jaroslav. *The Lyrical and the Epic: Studies of Modern Chinese Literature.* Edited by Leo Ou-fan Lee. Bloomington: Indiana University Press, 1980.

Reik, Theodor. *Masochism in Modern Man.* Translated by Margaret H. Beigel and Gertrud M. Kurth. New York: Farrar, Straus, 1941.

Ren Fangqiu. *Zhongguo jindai wenxue zuojia lun* (Essays on modern Chinese writers). Zhengzhou: Henan renmin, 1984.

Richett, Adele Austin, ed. *Chinese Approaches to Literature from Confucius to Liang Ch'i-ch'ao.* Princeton, N.J.: Princeton University Press, 1978.

Rose, Gillian. *Feminism and Geography: The Limits of Geographical Knowledge.* Minneapolis: University of Minnesota Press, 1993.

Rose, Jacqueline. *Sexuality in the Field of Vision.* London: Verso, 1986.

Rowe, Colin, and Fred Koetter. *Collage City.* Cambridge, Mass.: MIT Press, 1978.

Roy, David T. *Kuo Mo-jo: The Early Years.* Cambridge, Mass.: Harvard University Press, 1971.

Schram, Stuart R., ed. *Authority, Participation and Cultural Change in China.* Cambridge: Cambridge University Press, 1973.

Schudson, Michael. *Advertising, the Uneasy Persuasion: Its Dubious Impact on American Society.* New York: Basic Books, 1984.

Semsel, George S., Hou Jianping, and Xia Hong, eds. *Chinese Film Theory: A Guide to the New Era.* New York: Praeger, 1990.

Sennett, Richard, ed. *Classic Essays on the Culture of Cities.* New York: Meredith, 1969.

Sit, Victor F. S., ed. *Chinese Cities: The Growth of the Metropolis Since 1949.* Oxford: Oxford University Press, 1985.

Soja, Edward W. *Postmodern Geographies: The Reassertion of Space in Critical Social Theory.* London: Verso, 1989.

Sontag, Susan. *Illness as Metaphor and AIDS and Its Metaphors.* New York: Doubleday, 1990.

Sorlin, Pierre. *European Cinemas, European Societies, 1939–1990.* London: Routledge, 1991.

Sparke, Penny. *An Introduction to Design and Culture in the Twentieth Century.* London: Allen and Unwin, 1986.

Spence, Jonathan D. *The Gate of Heavenly Peace: The Chinese and Their Revolution, 1895–1980.* New York: Penguin, 1981.

———. *The Search for Modern China.* New York: Norton, 1990.

Spivak, Gayatri C. *In Other Worlds: Essays in Cultural Politics.* New York: Methuen, 1987.

Strassburg, Richard E., and Waldermar A. Nielsen, eds. *Beyond the Open Door: Contemporary Paintings from the People's Republic of China.* Pasadena, Calif.: Pacific Asia Museum, 1987.

Su Tong. *Raise the Red Lantern.* Translated by Michael Duke. New York: William Morrow, 1993.

———. *Qiqie chengqun* (Wives and concubines). Taipei: Yuanliu, 1990.

Tang, Xiaobing. *Global Space and the Nationalist Discourse of Modernity: The Historical Thinking of Liang Qichao.* Stanford, Calif.: Stanford University Press, 1996.

———, ed. *Zai jiedu: dazhong wenyi yu yishi xingtai* (Rereading: people's literature and arts movement and ideology). Hong Kong: Oxford University Press, 1993.

Taylor, Charles. *Sources of the Self: The Making of the Modern Identity.* Cambridge, Mass.: Harvard University Press, 1989.

Taylor, Ronald, trans. *Aesthetics and Politics: Debates Between Ernst Bloch, Georg Lukács, Bertolt Brecht, Walter Benjamin, Theodor Adorno.* London: NLB, 1977.

Wakeman, Frederic, Jr. *Policing Shanghai, 1927–1937.* Berkeley: University of California Press, 1995.

———, and Wen-hsin Yeh, eds. *Shanghai Sojourners.* Berkeley: Institute of East Asian Studies, University of California, 1992.

Wang Anyi. *Baotown.* Translated by Martha Avery. New York: Penguin, 1989.

———. *Fuxi yu muxi de shenhua* (Patrilineal and matrilineal myths). Hangzhou: Zhejiang wenyi, 1994.

———. *Huangshan zhi lian* (Love on a barren mountain). Hong Kong: South China Press, 1988.

———. *Jishi yu xugou—chuangzuo shijie fangfa zhi yizhong* (Records and fiction: one method of creating the world). Beijing: Renmin wenxue, 1993.

———. *Pugongying* (Dandelions). Shanghai: Shanghai wenyi, 1988.

———. *Xianggang de qing yu ai* (Love and sentiment in Hong Kong). Beijing: Zuojia, 1996.

Wang, Ban. *The Sublime Figure of History: Aesthetics and Politics in Twentieth-Century China.* Stanford, Calif.: Stanford University Press, 1997.

Wang, Chi-chen, trans. *Ah Q and Others: Selected Stories of Lusin.* New York: Columbia University Press, 1941.

Wang, David Der-wei. *Fictional Realism in Twentieth-Century China: Mao Dun, Lao She, Shen Congwen.* New York: Columbia University Press, 1992.

———. *Fin-de-siècle Splendor: Repressed Modernities of Late Qing Fiction, 1849–1911.* Stanford, Calif.: Stanford University Press, 1997.

Wang Guowei. *Wang Guowei xiansheng sanzhong* (Three works by Wang Guowei). Taipei: Guomin, 1960.

Wang, Jing, ed. *China's Avant-Garde Fiction.* Durham, N.C.: Duke University Press, 1998.

———. *High Culture Fever: Politics, Aesthetics, and Ideology in Deng's China.* Berkeley: University of California Press, 1996.

———. *The Story of Stone: Intertextuality, Ancient Chinese Stone Lore, and the Stone Symbolism in "Dream of the Red Chamber," "Water Margin," and "The Journey to the West."* Durham, N.C.: Duke University Press, 1992.
Wang Shiqing. *Lu Xun: A Biography*. Translated by Zhang Peiji. Beijing: Foreign Languages Press, 1984.
———. *Lu Xun zhuan* (Biography of Lu Xun). Beijing: Zhongguo qingnian, 1959.
Wang Xiaoming, ed. *Ershi shiji Zhongguo wenxue shilun* (Essays on twentieth-century Chinese literary history). 3 vols. Shanghai: Dongfang chuban zhongxin, 1997.
Wang Yao, ed. *Beijing daxue Lu Xun danchen yibai zhounian jinian wenji* (Commemorative essays on the centenary of Lu Xun from Peking University). Beijing: Peking University Press, 1982.
Wasserstrom, Jeffrey N. *Student Protests in Twentieth-Century China: The View from Shanghai*. Stanford, Calif.: Stanford University Press, 1991.
Wei, Betty Peh-T'i. *Shanghai: Crucible of Modern China*. Hong Kong: Oxford University Press, 1987.
Wei Shaochang, ed. *Wu Jianren yanjiu ziliao* (Research materials on Wu Jianren). Shanghai: Shanghai guji, 1980.
White, Gordon. *Riding the Tiger: The Politics of Economic Reform in Post-Mao China*. Stanford, Calif.: Stanford University Press, 1993.
Whyte, Martin King, and William L. Parish. *Urban Life in Contemporary China*. Chicago: University of Chicago Press, 1984.
Widmer, Ellen, and David Der-wei Wang, eds. *From May Fourth to June Fourth: Fiction and Film in Twentieth-Century China*. Cambridge, Mass.: Harvard University Press, 1993.
Williams, Raymond. *The Country and the City*. New York: Oxford University Press, 1973.
———. *The Politics of Modernism: Against the New Conformists*. Edited with introduction by Tony Pinkney. London: Verso, 1989.
Wong, Yoon Wah. *Essays on Chinese Literature: A Comparative Approach*. Singapore: Singapore University Press, 1988.
Wu Jianren. *Qing bian* (Passion transformed). Shanghai: China Eastern Normal University Press, 1993.
Xiao Ye. *Wudi haixing* (Legless starfish). Taipei: Yuanliu, 1989.
Yang, Gladys, and Hsien-yi Yang, trans. *Lu Xun: Selected Stories*. New York: Norton: 1977.
Yeh Chia-ying. *Wang Guowei ji qi wenxue piping* (Wang Guowei and his literary criticism). Hong Kong: China Books, 1980.
Yu Hua. *The Past and the Punishments*. Translated by Andrew F. Jones. Honolulu: University of Hawaii Press, 1996.

———. *Shibasui chumen yuanxing* (On the road at age eighteen). Taipei: Yuanliu, 1990.
———. *Shishi ru yan* (This world of clouds). Taipei: Yuanliu, 1990.
Yu Simu. *Zuojia Ba Jin* (On the writer Ba Jin). Hong Kong: Nanguo, 1964.
Yuan Jin. *Yuanyang hudie pai* (The mandarin duck and butterfly school). Shanghai: Shanghai shudian, 1994.
Yuan Ke. *Zhongguo gudai shenhua* (Ancient Chinese myths). Shanghai: Commercial Press, 1951.
Yuan Liangjun, ed. *Ding Ling yanjiu ziliao* (Research materials on Ding Ling). Tianjin: Tianjin renmin, 1982.
Zeitlin, Judith T. *Historian of the Strange: Pu Songling and the Chinese Classical Tale*. Stanford, Calif.: Stanford University Press, 1993.
Zhang Ailing. *Zhang Ailing quanji* (The complete works of Zhang Ailing). Vol. 3. Taipei: Huangguan, 1992.
Zhang Geng, ed. *Zhongguo xin wenyi daxi, 1949–1966: xiju ji* (Compendium of new Chinese arts and literature, 1949–1966: the drama collection). Beijing: Zhongguo wenlian, 1991.
Zhang Minquan. *Ba Jin xiaoshuo de shengming tixi* (The life forms in Ba Jin's fiction). Shanghai: Shanghai wenyi, 1989.
Zhang Ruoying. *Zhongguo xin wenxueshi ziliao* (Documents from the history of Chinese new literature). Shanghai: Guangmin shuju, 1934.
Zhang, Xudong. *Chinese Modernism in the Era of Reforms: Cultural Fever, Avant-Garde Fiction, and the New Chinese Cinema*. Durham, N.C.: Duke University Press, 1997.
Zhang, Yingjin. *The City in Modern Chinese Literature and Film: Configurations of Space, Time, and Gender*. Stanford, Calif.: Stanford University Press, 1996.
Zhang Zhanbing and Song Yifu. *Zhongguo: Mao Zedong re* (China: Mao Zedong fever). Taiyuan: Beiyue wenyi, 1991.
Zhao Jiabi, ed. *Xiandai Zhongguo wenxue daxi* (Compendium of modern Chinese literature). Shanghai: Liangyou, 1935–36.
Zhejiang Lu Xun Studies Society. *Lu Xun yanjiu lunwen xuan* (Essays from Lu Xun studies). Hangzhou: Zhejiang wenyi, 1983.
Zito, Angela, and Tani E. Barlow, eds. *Body, Subject, and Power in China*. Chicago: University of Chicago Press, 1994.

INDEX

A Ying, 15, 24–25, 32, 38
Adorno, Theodor, 273, 312n, 314n
All Story Monthly (Yueyue xiaoshuo), 14, 15
Althusser, Louis, 171
Anderson, Marston, 69–70, 72, 91–92
anti-imperialism. *See* imperialism
anxiety: in *Black Snow,* 255–58, 261; in *Cold Nights,* 140, 145, 147, 152; in *Diary of a Madman,* 68; of everyday life, 4, 154, 214, 283–84, 292, 311, 312–15; and history as mirror, 228, 239, 335; and homesickness, 85; and idealism, 325; in the lyrical age, 3, 167, 179, 193; and modernism, 199, 207n, 224; and postmodernism, 197, 199, 267n; post-utopian, 257, 261, 332; and revolution, 106, 113; in *The Sea of Regret,* 32, 34–47
avant-garde fiction (experimental fiction), 198–224, 225–44, 302, 304, 331

Ba Jin, 2, 131–32, 134, 137–38, 144, 159–60. Works: *Family* (Jia), 81, 137, 144; *Leisure Garden* (Qiyuan), 138–39, 144; *Little People and Little Things* (Xiaoren xiaoshi), 137. See also *Cold Nights*
Balzac, Honoré de, 203, 219, 231
Barlow, Tani, 99n, 104, 113
Barthes, Roland, 80, 201, 225, 233n, 302
Baudelaire, Charles, 5, 201, 216, 221, 338
Baudrillard, Jean, 242n, 298–300, 305, 307, 308
Beijing, 22, 33, 245–46, 273; in cinema, 4, 246–47, 249–51, 253–72
Beijing nizao. See *Good Morning, Beijing*

Benjamin, Walter, 201–2, 206, 207n, 219, 221, 268, 276n, 328, 338
Benming nian. See *Black Snow*
Berman, Marshall, 56
bildungsroman, 200, 202–4, 205, 206, 334
Black Snow (Benming nian), 249, 250–51, 253–61; and aesthetics of depth, 257–61, 271; compared with *Good Morning, Beijing,* 271–72; intellectualizing in, 256–57
boredom: in avant-garde fiction, 213, 217, 223; in Ding Ling's fiction, 101, 102, 104, 121
Boxer Rebellion, 22–23, 28–30, 32, 33, 34–38
Brown, Wendy, 155–56

Calinescu, Matei, 53
Cao Yu, 152, 189
capitalist realism, 3, 290, 292
catastrophe (*haojie*), 206, 212
Chambers, Ross, 339, 340n
Chang, Eileen. See Zhang Ailing
Changsha, 284, 286, 290, 296, 297, 301, 304, 306, 307
cheng. See sincerity
Chen Pingyuan, 11–12, 345n
Chen Ran, 339n, 342
Chen Sihe, 55n, 320n, 322, 345n
Chen Xiaoming, 256n, 257–58, 301–3, 305–6
Chen Yun, 167–69, 177n. See also *The Young Generation*
Chinese Youth (Zhongguo qingnian), 174–75, 189, 277
Chongqing, 131, 134, 149, 150, 155. See also *Cold Nights*

Chow, Rey, 16n, 44–45, 119n
cinema, 121–22, 166, 167, 194, 246–72; Fourth Generation, 249–50; Fifth Generation, 249–50; in *The Town of Olive in 1944,* 226–34. See also *Black Snow;* cinematographic representation; *Good Morning, Beijing*; New China cinema
cinematographic representation: in *Nineteen Thirty-four Escapes,* 241; of Shanghai, 100–101; in *The Town of Olive in 1944,* 230–32, 234. See also cinema; visuality
city, 4; and cinema, 246–72; in Ding Ling's fiction, 98–99, 105, 111–12, 122, 129; and narrativity, 219–20; and nationalism, 106–7; and native-land literature, 85; and "new fiction of the city dwellers" (xin shimin xiaoshuo), 301; in lyrical age, 177–78, 180–83; in postrevolutionary age, 246–72, 274–78, 283–90, 292, 297, 300–302, 306–15; in Su Tong's fiction, 214–17, 218–23, 235–36; in Yu Hua's fiction, 212–15. See also Beijing; *Black Snow*; country; *Good Morning, Beijing*; He Dun; Shanghai; *Shanghai, Spring 1930*; urbanization
Clark, Paul, 252
A Classified History of Passion (Qingshi leilüe), 26, 29
Cold Nights (Hanye), 131–60; and deconstructive writing, 154; and individual failure, 133–35, 138–40, 147–50, 154–56; legacy of, 159–60; and masochism, 135, 140–53, 156; moral discourse of, 157–58; and *ressentiment,* 135, 152–56; and tuberculosis, 134, 135, 140, 145–47, 152, 153–54, 156
collectivism, 159, 165, 175, 179, 181, 184, 196, 211, 244, 246, 248, 258, 270, 279, 290, 301, 303, 304, 335, 339
collectivization, 164, 194
colonialism, 28, 53, 99, 101, 334
comedy, 26–27, 28, 30
Confucianism, 23, 26, 58, 144, 152, 179, 336n
consumer society, 3, 13, 106, 199, 232, 290; in avant-garde fiction, 212, 213, 222; in Ding Ling's fiction, 109, 121–23, 126; in He Dun's fiction, 285, 298–300, 304, 307; in lyrical age, 177; in postrevolutionary age, 260, 261, 265, 273–77, 280, 283–84, 292, 294, 308–15; in Wang Anyi's fiction, 321
cosmopolitanism, 174, 345
country, 4, 75; in cinema, 248, 250, 252; as the city's other, 111–12, 284; in postrevolutionary society, 274–75; in revolutionary society, 282–83; in Su Tong's fiction, 214, 217, 218, 223, 235–36; in Yu Hua's fiction, 214. See also city
Cultural Revolution, 4, 54, 55, 165, 167, 173, 175, 181, 182n, 206n, 208, 212, 213, 236, 242, 250, 273, 276, 296, 324, 345

Dai Jinhua, 98, 113, 116, 144, 187n
Deleuze, Gilles, 143, 145, 148, 149, 151, 152–53
Derrida, Jacques, 64, 329n, 337, 342
De Sica, Vittorio, 251–52
desire: in *Black Snow,* 255, 257, 260; in *Cold Nights,* 145, 150, 152, 154–55; in *Diary of a Madman,* 68, 73; in *Good Morning, Beijing,* 264; and the mirror of history, 242; and nostalgia, 86; postrevolutionary, 213, 285, 294, 297, 298–300, 302, 306; in *The Sea of Regret,* 2, 39, 41, 45; in *Shanghai,*

Spring 1930, 116–18, 121, 127; "spectacles of," 302–3, 305, 307; tragedy, 27; urban setting, 110–12. *See also* passion; sexuality; utopianism
"Diary of a Madman" (Kuangren riji), 2, 42n, 49, 54; absent father in, 81, 144; deconstructive reading in, 64–66, 67, 70, 73; dual ending of, 68–69; *feng* and *kuang* (madness), 57–60; history in, 64–65, 68–69, 72, 73; legacy of, 62–63; and New Culture movement, 66–67; paranoia in, 49, 57, 69, 72; and realism, 60–61, 69–70, 72
Di Baoxian (Pingdeng ge), 28, 29. *See also* "Tang Sheng"
Ding Ling, 2, 3, 97–99, 102–3, 107–9, 113–14, 128–30, 138, 155, 160, 343. Works: "Daylight" (Ri), 100–102; "Diary of a Suicide," 102–3; *Flood* (Shui), 129; *In Darkness,* 114; "In the Hospital" (Zai yiyuan zhong), 130; "Mengke," 98, 99; "Miss Sophia's Diary" (Shafei nüshi de riji), 98, 111, 158; "One Day" (Yitian), 128n; *Wei Hu,* 110n. See also *Shanghai, Spring 1930*
Dittmer, Lowell, 171n, 175n, 189
Doleželová-Velingerová, Milena, 30, 47
drama, 3, 4, 12, 26, 27–28, 55, 194–95, 345; golden age of, 166; "model theater," 167; opera, 167; spoken (*huaju*), 166; *tanci,* 167. See also *The Young Generation*
Dream of the Red Chamber (Honglou meng) (The Story of the Stone), 19, 27, 46
Duras, Marguerite, 316, 317, 338

Egan, Michael, 31
Enlightenment, 11, 52, 301, 302, 304

epistemology: and Chinese modernism, 54; and "Diary of a Madman," 59, 72; "epistemic violence," 50–51; and late Qing fiction, 12–13
ethnic minorities, 227–28, 229, 244
experimental fiction. *See* avant-garde fiction
exteriority: aesthetics of, 3; in avant-garde fiction, 209; and interior design, 296; in painting, 282; and the "politicized body," 127–28; revolutionary desire for, 123; transition from interiority to, 97, 159–60

father figure: in avant-garde fiction, 203, 204, 209, 305; in *Cold Nights,* 143–45; in "Diary of a Madman," 81, 144; in "My Native Land," 81; in *Sadness for the Pacific,* 330–36; in *The Young Generation,* 181, 185, 187
femininity, 16, 38–46, 107, 109, 116, 121–26, 151, 342. *See also* feminism; gender; masculinity
feminism, 20, 98–99, 186–87. *See also* femininity; gender; masculinity
feng (madness), 58–59, 217. See also *kuang*
Feng Menglong, 29; *A Classified History of Passion* (Qingshi leilüe), 26, 29; and "passionism," 26
Ferguson, Priscilla Parkhurst, 122
Feuerwerker, Yi-tsi Mei, 70, 97, 103n, 128n
fiction (*xiaoshuo*), 11–12, 14–15, 129, 301, 345. *See also* novel
Fifth Generation. *See* cinema: Fifth Generation
Flaubert, Gustave, 103n, 340
folklore, 165, 186
Foucault, Michel, 59, 118
French Revolution, 16, 52, 123, 137, 208

Freud, Sigmund, 23, 34, 37, 39, 40n, 41, 66, 114, 116, 327
Fu Lin, 21, 24, 26, 28, 30, 31, 32; *Stones in the Sea* (Qin hai shi; Bird, sea, stone), 21–24, 28, 31–33, 43

Ge Fei, 214, 301
gender: in *Cold Nights,* 151; in Ding Ling's fiction, 104, 107–109, 116, 119–21; and feminist writing, 98–99; in *Hello, My Younger Brother,* 313; in late Qing, 16; and postmodern melancholy, 339; and revolution, 123–26; in *The Sea of Regret,* 33, 38–46; in *The Young Generation,* 185–87. *See also* femininity; feminism; masculinity
Gilman, Sander, 145, 148
Gissing, George, 154–55
Gogol, Nikolay, 57
Goldblatt, Howard, 258n, 274n
Good Morning, Beijing (Beijing nizao), 250, 253, 261–72; and the "collage city," 267–68; compared with *Black Snow,* 271–72; and legitimation of the market, 262–64; and rhetoric of compromise, 264–65, 271; and self-transformation, 268–70; and temporality, 265–66; and Third World condition, 266–68
Great Leap Forward, 171, 173
Guangzhou, 276, 294, 297
guilt: Nietzsche on, 66; in postrevolutionary culture, 286; in *The Sea of Regret,* 39, 40–42, 44, 45; and *The Young Generation,* 189
Guomindang (KMT), 185. *See also* Nationalist government
Guo Moruo (Kuo Mo-jo), 112, 163–64, 172n
Guo Zhenyi, 46
guxiang. See native land
"Guxiang." *See* "My Native Land"

Habermas, Jürgen, 52
hagiography: and pathography in *The Sea of Regret,* 2, 20–21, 39, 42, 47, 48
Hanan, Patrick, 16, 21
Hanye. See Cold Nights
haojie. See catastrophe
Harvey, David, 270
He Dun, 284, 290, 296, 297, 300–303, 304, 306, 314–15. Works: *Hello, My Younger Brother* (Didi nihao), 296–300, 306–7, 313–15; *I Don't Care* (Wo bu xiangshi), 284, 306; *Life Is Not a Crime* (Shenghuo wuzui), 284–87, 288, 296n, 301n, 306
Hegel, G. W. F. (Hegelianism), 51, 52, 113, 153, 208, 303, 344
Heller, Agnes, 278–79
Henhai. See The Sea of Regret
heroic, the: in Ba Jin, 138; in "Diary of a Madman," 72; "heroic melancholy," 328, 337–38; and Mao Zedong's poetry, 165; in "My Native Land," 82, 95; and New China cinema, 227, 248; and postrevolutionary self-transformation, 270; and quotidian dialectic, 1, 3, 4–6, 47, 344; and revolutionary mass culture, 175, 184, 189, 283; in *Shanghai, Spring 1930,* 116, 126; and socialist realism, 274; in Wang Anyi's fiction, 322, 323, 324, 332, 335; and Xiao Ye, 229. *See also* quotidian
Hiroshima, 229–30, 338
Hong Kong, 287–90, 346, 347
Hsia, C. T., 134, 187n
Hsia, Tsi-an, 97, 107n, 108
Hsiao Yeh. *See* Xiao Ye
Hsü, Kai-yu, 177
Huang Zongying, 194
humanism, 90, 128, 149–50, 186–187, 304, 312, 334, 342. *See also* liberalism
Hu Shi, 67

Hu Yepin, 107–08
hyperstimulation, 3, 33–38, 47. *See also* trauma

ideology, 3, 51, 52, 54, 56, 61–62, 99, 113, 160, 233, 290; of asceticism, 116, 126, 128; in *Cold Nights,* 135, 150, 152, 153–55; of compromise, 264–65, 271; of consumption, 298–300; critique from margins, 227–28, 244; of everyday life, 236, 294; ideologeme, 139–40; and Lu Xun studies, 60–61; in lyrical age, 171, 174, 183; of marketization, 273; of modernism, 199, 201, 210, 217, 223; of modernity, 105, 341, 347; of postmodernism, 198, 267n, 339; in postrevolutionary society, 197, 222, 261, 272, 280, 294; of realism, 138, 252; of seeing, 234, 235; and *The Young Generation,* 169, 182, 189, 190n, 192–94
imperialism, 38, 53, 99, 105, 106, 155, 174
"I-novel," 21, 32
interior design, 295–99, 306–15
interiority, 160; in avant-garde fiction, 203, 205, 208–9, 213, 216, 217, 223; in *Black Snow,* 257–61, 271; in *Cold Nights,* 133, 145, 154–59; "dialectic" of, 314; in Ding Ling's fiction, 97, 101, 121, 128; and interior design, 296, 306, 308–15; in lyrical age, 181; in "My Native Land," 76, 91; postmodern lack of, 302; in pre-1949 works, 2; in *The Sea of Regret,* 15, 30, 31, 38, 43; in *Stones in the Sea,* 21; and "subjectivity" in 1980s, 303–5, 312. *See also* exteriority; interior design; subjectivity
Italy, 251, 272, 298. *See also* neorealist cinema

Jameson, Fredric, 53–54, 61–62, 68–69, 139, 154–55, 197–98, 211, 232, 242n, 257, 269n, 280, 348n
Japan, 11, 172, 334; and criticism of Chinese theater, 27; literature of, 6, 21, 159, 347; and *The Town of Olive in 1944,* 226, 227, 229–30, 233; translations in, 12. *See also* Sino-Japanese War
Jiang Guanyun, 27
Jiang Qing, 166, 167
Jingwei, 19–20, 21
Jin Songcen, 17–20
Joan Haste (H. Rider Haggard), 16–18, 32

Kafka, Franz, 131, 145, 148, 197, 200, 202, 210, 211, 216
Karatani Kojin, 159
Kiely, Robert, 54–55
Kristeva, Julia, 316–17, 322, 326, 329, 337, 338
kuang (madness), 58–59, 63, 70. *See also feng*
"Kuangren riji." *See* "Diary of a Madman"

Lacan, Jacques, 83, 86, 87, 88n, 139, 145
La dame aux camélias (Alexander Dumas *fils*), 16, 17, 18
Lang, Olga, 132n, 137
League of Communist Youth, 174, 277
League of Left-wing Writers, 108
Lee Kuan-yew, 334, 335–36
Lee, Leo Ou-fan, 70–71, 110, 115n
Lei Da, 272
Lei Feng, 173
Lenin, V. I. (Leninism), 163, 179, 181n
Liang Qichao, 11–14, 16n, 19–20, 27, 341, 342–43; "Ode to Young China," 341, 342–43

Liaozhai zhiyi (Records of the strange from the liaozhai studio), 28
liberalism, 99, 160, 186–87, 334; in *Cold Nights,* 149–50, 152, 155–56. *See also* humanism
Li Jiefei, 320
Lin Gang, 311, 312
Link, Perry, 47
Lin Shu, 16n, 17
Lin Yaode, 236, 244
literary production: commodification of, 300; instrumentalization of, 56, 303; in late Qing, 11–15; in lyrical age, 165, 194; proletarianization of, 128–29; socialist reorganization of, 3; in Third-World culture, 54
Li Tuo, 201
Liu Heng, 243, 254, 258n, 274n
Liu Shaoqi, 182
Liu Zaifu, 208, 303–4, 312
Li, Wai-yee, 26
Li Yang, 164n, 165
Li Zehou, 51n, 312n
Louie, Kam, 345–46
Lukács, Georg, 56, 208n, 230, 278, 279, 348n
Lu Xun, 2, 14, 42n, 49–50, 51, 52, 57, 78, 81, 97, 121, 138, 144; on "awakening," 70, 71; and native-land literature, 85–87; state-sponsored studies of, 60. Works: *Call to Arms* (Nahan), 71, 78; "Medicine" (Yao), 158; "On the Power of Mara Poets" (Moluo shili shuo), 58; *Wild Grass* (Yecao), 72. *See also* "Diary of a Madman"; "My Native Land"
Lynch, Kevin, 245, 249, 257, 276n
lyrical age (shuqing shidai), 3, 164–67, 169–76, 179, 182. See also *The Young Generation*

madness: in avant-garde fiction, 212–13, 217; *kuang/feng* in "Diary of a Madman," 58–59, 63
Mandarin Duck and Butterfly fiction, 47
Mao Dun, 98. Works: *Midnight* (Ziye), 99–100, 111; "Suicide" (Zisha), 112
Mao Zedong, 163–65, 166, 168n, 171–72, 173, 181, 273, 279, 283
Marcus, Millicent, 252n, 262n
marketization, 196–97, 203, 251, 261, 263–65, 271, 273–78, 283
Marx, Karl, 66, 277, 302, 307n
Marxism, 56, 277
masculinity: in Ding Ling's fiction, 107, 116; in late Qing, 16; and masochism in *Cold Nights,* 146, 151; in "My Native Land," 77; and revolution, 123–25. *See also* femininity; feminism; gender
masochism: in *Cold Nights,* 135, 140–46, 147–53, 156; and residual modernism, 200; in *The Sea of Regret,* 41–42, 44
May Fourth movement, 13, 49, 67, 111, 112, 128, 138, 144, 146, 149, 157, 186, 198, 333–34, 345
McDougall, Bonnie S., 345–46
melancholia, 316–17, 318, 327, 337–38, 340. *See also* melancholy
melancholy, 3, 4; in *Black Snow,* 256; in Ding Ling's fiction, 103, 114; and *guxiang,* 75; in He Dun's fiction, 313; heroic, 328, 337–38; historical or "postmodern," 338–40, 342; Walter Benjamin on, 328, 338; in Wang Anyi's fiction, 318, 321, 330–40, 341; in Yu Dafu's fiction, 111, 333. *See also* melancholia
melodrama: in cinema, 252
Meng Yue, 98, 113, 116, 144, 187n, 214, 234–35, 242, 289n
"misty poetry," 62

model theater, 167, 186n, 190, 283
"modern girl," 98, 99
modernism, 50–57, 210–11, 279, 294, 316, 326, 339; in *Black Snow,* 248, 257, 271, 272; in "Diary of a Madman," 49–50, 65, 70, 73; European, 50, 52, 223; and interior monologue, 304; residual, 4, 197–224, 287, 343. See also *Black Snow*; "Diary of a Madman"; Su Tong; Xiao Ye; Yu Hua
modernity, 1, 7, 52, 167, 179, 280, 284, 307, 336n, 347; and bildungsroman, 203; in cinema, 249, 264; and disease, 135–36, 159, 316; and everyday life, 212, 279, 292, 294; and hyperstimulation, 33, 34; and ideology, 3, 105, 339, 341, 347; and late Qing new fiction, 13–14; and nonsynchronic synchronicity, 246, 343; and postmodernism, 197, 198, 328; and residual modernism, 211, 215, 218, 220, 223–24, 287; and Shanghai, 99, 100; socialist, 173; utopian, 342; Western, 49–53, 99, 315
modernization, 52, 56n, 105, 216, 218, 236, 245, 338, 342; in cinema, 249, 252, 266, 268–70, 271; incomplete, 211, 214, 217, 223; in lyrical age, 164; and narration, 221; in post-revolutionary age, 274–79, 296; revolution as, 106; Singapore model of, 335, 336n; and "twentieth-century Chinese literature," 345
Moretti, Franco, 203–4, 219
mother figure: in *Cold Nights,* 144, 148–52; in "My Native Land," 89; in *The Young Generation,* 185–86
Mo Yan, 243, 274n, 331
Mulvey, Laura, 104, 263n
"My Native Land" (Guxiang), 74–96; and homesickness, 77, 85–87, 96; and landscape, 93–96; and leaving, 93–94; and misrecognition, 87–90, 92; and realism, 76–77, 80–81, 90–91; and reality/memory gap, 79–81, 92; sexuality in, 89; and utopianism, 94–96

nationalism, 28, 29–30, 38, 99, 105, 106, 132, 153–54, 156, 165, 179, 228, 234, 332, 341
Nationalist government (Republic of China), 105, 108, 131, 163, 185, 222
native land (*guxiang*), 74–76, 78, 85. See also "My Native Land"; native-land literature
native-land literature (*xiangtu wenxue*), 85–87, 96. See also "My Native Land"
neorealist cinema, 6, 251–53, 262, 270–72. See also *Good Morning, Beijing*
neurosis: as a meaning of *feng,* 58; in *The Sea of Regret,* 2, 20, 33–47; in *Stones in the Sea,* 23
Never Forget (Qianwan buyao wangji), 170, 181n
New China cinema, 247–48, 250
New Citizen Journal (Xinmin congbao), 27
New Culture movement, 49, 67, 144
New Fiction (Xin xiaoshuo), 11, 12, 14, 17, 28
New Life movement, 105, 106
New Literature movement, 13
New Sensationists (Xin ganjue pai), 130
New Youth (Xin qingnian), 49
Nietzsche, Friedrich, 58, 64, 65–66, 136, 152, 153, 155
nostalgia, 3; for Maoist era, 283; and native-land literature, 75, 83, 86, 96; in *Nineteen Thirty-four Escapes,* 226, 236, 244; and residual modernism, 211, 223; in *Stones in the Sea,* 21; in *The Town of Olive in 1944,* 226, 232; in Wang Anyi's fiction, 287, 321, 328, 332; in Zhang Ailing's fiction,

376 *Index*

nostalgia (*continued*)
5, 130. *See also* "My Native Land"; native land (*guxiang*); native-land literature; *Sadness for the Pacific*
novel, 280; in late Qing, 11–15, 30; in lyrical age, 194. *See also* fiction
Nüwa, 18–20, 21

passion, 4, 47, 342; and Ba Jin, 137; vs. "benevolence," 24; and Cultural Revolution, 213, 278; in Ding Ling's fiction, 98, 101, 115, 127; in *Good Morning, Beijing*, 263; vs. lust (*yu*), 17; of lyrical age, 165, 172, 174–75, 180–84, 195, 278; mythology of *qing*, 18–20; and revolution, 112–13; and romanticism of 1920s, 110–12, 116–18; in *The Sea of Regret*, 2, 4, 16, 24–26, 32, 39, 41–46; in *Stones in the Sea*, 24, 28, 32; and tradition of "passionism" (*qing jiao*), 26–27; in Wang Anyi's fiction, 321, 322, 326, 328, 332, 335, 336, 339
pathography. *See* hagiography: and pathography in *The Sea of Regret*
pathos: of Ba Jin, 160; and "native land" (*guxiang*), 74–75, 85; in *The Sea of Regret*, 16, 33, 47; of Wang Anyi, 331, 339
patriarchy. *See* father figure
Peng Wen, 249n, 250, 255
Pensky, Max, 328, 338
People's Liberation Army (PLA), 163, 173, 184, 188
People's Republic, 181; founding of, 1–2, 163; "peaceful construction" of, 164
poetry, 51, 62, 345; in lyrical age, 166, 194; of Mao Zedong, 163–65
Poetry (Shikan), 164, 176n
Popular Cinema (Dazhong dianying), 272

popular music, 254, 260. *See also* rock and roll
postmodernism, 52, 55, 290, 343; and Chen Xiaoming, 301–3, 305; and cinema, 252, 267n, 268–69, 270; and melancholy, 4, 316–18, 322, 326–28, 336n, 337; and reemergence of everyday life, 342; and residual modernism, 196–200, 218, 224; and "society of the spectacle," 232, 241–423
postrevolutionary culture, 4, 195, 196, 205, 208, 213, 222, 243, 283, 284, 289, 304, 339
Proust, Marcel, 50, 201–2
Průšek, Jaroslav, 6, 103n
psychological realism, 31, 32, 38, 47, 134, 139, 254
Pu Songling, 28, 29n

Qiu Jin (*Jingwei shi*; *The Stones of Jingwei*), 20
Qiu Tao (*Dream Girl*), 292–94
quotidian, the (everyday life): anxiety of, 154, 283–84, 292, 294, 311, 312–14; in cinema, 251, 260, 267; and the city, 106, 108–9, 283–84, 287; in *Cold Nights*, 131–32; and heroic dialectic, 1, 3, 4–6, 106, 344; in lyrical age, 165, 166, 170, 177–79, 184, 195; its negation in *Flood*, 129; and postmodernism, 295; and postrevolutionary society, 277, 290; revolutionary impoverishment of, 278–80; in *Shanghai, Spring 1930*; and Su Tong's fiction, 236; in Wang Anyi's fiction, 289, 318, 326, 342; in Yu Hua's fiction, 210, 212–13. *See also* heroic, the

race, 29–30
realism, 51–56, 100, 348n; and Ba Jin,

138–39; and Lu Xun, 50, 59–60, 69–70, 72, 76–77, 80–81, 90; and moral commitment, 252, 253; and native-land literature, 87; revolutionary, 165, 248. See also capitalist realism; psychological realism; socialist realism

Reik, Theodor, 142, 156

residual modernism. See modernism: residual

ressentiment, 135, 136, 152–56, 160

revolution, 49, 52, 97, 163–64, 334, 335, 341, 342; and avant-garde fiction, 207, 221–22, 223; and Ba Jin, 137; and the body, 109, 116–19; and cinema, 248; and "Diary of a Madman," 72; and end of 1920s romanticism, 112–13; and exteriority, 122–23; global, 172, 174, 176; memory of, 300; as modernization, 106; in peacetime, 172, 182. See also *Shanghai, Spring 1930*; *The Young Generation*

"revolution and love" fiction, 97, 105, 106, 115n. See also *Shanghai, Spring 1930*

"revolutionary literature," 113

revolutionary mass culture, 3, 194–95, 247–48, 279, 280–83, 284. See also *The Young Generation*

revolutionary romanticism, 2, 51, 165, 248, 283

rock and roll, 247, 264, 271. See also popular music

romanticism, 28, 47, 48, 52, 130, 136, 137, 164, 283, 325, 333, 335; combined with realism, 56n, 165; in Ding Ling's fiction, 119, 121, 128, 343; of 1920s, 110–12, 115, 119. See also lyrical age; passion; revolution and love fiction; revolutionary romanticism; *The Sea of Regret*; *Stones in the Sea*

root seeking (*xungen*), 250, 330, 331

Rose, Jacqueline, 240–41

Rosenfelt, Deborah, 98n, 129n

Sacher-Masoch, Leopold von, 148, 149, 153

sadism, 152

Saussure, Ferdinand de, 139, 326n

The Sea of Regret (Henhai), 2, 4, 15–16, 20–21, 24–26, 28, 30–38, 343; legacy of, 46–48; and trauma, 32–38, 43, 45, 47; virtue and sexuality in, 38–46, 47

sexuality: in *Cold Nights,* 150; in Ding Ling's fiction, 98, 115–19; in "My Native Land," 89; in 1920s fiction, 110–11; in *The Sea of Regret,* 38–41, 45, 47

Shanghai, 2, 17, 130, 166, 176, 276, 288, 289, 331, 334; in Ding Ling's fiction, 99, 100–01, 343; interior design in, 309–10; 1930s descriptions of, 99–100; politics of, 105–06; in *Stones in the Sea,* 22. See also *Shanghai, Spring 1930*

Shanghai Literature (Shanghai wenxue), 301

Shanghai, Spring 1930 (Yijiu sanling nian chun Shanghai), 97, 102, 103, 155; conclusion of, 125–27; and discourse of revolution, 103–05, 112–13; femininity and consumption in, 119–23, 126; gender and revolution in, 122–28; and the pre-revolutionary body, 106–12; and training the male body, 114–19

Shi ji (Records of the historian), 74

Shi jing (The book of songs), 58

Sima Qian, 74

sincerity (*cheng*), 42–43

Singapore, 329, 330, 332–36

Sino-Japanese War, 5, 131, 156, 222, 226, 227, 233, 329, 334, 335. See also World War II

socialist realism, 3, 51, 55, 159, 247–48, 250, 252, 274, 282, 290, 292, 304. *See also* realism; revolutionary romanticism
Soja, Edward, 265
Sontag, Susan, 135–37
Sorlin, Pierre, 251, 252
Soviet Union, 171, 172, 174, 247–48, 334
Sparke, Penny, 308
spectrality, 221, 223, 287, 329, 342
Spence, Jonathan D., 108, 130n
Spivak, Gayatri, 50–51
Stalinism, 172, 247–48
The Story of the Stone. See *Dream of the Red Chamber*
stream of consciousness, 54, 55
subjectivity: in avant-garde fiction, 202, 205, 207–9, 215–17, 219; in cinema, 249, 256, 257, 261, 268, 270, 271; in *Cold Nights,* 135, 139, 140, 141, 148, 154–55; collective, 112–113; 159, 165, 181; female, 342; and guilt, 39–42; and Hegel, 208; illness and, 136; imprisoning urban, 101–2, 111–12; and interior homeland, 78–81; lyrical, 171, 186–87; melancholy, 318, 335, 336–38, 339; in Ming Dynasty, 26; and the mirror of history, 233, 234, 240–41; and (mis)recognition, 86–93; modernist, 52, 53, 57–60; in 1980s intellectual debates, 62, 208, 303–5, 312n; and postrevolutionary self-transformation, 285; and realist orthodoxy, 56; "subjection" of, 118–19, 126–27; traumatized, 16, 36, 38, 41. *See also* collectivism; exteriority; interiority
sublime, 234, 323, 329
suicide, 29, 32, 98, 102–3, 324
Su Tong, 203, 204n, 214, 223, 225, 233, 234, 274n, 301, 331, 332, 347. Works: "As Serene as Still Water" (Pingjing ru shui), 214–15, 220, 236; "Hello, My Beekeeper" (Nihao, yangfengren), 214–23, 236; *Nineteen Thirty-four Escapes* (Yijiu sansi nian de taowang), 204n, 214, 218, 234–44, 332
Symbolism, 52, 55

Taiwan, 172, 213, 225, 226, 227, 228, 233, 236, 244, 346, 347
"Tang Sheng," 28–30, 39
Tan Sitong, 24
Taylor, Charles, 279, 280
teleology, 51
totality, 347–48
tragedy, 27–28, 30–31, 47–48
tragicomedy, 28, 322, 327
trauma, 342; and Cultural Revolution, 4, 236; and hyperstimulation, 3, 33–38, 47; and melancholy, 327, 339; in *The Sea of Regret*, 2, 15, 30, 32–38, 43, 45, 46, 47; in *Stones in the Sea*, 22
Troubleshooters (Wanzhu), 346–47, 249, 251
tuberculosis, 131; in *Cold Nights,* 134, 135, 140, 145–47, 152, 153–54, 156; as desire, 145; and Ding Ling's heroines, 98; as metaphor, 135–6, 158; after 1949, 159–60; as psychosomatic illness, 140, 145, 152

United States, 28–29, 54, 97–98, 164, 172, 174, 196, 264, 287, 295, 298, 299
Urbach, Henry, 295
urbanization, 275–77, 284, 290. *See also* city; country
utopianism, 1, 3, 4–5, 80, 136, 137, 150, 159, 273, 341, 342; and anxiety, 267n, 292–94; and economics, 171; and everyday life, 280, 284; failure of, 280; in *Good Morning, Beijing,* 265,

267, 270; and interiority, 312–13; in Maoist era, 164, 173, 190, 195, 279–80, 283; and melancholy, 337, 339; in "My Native Land," 80, 82–83, 85; in native-land literature, 85, 87; and postrevolutionary culture, 283, 286, 292; and residual modernism, 217, 218, 221; and revolution, 106, 129; and subjectivism, 257; and writing 138. *See also* heroic, the

Viladas, Pilar, 295
virtue: in "Diary of a Madman," 60; in *The Sea of Regret*, 2, 39, 42–45, 46, 47
visuality: in *Nineteen Thirty-four Escapes*, 234–44; in *The Town of Olive in 1944*, 228–34

Wang Anyi, 4, 287, 288n, 317–21, 328, 330, 331–32, 339, 341, 342. Works: "Baotown" (Xiao Baozhuang), 330n, 331; *Love and Sentiment in Hong Kong* (Xianggang de qing yu ai), 287–90, 318n, 320n, 321; *Our Uncle's Story* (Shushu de gushi), 318–20, 321–28; *Records and Fiction* (Jishi yu xugou), 331n, 332n; *Sadness for the Pacific* (Shangxin Taipingyang), 4, 318, 321, 328–36
Wang, Ban, 165n, 166
Wang, Chi-chen, 75–76, 94n
Wang, David Der-wei, 12, 70n, 85n, 98n, 346n
Wang Guowei, 27
Wang, Jing, 19n, 303n, 304–5
Wang Meng, 274n, 304
Wang Shiqing, 26, 72
Wang Shuo, 247, 300
Wang Zheng and Xiao Hua, 203, 218n, 236n
Wilhelm Meisters Wanderjahre, 203–4

Williams, Raymond, 192n, 199, 200, 201, 215, 276n, 287–88
World War II, 2, 131, 156, 226, 334. *See also* Sino-Japanese War
Wu Jianren, 28, 30, 32, 46, 47, 343; criticism of new fiction, 14; on passion (*qing*), 24–26; on role of the novel, 15. Works: *Ashes After the Catastrophe* (Jie yu hui), 24n; *Passion Transformed* (Qing bian), 25n, 44n; *Strange Things Witnessed in the Past Twenty Years* (Ershi nian mudu zhi guai xianzhuang), 14. *See also The Sea of Regret*

Xiao Ye (Hsiao Yeh), 225, 226, 241, 244, 347; *The Town of Olive in 1944* (Ganlan zhen 1944), 225–34, 236–37, 242, 244
Xie Fei, 250–51, 253, 255, 256n, 257, 259. *See also Black Snow*
Xin Xiaoshuo. *See New Fiction*

Yao Wenyuan, 166, 177n
Yin Bansheng, 32
The Young Generation (Nianqing de yidai), 3, 164n, 166–71, 176–94; "bourgeois quagmire" in, 177–80, 187; climax of, 191–94; family as symbolic order in, 184–91; historical context of, 170–76; indebtedness in, 189; and urban youth, 180–84. *See also* lyrical age
Yu Dafu, 111, 138, 333–34; "Blue Smoke," 158
Yu Hua, 200–203, 209–10, 223, 301, 304. Works: "Classical Love" (Gudian aiqing), 209; "Narrative of Death" (Siwang xushu), 211n; *1986* (Yijiubaliu nian), 212–14; "One Kind of Reality" (Xianshi yizhong), 209; "On the Road at Age Eighteen"

Yu Hua (*continued*)
(Shibasui chumen yuanxing), 200–211, 212n, 215; "This Story Is Dedicated to a Girl Named Yang Liu" (Ciwen xiangei shaonü Yang Liu), 213–14; "This World of Clouds" (Shishi ru yan), 209

Zhang Ailing (Eileen Chang), 5–6, 130, 287, 289; *Love in a Fallen City* (Qingcheng zhi lian), 287

Zhang Minquan, 138
Zhang Nuanxin, 250, 261–62, 265. See also *Good Morning, Beijing*
Zhang, Xudong, 55n, 214n, 248n, 250
Zhang Yimou: *Ju Dou*, 267n; *Raise the Red Lantern*, 267n; *Red Sorghum* (Hong gaoliang), 248
Zhang Yiwu, 198
Zhou Zuoren, 57–58

Xiaobing Tang is an Associate Professor in Modern Chinese Literature, University of Chicago. He is the author of *Global Space and the Nationalist Discourse of Modernity: The Historical Thinking of Liang Qichao* (Stanford, 1996). He edited the following books: (with Stephen Snyder) *In Pursuit of Contemporary East Asian Culture* (Westview, 1996); (with Liu Kang) *Politics, Ideology, and Literary Discourse in Modern China: Theoretical Interventions and Cultural Critique* (Duke, 1993).

Library of Congress Cataloging-in-Publication Data
Tang, Xiaobing
Chinese modern : the heroic and quotidian / Xiaobing Tang.
p. cm. — (Post-contemporary interventions)
Includes bibliographical references and index.
ISBN 0-8223-2412-1 (alk. paper). — ISBN 0-8223-2447-4 (pbk. : alk. paper)
1. Popular culture—China.   2. Chinese literature—20th century—History and criticism.   3. Postmodernism—China.   I. Title.   II. Series.
HM101.T33   2000
306'.0951—dc21   99-36866

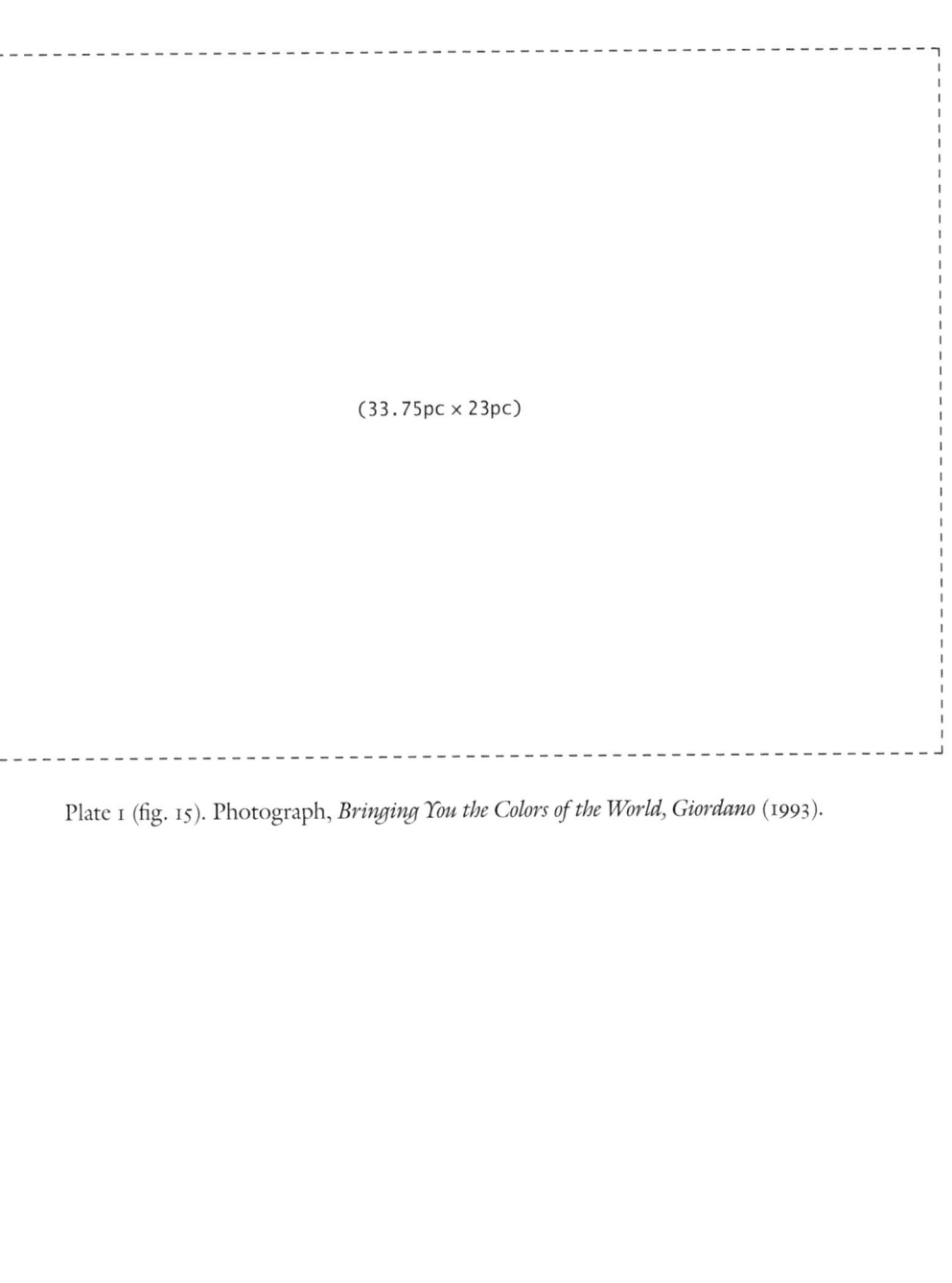

Plate 1 (fig. 15). Photograph, *Bringing You the Colors of the World*, Giordano (1993).

Plate 2 (fig. 16). Oil, *Dream Girl,* by Qiu Tao (1985).

www.ingramcontent.com/pod-product-compliance
Lightning Source LLC
Chambersburg PA
CBHW061342300426
44116CB00011B/1953